Music, Life, and Changing Times

At this book's core is a critical edition of letters exchanged over 50 years between Anglo-Irish composer Elizabeth Maconchy (1907–1994) and the Welsh composer Grace Williams (1906–1977). These two innovative and talented women are highly regarded for their music, their professional activities, and their roles in British musical life. The edition comprises around 353 letters from 1927 to 1977, none of which have been published before, along with scholarly introductions and contextualisation. Interwoven commentaries, in tandem with carefully constructed appendices, frame the letter texts. Moreover, the commentaries and introductory essays highlight and track the development of important themes and issues that characterise the study of twentieth-century British music today. This edition presents a dialogue, through both sides of a unique correspondence that offers an alternative commentary on musical and cultural developments of this period.

Sophie Fuller studied music at King's College London and works at Trinity Laban Conservatoire of Music and Dance. She is the author of *The Pandora Guide to Women Composers: Britain and the United States, 1629–Present* (1994). Her research interests and writings explore many different aspects of music, gender, and sexuality but focus in particular on musical life in late nineteenth- and twentieth-century Britain. Her work in this area includes essays on the significance of the private musical world in the life and career of Edward Elgar and on women musicians and professionalism in the late-nineteenth and early-twentieth centuries. Together with Phyllis Weliver, she has established the digital resource 'Sounding Victorian' (www.soundingvictorian.org).

Jenny Doctor is a musicologist intrigued by social aspects of British culture in the twentieth century. After being awarded a Fulbright Grant to the UK in 1989–90, when she was affiliated with the Music Department at King's College London, she later was affiliated with St Hilda's College, Oxford, where she archived and catalogued the music manuscripts of Elizabeth Maconchy, which are held in the College Library. She has researched and written on British music and composers of the twentieth century, in particular Benjamin Britten, Elizabeth Maconchy, Grace Williams, Ralph Vaughan Williams, and Edward Elgar, often investigating their relationships with the BBC and other sound technologies of their day. Her investigations led to *The BBC and Ultra-Modern Music, 1922–36: Shaping a Nation's Tastes* (Cambridge University Press, 1999). With Sir Nicholas Kenyon and David Wright, she co-edited *The Proms: A New History* (Thames & Hudson, 2007), contributing an essay on the interwar period. More recently, she co-edited with Björn Heile and Peter Elsdon *Watching Jazz: Encounters with Jazz on Screen* (Oxford University Press, 2013), contributing an essay on jazz on early BBC television. She is currently the Head of the Albino Gorno Memorial Library and Associate Professor of Musicology at the College-Conservatory of Music, University of Cincinnati.

Music, Life, and Changing Times
Selected Correspondence Between
British Composers Elizabeth Maconchy
and Grace Williams, 1927–77

Volume 1

**Edited by
Sophie Fuller and Jenny Doctor**

LONDON AND NEW YORK

First published 2020
by Routledge
2 Park Square, Milton Park, Abingdon, Oxon OX14 4RN

and by Routledge
52 Vanderbilt Avenue, New York, NY 10017

Routledge is an imprint of the Taylor & Francis Group, an informa business

© 2020 selection and editorial matter, Sophie Fuller and Jenny Doctor; individual chapters, the contributors

The right of Sophie Fuller and Jenny Doctor to be identified as the authors of the editorial material, and of the authors for their individual chapters, has been asserted in accordance with sections 77 and 78 of the Copyright, Designs and Patents Act 1988.

All rights reserved. No part of this book may be reprinted or reproduced or utilised in any form or by any electronic, mechanical, or other means, now known or hereafter invented, including photocopying and recording, or in any information storage or retrieval system, without permission in writing from the publishers.

Trademark notice: Product or corporate names may be trademarks or registered trademarks, and are used only for identification and explanation without intent to infringe.

British Library Cataloguing-in-Publication Data
A catalogue record for this book is available from the British Library

Library of Congress Cataloging-in-Publication Data
Names: Maconchy, Elizabeth, 1907–1994, author. | Williams, Grace, 1906–1977, author. | Fuller, Sophie, editor. | Doctor, Jennifer R. (Jennifer Ruth), 1958– editor.
Title: Music, life, and changing times : selected correspondence between British composers Elizabeth Maconchy and Grace Williams, 1927–77, volume 1 / edited by Sophie Fuller and Jenny Doctor.
Description: London and New York : Routledge, 2019. | Includes bibliographical references and index.
Identifiers: LCCN 2018052289 (print) | LCCN 2018054323 (ebook) | ISBN 9781315615042 (ebook) | ISBN 9781409424123 (hardback : alk. paper) | ISBN 9781409424123 (hardback : alk. paper) vol. 1 | ISBN 9780367244644 (hardback : alk. paper) vol. 2 | ISBN 9780429282621 (eBook)
Subjects: LCSH: Maconchy, Elizabeth, 1907–1994—Correspondence. | Williams, Grace, 1906–1977—Correspondence. | Composers—England—Correspondence. | Composers—Wales—Correspondence.
Classification: LCC ML410.M167 (ebook) | LCC ML410.M167 A4 2019 (print) | DDC 780.92/2—dc23
LC record available at https://lccn.loc.gov/2018052289

ISBN: 978-1-4094-2412-3 (hbk)
ISBN: 978-0-429-28260-7 (ebk)

Typeset in Times New Roman
by Apex CoVantage, LLC

Contents

Volume 1

List of figures   viii
List of music examples   ix

Editors' Preface   x

Introductory thoughts   xii
SOPHIE FULLER

Afterthoughts   xvi
JENNY DOCTOR

A friendship of fifty years   xxi
NICOLA LEFANU

PART I
Letters 1–49 (1927–Summer 1939)   1

I.1   Letters 1–9 (1927–August 1931)   3
I.2   Letters 10–23 (February 1932–March 1933)   14
I.3   Letters 24–34 (June 1933–March 1934)   30
I.4   Letters 35–41 (November 1934–March 1936)   43
I.5   Letters 42–49 (June 1937–Summer 1939)   51

PART II
Letters 50–93 (October 1939–April 1949)   59

II.1   Letters 50–64 (October 1939–June 1942)   61
II.2   Letters 65–81 (January 1943–December 1944)   80
II.3   Letters 82–85 (May 1945–January 1947)   100
II.4   Letters 86–90 (October 1947–June 1948)   105
II.5   Letters 91–93 (February 1949–April 1949)   111

PART III
Letters 94–146 (November 1949–December 1959)   117

III.1	Letters 94–104 (November 1949–July 1950)	119
III.2	Letters 105–113 (December 1950–November 1952)	135
III.3	Letters 114–122 (March 1953–March 1955)	147
III.4	Letters 123–136 (February 1956–August 1958)	157
III.5	Letters 137–146 (January 1959–December 1959)	173

PART IV
Letters 147–187 (August 1960–December 1965)   187

IV.1	Letters 147–151 (August 1960–May 1961)	189
IV.2	Letters 152–162 (December 1961–February 1963)	197
IV.3	Letters 163–173 (July 1963–April 1964)	210
IV.4	Letters 174–179 (July 1964–January 1965)	226
IV.5	Letters 180–187 (March 1965–December 1965)	234

Grace Williams: Works	xxiii
Elizabeth Maconchy: Works	xxvii
A Select Bibliography	xxxii
Writings by Elizabeth Maconchy	
(arranged chronologically)	xxxii
Writings by Grace Williams (arranged chronologically)	xxxii
Select writings about Maconchy, Williams, and their circle	xxxii
Index	xxxv

Volume 2

List of figures	viii
List of music examples	ix
Editors' Preface	x
Introductory thoughts SOPHIE FULLER	xii
Afterthoughts JENNY DOCTOR	xvi
A friendship of fifty years NICOLA LEFANU	xxi

Contents vii

PART V
Letters 188–268 (February 1966–November 1969)   1

V.1	Letters 188–198 (February 1966–December 1966)	3
V.2	Letters 199–220 (January 1967–May 1967)	19
V.3	Letters 221–238 (July 1967–January 1968)	41
V.4	Letters 239–254 (February 1968–December 1968)	65
V.5	Letters 255–268 (December 1968–November 1969)	86

PART VI
Letters 269–353 (January 1970–January 1977)   107

VI.1	Letters 269–285 (January 1970–December 1970)	109
VI.2	Letters 286–295 (January 1971–November 1971)	134
VI.3	Letters 296–305 (February 1972–January 1973)	149
VI.4	Letters 306–315 (March 1973–December 1973)	165
VI.5	Letters 316–326 (February 1974–December 1974)	181
VI.6	Letters 327–337 (January 1975–December 1975)	197
VI.7	Letters 338–353 (February 1976–January 1977)	215

Grace Williams: Works	xxiii
Elizabeth Maconchy: Works	xxvii
A Select Bibliography	xxxii
Writings by Elizabeth Maconchy	
(arranged chronologically)	xxxii
Writings by Grace Williams (arranged chronologically)	xxxii
Select writings about Maconchy, Williams, and their circle	xxxii
Index	xxxv

Figures

Volume 1

PI.1	Elizabeth Maconchy, 1925.	2
PI.1.1	Elizabeth Maconchy, *The Land* (1930), autograph manuscript, p. 1. (Letter 8)	10
PII.1	Grace Williams, date unknown.	60
PII.1.1	Elizabeth Maconchy, autograph letter, 18 April 1942. (Letter 63)	75
PIII.1	Elizabeth Maconchy and family, 1955. L to R: Nicola, Maconchy, Anna, William LeFanu.	118
PIV.1	Grace Williams and family, 1957, on the occasion of her father being granted Freedom of the Borough of Barry. Front row, L to R: Williams's sister Marian, her mother, her father, Williams, Williams's brother's wife Marjorie. Back row, L to R: Williams's brother Glyn, his sons, Marian's daughter Eryl, Marian's husband Glyn Evans.	188
PIV.3.1	Grace Williams, Trumpet Concerto (1963), autograph manuscript, p. 1. (Letter 172). Permission to reproduce kindly granted by Llyfrgell Genedlaethol Cymru/National Library of Wales.	221

Volume 2

PV.1	Grace Williams, date unknown.	244
PV.4.1	Grace Williams, autograph letter, [after 17] September 1968. (Letter 254)	324
PVI.1	Elizabeth Maconchy and Nicola LeFanu, 1977.	350

Music examples

Volume 1

PI.3.1	Elizabeth Maconchy, *The Leaden Echo and the Golden Echo* (1930–31, rev. 1933–34), excerpt. (Letter 30)	37
PI.3.2	Elizabeth Maconchy, *Deborah* (1933–34), oratorio, excerpt. (Letter 31)	38
PI.3.3	Elizabeth Maconchy, String Quartet no. 1 (1933), excerpt. (Letter 34)	42
PI.4.1	Grace Williams, imitation of Vaughan Williams. (Letter 38)	48
PI.5.1a and 5.1b	Elizabeth Maconchy, String Quartet no. 2 (1937), excerpts. (Letter 46)	55
PII.1.2a and 1.2b	Elizabeth Maconchy, String Quartet no. 2 (1937), excerpts. (Letter 63)	76
PII.2.1	Grace Williams, *Sinfonia concertante* (1940–41, rev. 1942–3), excerpt. (Letter 65)	81

Volume 2

PVI.1.1a and 1.1b	Elizabeth Maconchy, Concerto (Concertino) for piano and chamber orchestra (1928, rev. 1929–30), excerpts as recollected by Williams. (Letter 270)	354
PVI.1.2	Elizabeth Maconchy, String Quartet no. 9 (1968–9), excerpt. (Letter 279)	368
PVI.5.1	Alison Bauld, *Egg* for tenor, flute, cello, vibraphone, and drum (1973), excerpt as recollected by Williams. (Letter 320)	430
PVI.5.2	Grace Williams, *Fairest of Stars* (John Milton), aria for soprano and orchestra (1973), excerpt. (Letter 320)	431

Editors' Preface

Many difficult decisions have had to be made in preparing an edition of this remarkable correspondence. We have aimed throughout to make the two volumes easy to read and use. Through section headings, introductions to individual letters, and footnotes, we have explained things or people that may not be easily understood, as well as identifying performances and broadcasts.

The letters have been divided by decade into six Parts, and each Part divided into several sections. Each letter has been given a number and wherever possible a date – in square brackets where we have worked this out from evidence in the letter itself rather than a date given by the writer. Addresses have been given as they appear on the original letters.

People's dates, where they can be ascertained, are provided in the index. The index will also take the reader to the first time a person is mentioned in the correspondence, where a brief explanation of who they are can be found in a footnote.

For both Maconchy and Williams, we have given a list of all works mentioned or discussed, together with the relevant letter numbers (which may also refer to the introduction to a letter).

Not all the letters that the two women wrote to each other have survived, but even the surviving letters would have taken up several volumes if published in their entirety. Inevitably, much that they wrote we have reluctantly had to omit, something always indicated by [. . .]. Both women frequently added extra thoughts or explanations to the main flow of a letter, inserting them above a line or at the top of a page. We have included these in brackets. Full stops are frequently missing. Rather than indicate these by adding a cumbersome [.] we have simply kept the omission.

We would both like to thank Maconchy's daughter Nicola LeFanu for her unfailing support and invaluable contribution to this edition. Anna Dunlop (Maconchy's elder daughter) and Eryl Freestone (Williams's niece) have also provided important assistance. We would like to thank all three women, as executors of the Estates of Elizabeth Maconchy and Grace Williams, for allowing the reproduction of the correspondence and images.

We would also like to thank Stephen Ferre for his invaluable help inputting the musical notation into these volumes and Ethan John Davies at Tŷ Cerdd for help with images of Grace Williams's scores. We thank the Llyfrgell Genedlaethol Cymru/National Library of Wales for permission to reproduce the manuscript of Williams's Trumpet Concerto (Figure PIV.3.1).

Jenny Doctor would like to thank the Maconchy Estate for its unfailing support and guidance through all the years that I have worked on Elizabeth Maconchy's manuscript materials. Sincere thanks to Maria Croghan, Librarian at St Hilda's College, Oxford, for her help, support, and kindness for many years. I am grateful to the Malcolm Boyd Estate for invaluable research materials relevant to Grace Williams. I appreciate the support and research time that I received from Professor Jonathan Wainwright and the Music Department at the University of York, encouraging work on this project. As always, I am extremely grateful to Jeff Walden of the BBC Written Archives Centre (WAC) for his usual kind and efficient assistance, and to the BBC for allowing us to reproduce quotations from its written archives as illustrations in these volumes. I am thankful for the support and patience of my friends and family throughout the preparation of this edition. And, finally, I would like to express my sincere and deep gratitude to Sophie for her collaborative support, expertise, and friendship throughout this long project.

Sophie Fuller would like to thank the Maconchy Estate as well as Eva Rieger and the Marianne Steegman Foundation for invaluable financial assistance. Thanks also to all those friends and family, in particular Elaine, for their encouragement and support for this project over the years.

Introductory thoughts

Sophie Fuller

> It's amazing that we go on going on, I think – but don't let's stop!
> – Maconchy to Williams, 20 October 1974 – Letter 325

In the summer of 1977, as a teenage flautist, I took part in the Orchestral Summer School at Coleg Harlech in North Wales. The only musical work I remember from that week of intense rehearsing and frolicking on the beach was one that has stayed with me ever since, Grace Williams's *Penillion* (1955). It was not a work that any of my local Oxfordshire youth orchestras would have programmed, nor was I exposed to any more of Williams's music back in England. I knew nothing about the composer except that she was Welsh and, unusually for my youthful experience of orchestral music, a woman. Eleven years later, as a music student specialising in composition and musicology, I started researching a London concert series from the 1930s that promoted contemporary music and was organised by three women musicians. Two of the composers who featured most frequently in the programmes were Grace Williams and her close friend Elizabeth Maconchy, who was also the mother of my own composition teacher, Nicola LeFanu.

It was at this time that I first heard Maconchy's String Quartet no. 1 (1933), another memorable experience and one that raised a whole series of questions. Why had I never heard this remarkable piece of music before? Why didn't I know that Maconchy had written a series of thirteen string quartets throughout her life? Why weren't they part of the musical canon, along with the string quartets by, say, Bartók or Britten, recorded as a matter of course by many different ensembles or taught on undergraduate music programmes? How could music so powerful in its energy, drive, and passion be so little known? Exploring these questions set me on the path I have travelled for the last twenty-five years – a path on which I have uncovered a wealth of music created by women and tried to unpick the complex webs of their lives, careers, reception, and, all too often, their neglect.

Writing in 2017, ten and eleven years after the centenaries of Maconchy and Williams, there are signs that musicians and scholars are beginning to recognise the value of the music that these two talented composers produced throughout their long careers. For a long time, the short 1980 biography of Williams by

Malcolm Boyd, together with a few articles on (and by) both women, provided the only detailed information. But Rhiannon Mathias's 2012 book on Maconchy, Williams, and their contemporary Elisabeth Lutyens as well as two recent doctoral theses by Graeme Cotterill on Williams and Erica Siegel on Maconchy[1] have opened the doors to further scholarship. Cotterill's editions of key works by Williams have encouraged important performances of her music. In 2014, a symposium on Maconchy's life and work was held at the Graz Zentrum für Genderforschung in Austria, and the resulting collection of essays includes a variety of new scholarship on the composer.[2] The internet provides a wealth of useful information and performances, in particular the website created by French composer Corentin Boissier, 'Grace Mary Williams. Welsh classical composer (1906–1977)', which includes information, scores, and recordings, and Nicola LeFanu's authoritative biography of her mother, Elizabeth Maconchy.[3] Jenny Doctor, one of the two editors of this volume of letters, has written several articles on Maconchy, as well as a chapter about Williams and the sea.[4]

Elizabeth Maconchy and Grace Williams met when they were in their twenties and remained close friends until Williams's death, fifty years later. When she knew she was dying, Williams sent Maconchy's letters back to her, saying 'they are valuable because you've written so much about works in progress & I doubt if you've written to anyone else in such detail'.[5] This is not the only reason why this correspondence is so remarkable and so valuable for our understanding of many different aspects of these two composers' lives and careers and indeed of twentieth-century music and music making. But it is a central topic of the correspondence, often demonstrating the first tentative ideas of a work through to the revisions and reworkings that followed early performances. Both women valued the keen critical ear of the other as they read through drafts and scores or listened to rehearsals, performances, and broadcasts.

The unfailing support that Maconchy and Williams gave each other shines through these letters. Their long friendship took them both through periods of excitement and of depression and despondency. They always knew they could rely on each other for not only honest and insightful musical criticism but also

---

1 Rhiannon Mathias, *Lutyens, Maconchy, Williams and Twentieth-Century Music. A Blest Trio of Sirens* (Farnham: Ashgate, 2012); Graeme Cotterill, 'Music in the Blood & Fire in the Soul? National Identity in the Life and Music of Grace Williams', PhD (University of Wales: Bangor, 2012); Erica Siegel, 'Elizabeth Maconchy: The Early Years, 1923–1939', PhD (UC Riverside, 2016). See also select bibliography.
2 The collection will include Sophie Fuller, 'The Maconchy–Williams Correspondence, 1927–1977', in *'Passionately Intellectual, Intellectually Passionate': Elizabeth Maconchy (1907–1994)*, ed. Andreas Dorschel and Christa Brüstle (Vienna, London and New York: Universal Edition, 2017).
3 'Grace Mary Williams. Welsh classical composer (1906–1977)', http://gracewilliamscompo.wixsite.com/officialwebsite; Nicola LeFanu, 'Elizabeth Maconchy DBE (1907–1994): Some biographical and musical notes', www.musicweb-international.com/classrev/2007/Oct07/Maconchy_LeFanu.htm.
4 See select bibliography.
5 See Letter 355.

understanding and encouragement. Both were frustrated by any neglect of the other. In 1957, Williams wrote to Maconchy:

> You are right to feel dejected at lack of performances – & wrong, too, because the all important thing is that you have composed all these truly original & fine works & there must come a time (I'm sure it will come suddenly) when they will be recognized for what they are worth.[6]

Williams also expended a great deal of energy, especially in the 1960s, encouraging musicians she came in contact with to perform Maconchy's music.

Something else that comes over clearly is the sheer amount of time and effort each woman had to put into preparing and revising scores and parts in the days before Sibelius or easy access to photocopiers. A composer's relationship with a publisher in the twentieth century was very significant – as well as usually taking on the responsibility of providing scores and parts for a work they accepted, a publisher would also act as a promoter. Both women faced a series of disappointments and frustrations with various publishers. Equally frustrating could be the process of bringing a work to performance. Both women frequently commiserate on the offhand way in which they were so often treated by conductors, soloists, and other musicians as well as lamenting the lack of time given for effective rehearsal of their works.

The letters also demonstrate the many UK institutions and relationships that were critical in maintaining and building a successful composing career. For the fifty years of this correspondence, one of the most important of these institutions in this regard was the BBC. For much of the twentieth century, music was broadcast over the radio (and sometimes on television), providing a valuable performance space that could potentially reach thousands of listeners. The BBC also could and did commission works. Williams had a particular relationship with BBC Wales and was very involved in the politics of that institution, something that has been ably explored by Graeme Cotterill in his article 'Shall Nation Speak unto Nation? Grace Williams and the BBC in Wales, 1931–1950'.[7]

Maconchy played a key role in two significant institutions, the Composers' Guild (becoming 'chair' in 1959) and the Society for the Promotion of New Music (becoming president in 1976). These were organisations that did much to promote the work of British composers and to support their careers. Despite not living in London, always the British centre of new music, both women were always keen to keep in touch with musical developments, attending concerts when they could and listening avidly to BBC radio. Although they themselves had caused consternation by the perceived modernity of their music in the 1930s, by the 1960s and 1970s they were frequently bemused by the kind of new music that seemed to dominate BBC radio broadcasts.

---

6 See Letter 127.
7 Graeme Cotterill, 'Shall Nation Speak unto Nation? Grace Williams and the BBC in Wales, 1931–1950', *Women & Music: A Journal of Gender and Culture* 17 (2013), 59–77.

It is fascinating to read of their own attitude towards themselves and others as composers who were women. The early letters of both composers are marked by a youthful enthusiasm and confidence – the musical world was theirs for the taking. As time went on, they both faced the harsh reality of trying to maintain a career as a composer in a post-war world that was not particularly supportive of women. In their constant assessment of new music, they were somewhat ambivalent about the work of their contemporaries Elisabeth Lutyens and Phyllis Tate, but fascinated by the music of the younger composer Thea Musgrave. Inevitably, they followed the career of Maconchy's daughter, composer Nicola LeFanu, with particular attention.

The correspondence is full of details about domestic matters, such as spring cleaning or making jam. There is also plenty of recounting of news about family or close friends, such as composers Dorothy Gow or Ina Boyle. As well as discussing music, both women talk about books and plays, while Williams was impressed by the potential of television as an art form. Health is a recurring topic, especially following Maconchy's bouts of tuberculosis in the 1930s and Williams's ill health in the 1940s. Both maintained a keen interest in politics, with Williams particularly concerned by world events and political unrest in the 1960s.

Maconchy and Williams faced low points in their careers when they felt their creativity had dried up or that composing was simply too much of an uphill struggle, but neither of them ever stopped. Despite moments of discouragement and self-doubt, the overall impression that I am left with, after living and working with these letters for over a decade, is one of awe and admiration at Maconchy and Williams's sheer grit and deep-rooted belief in the glorious music that they were determined to continue to produce. From Williams's *Penillion* (1955) to the monumental *Missa cambrensis* (1968–71) or the evocative *Ave Maris Stella* (1973); from Maconchy's First String Quartet (1933) to her inventive operas *The Sofa* (1956–7) and *The Departure* (1960–61) or haunting song cycle *My Dark Heart* (1981), this is music that will be with us all for ever.

Afterthoughts

Jenny Doctor

>Your letter was like wine to the thirsty...
>– Maconchy to Williams, 24 February 1932 – Letter 10

>Betty I don't know why you want my opinions, <u>really</u>, because as soon as I've given them I feel they're thoroughly footling & I'm a sort of impostor. However – –
>– Williams to Maconchy, January 1934 – Letter 32

After more than twenty-five years of being involved with this fascinating and engaging collection of letters, and now that this editing project nears completion, I am struck strongly – and regretfully – by the realisation that this mode of exchange is unlikely to emerge from today's communication culture. We don't generally hand-write letters like this anymore, and we rarely send long letters to each other through the post. Clearly, this collection represents a communication style and phenomenon of the past. And I have to wonder whether the compass and depth of detail that characterise the exchanges may be hallmarks of that obsolete communication style, and so also be recognised as 'of the past'. The correspondence contains a life-time of engagement, sharing, and reminiscing about: education, friends, and experiences; narratives of family growth and progression; ideas, critiques, and professional encouragement relating to music, music composition, and the music industry; political and social thoughts and ideas; and the impacts of technological advancements and other cultural changes – all through pages and pages of hand-written correspondence. Both the letters, and the twentieth-century worlds of communications and music that are described within them, are of a time that ended with the advent of the digital age.

So, in this essay, expressing a few thoughts after years of interacting with these letters, I'd like to bring to the forefront of attention – especially for younger readers who have grown up in that digital age – the vibrancy, the expressivity, and the potential for nuance offered within a mode of expression that involves hand-written effort, a friendship spanning over five decades, and a willingness to engage with the topics-at-hand with honesty, reflection, and in painstaking detail.

Betty and Grace led extremely busy lives, yet each made the time – just before bed, while at the hair dresser, or during a few spare minutes elsewhere in their days – to sit down and let flow onto the page recent happenings in her life, about a recent performance she had attended, and/or about a radio performance of a work by the other that she had just heard. In fact, the radio was frequently a common denominator, a way that they heard the same music performances, either by each other or by other contemporary composers who interested them, and thus a catalyst prompting a letter to be written. Because Betty and Grace lived far from each other, and for much of their lives both lived in the countryside, away from the musical centres where the music activities and performances that interested them took place, the radio was especially significant as a unifying communication tool, keeping them in touch with the main performers of the day, as well as recent compositional developments.

Before the internet allowed shared experiences of music performances through streaming or downloading, the radio played that role for much of the twentieth century. In the UK, after it was founded in the early 1920s, the British Broadcasting Corporation (BBC) quickly became a primary impresario for new music, providing platforms for performance over its national and regional wavelengths and also its performing groups, such as the BBC Symphony Orchestra and the BBC Welsh Orchestra, as vehicles for performances of new works. As a BBC historian, for me one of the most intriguing aspects of these letters was the evidence they represent with respect to the role that radio came to play in the lives of composers over the course of the twentieth century. As musicologists working with BBC materials, we often explore a composer's relationship with the BBC, such as how Grace Williams was among the first groups of composers who worked professionally for the BBC, providing scripts and music for Welsh schools' programmes in the 1940s and 1950s, as well as doing other jobs for BBC Wales, including orchestrations and copying, throughout her career;[1] or we might research and write about either Williams's or Maconchy's many performances on BBC wavelengths.[2] But these letters provide extended evidence that permit us to see the relationship the other way around. It is fascinating to read these letters as demonstrations of just how vital it was for British composers to interact with their BBC contacts, gain BBC performances, and network to further BBC opportunities; the letters clarify that for British composers during this period, they believed that these interchanges with the BBC were central and necessary to advancing their careers. Just as significant, the letters provide insight into each composer as a consumer of BBC radio, glimpsing the role that the radio played in her daily life.

---

1 Graeme Cotterill, 'Shall Nation Speak unto Nation? Grace Williams and the BBC in Wales, 1931–1950', *Women & Music: A Journal of Gender and Culture* 17 (2013), 59–77.
2 See, for example, Cotterill, 'Shall Nation Speak unto Nation? Grace Williams and the BBC in Wales'; and Jenny Doctor, 'The Maconchy Seventh String Quartet and the BBC', *Musical Objects* 1 (1995), 5–8.

In addition to appreciating broadcasting as a significant theme that I glean from the letters, I'd also like to point out the writers' expressivity and individuality. Each composer has a writing style that was clearly reflective of her personality. Elizabeth Maconchy's elegant, consistent hand and quiet, measured tone images a caring thoughtfulness, honesty, and depth of insight that was enormously respected and treasured by her friend. It was over spans of letters that I, too, came to appreciate the deep value of Maconchy's discernments and observations, not only through the detailed critiques that she sent in response to Grace's scores, but also in commenting about their families' concerns, their respective professional developments, and the larger, often disruptive and destabilising cultural themes that their generation contended with over the decades. In contrast, Grace Williams's individual letters were often more impassioned and colourful. Grace's handwriting not only covered the page in rows, but circled around the edges, as she remembered more and more notes to add after signing off at the letter's end. As she encountered politics at work, within the BBC, and with other people and organisations that she interacted with as a professional earning her own way, she expressed to her friend detailed intrigue and often her bruised sense of fair play, as well as fervent and vivid descriptions and critiques of musical rehearsals and performances that she experienced. As the women aged and dealt with family illness and loss, Grace's letters reflect the richness of her creative life and thought-processes, but also the fiercely independent, and often solitary, way that she chose to live. Perhaps because the letters to Betty were a way for Grace to express pent up emotions and worries that she admitted to few others, her letters often repeated information from one to the next, especially in the 1960s.

This raises the practical issue of editorial decisions in this edition. In all, the collection of Maconchy–Williams correspondence consists of 367 letters and postcards, 201 by Elizabeth Maconchy and 166 by Grace Williams. Of course, it was not viable to publish the full exchange of letters, but 353 letters are represented, in whole or part, in this edition. As editors, Sophie and I decided from the beginning that we would omit repetition of information and private family matters. The hardest editorial decision-making was over what had to be cut. Sophie and I are very grateful to Routledge for enabling so much of the original text to be reproduced in this two-volume edition. Moreover, because the letters span a period of five decades, from 1927 to 1977, there are inevitably gaps in the narrative that require explanation. Our goal was to let Betty and Grace speak for themselves through their letters to each other and to readers today. Although we wanted the edition to be supportive for readers who may not yet be familiar with their worlds, we wished to keep explanatory footnotes to a minimum. Thus, we chose a narrative presentation, in which the letters are presented in groups, with framing editorial paragraphs to bridge the gaps and to introduce necessary details.

Finally, as a conclusion to these afterthoughts, I'd briefly like to summarise, in deep gratitude to Elizabeth Maconchy and Nicola LeFanu, my involvement with this project. In 1989, I was lucky enough to be awarded a Fulbright Scholarship for dissertation research in London and became affiliated with the music department at King's College London. Being part of that remarkable department and receiving guidance from such leading and thoughtful faculty as Profs. Arnold Whittall, Nicola LeFanu, and Curtis Price changed my understanding of the study of music and music history in profound ways. Moreover, the King's music students whom I met and worked with that year had an equally significant impact on my learning experiences, and several research areas that I began to explore with them then became serious interests that continue as writing and publishing areas for me now. I was particularly delighted to meet and become friends with Sophie Fuller while at King's. And it was during that year that I first became aware of the music of Elizabeth Maconchy as part of my research. In addition to hearing performances of several Maconchy works for the first time, I heard Nicola LeFanu talk about her mother's music – and began to converse with Nicola about her mother's archives of music scores, correspondence, and other materials.

Towards the end of that academic year, Nicola invited me to undertake a preservation project relating to a group of letters that had been exchanged between her mother, Elizabeth Maconchy, and the Welsh composer Grace Williams. Nicola was aware that prior to moving to England, I had worked in a music library and had received training in handling and processing archival materials. I was amazed at the number of letters in the collection and was concerned that some were quite fragile, written on poor quality, war-time paper. I began the slow job of making copies of the letters for preservation purposes. Of course, I read the letters as I copied them. It did not take long for me to fall under the spell of the intense domestic, social, and musical worlds that these composers and friends had confided to the many pages that they had scribed and shared with each other. Nicola invited me to Betty's home at Shottesbrook in Boreham, Essex, to meet her mother and father, William LeFanu (Billy), and it was truly an unforgettable experience for me to go there and talk to them about the letters, and also about other related musicians and BBC administrators of the period.

Nicola broached with me the idea of publishing an edition of the letters, and I agreed that it was a fantastic idea. But there were many references in the letters that needed to be researched. Maconchy's papers were held in the Library at St Hilda's College, Oxford, but the collection had not yet been processed. I agreed to organise and create a working catalogue of the collection of music manuscripts,[3] a task that I had the privilege of working on at St Hilda's College Library on a part-time basis over a number of years.

I also wished to research Grace Williams through archival documents. By that time, I was working as an editor on *The New Grove Dictionary of Opera*, and a fellow editor was Malcolm Boyd, the (now late) musicologist who had long lived and taught in Wales, and who had written a monograph on Grace Williams.[4]

---

3 The catalogue of Maconchy's works has since been published in *A Dictionary-Catalog of Modern British Composers*, ed. Alan Poulton (Westport, CT: Greenwood Press, 2000), 1107–45, and in *'Passionately Intellectual, Intellectually Passionate': Elizabeth Maconchy (1907–1994)*, ed. Andreas Dorschel and Christa Brüstle, Studien zur Wertungsforschung (Vienna, London and New York: Universal Edition, 2017).

4 Malcolm Boyd, *Grace Williams*, Composers of Wales, vol. 4 (Cardiff: University of Wales Press, 1980; re-issued 1998; digitised, University of Michigan, 2007).

Malcolm generously shared with me the papers that he had collected on Grace, and I am very grateful for all the lively conversations that Malcolm and I shared about her contributions to Welsh music. However, at the time when I tried to access her papers in the Welsh Music Information Centre, it was closed to researchers. It has long since reopened, and I am delighted that a number of other musicologists have done serious research and writing on Grace Williams and her remarkable contributions to music.[5]

When Nicola broached the idea of publishing an edition of the letters again some years later, we agreed that it would greatly benefit the project if Sophie Fuller were to co-edit the edition with me, given that Sophie has long been recognised as a leading writer and researcher on British women composers of the twentieth century. By then, Sophie and I had already discussed Maconchy-related research. Moreover, when it came time for Betty and Billy to move from Shottesbrook, we had together gone to the house to help the family clear out the remaining scores and materials that were to be held by St Hilda's College, Oxford, and we delivered them to the College Library. Therefore, it seemed natural that the edition would benefit from both our involvement. Sophie and I gratefully acknowledge that it has been a privilege, pleasure, and great advantage to the edition to have had the invaluable assistance and encouragement not only of Nicola and her late parents but also of her sister, Anna Dunlop, and of Grace's niece, Eryl Freestone.

The genesis of this edition has matured over a number of years, but all of us who have been engaged with the letters and know them well believe that it is at last the time for this correspondence to be issued. It is *now*, 90 years after Betty and Grace met and began to write to each other, that the time is finally right. It is *now* that the musical works of Elizabeth Maconchy and Grace Williams may be heard, acknowledged, and given retrospective recognition. Further, it is *now* that their significant contributions to the twentieth-century British musical landscape may at last be heard, given recognition, and understood in the contexts of their rapidly changing political and social times, compositional styles, and artistic and technological worlds.

---

5 For a summary, see Sophie Fuller's *Introductory Thoughts* to this edition.

A friendship of fifty years

Nicola LeFanu

The friendship between Grace Williams and my mother Elizabeth Maconchy lasted over fifty years. Their correspondence chronicles the great changes in the world they lived in. There are many accounts of music in Britain during the twentieth century, but from the letters gathered in this volume we gain a new perspective. The letters illuminate what it was like to be brilliant women who had to contend with a man's world. Both Maconchy and Williams became successful professional composers who nevertheless were often marginalised or patronised.

My mother arrived at the Royal College of Music in 1923, a shy girl from Ireland. Grace Williams, from Wales, came some years later, already a BMus from Cardiff. They rapidly became close friends and began to discuss their musical ideas, a practice that continued until Williams's death in 1977.

The early letters are full of youthful exuberance, excitement at their musical discoveries, and impatience with anything perceived as conservative. They both won scholarships for study overseas – Maconchy in Prague and Williams in Vienna – and this confirmed an appetite for new music from Europe which they never lost. By inclination (they were Welsh and Irish, after all), they never felt part of the 'English pastoral school'.

Neither young woman doubted her vocation as a composer. Professional to their fingertips, both had long working lives. The letters indicate the successes and opportunities of their careers, but show all too clearly the difficulties they encountered. Prejudice against women was sometimes overt ('publish a young woman? songs, yes, but not symphonic works') and more often covert. Their music, Maconchy's in particular, was deemed 'unfeminine', 'too virile'.

There were practical difficulties that prevented them doing what is now called 'networking': Williams had supported her composing career by teaching but had to leave London to care for her elderly parents. Maconchy had to leave London because she contracted tuberculosis. The years of the war were isolating and both suffered depression and self-doubt as their domestic duties grew and their music became neglected. Yet they never gave up.

There are inevitable gaps in the correspondence. In 1939, Maconchy and her husband destroyed their personal papers; living close to the Kent coast, Maconchy would have been a target for the Nazis, in the case of an invasion, for she was active in left-wing politics during the 1930s. There are lacunae due to Williams's ill health, or simply letters that are lost.

The selection published here and so skilfully edited gives an enthralling picture of their daily lives. Both lived and breathed music, even when coping with domestic crises: trying to hold the sound world of a new composition in the mind's ear while caring for a sick child or an aged parent. All tasks were manual – copying parts, binding scores, dressmaking and mending, picking and preserving summer fruit for winter meals. They did have 'a room of one's own', but they never had enough *time* of their own.

Although they were shy, they were forthright in their opinions, never afraid to speak up for their beliefs. As they grew older, both became quite public figures, Maconchy especially, working hard for other composers. They were commissioned by leading performers and ensembles and still continued to share their hopes or fears: delight in a good performance, fury at an ill-prepared one.

I remember them both as extraordinarily positive people. Despite the self-doubt expressed in the letters, Williams and Maconchy radiated energy. They were always active and involved in what was new: music above all, but also poetry, politics, new scientific ideas. They kept up with the new music being composed in Britain, listening every night to the BBC Third Programme and attending concerts when they could. They didn't suffer fools gladly, but they always made time for the young. They had beautiful musical speaking voices – a hint of Welsh and Irish still present – and they were very attractive, taking care with their appearance, unlike many of their colleagues.

After being with Maconchy or Williams, you felt more alive. Readers of these letters will come to know two remarkable people and be led, I trust, to rediscover their wonderful music.

Part I
Letters 1–49 (1927–Summer 1939)

Figure Pl.1 Elizabeth Maconchy, 1925.

I.1 Letters 1–9 (1927–August 1931)

The correspondence between Maconchy and Williams dates back to 1927, when they were both studying composition at the Royal College of Music (RCM) in London. Maconchy had been a student there since 1923, and Williams arrived in 1926, having previously completed a BMus at the University of Cardiff. Their RCM composition teacher was Ralph Vaughan Williams – known to his students as 'Uncle Ralph'.

Very few letters from Williams to Maconchy survive from this earliest period of their friendship, but those from Maconchy to Williams clearly show their growing friendship, strengthened by their love for their native Ireland (Maconchy) and Wales (Williams) as well as the excitement of studying in Prague (Maconchy) and Vienna (Williams). Williams's visit to Prague to hear one of Maconchy's earliest significant professional performances was to be remembered and marked as an important anniversary for years to come.

Although so much time was spent on their musical activities – such as listening to music and copying parts for performances of their own works – Maconchy found time to fall in love and get married.

1) [?1927]

Friday

Dear Grace,

The idea we had yesterday of our meeting and playing our work to each other, is assuming a definite shape. – I met David Evans and told him of the idea, and he was very keen about it – then we discussed it with Imogen Holst[1] – and finally we three went to the Director[2] to ask if about 11 of us (all enthusiastic composers at College) could meet every fortnight on Thursday evenings, at College, to discuss things and play our own music to each other, and if we could have a room at College and have tea brought to us. – he was very interested and said he would start by giving a composers' party, next Friday. I imagine all the composers would be

---

1 David Moule-Evans and Imogen Holst, daughter of composer Gustav Holst, were fellow students at the RCM.
2 Hugh Allen, director of the Royal College of Music 1919–1937.

invited to this, but I hope that our meetings could be confined to a few, who are really keen, and in earnest, – or else nobody would benefit by it.

Imogen Holst, and David Evans and I then went out & had tea and discussed the situation for hours, – I must tell you about our deliberations on Wednesday – but I do think it is a real need in college, and would be a very good and beneficent thing, don't you?

Yrs ever

Betty Maconchy.

Maconchy spent her summer holiday at Santry Court, near Dublin, at the home of her grandfather, Captain George Leslie Poe, writing to Williams en route.

2) [Summer 1927]

London Midland and Scottish Railway Company
Holyhead, Kingston, and Dublin, Express Steamers,
Royal Mail Route, S.S.

My dear Grace

This is being written at 2.30am on the mail boat on the way to Ireland.: – at least, at the moment we are not actually on the way because the boat has not started – when it does I shall go up on deck and watch the lights going away in the distance. I love doing that. I am one of the many who haven't applied for berths in time, so I'm stationed in a hard chair in what is ironically termed the 'lounge'; – the chairs are fixed to the floor – so are the tables, but the two are so far apart – (to allow, I suppose, for being very fat), that writing is almost an impossibility!

I'm surrounded by the weirdest looking people. Quite ordinary beings look very odd when they are going to sleep in extraordinary positions. I feel rather as if I was in another world – perhaps the Moon – among a strange race. There is a very picturesque row of nuns behind me, – sitting calmly and very still, in a long row on a sort of settle along the wall; – and looking so much more beautiful than ordinary people.

This is tomorrow morning, – or rather the same morning, I suppose, – but I have had a night in between because a nice stewardess got me a berth and I slept nearly all the way over.

I've been looking at you for the last ten days. – You see I've been staying at a house, near Bath, which stands right up in the Cotswolds, and looks right out for miles and miles, and over a large wooded country, and through a gap in the hills there is a little bit of sea, and on the other side is Cardiff. So each time I looked out at the view I thought about you.

I suppose you've heard that you have got £10 of the Foli scholarship?[3] – College never lets you know these things, – and I thought that possibly you may not have seen it. Best congratulations about it, – it is a splendid effort – a man called Shields had some of it, and I got some too, – so isn't that fun?

---

3 An RCM award. Maconchy was also awarded a Foli Scholarship at this time, of £20.

I'm going to the Horse Show to-day, and the next two days, – and then straight off to Connemara on Saturday morning – how heavenly it will be. I've had the most lovely time in Somerset; we went all sorts of expeditions, and saw thrilling places and things. I feel about fifty times the person I was at the end of term, – and I'm getting so fat!

I've begun writing a violin sonata and I'm so thrilled about it; – I shall have no piano for the next few days, but there is one (of sorts) in the house in Connemara, I believe – but it will probably be rather hard to be alone there as there will be a large party.

This is Friday evening, and I've had three ripping days at the Horse Show. The most thrilling jumping, – I got terribly excited over it. – To-morrow I'm off to Connemara – mountains and sea, and miles of bog, and low white tumble-down cottages, and the smell of turf-smoke, which is the most wonderful smell in the world.

I'm staying at my Grandfather's house at the moment; it is rather lovely, and I'm awfully fond of it, and the place, and all the people round here, specially the poor people, but I'm rather glad I shan't be here for long. – In the summer there's just an unending round of tennis parties – different places, but all the same people, mostly rather boring, and I nearly die of it after a bit.

I want to be either very gay, – or else quite wild, – but a rather dull and conventional middle course is awful, don't you think?

You will write to me and say when you're coming to see me in London won't you? I shall be coming back on Sept 7th, I think. [. . .]

I'm going to the Proms[4] every night this time: we must do some together.

But love – (how many more quartet pieces have you written?!)

yr affectionate

Betty.

In 1903, Ernest Palmer had set up the Patron's Fund at the Royal College of Music for 'the encouragement of native composers by the performance of their works'. The fund was used to give public concerts and rehearsals of new chamber and orchestral works by young composers. The rehearsal on 16 March 1928, conducted by Malcolm Sargent, included Dance of the Dryads *by Sybil Barlow of the Royal Academy of Music.*

3) 16 March 1928

[Maconchy to Williams]

[. . .][5]

Rather a terrible Patrons Fund this morning – sea dreams and things – and the dance of the dryads of the mysterious Sybil Barlow – was mostly Debussy and

---

4 The Henry Wood Promenade Concerts, a London summer festival of concerts planned and conducted by Henry J. Wood and produced and broadcast since 1927 by the BBC.
5 The first page of this letter is missing.

some (very mild) Delius – and a large chunk of Wagner, – (and not at all like a dance) so I didn't feel as jealous as I was afraid I might! But then I went and chose rather a darling little gold watch which I'm being given for my birthday, which cheered me up again

Very nice to be told one looks seventeen when one's going to be – you know how much!

Love from
Betty

Maconchy's Concerto for piano and chamber orchestra (1928, rev. 1929–30) was played on 30 November 1928 at a Patron's Fund rehearsal, with fellow RCM student Gwendo Paul at the piano and conducted by Adrian Boult. In preparation, Maconchy and Williams played a two-piano reduction to Vaughan Williams and the composer Herbert Howells, and also at Maconchy's orchestration lesson with composer Gordon Jacob.

4) 25 November 1928

[Maconchy to Williams]

188c Gloucester Terrace, Hyde Park, W2
Sunday.

My dear –

– Sir Hugh[6] has promised that my Concerto shall be tried over with the orchestra (Friday one) – isn't it thrilling – he wanted them to do it straight away after the last concert – but it wasn't even finished then – (I hope I've got it all right now) – so of course that was impossible. – But I've worked like mad at it the last few days. – I'm in the middle of making a two piano arrangement – <u>could</u> you play it with me on Wednesday, to Uncle Ralph & Herbert Howells? – He's coming to hear it. –

I thought we might do it at composers on Tuesday, and <u>if</u> you could come during my lesson with Gordon Jacob on Monday, we could play it to him – at least as much as I've got done – as he's not at College on Wednesday.

We'll have to try & transfer to a room with two pianos.

If it's too much trouble to play it you must honestly say so. – But I had to ask you, because I'm sure no one else could either read it (although I'm making a superb copy –) or anyway understand it. [. . .]

Much love from
Betty
P.S. Isn't it exciting?

6 Hugh Allen, the RCM Director.

Both Maconchy and Williams were awarded Octavia travelling scholarships by the RCM; these offered composition students the invaluable opportunity to study overseas. In 1929, Maconchy travelled to Prague to study with Karel Jirák, and in summer 1930 Williams went to Vienna to study with Egon Wellesz.[7]

At the same time as all this professional activity, Maconchy became secretly engaged to Irish scholar and librarian William LeFanu, known as 'Billy'.

5) 3 December 1929

Chez Mme Herlenn, 110 Boulevard Malesherbe, Paris 17e
December 3rd

My dear Grace.

I hear from Uncle Ralph that you've got the Octavia, too. How simply splendid: my dear, I <u>am</u> so glad. You said you wanted perhaps to get a job abroad and work – and how <u>much</u> better you'll be able to do that if you don't have to use up your time and energy & 'brain-power' with a job. It is <u>grand</u>. I wonder where you'll go?

[. . .] The rumour you heard (I wonder how?) about me being engaged is true – in fact it has been true for nearly a year, though it seems impossible to realise that it is as long as that, – and in another way seems <u>miles</u> longer: and I am <u>very</u> glad that you 'most thoroughly approve' of the 'nice tall fair man' because it is to him. Of course the trouble is that neither of us have any money – and so no-one is supposed to know about it (don't tell anyone else will you?) – because it is so hopeless to have a formal sort of engagement and for people always to be saying 'when are you going to be married' when one doesn't know. So the best thing seemed to be for me to fill in some time by going abroad: and it is not easy for either of us to work when we are both in London and I thought it would be easier for both of us if I was away. But <u>nothing</u> could have been harder than to try and work, – or even to try & stay in Prague! So I did what I could as fast as possible about seeing people and showing them my things, and getting introduced to conductors and things – (I had about 7 lessons from Jirak, too, who I think is <u>extremely</u> good;) and then I had a marvellous ten days in London before coming here: nobody knew I was home except Uncle Ralph – and Mummy (I didn't tell her till the last minute that I was coming!) who is in Ireland for the winter, but was in London at that moment.

[. . .] Well, then I came here, – and though I have had a wonderful time at the Louvre – and still there are lots of things to see there – and there is lots to see and hear in Paris – I haven't met <u>any</u> interesting musical people. I really don't feel I want to a bit – but was rather worried by feeling that perhaps I ought to and both[er] all sorts of people who didn't want to see me: however Uncle Ralph (he is <u>wonderful</u>) reassuringly says it doesn't matter. I have heard two <u>wonderful</u> performances of the Debussy Fêtes since I've been here: and two of Nuages, and one of Sirènes – (with sirens who were even solider and less seductive than the

---

[7] Williams wrote of her experience in 'A Letter from Vienna', published in *The R.C.M. Magazine* 26/2 (1930), 64–67.

8   *Part I. Letters 1–49 (1927–Summer 1939)*

ones at the R.C.M.)[8] Do you remember how excited we were by Fêtes that day at College[?] Other things have been good too – but a new Aubade for Piano & 18 orchestral instruments by Poulenc, which I heard on Sunday was so bad in every conceivable way (except in his immense command of instrument technique) that I have hardly yet recovered from the fury & indignation it aroused in me. I do think that most of these new French people are just 'damned silly'!

You said in your letter that you might go to Vienna, – do you think you will? – I shall be going out to Prague in March – because they are going to do my Concerto with the Philharmonic Orchestra: Jirak is going to conduct it, & Erwin Schulhoff is playing it: won't it be thrilling? and it is on March 19th – my birthday – which I feel to be a good omen! Also Jeremias, the wireless conductor, is going to do the Fantasy for Children (which I don't think you like much!) on the wireless at the beginning of March – and the Variations[9] later – either in April or May – pray heaven it is April – & that he won't cry off – it is always rather risky when dates are vague!

I must come to Vienna if you are there – I want to go from Prague – (though I shan't when it comes to the point because it will mean staying away longer!) but I would like to see it – and it is very cheap to go from Prague, under £2 for the return ticket, I think – and it would be splendid if you are there.

I have been working quite hard here at a string quintet – I want to send it in for the Cobbett, I think – (though I think it's rather bad, I can't tell,).[10] The president of the German Chamber Music Society in Prague asked me to write a quartet for them to have played at one of the society's concerts next season. This was meant to be a quartet, but turned, accidentally, but quite inevitably, into a quintet, so I don't know if it will do!

I must stop. – I am going to Ireland for Christmas – I must keep Mummy company as Sheila has gone to Canada for 2 or 3 months, and Maureen of course is in Cairo, so she is rather deserted by her family.[11] [. . .]

The prospects of getting married are not so far off as they were – as Billy has a new job, which is £400 a year,[12] – and I want to start trying to get some pupils when I come back to London, and make some money too.

Goodbye for the present – I am so glad about the Octavia –

Much love from Betty

Maconchy returned to Prague for several important performances of her works: on 19 March 1930, Jirák conducted the Prague Philharmonic Orchestra in a

---

8   The three movements of Debussy's orchestral *Nocturnes* (1899).
9   Maconchy's Theme and Variations for orchestra (1928) was apparently not performed.
10   W. W. Cobbett had been holding competitions annually since 1905 to generate the creation of chamber music 'phantasies'. Maconchy's two-movement *Phantasy Quintet* for strings (1929) was awarded this prestigious prize in 1930.
11   Sheila and Maureen were Maconchy's sisters.
12   In 1929, William LeFanu was appointed assistant to Sir D'Arcy Power, Honorary Librarian of the Royal College of Surgeons. He was to remain librarian of the RCS for the rest of his working life.

performance of a revised version of her Piano Concerto, with the eminent Czech composer–pianist Erwin Schulhoff, and on 25 March Otakar Jeremiáš conducted her chamber orchestra work, Fantasy for Children *(1927–8) on Prague Radio.*

6) [Between 2 and 7 March 1930]

Hotel Atlantic, Spretova ulice 13, Prague xii
Thursday

My dear Grace,

It is <u>grand</u> of you to say you'll come – I wish you could come sooner – now – I'm so lonely – : but I shall survive no doubt, and it will be grand to have you for the Concerto. I'll book a room for you from the Tuesday night, and of course I'll meet you when I hear what time you arrive.

[. . .]

There's a good deal of music going on for me to hear, and the people I knew before are <u>very</u> nice and seem pleased to see me again, and so on, which all helps, but I do rather curse myself for coming.

I think it would be <u>much</u> nicer to be in the room in your house, even if it's hideous. (My wall paper here is red with a pattern of leaves and umbrellas on it, in 2 shades of green, apple & emerald.) – if that would really be possible.

[. . .] This really is quite a nice place, I think, – though it is rather complicated to have a bath. It is too expensive to have a room with a bath-room, and there aren't any sort of public bathrooms; – when you ask for one you have it in the private one belonging to a room that isn't taken: if they're all taken while you're here, which is the week of the Fair, we'll have to devise some other means.

Wasn't it sickening? My <u>nicest</u> evening dress was stolen on the way here – they must have bent up the side of the lid of my suitcase & pulled it out: the one I was going to wear on the 19th: but it can't be helped – I'm insured, & so I hope I'll get something.

[. . .] I do hope the Spring will come soon: there is a drought here, and the grass is dark grey and the trees look as if they never could come into leaf, but perhaps they will.

Much love from
Betty

7) 7 March 1930

Společenský Klub, V Praze, Na Příkopě, Číslo 12, Telefon 268.33. 330449
V Praze
Friday

My dear – I heard last night that the rehearsals of the Concerto aren't till the mornings of the 18th and 19th – and I have nothing definite to be here for except a preliminary rehearsal, with just piano, of the thing on Monday next at 11.30. – So

Figure PI.1.1 Elizabeth Maconchy, *The Land* (1930), autograph manuscript, p. 1. (Letter 8)

I suddenly thought 'now is my chance to go to Vienna' – so I fired off a wire at you – I don't expect I'll get an answer till the morning because everything is shut this afternoon for Masaryk's[13] birthday party. But I do hope it will be all right – [...] I feel very much excited by the idea, and immensely cheered up. I shall just bring a small suitcase. – I <u>wonder</u> if they're doing a Mozart opera in the next week – ? it's one of my chief ambitions to hear Don Juan or Figaro in Vienna.

I wonder if the room in your house is free now – I <u>hope</u> so. Is it warm?!! You know how cold I am, – but you are, too: and anyway it will soon be spring. – I'm longing to hear that it will be all right, and to see you soon

Best love Betty.

Maconchy later recalled her Vienna visit: 'We went three times to the opera in Vienna, as cheaply as possible: to Meistersinger, Die Entführung, and Salomé, and we looked at Pictures in the Kunsthistorisches and the Albertina, walked in the Wiener Wald, and even had coffee (we couldn't afford more) in the smartest Viennese cafe – where we smoked a cigar'.[14] *Williams then came to Prague, as promised, for the performance of Maconchy's Piano Concerto. It is telling of Williams's finances, outlook, and determination that she chose to travel third class for her return to the UK.*

Maconchy was to marry Billy on 23 August at Santry Parish Church in Ireland. Her orchestral suite, The Land *(1929), after Vita Sackville-West's poem, was performed a week later, on 30 August at the Promenade Concerts, conducted by Sir Henry J. Wood and broadcast by the BBC.*

8) 21 July [1930]

Heath Cottage, Layer de la Haye, near Colchester.
July 21st

My dear Grace.

It was grand to get your postcard this morning – but alas, I'm not coming up to London any more I fear before I go over to Ireland. [. . .] I wish I could see you – when do you go back? (to Vienna, in the autumn, I mean) You are going back all right aren't you, as they have extended your thing? (upon which congratulations) or will you go somewhere else? – I <u>suppose</u> you will have gone before the beginning of October, when we shall get back from our honey-moon? (in Connemara, my dear, won't it be superb?) We've got a flat at 28 Upper Addison Gardens – and it would be lovely if you could come and see us there. So if you haven't gone, you <u>must</u>. But stay! – if you <u>really</u> could be at the Queen's Hall to hear the Land I shall see you then. It is on August 30th: (Saturday) but you really mustn't come all the way up if you are at home then – you could listen in from there. It would be lovely if you could hear it though: and you are

---

13 Tomáš Garrigue Masaryk, first president of Czechoslovakia.
14 Maconchy, contribution to 'Grace Williams: A Symposium', *Welsh Music* 5, no. 6 (Summer 1977), 18.

a <u>marvellously</u> valuable person to discuss things with. The concert is exactly a week after the wedding – won't I be cross and awful after <u>both</u>? – <u>you</u> know the disastrous effect that just the concert in Prague had on me! You were noble to bear with me as you did.

There's such a lot I want to hear from you. <u>Is</u> your Suite going to be done?[15] & if so, where? Do tell me – & of everything else. How is Wellesz? How <u>stoic</u> to come home third. Billy and I will have to go to Prague like that some time. –

My dear I would <u>love</u> it if you gave me a handkerchief to use at my wedding – (I don't mean that I shall weep! – but I can flaunt it.) I haven't got a nice one, and I'd like to have one you gave me.

Best love from Betty.

On 6 August 1931, Williams's overture, Hen Walia (1930), *was given its first performance at the Eisteddfod in Bangor by the London Symphony Orchestra, conducted by Evan Thomas Davies and broadcast on the BBC's National Programme. It is interesting that Maconchy and Williams were composing operas this early in their careers and at a time when there were few opportunities for performances of British operas.*

9) 10 August 1931

28, Upper Addison Gardens, W.14. Park 5932
August 10th 1931

Dearest Grace.

I've meant to write to you ever since Thursday night: – we heard 'Hen Walia' – (what does it mean by the way? –) <u>very</u> clearly, on a borrowed set; and I was frightfully impressed by it. It seemed to me to be just what an Overture ought to be – awfully good stuff, and all very much to the point. – It sounded – although it's much harder to tell that on the wireless than in the flesh – as if it would have benefited by more rehearsal – the joins sounded a bit precarious – I thought: – though no doubt they are perfectly safe, really. The opening was splendid, I thought – and I thought you worked the Welsh tune, with the horn counterpoint, up to a point when it was very moving. I did feel doubtful about one thing – and that is – does the second half really balance the first part, with its very vigorous beginning and all that slow part, which seemed to make it very big and solid? [. . .] But I expect I got that impression largely because it wasn't an ideal performance – I suspect that they didn't get nearly a big enough climax near the end? – and anyway I'm probably all wrong about it. I thought the scoring was <u>brilliant</u> – you <u>are</u> good at it!

[. . .]

I'm so sorry I didn't write at once – as I meant to. But I've been more or less doing parts incessantly. However, I shall have them done before we go to Ireland – and that is on Friday week. [. . .] It will be grand to get to Ireland – though this

---

15 Probably the Suite for orchestra (*c.* 1931–2).

isn't my idea of what London in August would be like – I am shivering in front of a fire! – It was fun that you came here last week – and I loved seeing your opera – and showing you ours.[16] – Is the music <u>too</u> rubbishy? – and what do you really think about 'Goodbye summer, good-bye goodbye' – ? it might be very hard to make the skit convincing enough with a small orchestra – which I think we <u>must</u> limit ourselves to. But yet it comes in so naturally there!

I wish you weren't going to Vienna – I must stop. – Do have a good holiday before you go – and don't ruin your touch by too much typing!

Best love – and I did think the overture was <u>grand</u> – ('More Power to your – – ')
Betty

---

16 Neither of these two early operas have been traced.

I.2 Letters 10–23
(February 1932–March 1933)

In early 1932, it was discovered that Maconchy had contracted tuberculosis, the disease which had killed her father, Gerald Maconchy, ten years earlier. Rather than relocate to Switzerland, she moved first to the fresh air of Brighton and then to a house ('Chart Corner') near Sevenoaks in Kent. Cut off from London's musical life, correspondence with friends and the wireless both became increasingly important. Meanwhile, Williams found employment teaching part-time at Southlands Training College in south London, as well as copying parts for Oxford University Press, the Music Department of which was under the direction of Hubert Foss.

Both Maconchy and Williams were involved from the start of the 'Ballet Club Concerts', as they were initially known, instigated by their friends: violinist Anne Macnaghten (leader of the Macnaghten String Quartet), conductor Iris Lemare, and composer Elisabeth Lutyens in December 1931. The concerts became formally known as the Macnaghten–Lemare Concerts and provided invaluable performance opportunities for the generation of British composers that included Britten, Lutyens, Maconchy, Williams, and many others.[1]

Another important series of concerts was the International Society for Contemporary Music (ISCM) Festivals, which had been started in 1922. These became an important annual fixture for composers interested in recent European developments.

10) 24 February 1932

4 Kingscliffe Court, Marine Parade, Brighton
February 24th

Dearest Grace.

Your letter was like wine to the thirsty & pleased me a lot. Your musical adventures at Putney seem to have been rich: the music mistress sounds a rare

---

[1] See Sophie Fuller, '"Putting the BBC and T. Beecham to Shame": The Macnaghten–Lemare Concerts, 1931–7', *Journal of the Royal Musical Association* 138, no. 2 (2013), 377–414.

Section I.2. Letters 10–23 (February 1932–March 1933) 15

and interesting specimen (or perhaps this species of temperamental composer is frequently to be met with?) I should think she would be best in small doses – & I hope you won't have to see too much of her!

[. . .]

I am <u>furious</u> about the Patron's Fund. It is absolutely <u>mad</u> to have rejected your Psalms.² Who can they have to select the things? – unless, as you say, it is Claude Aveling³ – (but seriously it could <u>hardly</u> be him!) And it is more maddening to think of some of the tripe, and the obviously incompetent things they do do. – It is dreadful that such a laudable (& expensive) scheme should be so wasted – & not only wasted but perverted and misapplied. I wish Uncle Ralph would seriously agitate for its reform. I think it is very important.

It is grand that you are getting jobs – though I don't like to think of your doing 84 pages of part copying in 3 days. They must have been perfect if Hubert Foss wrote himself about them – & I expect you'll get lots more if you want them. <u>Don't</u> go and strain your eyes over them, whatever you do – as, once strained, they are a fearful bore.

Well, Brighton is far nicer than I expected: this flat is really awfully nice, and the drawing-room & our bedroom have big windows looking over the sea, & get all the sun there is, (there has been a certain amount, & one completely perfect day, but a lot of mist and greyness –). So far I haven't done much – Billy propels me (very rapidly) in a bath-chair at the weekend, & Mummy (much slower!) on weekdays – also a <u>charming</u> old man (82 years old) who has been a coachman in Brighton since '79 & tells me his life-story & all about his relations (I have got as far as the in-laws, now) with hardly a pause. I meant to answer your letter sooner, but, though it sounds paradoxical, while I lead this life of idleness I don't seem to get time to do anything! I get up at 11 – go out in the bath chair from 11.30 till 12.30 – rest after lunch – go out in the chair again before tea – & spend most of the rest of the time on the sofa, which makes one feel too comfortably lazy to do much – (I'm there now, so this letter will probably be idiotic.) Mummy & I play numerous games of backgammon!! & Billy gets home at 7, or sometimes a few minutes earlier. (Thank goodness the trains are very good – only an hour for 56 miles – & he doesn't find the journey very tiring – he is looking much better already, too.) I went for a short walk this morning, & hope soon to be able to kick the bath-chair into the sea. It amused me so much at first – & Billy & I laughed a lot at ourselves when he pushed me along in it – but by now all the novelty has disappeared & I hate the thing. – I've done a small alteration to the quintet⁴ (which Anne Macn. is going to play at a party of her mother's after Easter –) but otherwise no work yet, except a little piano practice – there is a rather good grand piano here, which is <u>great</u> luck.

---

2 Williams, Two Psalms for soprano and chamber orchestra (1927, rev. 1935).
3 Claude Aveling was a lyricist and translator.
4 Maconchy's prize-winning *Phantasy Quintet* for strings (1929) had already received several performances, including one by the Macnaghten Quartet with Joyce Cook on 14 December 1931; see Letter 5.

16   Part I. Letters 1–49 (1927–Summer 1939)

I really feel <u>practically</u> all right now – & at the end of 2 months health-promotion I should think I ought to be in the rudest health.

The X-ray showed traces of a small patch on my right lung, apparently – but the London doctor & the one here, & Sir Percival Hartley, who we had once, were all certain of it clearing up quickly, & with all the listening-in & thumping they've done to my chest they can hear absolutely <u>nothing</u> now & so I expect it's cleared up already. It was very sad not to see you that day at the Home – I hope you got quite successfully over the chill, which sounded nasty. But it was grand seeing you the other time, & frightfully good of you to come.

[. . .] I seem to be missing <u>such</u> good concerts, (& up till Christmas they were so dull!) all that week of the Busch quartet[5] & every sort of thing. I had the wireless at the nursing-home the night Busch played the Brahms at Queen's Hall – & heard about 2 thirds of the first movement – absolutely <u>superb</u> – when the b — y batteries gave out. Comment is superfluous. I wanted to hear the Bax badly, too – was it good?[6] (By the way did you come across the picture in the Evening Standard (Billy discovered it) of 'Miss Harriet Cohen in hiking costume'?) Mummy is preparing for backgammon, & seems anxious for me to play – so goodbye, my dear, forgive this aimless scribble. – (I played through one of my 8-part things 2 days ago,[7] & thought it good – I must show them to you some time.)

Best love from
Betty
My love to any of the nice people you happen to see.

Maconchy's Suite for chamber orchestra (1930) had received its first performance by the London Chamber Orchestra, conducted by Anthony Barnard, at Aeolian Hall in London on 10 February 1931, and was given its first broadcast on the BBC London Regional Programme by the BBC Orchestra, conducted by Adrian Boult. Her Symphony (1929–30) was played through on 30 March 1932 by the BBC Orchestra, conducted by Aylmer Buesst, but was later withdrawn.

11) 11 March 1932

4 Kingscliffe Court., Marine Parade, Brighton
March 11th

Dearest Grace,

This is just to tell you of very good news I've had from the B.B.C. They're going to do my 'Suite for Chamber Orchestra' – (I don't think you've seen it – it's not a very good work – Anthony Bernard did it a little over a year ago – or were you at that concert – my memory is confused & I can't remember.) Anyway they're doing it on

---

5   The Busch Quartet, led by violinist Adolph Busch, was then a leading European string quartet.
6   On 10 February 1932, Arnold Bax's 'Symphonic concerto for piano and orchestra', *Winter Legends*, was first performed by pianist Harriet Cohen at a BBC Symphony Concert and broadcast on the National Programme.
7   Maconchy's Two Motets (John Donne) for double chorus (1931).

the 21st (Monday week) in studio No. 10 for the regional programme, between 9 & 10.15. The rehearsal is at 2.30 that day, & I'm coming up for that & the concert & staying the night. Could you come to the rehearsal? I'd love it if you could – they said they 'hoped I wouldn't hesitate to bring anyone who particularly wished to hear it' to the rehearsal – so I take it they don't want people to come in the evening!

It <u>would</u> be nice if you could come, as it nearly hits off the 2nd anniversary of the Concerto in Prague. – <u>Also</u>, they're going to rehearse the Symphony – just a try-over, I imagine, at what they call a 'special rehearsal' on the 30th – Wednesday – and they say I can invite people if I let them know beforehand how many – so would you like to hear it? I am wildly excited about it – it has been my chief ambition for some time to hear it – more especially in Studio 10 (the Waterloo Bridge one –) & even though it will probably be just a run through & will sound pretty inadequate, it's thrilling, isn't it? [. . .]. I'm feeling miles better (& am allowed to walk for quarter of an hour!) The doctor didn't much want me to go to London – but I got him to say I could!

We're going to stay here till the end of April, I think – & we are looking for a little cottage or house in the country as the doctor thinks I ought to live there for a year or two, & are trying to get rid of the end of our lease of the flat.

Best love – I <u>hope</u> I may see you & hear your news
Betty

12) [After 21 March 1932]

9. Old Village Road, Barry, Glamorgan

Dearest Betty

The Suite is brilliant: It's got such <u>stuff</u> in it & it all comes off <u>superbly</u> – it's much the most professional thing you've done – the scoring is heavenly so new & so <u>vital</u>. Of the Allegros I like No 3 (<u>Mvt 3</u>) best; though the last is amazing – & such a Fugue! – it doesn't come off <u>quite</u> as well as the others does it? It comes off frightfully well, but it isn't quite as brilliant as 1 & 3 – because a fugue is the most damnably devilish sort of music to score isn't it? – But I loved your subject in augmentation.

Both your slow mvts – were <u>lovely</u> – I can't say more.

I should have liked No. 1 to have been <u>much</u> longer. There is so much stuff there – it could easily be lengthened –

And I thought the finish of No. 5 a bit too abrupt & unprepared. I do feel something <u>vital</u> ought to happen before a finish. Either that or a gradual dying away. I don't like things being cut off suddenly unless they have some <u>terrific</u> force behind them. One's physical reaction is so much grander if the music ends brilliantly & <u>definitely</u> – it's so lovely getting worked up for the end – it's equally lovely when a thing ends on a suspended pianissimo. I fear I'm horribly conventional about this point. Please forgive me for harping so much about it. If there had been a stringendo & a crescendo before that final snap, I should have been so terribly thrilled. As it was Marian said it was a pantomime to watch me listening. Yes it is a brilliant work & I hope & hope that Adrian realised it & that now you'll be a B.B.C. fixture. I wish I could be in London on the 30th: oh dear it is sad to think I was in

London all those weeks when they didn't do it. Do you know when the broadcast performance is to be? Perhaps they will have a second rehearsal later, when I am back in town.

It's <u>heavenly</u> being at home. I am a free soul again.

Look after yourself well. I hope you didn't get over excited yesterday.

– Best love from

Grace

13) 18 May 1932

Chart Corner, Seal Chart, near Sevenoaks
Seal 106.
May 18th 1932

Dearest Grace.

I am a <u>pig</u> to have left you so long without a letter – & I have two letters of long standing to thank you for. The first was about the Suite, – which seems about a hundred years ago now! – I'm so glad you liked it – I agree that the last movement is <u>not</u> right – & I shall overhaul it – but I haven't yet begun to work. The other was about the Symphony – I wish you'd heard it – because it was probably the first & last 'world performance' there will ever be! The B.B.C. <u>aren't</u> going to perform it, alas! – however – it was a great thing to hear it, & good of them to give it a try-over. I must wait & tell you all I thought about it when we meet. On the whole, I was pleased – given a more vigorous conductor than Mr Buesst (how I longed to conduct it myself!) I think most of it would go all right, though I'm not happy about the last movement: it really looks rather good on paper but it's <u>too</u> contrapuntal for orchestral writing, I believe – or, I suppose, contrapuntal in an ineffective way. The slow movement pleased me very much. [. . .][8]

Williams's Two Psalms for soprano and chamber orchestra (1927, rev. c. 1935) were first performed at a Patron's Fund rehearsal at the RCM on 1 July 1932, sung by Meriel Green and conducted by Iris Lemare. Her Suite for orchestra (1932) was performed at the 1932 Eisteddfod by the London Symphony Orchestra and broadcast by the BBC's National Programme.

14) 23 June 1932

Chart Corner, Seal Chart, Kent, Seal 106
June 23rd 1932

Dearest Grace

It is absolutely grand about the Eisteddfodd (is that spelt right?) and about Patron's Fund. I am almost sure that I shall be able to come up & hear the Psalms

---

[8] The end of this letter is missing.

Section I.2. Letters 10–23 (February 1932–March 1933)   19

on the 1st – which will be lovely. We <u>must</u> get a wireless before the Eist. . ., it is disgraceful that we haven't got one yet, but there are such a lot of things (like a revolving summer house, which we're just getting) that we want! In the meantime, of course, I hear no music. – I hope the Psalms are going well, & that Meriel is in good voice – or will be next Friday. Perhaps she will strike one of those days – oh, how rare for a singer – when she has not got a sore throat, or a cold, or hay fever, or flu, or indigestion, or bereavement.

I also have a bit of good news – The B.B.C. are doing the Piano Concerto on the 7th of July – about 8. p.m. & Kathleen Long is playing it.[9] She has been frightfully nice – I went up to London just over a week ago & we did it on two pianos, <u>very</u> thoroughly & she is going to play it frightfully well – much better than Schulhoff.[10] There's only going to be one (short) orchestral rehearsal for an all-modern programme – so she's going to try & get Stanford Robinson,[11] who's conducting it, to rehearse it with us on two pianos – I hope to goodness he can. You must meet us that evening & we will feed together to commemorate our meal before the concerto in Prague – & come on to the Studio – as I expect I'll be allowed to bring people.

Do tell Uncle Ralph about this if you see him – I've been meaning to write to him daily but I want to send him my 2 8-part hymns (Donne words –) & I must do a little to them first, which never gets done. I'd like to play them to you – sometimes I think they are <u>good</u> – & sometimes alas! very bad. There was an idea that Iris' choir should do them at the Ballet Club Concerts in the autumn – but Anne thinks they'd be too difficult[12] – I am rather glad, as I'd like them to be very well done, if at all. – Have you started your 'piece'[13] for them yet? I've just started to get to work again properly – I'm finding it extremely difficult to get back into my stride – (or perhaps I should [be] saying 'toddle') & am wondering if I'll ever write a good bar again. I'm doing an overture[14] – probably it will have to be to 'an unwritten comedy' – as I don't think the opera is going to come off (the overture is intended for it – I think it's a good plan to have some tunes to work on when one's trying to 'write oneself in') Jack Gordon[15] thinks the libretto ought all to be altered, which has discouraged us. Gwen Raverat (who designed the décor for Job –)[16] is 'doing' a ballet from a Hans Andersen fairy story (for a children's school, I believe) & wants me to do the music, which sounds good.[17]

---

9 Broadcast on the London Regional Programme.
10 See Letter 5.
11 Stanford Robinson was a BBC staff conductor.
12 Conductor Iris Lemare and violinist Anne Macnaghten, organisers of the Ballet Club (Macnaghten–Lemare) concerts.
13 Williams's Movement for trumpet and chamber orchestra (1932).
14 Maconchy's Comedy Overture (1932–3).
15 John Barritt Gordon was an opera producer who acted as manager of the opera class at RCM from 1930 to 1937.
16 Wood-engraver Gwen Raverat (born Darwin) had worked on Vaughan Williams, *Job: A Masque for Dancing*, premiered at the Old Vic Theatre, London in 1931.
17 Maconchy's ballet, *Little Red Shoes* (1935).

It must have been grand seeing Wellesz – (how foul missing Oxford –) – I'd love to have met him again. Don't you wish you were at the International Festival now?[18] Anne Macnaghten is there – I had an amusing letter about it from her yesterday. It's going to be in Amsterdam next year I believe – ; we must force them to do something of ours, & go. It's so get-at-able.

[. . .]

I've been given a 'clean bill of health' by the doctor – which is marvellous. He says I've only got to get strong again, & always be careful of colds etc. I feel marvellous, but still get tired absurdly easily. It is absolutely divine here. Best of best love Betty.

Do send a p.c. as to where in the Patron's programme your Psalms come. Could we lunch together afterwards?

You mustn't be so indignant about the Symphony! I'm quite resigned.

Maconchy's Sonata for violin and piano (1927) was given its first performance at a Macnaghten–Lemare concert on 18 October 1932, with Anne Macnaghten on violin and Helen Perkin[19] on piano. The other works on the programme included a Haydn string quartet, songs by amateur composer Oliver Horsley Gotch, and the first performance of the Fantasy string quartet (1932) by Dorothy Gow (a very close friend of both Maconchy and Williams, known as 'Dolly' and later 'Dorrie'). The Macnaghten Quartet played this quartet, and all works they performed, from memory. At this time, Williams was preparing parts for her Sextet for oboe, trumpet, violin, viola, cello, and piano (1931) for the prestigious Daily Telegraph (D.T.) *competition.*

15) 22 October 1932

Chart Corner
October 22nd

Dearest Grace.

I don't quite know what to feel about the sonata either. – For one thing I found I couldn't 'get away' from it & hear it as a whole – as one almost always can at a performance – so that I still don't know if it's a good work or not. It did go well; – but I was left feeling flat & rather disappointed. I think Helen P. didn't know it well enough to let herself go – and of course that held Anne back too. I wish you had been playing it. – It was chiefly the slow movement that was disappointing – wasn't it? It wasn't slow enough for one thing – and I thought Helen was rather perfunctory – specially in the quiet parts – so that her part

---

18 The ISCM Festival in 1932 was held in Vienna.
19 English composer and pianist Helen Perkin was closely associated with the composer John Ireland; she gave the first performance of his Piano Concerto in the 1930 Proms. See also Letter 317.

sounded a bit meaningless. – The last movement went well, didn't it? & seems to come off all right, I think. I want to see you and talk about it – and lots of other things. Don't regard yourself as a fault-finder! You're not – and you're much the best critic I know.

<u>Do</u> come on either the Monday or Tuesday after next, (31st or 1st, I suppose that is –) both are equally good for me – so let me know which. It will be grand – it was sickening only seeing you for a second. I went before the Haydn. – the only condition on which I was allowed to come was that I left directly my piece was over – and eat lozenges all the time – & walked out if it was hot! I longed to walk out during the Gotch – because they <u>were</u> terrible and it <u>was</u> hot – but I hadn't the face to! (Anyway, I'm all the better for the expedition.) I liked Dolly's quartet very much – I don't think it unoriginal – but of course there <u>are</u> a lot of clichés in it: but she is good; – and I thought they played it excellently (I hadn't heard it before, of course). I <u>do</u> approve of playing without music, don't you?

Well, all news & talk when we meet. – I wish I could hear your D.T. sextet. You must be having an awful time over the parts. Much love from Betty.

The Macnaghten–Lemare concert on 15 November 1932 included Gordon Jacob's Second String Quartet (1930) and Maconchy's 'The Woodspurge' (1930), a setting of D.G. Rossetti, sung by Muriel Herbert, with Alannah Delias accompanying. Maconchy continued work on her Comedy Overture, *while Williams was working on her Movement for trumpet and chamber orchestra (1932) and a Suite for nine instruments (1932). Benjamin Britten, then a young composer at the RCM, was a good friend of Williams's during the 1930s.*[20]

16) 18 November 1932

Chart Corner
November 18th

Dearest Grace.

It was marvellous getting your letter this morning – and I've devoured it more than once, (which proves you can eat your cake – and have it. . .) You tell me all the things I want to know: – and you have of course hit the nail on the head about my song – the accompaniment is the thing. What happened was – (this is a confession) I wrote it as a small piano piece (supposed to be one of a suite) in Prague – but it didn't feel satisfactory somehow and I couldn't get it to feel so – then, nearly a year later, when we were on our honeymoon, I was reading those words & thought 'that's just the thing – it ought to be a song – ' I took the piano

---

[20] See Malcolm Boyd, 'Benjamin Britten and Grace Williams: Chronicle of a Friendship', *Welsh Music* 6, no. 4 (1980).

part almost as it stood, (lengthening it a bit, etc) and of course the voice part is consequently negligible; but I liked the result, rather. (Not, of course, the right way to write a song – . . . But then Petrouchka[21] was a piano concerto – – –) I <u>am</u> glad you liked it – (and that Alannah played it so well)

The one time I heard Gordon's 2nd quartet (at his chamber concert) I also thought it was <u>deadly</u>: poor Gordon. I think Mrs G's (I never <u>can</u> succeed in calling her 'Sydney') remark about 'not the right thing for young girls' is absolutely <u>superb</u>. I hope they'll come here and see me – I'd like it. Have they got a car? Gordon once talked of getting one, I know

So glad you've started on the trumpet piece – <u>please</u> let me see it. I haven't seen anything of yours properly for ages. I'd love to see your suite – but I <u>hope</u> you sent it in for the International Festival? I'm scoring my overture. I'm aiming at effectiveness above all (I <u>must</u> try & produce a 'successful piece') & I wondered if I was sacrificing any vision I ever had to competence (of a sort) when I read your letter. I do think you are so right about that – scoring, I mean. Competence is <u>not</u> everything, and there ought not to be a rule of thumb way or even a 'right' way of scoring any particular sort of passage. I remember Gussie[22] saying the same thing about Gordon's scoring – (only rather diffidently and 'in confidence' so don't say he said so!) It's such a temptation, if you know or think you know the 'proper' & effective way to score some bit – just to <u>do</u> it like that swiftly and competently – instead of listening to it in your head how you imagine it sounding & then boiling it laboriously down on to paper from that – if you know what I mean.

I'm very glad to know about Britten. The college staff are such <u>sheep</u> aren't they? (Hear the way they all follow if one leads: they're so lazy at finding out for themselves if people are any good (apart from their own pupils) that if someone else whispers the word 'genius' (as you describe) they're only to[o] glad to concur.

I hope they won't spoil Britten, he sounds good. I daresay that partly the reason why he has sprung into prominence so quickly is that he came to College after or during a bad patch. There hasn't been anyone much at the RCM since the departure of all our distinguished selves, has there?

O – how I wish I could have heard Fêtes <u>and</u> Sacre last night.[23] I nearly wept when I first saw the programme. Were they lovely? – O – I <u>am</u> glad about the cod-liver oil; you are very good, – but fancy liking it! Do go on with it and get fat. I weigh 8 stone <u>6</u> now. I can just get up my hair now, but it takes ¼ of an hour to put it up, and it only stays for 10 minutes; but I think it won't look bad when it's longer. [. . .]

<u>Do</u> come down again soon. [. . .] And you <u>must</u> bring your trumpet piece and your Bach fugue – and I much want to show you the little I've done of the overture.

Very much love from
Betty

---

21 Stravinsky's ballet *Petrushka* (1910–11).
22 Gustav Holst.
23 The BBC Symphony Concert on 16 November 1932 included Debussy's *Nocturnes* (with first movement, 'Fêtes') and Stravinsky's *Le sacre du printemps*.

Despite the women's enthusiasm, the works both Maconchy and Williams submitted to the ISCM reading panel were rejected. Maconchy was unable to attend the next Macnaghten–Lemare concert, on 12 December, featuring a choir conducted by Iris Lemare.

17) [Before 12 December 1932] – postcard

Chart Corner, Seal Chart, Kent. Seal 106
Monday

Dearest Grace.

It is grand that you can come down [. . .]. I <u>am</u> sorry about the international – how devilishly rude just sending them back like that: I fared no better, & have all my three children back again (I got a postcard from D. Wadham[24] saying 'The committee are interested in your work & hope you will send in again'). It must have been fun Wellesz being over – & superb about the opera. – I doubt if I shall come up to Anne's next concert – though I should much like to hear Iris' choir. <u>Do</u> bring down your suite with you – and anything else you can share. Much love
 Betty.
You must go on with the cod liver oil. I have now achieved 8 st 8lbs. [. . .]

18) [Late 1932 or early 1933]

6 Arundel Terrace, Brighton
Saturday

Dearest Grace

HURRAY HURRAY it will be <u>lovely</u> to see you on Thursday. [. . .] Your suggestions about the Overture are excellent. [. . .] I nearly screamed when I came to what you said about the last 8 bars. I've had a devil of a time with the end – trying to get it quite right – and in my heart of hearts I've always had my doubts about it! and you're right about that modulation before the return of the 1st theme: but Uncle Ralph has suggested a cut just before that – I'm not quite sure about it yet – but have done an alternative version, which makes it 8 bars shorter – & it obviates that difficult modulation. I want to discuss that & all the other things with you on Thursday with the score <u>fully</u>. You are so <u>enormously</u> helpful.

There's heaps to say – but it must keep till Thursday. – It is so lovely here that B. & I are just going for a sudden expedition on to the Downs taking lunch and I hear him with the car at the door.

---

24 Dorothy Wadham, secretary of the ISCM.

I hope it will be a good day when you come. It will be simply grand to see you. Are you taking your cod-liver oil??

Very much love from
Betty

Please bring your trumpet thing (I don't believe what you say about it) & your Suite on Thursday.

Williams's Movement for trumpet and chamber orchestra was performed at a Macnaghten–Lemare concert on 31 January 1933, alongside Britten's Sinfonietta, Op. 1 (1932). In addition, she had written an opera (which can no longer be traced) that Maconchy was studying, along with Britten's Sinfonietta. In February, Maconchy had heard a BBC Concert of Contemporary Music broadcast with Britten's Phantasy in F minor for string quintet (1932), along with Christian Darnton's String Trio and Erik Chisholm's dissonant Double Trio.

19) 8 March 1933

6 Arundel Terrace, Brighton
March 8th '33

Dearest Grace.

I am sitting in one of those little shelters in the garden near the sea, & the sun is so hot it is hardly bearable, & I long to take off my clothes & sunbathe – but as I am in full view of several people on the shore I can't very well. I wish you were here to share the sun – are you coming down again? [. . .]

I've been going through the opera a good deal – though as yet, not nearly enough – & I do think it's brilliant. I think the way you've managed the material is astonishing (& it did need some managing!) & it ought all to be really effective from a 'stage' point of view. The way you've built up the scenes and managed the climaxes etc seems masterly to a degree.

I'm going over the Britten Sinfonietta carefully. I still think some of the material is rather uninteresting in itself (though always just the right kind of theme in the right place) but he does know how to make something out of it. He is accomplished. I listened to the quintet & liked the early part immensely – lovely things in it – also the end; a lot of the middle I did certainly think dull, (– I think you're right, that when he is most brilliant technically the music is least interesting & vice versa) – My God the Chisholm! – the tragedy is that people are taken in by it . . . Dear oh dear oh dear.

I have no particular news – The overture has gone to H. Wood in a superb blue cover – & I've tidied up 'The Land' score – I'd slurred the brass far too much all the way through (I must have scratched out half a mile of slurs!) & I hadn't bowed it properly before, – & I've sent it to the B.B.C. now

I'm looking forward to hearing Busch playing the Bach E major to-night.[25]

25 Violinist Adolph Busch, broadcasting the Bach E major Violin Concerto.

We go back on the 27th – the time here has gone incredibly fast. I hope the frost hasn't killed our pot plants at Chart Corner. [. . .]
Very much love from
Betty.
This is a stupid letter but the sun has made me quite idiotic!

Both Maconchy and Williams entered the 1933 Daily Telegraph *Chamber Music competition, Maconchy with a Quintet for oboe and strings (1932) and Williams with her Sextet for oboe, trumpet, violin, viola, cello, and piano (1931). Rumours abounded regarding the results, but it turned out that Maconchy won third prize, behind Edric Cundell and Cecil Armstrong Gibbs, while Britten's Phantasy, Op. 2, for oboe and string trio and Victor Hely-Hutchinson's Sextet were highly commended. The three winning works were performed and broadcast from the Concert Hall, Broadcasting House, on 13 May 1933, and recordings were issued soon after.[26] Maconchy's quintet was played by Helen Gaskell (oboe) with the Griller String Quartet.*

20) [Before 13 March 1933]

51 Warwick Rd, SW5

Dearest Betty,

How <u>HEAVENLY</u>! – ! When I got your postcard I felt convinced you'd got 1st prize. It didn't enter my head – not for a moment – that it could be anything but first but then I rang up Anne to tell her the glad tidings & she tells me that Gerrard Williams has topped the list with that 'Accomplished' quartet – blast him he <u>is</u> an accomplished craftsman of the first order, I know – he does all those military band arrangements for the B.B.C. – & his school music arrangements are quite well done.[27]

[. . .]

However £75 will be very nice for you & then your quintet <u>will be broadcast</u> – I'm <u>longing</u> to hear it – I howled when I read that it was 'young man's music' didn't you? I wonder who'll get the 3rd? Anne hasn't the slightest idea. I strongly suspect the 'little trio' – the 'delightful musical toy'. I wonder whether the oboe quartet was Benjamin's. He's away for the weekend so I can't ask him. – I am just a <u>bit</u> jealous of the other sextet. My heart missed a beat when I read about it. – Piano & wind – & then a full stop. <u>But</u> no strings (& I had 3) mentioned – and the description did so fit <u>most</u> of my thing it was nothing but a string of tunes which I wrote mostly when I was sunbathing – nevertheless lots of my first & last mvts. were a bit fiery – so – I have a nasty little serpent within me when I think of this other person's sextet – but it will soon be subdued.

---

26 See Letter 24.
27 In the semi-finals, the top six pieces were played without identification for the judges and critics. In fact, the piece by Gerrard Williams did not receive a prize.

Write & tell me everything <u>at once</u>. Bless you if <u>ever</u> any one deserved to win it's you & I'm absolutely delighted – so will everyone else who knows you be. I'll write again when I hear the verdict. This is my last sheet of notepaper – can't write anymore. Isn't Billy wound up about it. I could just imagine you having a <u>perfect</u> day yesterday. Best love Grace

21) 13 March 1933

Monday, March 13th '33
6 Arundel Terrace

Dearest Grace. It was lovely getting your letter this morning. But I can't tell you how I wish & wish you had got a prize too. Then it would be marvellous. You'll have seen this morning that I wasn't even 2nd – only 3rd! but still. <u>Comic</u> Armstrong Gibbs being 2nd! – how did Anne get hold of Gerard Williams' name as the winner? (Perhaps he's the sixth one who isn't mentioned – or perhaps she's just muddled him up somehow with Edric Cundell – who I know only by name – do you know anything about him?) I'm sorry Britten didn't get a prize too – though I should I'm afraid have been really <u>jealous</u> if his oboe piece had got it instead of mine!

Well, the two <u>very</u> urgent telegrams I got on Friday – & the fact that Wortham[28] was coming down here to see me made me think – I couldn't help it – that I really might have got the 1st prize – so it was just a bit of an anti-climax when I got a letter on Saturday morning, & a cheque for £50 (though the latter is very nice!) However – – Wortham was quite nice – though he really got <u>nothing</u> out of coming down to see me – when I started to tell him that I'd got a scholarship at the College – for instance, – he waved it away, & said he must say some 'personal' things about me – however he didn't get any from me – (I hope he won't make them up – he asked me who my favourite composer was!! – (rather shamefacedly, it's true!) – but I said he really <u>couldn't</u> ask me questions like that & anyway I didn't know –) But really he's quite a nice man, & I don't think he in the least <u>wanted</u> to write rubbish, but had been told to. The 'chat' will be in tomorrow's paper. The judge's comments don't tell one much, do they?

Wortham said they'd disagreed a lot (in spite of what Sir Hugh[29] said); also that you'd be <u>amazed</u> at the people who sent in, apparently and that one person had sent <u>20</u> things!!

'Fresh-hearted, unselfconscious young man' was good! – I'm <u>sick</u> of being told I'm immature though, (<u>and</u> Vaughan-Williamsian: they didn't know I was his pupil this time – is it very obvious?)[30]

---

28 Journalist Hugo Evelyn Wortham.
29 Hugh Allen was one of the judges.
30 'An Oboe Quintet. Vaughan-Williamsian. Fresh air and Folk Song. To Write Like This One Has a True Composer's Instinct. Ideas, Atmosphere. Immaturity, No Doubt, Too, and Uncertain Balance.

I must go in to lunch – I've written about nothing but this thing – ; but you <u>did</u> say you wanted to hear, & it's fun to pour it out to you. I do wish you'd got 1st prize: but these things are just bound to be chancy & unreliable & wrong.

It is very sad that I shan't see you till next term – but you must come and stay then. I hope that 4tet do play your variations[31] 'decently' & will broadcast them... (Wortham said he <u>thought</u> they would broadcast the 2nd and 3rd works a bit later.)

All best love
Betty.
Yes, B. is <u>frightfully</u> pleased.
I had a lovely letter from Uncle Ralph this morning.

Discussion about the competition continued, but Williams also described going with Britten to the BBC Concert Hall on 13 March 1933 to hear Samuel Dushkin (violin) and Igor Stravinsky (piano) perform a programme of Stravinsky's works, including the Duo Concertant *(1931–2) and the* Pulcinella Suite *(1925).*

22) [Between 14 and 17 March 1933]

51 Warwick Rd, SW5

Dearest Betty

It was <u>terribly</u> kind of you to write so soon; & <u>such</u> a letter telling me everything I wanted to know. Of course they'll broadcast the quintet – I'm sure Bliss[32] will see to that – he said in his first article that he hoped all six would be performed soon & I do think he'll do his best to see that they are because he is a nice kind person & thank God he at least was a sane adjudicator. I feel it in my bones that he fought hard for your work & I suspect that he'd have liked it to have been first – but the other three old fossils <u>would</u> fall for something which came off perfectly at first go. They <u>must</u> have had a shock when they read about 'Serbia' & 'Deirdre'[33] – & now Henry & Adrian[34] will have to perform them!! My dear, Benjamin once heard some Cundell at a Patron's & he says it was frightful. Brahms & Elgar. I don't know – he seems rather a nice unsophisticated humble sort of chap though – but again I don't know. Anyhow it isn't his fault that he got first prize. So Armstrong Gibbs still preaches the same old Gospel that he preached to us at that scholarship exam. years ago. Do you remember? A blaring hot afternoon & he with his orange hair & raspberry face & loud check suit holding forth on Beauty. Oh dear – yes

---

The Oboe Overworked. A Fresh-hearted, Unselfconscious Young Man's Music', *Daily Telegraph*, 11 March 1933.
31 Probably Variations for String Quartet ('Veni Emmanuel') (1920s).
32 Composer Arthur Bliss, on the judging panel.
33 Edric Cundell, the winner, was a teacher at Trinity College of Music and had written two symphonic poems, *Serbia* (1919) and *The Tragedy of Deirdre* (1922). He was later to conduct the première of Maconchy's Bassoon Concertino.
34 Conductors Henry Wood and Adrian Boult were both on the judging panel.

it is comic, as you say that he was 2nd. But thank God for you & Benjamin (who is very pleased about you & sends his congratulations) – you really have saved the whole thing. What does Uncle Ralph say? – have you heard from him since he heard the whole result? Bless him he'll be delighted about you anyhow. About your work being Vaughan-Williamsan – NO, of course not only inasmuch as Debussy resembles Moussorgsky. I'm going through Pelleas again & when I look right into the texture of Pelleas I do realise how immensely indebted to Boris he was.[35] – The part where they discover the paupers in the cave – & the introduction to Act IV & one of the Yniold scenes – all originate in Boris. But nevertheless Pelleas is DEBUSSY – similarly I think when one looks into your work one sees how much Uncle Ralph has helped – nevertheless the general impression is that it is all very much Elizabeth Maconchy. More & more I regard Uncle Ralph as a pioneer whose work will be finished by someone else; don't you? Really, if it hadn't been for him, where would we all have been. We might all have been self-satisfied reactionaries – Elgarians? ? Delius wouldn't have been any good to us – He is small & complete – doesn't lead anywhere. In a way I feel the same is true of Holst. There's something much bigger about Uncle Ralph's attitude of mind – freer & more progressive so that I think it's a fine thing to be influenced by him. After all one has to be influenced by somebody – all the greatest composers have been influenced by other composers (which is a trite thing to say.).

I went to Stravinsky at the B.B.C. on Monday (Benjamin gets free tickets simply by asking for them & he is a comic kid taking an old dowager like me but he says I don't make insane remarks so –) I liked parts of the Duo – especially the last sections – but I felt lots of it absolutely manufactured. It seems to me that Stravinsky is the sort of person who'll write one great work & then go completely phut for a few years – then another masterpiece. Parts of the Duo seemed so tired. He himself is a Sphinx isn't he! So stony & repressed & self-conscious. His playing, I feel, is terribly self-conscious – he just can't let himself go – no rhythm!!! But I can understand that his platform manner is absolutely no indication to the real character of the man.

Now I must rush away & teach once again. I've had some really lovely Glamorgan folk songs sent me with a request for accompaniments. I've done nine since yesterday. Nice work.

Betty could you let me have the opera some time before Apr. 4th? I want to try & arrange the fountain song for voice & str. quartet.[36] There is supposed to be a fairly gd. quartet at Bangor Univ. & there are loads of singers there – they've just written to me to ask if they can do the variations (which they heard had been done at Cardiff) – but I thought they might do songs instead. I could meet Billy at Victoria next week on Mon. Tues. or Thurs. – is it at about 5 p.m.?

Have a lovely birthday on Sunday. I'll think about you. It's three years since Prague – & two since I came back from Vienna! We are growing up!

Best love from
Grace

---

35 Debussy's opera *Pelléas et Mélisande* (1902) and Musorgsky's opera *Boris Godunov* (1873).
36 This does not appear to have survived.

23) 18 March 1933

March 18th '33.
6 Arundel Terrace.

Dearest Grace

Your letter was grand. Of course you shall have the opera back next week – have I kept it too long? – the fountain song ought to be very nice as a separate song with string 4tet. Billy says could you lunch with him on Thursday, & he will give you the score then? [. . .]

Why did you think I 'condemned lots of the music' of the opera? Because indeed I don't. I said those things about the dramatic & 'stagey' side because they are so vitally important & where so many otherwise good operas (specially English) fail, I think, & yours doesn't. But you know what I think about your music – and I don't think this falls below. – It is of course (in places) more 'operatic' & therefore in a way less 'profound' (these are quite the wrong words, but the right ones don't exist for writing about music –) than when you are being purely pure, (!!) I think – but I also think it's all very good.

I must have some more good sessions at it before B. takes it back.

How sickening Victor H-H writing that sextet – (my heart jumped like yours when I read 'sextet' at the top of the list – I was just going to have a bath when the paper arrived – & I was sitting on the edge of it and nearly fell in!) It was very nice of Britten to send his congratulations – please thank him. He's very lucky to be able to have you to go to concerts with – and also I think it's frightfully good for him to have someone who doesn't flatter him, & knows more than he does, and is also very nice, to talk to!

They are going to broadcast the quintet – it was in the paper on Wednesday – but I've heard nothing else – or when it will be. No doubt it will be the Griller 4tet as they know all the works. I'd like Sylvia to do the oboe.

I got the comicest letters from the Women Musicians[37] – 'So glad the men haven't had it all their own way' – 'such a result is splendid in open competition'!!! etc

Sunday night – I meant to write more but am just too absolutely sleepy. We went for a drive and had tea with Mummy – who had a beautiful pink birthday cake for me!

Yes, three years since Prague – & we are growing up . . . It was good having you in Prague.

Very much love from
Betty

---

[37] The Society of Women Musicians (S.W.M.) had been founded in 1911 with the aim of providing women composers and performers opportunities to meet and enjoy the benefits of mutual cooperation. In later years Maconchy was to be an honorary Vice-President of the Society.

I.3 Letters 24–34
(June 1933–March 1934)

This ten-month period was a prolific time for both women, despite the recurrence of Maconchy's TB, which led to her spending more time in Brighton. They both continued to be involved in the Macnaghten–Lemare concerts as well as having works performed by ensembles such as the Bournemouth Symphony Orchestra, entering competitions, and hearing works broadcast on the BBC.

That summer, Maconchy's Quintet for oboe and strings (1932) became her first work to be issued as a recording. She spent much of this time on her oratorio *Deborah*,[1] working closely with her husband, Billy, and on her ballet *Little Red Shoes* (1935). Williams was working hard as a teacher, as well as continuing to compose music such as her Concert Overture for orchestra (1933–4) and vocal works for Welsh tenor Gwynn Parry Jones.

Maconchy held a private concert party at Chart Corner on 1 July 1933, at which the Macnaghten Quartet and Sylvia Spencer (oboe) performed her prize-winning Quintet for oboe and strings (1932), as well as Purcell's Fantasias and Haydn's String Quartet op. 76 no. 4. Two weeks earlier, on 17 June, the same players had played the quintet at a Society of Women Musicians concert at 74 Grosvenor Street, London, alongside recent works by other society members. At this time, Maconchy embarked on her First String Quartet (1933).

Meanwhile, Maconchy had lent Williams her score of Janáček's Jenůfa, *an opera she had seen in Prague but which was not yet known in Britain, remaining unstaged until 1957. Similarly, Musorgsky's* Khovanshchina *was relatively unknown, having been produced in London in 1919, but not restaged until 1959.*

24) 15 June 1933

Chart Corner
June 15th

Dearest Grace

Here is your party-invitation; – it has got delayed for two or three days, waiting for a letter to be written with it! – There is to be a place for you in

---

1 A manuscript of this work survives in the Maconchy Archive at St Hilda's College, Oxford.

someone's car (Sylvia or Mary (the 'cellist's) – or someone's –).² Anne will probably do the arranging of transport later – so will you communicate with her about it, later. She is in bed with a septic throat & temperature – but I heard this morning that she is better – but they <u>may</u> not be able to play at the S.W.M's on Saturday. (I shan't come up if they can't) Presumably you don't want to hear the other S.W.M's efforts (if they are anything like last year!) – so perhaps you'd ring her up to find out if it's all right – I'm going to, on Friday. If all is well – will you meet us at 74 Grosvenor Street at 4? (tea is at 4) the concert is at 4.30.

I'm so glad you're enjoying Jenufa, & agree with me in thinking it a <u>wonderful</u> opera. On the actual stage, it seemed to be really dramatic (& terribly moving) without being typically 'operatic' at all. I'd give anything to see it again; I wish I could hear Khovan – – – however you spell it – too.

I hear my records are out as Lucie (B's sister) has got them.³ I haven't been sent any, yet, so must order them. They are not in the early June catalogues – so will be in the mid-June ones, I suppose.

The weather is glorious here again – Maureen & the dress maker have been here since I last saw you – so I've only done a little work. The latter has made me (I think) a very nice dress for '<u>the</u>' party. Sheila comes to-day to fetch Maureen away, & then I really must work hard again. I've finished the 1st movement of the 4tet & would like you to see it. I will send it to you, when I've made a decent copy – if you don't mind. I've had a good deal of trouble with the end – and I'm not sure I haven't got too much almost exact repetition in the recapitulation section: & yet in a way I feel it needs it. I want to know what you think. I don't approve of always dressing one's themes up in a new disguise when they appear again, do you? In this movement I think they would lose their character if one did. . . (I think personally people do it too much, at present.)

I have washed my hair, & am drying it in the sun – but unless I move, I shall get sunstroke (not having such a good head as you!)

I <u>hope</u> you are writing again – & your idle fit passed??

Very much love from Betty.

25) [After 1 July] 1933

51 Warwick Rd, S.W. 5

Dearest Betty

Once more <u>lots & lots</u> of thanks for the lovely party. I think it was about the nicest I've been to – everyone said the same. – Anne's Quartet <u>has</u> improved! LOADS, hasn't it? I thought they played your first mvt. terribly well & <u>all</u> of it was good. The records of the last 2 mvts. impressed me frightfully – I felt I'd

---

2 Mary Goodchild, cellist of the Macnaghten Quartet.
3 Maconchy's Quintet for oboe and strings was issued by HMV (B4448–9), performed by the Griller String Quartet and Helen Gaskell (oboe).

really got hold of them thoroughly at last – I'll get the records as soon as I get home at the end of the week & work away at them. V. nice prospect!

– We had a thrilling drive home – the air was so warm – but we all felt hungry again & almost turned back in order to creep like sleuths into your larder & steal all that was left over (I bet there wasn't much –) Betty you are a marvel to be able to produce those heavenly asparagus sandwiches – & those dear little round brown ones – Even Dorrie (!!) Gow forgot all about her special diet & just stuffed. (And when I said 'I'm going inside in search of another meringue', she said 'Let me come too'.)

Have a lovely time in Ireland.

Best love from Grace

I loved your blue frock. And Sheila's and Maureen's (I just devoured those reds.)

P.S. I'll look after Jenufa v. carefully. Thanks so much for letting me have it for the holidays.

Both Maconchy and Williams received premières at the first Macnaghten–Lemare concert of the season, given on 6 November 1933: the Macnaghten Quartet played Maconchy's String Quartet no. 1, while John Francis (flute) and the composer (piano) played Williams's Sonatina for flute and piano (1933). At the second concert in the series, on 11 December 1933, Maconchy's Two Motets for double chorus (1931), settings of John Donne, was first performed, conducted by Iris Lemare.

26) [Before 17 October] 1933

Chart Corner, Seal Chart, Kent. Seal 106
Wednesday.

My dearest Grace

It is ages since I have heard anything of you. Did you have a good holiday? – you must be back in London by now. Did you write much during the holidays, or just bask? (it was a particularly good opportunity to do the latter, wasn't it?)

We had a long holiday in Ireland – the only pity being that when we went to Connemara for a week it rained every day except one, though the drought went on everywhere else. But it was lovely all the same. It was grand getting back here too – it is a nice little house to come back to. And then when we'd been back just a fortnight, & without the slightest warning I again got a (very slight) haemorrhage. There appears to have been no reason for it, and I'd no temperature, & there's nothing to be heard in my lung. However, it was very slight indeed – that was only just over a week ago – & yesterday I was in the garden most of the day, & shall be again to-day. I'm going to London next week to be X-rayed (– the doctor thinks it's a minute blood-vessel which gives way – & doesn't affect my 'general health') But it's a curse, of course – though I feel perfectly well. I'd looked forward to a really good winter of hard work and coming up to London often – but I suppose I shall have to modify my programme a bit! – Iris's choir is starting to rehearse my motets on the 17th, & it's a bit of a problem getting the parts done as I'd only done two when this happened! However I think it can be managed.

Anne's 4tet have apparently worked very hard at my 4tet – I haven't heard it yet. They are altogether going to play it eight times before Xmas! – the chief times being the Ballet Club, the Grotian Hall (at a series of concerts that Arthur Bliss is somehow mixed up with) & the Oxford Univ. Music Club.[4] – (The others are lunch time concerts etc.) I'm being anxious to hear it soon, of course.

Nothing else has happened about prospective performances since I saw you – except that I heard from Harriet Cohen that she 'liked my Concerto very much indeed' & would like to play it – which was a great surprise. I don't know if anything will come of it. We are trying the Hallé Orchestra.

Have you anything exciting in view? Do write & tell me your news – & will you come down here when I'm a bit more active? (which will be very shortly) I must stop and get up.

Very much love from
Betty
Forgive a dull letter.

Maconchy's illness prevented her from copying the parts for her Two Motets herself. When a copyist let her down, Williams and other friends stepped in.

27) [Before 17 October] 1933

Chart Corner
Sunday.

Dearest Grace.

I am so sorry about what has happened about the parts of my wretched motets. Iris was here on Friday (Anne's 4tet came down to me to hear a rehearsal of my 4tet) & tells me that the FOOL who was to have done the 2nd choir parts has been completely useless – said when we saw the thing last Monday that he'd be able to do them quite easily – then took four days to do ONE and left a note to say he couldn't do any more!!! (– But presumably Iris told you all this –) & then apparently she just shipped them on to you – my dear, I do hope you're not having an awful and hectic week-end – and I hope to goodness you aren't trying to get them all done – because I know what a long time they take – and that it would be impossible and exhaust you. I feel furious about it all – chiefly with myself for getting ill (I had it all mapped out to get them done in nice time –) and partly with Iris for not arranging something more satisfactory, when she really had time

---

4 Early performances of the quartet included: 7 November, at a Grotrian Hall Chamber Concert (at Steinway's concert hall in Wigmore Street, London), and 14 November, at the Holywell Music Room, Oxford.

to – & then with this idiot of a man – and lastly because it has fallen on you. One bright spot is that they will be well done – (which they mightn't have been by Iris' man!) & mind you make out a good adequate bill for them. (I wonder if they will be able to sing that first one?)

I went to London on Thursday to a specialist, who also X-rays, & he gave what was really a very good report of me – the X-ray photograph shows virtually nothing – & they can hear virtually nothing – & apparently it is really nothing to worry about having had this go –; but I have to go on with this same old 'regime' of existence – being allowed an occasional visit to London.

– Billy is waiting to go to the post – Let me know which day you can come down, won't you? soon –

I was very pleased with the 4tet on Friday: – I want you to hear it & tell me what you think of it. They have got hold of it very well, I think.

Very best love from
Betty

I haven't said what an angel I think you are about the parts – but you know what I think about it –

28) 17 October 1933 – postcard

17 October 1933

Dearest Grace – You are MARVELLOUS – I don't know how to say thank you to you – and Dolly – and 'Eleanor' (who I know – but I don't know the rest of her name –)[5] and B. Britten. I feel very ashamed at my dirty work being done for me – but it is simply grand that they're done, and, miraculously in time.

I hope to see you soon, when the flute sonata is off your chest – but of course these parts must have kept it back – as well as terribly overworking you. 100000000 thanks, and all love from Betty.

The Macnaghten–Lemare concert on 11 December 1933, included, in addition to Maconchy's difficult motets, first performances of Litanie, *another John Donne setting for double chorus, by John Sykes, an RCM student, and Britten's Two Part-Songs for mixed choir, 'I loved a lass' and 'Lift-boy', as well as three movements from his string quartet* Alla Quartetto Serioso: 'Go play, boy, play'. *Maconchy continued to work on her ballet* Little Red Shoes[6] *and had started a new project, an oratorio,* Deborah, *for soprano (Deborah), baritone (Narrator), bass (Barak), double chorus, and orchestra. As well as teaching at Southlands Training College, since September 1932, Williams had been music mistress at Camden School for Girls in north London.*

5 Eleanor Bevan Ramsbotham, Dorothy Gow's partner.
6 See Letter 14.

29) [After 11] December 1933

Chart Corner
Friday.

Dearest Grace.

It <u>was</u> nice getting your letter. I'm awfully glad you heard the rehearsal of the motets though I wish you had been there and I could have seen you on Monday – (I should like to hear you conduct five hundred school children, it must be very inspiring) Apparently the performance was better than the rehearsal – but I was disappointed. When I'd heard them about 3 weeks ago at a rehearsal – they didn't know them properly – but the effect, in a smallish room, with them all singing fortissimo all the time (so as to be sure of sticking to their notes!) was <u>exciting</u>, and on Monday it wasn't – just rather flat. After the rehearsal I hadn't expected more than a performance that would show what they were all about – and when the element of excitement was lacking I didn't think she could tell very clearly what it was all about! However –

The physical and mental strain involved in waiting for the next ♭A, ♮A or ♭B in the sopranos ought to cure me of writing a part like that again! – <u>but</u> I like lots of high notes – or at least a <u>high texture</u> – in choral writing – it seems to me one can get a sort of suspended-in-mid air feeling – (less 'of the earth' than choral writing in the middle & low registers –) hard to explain, – but do you feel it, too?

Cuthbert Bates (the Tudor Singers conductor)[7] was there, and was <u>most</u> enthusiastic and said on the spot that he would do the motets with the Tudor Singers (who I believe are really good – have you heard them?) – so I do hope he will – and won't be put off by the difficulties he will find in the score! I think he'll stick to it. It <u>would</u> be lovely to hear them sung as I imagine them; – Iris's poor choir <u>did</u> work so hard – and she hardest of all –. I think it was very courageous of them to tackle them, and of Iris to go on and make something of them out of the chaos there was for ages, apparently! But indeed the standard of choral singing is abysmal, as you say. – I would <u>love</u> you do [sic] them with your students – (I bet they're very good, under your coaching –) [. . .].

Arthur Bliss was at the concert, and was <u>most</u> pleasant – (I thought him just a bit too much! –) I said I really wanted a big choir for the motets and he murmured 'O yes, we must see about that, for certain – ', but I doubt if it meant much!

I also talked to Britten for the first time and liked him – I didn't like his appearance, but then I did like him when talking to him.

– Rather funny, he said something about what did I think of the performance (implying that he thought it awful –) and there was one of the most hardworking and worthy of the soprano's [sic], looking very pathetic just beside us! – so I <u>had</u> to be kind – he must have thought me a bit odd, & very easily satisfied – !

---

7 In 1923, the amateur choral conductor Cuthbert Bates had founded the Tudor Singers.

36   Part I. Letters 1–49 (1927–Summer 1939)

Has Uncle Ralph gone back to Dorking yet? – I must write to him

I wish I could see you – there's such a lot I want to talk about, and I've embarked on my Oratorio, and badly want to show you what I've done – (only the 1st chorus,, actually) and the Little Red Shoes ballet, of which I've only done about a third. I do go slowly – What are you doing, and going to do? You must have had a most hectic term, and I hope will have a good holiday. (I'm glad the money's rolling in now!)

[. . .]

I am very well – the cold weather suits me, I think. (it has been cold here) I got one awful fit of depression this autumn, – nothing seemed any good at all for ever more – ; but I got over it, as one does.

I believe the reason the choir sang the Sykes so badly was that they'd given all the time to my things – which makes me feel rather bad. – I enjoyed the last movement of Britten's 4tet, but thought the first two not good. I also enjoyed the lift-boy a lot – really witty –, I think.

Much best love from Betty.

Maconchy continued work on the oratorio, Deborah, *over Christmas and also began revising her Gerard Manley Hopkins setting,* The Leaden Echo and the Golden Echo *(1930–31) for chorus and chamber orchestra. She awaited news about whether her First String Quartet was to be selected for the ISCM Festival in 1934.*

30) 8 January 1934

Chart Corner, Seal Chart, Kent. Seal 106
January 8th '34.

Dearest Grace.

I do so want your criticism and advice about this – which is my Oratorio – or Cantata – as far as I've got with it.

I was much excited while I was doing it (till a few days ago –) and thought it splendid as I suppose one usually does while writing something! – now I feel very despondent about it, & fear it is very bad. [. . .][8] Is it worth doing this, if the first chorus, which I send, is an example of what it will be like?

– All this, and I haven't said thank you for the darling little handkerchief you sent me. It was very nice of you, and thank you so much. Did you have a good Christmas? We had a very good one, with Maureen, and now I'm getting a certain amount of work done. I've raked out my setting of Hopkin[s]'s 'Golden Echo & Leaden Echo' did you ever see it? (I did most of it just three years ago) I had done it for small chorus and strings – which was quite wrong. I am now re-scoring it for small chorus & chamber orchestra, and giving far more help to the voices.

8 Detailed description of the oratorio's structure follows.

I had given them very difficult things without any support – and I don't think I realised that – for instances – sops & altos don't sort of hit a chord like this – [musical notation]⁹ with the clarity & precision one essentially wants. But with a little help and support from wind – I think they more or less can get the right effect, don't you? – This Hopkins thing is certainly very hard – & goes high, too, but doesn't stay high in such a cruel way as the Motets. I want to send it to the B.B.C. next month which is the right sending-in time, I believe, – as no-one has seen it except Anthony Bernard¹⁰ – who expressed a desire to 'live with' the score two years ago – & is still doing so! I can't get it back – so am re-scoring it from my rough copy.

I am longing and dreading to hear about the fate of my quartet from the I.S.C.M. I thought I should have heard by now – as the Internat. Jury should have finished sitting last week, I think. Very unsettling!

You didn't say why you came back to London. But I do hope you will be able to come for a day before we go off on the 24th, – as you said you would. – A superb day to-day, and I'm writing in the hut, which it has been too horrid to do much lately. – I hope you've had some decent weather for your holiday, and been able to be by the sea a bit. I think you belong to the sea.

All best love from your loving
Betty.

With time during the Christmas holidays, Williams tried to work on her Concert Overture for orchestra (1933–4), to enter for the second Daily Telegraph *competition, which focused this time on new concert overtures, but also began thinking about works for tenor, leading to 'Oh! weep for those that wept' (1934) to join the already written 'Oh! snatch'd away in beauty's bloom' (1933), both settings of Byron for tenor and orchestra.*

31) [After 9] January 1934

51, Warwick Road, S.W.5

Dearest Betty,

Many thanks for the score, which I got just before leaving home yesterday [. . .].

I read it through several times in the train & each time I wasn't quite satisfied with the first part – as far as 'They break in pieces' – but all the rest I found thrilling. [. . .] it all gets going marvellously at 'They break in pieces' – & 'Adder's poison' is magnificent – & the return to the first theme seems to have more bite in it – e.g. 'Wicked triumph'!

---

9 Ex. PI.3.1. Elizabeth Maconchy, *The Leaden Echo and the* Golden Echo (1930–31, rev. 1933–34), excerpt.
10 Conductor Anthony Barnard.

– And then the rest of it just made me say 'Now here, <u>here</u> is the real Betty once more' – that ♩ 𝄾 ♪[11] figure is marvellous & the <u>gorgeous</u> part when Deborah hits top G ('and I – ') – that's the finest bit for me so of course you must go on & finish the work at once.

Think a lot more about the opening – I shall, too, & perhaps I'll be able to suggest something more – not that you'll need any stupid suggestions from me. I think that if you just read it through <u>a lot</u> & <u>hear</u> it <u>exactly</u> as you've written it, you'll feel <u>instinctively</u> that certain parts need just one or two extra touches to make the whole thing <u>bigger</u>. It is big as it stands but not quite <u>arresting</u> enough.

So endeth the school-marm. Betty I don't know why you want my opinions, <u>really</u>, because as soon as I've given them I feel they're thoroughly footling & I'm a sort of impostor. However – –

I'll do my best to come down before you go to Brighton, but I'm a bit desperate now about my Overture. I couldn't do a thing at the beginning of the holidays & thought I was done for forever – & then on the last day of the year I got the old feeling of wanting to write having something on the tip of my tongue – <u>but</u> I <u>still</u> couldn't <u>write</u> a note – it was an <u>awful day &</u> New Year's Eve at that. Then I tried to will myself to get going & even made a sort of new year's resolution to that effect! And wonder of wonders I did get going as soon as I awoke on New Year's day! & I've been at it ever since, but I'm so <u>slow</u> at scoring; I felt thoroughly rusty at first –

I've done only 3 mins. worth – & it must be 'not less than 7' (– which I think is <u>long</u> for an overture don't you? i.e. if it's a light one – & mine is v. light.).

I'll let you know later how it goes – Then I've just met Parry Jones & he's going to broadcast some songs of mine when I've written them (I've only got one for him at present) & scored them.[12] I think I hate his voice – & yet, I don't know – he sings the Tristan Seaman song beautifully & the Beethoven 'Adelaide'[13] & he gets all the best tenor jobs in England so –

best love from

Grace

<u>P.S.</u> Do you want the score back soon?

<u>P.P.S. Please</u> let me have the part of the motets at the end of the month. My seniors are on school practice until then.

Williams began to teach Maconchy's Two Motets to her student choir, while she continued to work on her Concert Overture. Maconchy's Comedy Overture *(1932–3) was first performed and broadcast on 7 March 1934 by Dan Godfrey conducting the Bournemouth Symphony Orchestra, which was well known for*

---

11 Ex. PI.3.2. Elizabeth Maconchy, *Deborah* (1933–4), oratorio, excerpt.
12 Gwynn Parry Jones was a leading Welsh tenor, who was known for undertaking new works by living composers.
13 The Young Sailor singing at the beginning of Wagner's opera *Tristan und Isolde*, and Beethoven's *Adelaïde*, Op. 46, for voice and piano.

performing new works by British composers. News finally arrived about the 1934 ISCM Festival: Britten's Phantasy, Op. 2, for oboe and string trio was selected but Maconchy's First String Quartet was not.

32) 15 February 1934

6 Arundel Terrace, Brighton
Feb. 15th '34.

Dearest Grace

It is grand of you to have embarked on the motets. – (I thought of you doing them last night) I should much like to hear them, if I might, later on. (I've never heard, by the way, if the Tudor Singers are rehearsing them – but I suppose they are – if you see any of them, do ask them – –)[14] I frightfully want to hear your Overture, can you bring your rough copy when you come down? I feel sure that it's very good! And have mentally allotted £100 to you – I hope the Jury will have enough sense to!

I haven't been able to do any writing for ages, as I'm doing the parts of my Overture for Dan Godfrey – they are nearly done, now: he wants them in a few days time, and the concert isn't till March 7th, so <u>perhaps</u> he will give it several rehearsals. I'm going to have rather a sweat finishing the score of my 'Leaden Echo & Golden Echo' (I think I told you I'd raked it out, and am rescoring it.) as I want to send it to the B.B.C. before the end of this month,[15] and I still have a lot to do, as I have had to stop it completely for these parts. It has been lovely here most of the time, so far, – a lot of sunny days when it's almost as hot as summer. It's been very nice having Anne here – she is a lot better, I think – she looked perfectly ghastly when she came here, but looks more normal now.

Yes, Britten is frightfully lucky isn't he? I was disappointed about my quartet – but it can't be helped. – The Festival has got reduced to only 2½ concerts of contemporary music – all the rest is Italian propaganda – concerts of modern Italian music, old Italian music, Italian opera etc – which is rather sickening.

Dorothy Wadham[16] wrote to me about a fortnight ago asking me [to] send a chamber work for a 'possible performance in Denmark' – so I've sent the 4tet – I don't know what it's for – they want some English works to select from, I believe, for a State festival or something.

Anne's quartet is broadcasting the quartet on March 20th which is good[17] – the Overture at Bournemouth will be broadcast too – they always do those Wednesday concerts.

---

14 See Letter 29. The Tudor Singers performed Maconchy's Two Motets on 17 June 1934, at St Margaret's, Westminster.
15 Maconchy submitted the score to the BBC on 27 February 1934. See BBC WAC RCONT1, Maconchy, Composer file 1, 27 February 1934.
16 ISCM secretary.
17 Broadcast at 4.30 pm, 20 March 1934, on the BBC National Programme.

We listened to Job[18] last night – I thought it was a very dull performance – frightfully unrthmymical [*sic*] – also uninspired. Did you hear it?

[. . .]

Well – I must stop & go for my daily walk

All best love from

Betty

In addition to growing attention from London-based BBC programmes, Maconchy began to be noticed by Irish radio stations, including the BBC Belfast Station, under director Godfrey Brown.

33) 19 March 1934

6 Arundel Terrace, Brighton
March 19th '34.

Dearest Grace

I've been meaning to write for some time – about the Overture for one thing – and to thank you for writing about it. The performance was definitely <u>bad</u> – the orchestra (as you had gathered on the wireless) really is very bad now – I believe it used to be better – and Dan Godfrey was in the middle of having a dispute with them, and everything was at sixes & sevens, and everyone on the worst possible terms with each other. He just found fault & railed at them, and didn't <u>attempt</u> to get the best out of them. He was in an incredibly 'rattled' state all the time – and just kept saying 'I'm totally out of sympathy with your work – I don't like it' – and then 'what can one do with this damned orchestra', 'I've no time, no time – – ' – so I just had to make the best of a bad job, and by disregarding his continuous obbligato of remarks such as the above, managed to tell him most of the things I wanted to and in the end it went a lot better than I thought it would! [. . .] I absolutely agree that the end is not right – damn it! I know you thought last year that it wasn't right – and I had an uncomfortable feeling about it, but couldn't make up my mind. But I know now that I must do something to it – the devil of it is that I don't know what – I shall have to laboriously work myself back into the 'spirit' of the wretched thing, and find some way.

I'm far from sure that it is a good work, but I should like to hear it again, played properly, before deciding. I'm not sure that it isn't scrappy in effect – perhaps because all the things in it only go on for such a short time.

It is very sad that you can't come down – but you must be fearfully busy, and the reason is <u>grand</u>. It is splendid about Parry Jones[19] – he is very important. What songs are you scoring for him – & what date is it to be? I expect he will sing them often. You must make him do <u>a lot</u> of your songs. [. . .]

---

18 Vaughan Williams's *Job: A Masque for Dancing*, broadcast on 14 February 1934 from a BBC Symphony Concert in Queen's Hall, London, conducted by Adrian Boult.

19 See Letter 31.

Four years to-day since the Land in Prague.[20] I often think how good it was of you to come, and what a difference it made. I wish I wasn't so old! You'll listen to the Land on Easter Sunday won't you?[21] I now hear it's at 4.30 with the L.S.O. (& Boult) not 9.0 – (as I'd thought it would be, as it is Boult.) Will you be able to listen to my quartet tomorrow? (4.30 on the National)

I had a pleasant surprise on Saturday – a letter from the B.B.C. music director in Belfast, saying that they are 'contemplating giving a short programme of my works' – and that they have a 'full orchestra, so can do works of almost any dimensions' – which sounds hopeful, – but I wonder how good they are? Also if the man who wrote (Godfrey Brown) who seems to be their conductor, is any good. Sometimes I think what a good thing it would be to conduct oneself. I immensely enjoyed writing him a list of my works!![22] [. . .]

Have you ever thought of sending anything to Tovey?[23] I've written to ask him if I may send him something.

I suppose you're too busy with scoring & your exam. papers etc to be writing much? I've hardly done any here – as first I had the Overture parts to do, then the score of my 'Leaden Echo & Golden Echo' to finish, & then a few details to be done to the Land parts. But now I'm working a bit, & writing a first chorus for the Oratorio, instead of that other one.[24] I want you to hear this one when we can meet.

The B.B.C. have sent me £3.3.0 for the hire of the Land – which doesn't seem excessive. Perhaps I'll be able to get something for Belfast, if it comes off.

I must stop. We have been having <u>tremendous</u> gales here, with perfectly lovely waves on the cliffs But I'm beginning to get tired of the wind.

All my best love from Betty.

34) [After 20] March 1934

51, Warwick Rd, S.W.5.

Dearest Betty,

I was quite bowled over by the quartet on Tuesday. The last three mvts are magnificent, <u>especially</u> the slow mvt.

I feel you've got a much broader grasp in these mvts than in the first. The theme of the 1st is of course very arresting but somehow I think there are just a few

---

20 It was in fact the Piano Concerto that was performed rather than *The Land*. See Letter 5.
21 On 1 April 1934, *The Land* was broadcast from a studio concert on the London Regional programme, by the London Symphony Orchestra conducted by Adrian Boult.
22 Maconchy sent scores for the Piano Concerto, *The Land*, and Comedy Overture, but Brown 'found there was nothing Irish about your work' and only her Suite for chamber orchestra was aired from Belfast, on 11 July 1934. See BBC WAC EM1, 21–2 September 1934.
23 Donald Francis Tovey was a noted musical commentator and director of the Reid Symphony Orchestra Concerts in Edinburgh.
24 Maconchy's oratorio *Deborah* (1933–4).

things (2 or 3 bars near the opening – rhythm something like ♪♩ ♪♩ ♩[25]) & some of the pizz. chords that don't seem quite up to standard – but I think I'm going to like the slow mvt. more & more – you <u>must</u> lend me the score when you can possibly spare it.

I was sorry to hear of Dan G's rudeness. But honestly the performance didn't sound 'definitely bad' over the wireless.

Here is your oratorio. So sorry I've kept it so long – I'm eager to see your new chorus. I <u>must</u> come down to the cottage next term.

In a desperate rush – going to Vienna on Saturday – until about April 23rd or 24th.

Best of luck for the Land – I'll <u>try</u> & listen in Vienna.

Love from Grace

May we keep the motets over the holidays? Do hope so.

---

25 Ex. PI.3.3. Elizabeth Maconchy, String Quartet no. 1 (1933), excerpt.

I.4 Letters 35–41 (November 1934–March 1936)

Since 1933, Williams had been receiving more broadcasts of her music on the BBC, mainly on the West Regional programmes. During this period (1935), such exposure continued, including the broadcast of her revised Two Psalms for soprano and chamber orchestra (1927, rev. 1934) on 5 November 1934 and a broadcast dedicated to her works (*Rhaglen o Weithiau Grace Williams*) on 23 November 1935 given by the Western Studio Orchestra conducted by Reginald Redman.

Maconchy's music continued to be broadcast on the BBC. The first performances were given of her ballet *Great Agrippa (or the Inky Boys)* (1933), at a Macnaghten–Lemare concert, and her Prelude, Interlude and Fugue for two violins (1934) at the 1935 ISCM Festival in Czechoslovakia. Other important performances during this period included her orchestral suite *The Land* played in Edinburgh by the Reid Symphony Orchestra, conducted by Donald Tovey, while her Piano Concerto was finally broadcast by the BBC.

On Monday, 5 November 1934, Williams's Two Psalms for soprano and chamber orchestra (1927, rev. 1934) received their first broadcast, on the BBC's West Regional programme, performed by Megan Thomas and the small Western Studio Orchestra, conducted by Reginald Redman; in addition, the programme included Williams's orchestral arrangements of folk songs and dances, as well as songs by other Welsh composers. By this time, Maconchy had written her Six Short Pieces for violin and piano (1934).

35) [Before 11 November 1934]

Chart Corner, Seal Chart, Kent. Seal 106
Tuesday

Dearest Grace

I managed to hear <u>most</u> of your broadcast last night – (in spite of a spirited dialogue in German on one side, and a maddening French tenor the other, & some hot jazz from goodness knows where –) I did <u>rejoice</u> to hear the psalms again – because I do think they're really most beautiful – they give me a feeling that hardly anything else does, I can't quite describe it, but I got exactly the same feeling

44   Part I. Letters 1–49 (1927–Summer 1939)

when I heard them at Patron's Fund, that time. I thought Megan Thomas was excellent, as far as I could tell – and dramatic, (which you said you were doubtful about I remember) that is <u>the</u> setting for the waters of Babylon psalm – I can't imagine it any other way now: (and the Belshazzar setting of it is laughable)[1]

I loved the Folk-dances – just right. And you have made <u>marvellous</u> use of the limited orchestra. That impressed me very much. Megan Thomas <u>must</u> do the Psalms again – with a big orchestra.[2] [. . .] I've written another easy violin piece (instead of the one we mutually decided ought to be scrapped!) & will try Boosey & Hawkes, I think, as you suggested.[3]

I mustn't write more, as there are endless rather tiresome things to do.

Ina Boyle[4] was here at the weekend – she will be in London till about the 15th (or 14th) & would love to see you I know, if you have time. [. . .] They're going to do a song-cycle of hers at Cardiff, which she owes to you, she says.

All best love from
Betty

Williams's Suite for chamber orchestra[5] was given its first performance by the Western Studio Orchestra, conducted by Reginald Redman, on 14 January 1935 as a broadcast from the BBC Cardiff Station. Two days later, her overture Hen Walia *(1930) was aired in a studio performance from London, performed by the BBC Symphony Orchestra, conducted by Charles Woodhouse. Maconchy was working on parts for her ballet,* Great Agrippa (or the Inky Boys) *(1933), for performance at a Macnaghten–Lemare Concert in February, and she received news that her Prelude, Interlude and Fugue for two violins (1934) had been accepted for the 1935 ISCM Festival that year, originally planned for Carlsbad, but in the end held in Prague.*

36) 17 January 1935

Chart Corner
Seal Chart, Kent
Seal 106
Thursday –

Dearest Grace.

I heard the Suite on Monday & the Overture last night – & was <u>thrilled</u>. (I couldn't get the Suite perfectly – but heard most of it pretty well – there

---

1   Walton's *Belshazzar's Feast* (1931).
2   In fact, Thomas broadcast them again on 28 December 1934, when Vaughan Williams conducted the BBC Symphony Orchestra in a studio broadcast that began with Maconchy's Comedy Overture and continued with Williams's Two Psalms.
3   This work remained unpublished.
4   Irish composer Ina Boyle was another pupil of Vaughan Williams and a close friend of both Maconchy and Williams. See Ita Beausang and Séamas De Barra, *Ina Boyle 1889–1967: A Composer's Life* (Cork: Cork University Press, 2018).
5   Also known as Suite for nine instruments.

was some 'failure' & a few interruptions) I like them both immensely – I think the most striking thing (which also struck Billy most forcibly) is the utmost sureness of touch – & complete (musical as well as technical) assurance. – (Most un-English! My dear) Can you see any of the 'grown-up' composers of this country writing anything that came-off (I mean musically as well as practically) <u>anything like</u> so well? B. & I laughed, thinking of fumbling people like Bliss, & what a mess they make! – I like the stuff of the Suite best, I think – (& frightfully want to hear it again, at Iris's concert –) I do <u>wish</u> one could hear things twice straight away, don't you? Because it <u>is</u> hard to get hold of them at first hearing – (even when there aren't idiomatic difficulties such as all the old-fashioned critics came up against – & of course never get beyond.) I wondered if there perhaps wasn't enough <u>variety</u> in the material of the Overture? But one can't really tell after one hearing on the wireless, I think. Certainly the <u>unity</u> & the way it hangs together is excellent. I think your scoring is <u>brilliant</u>: I don't know how you achieved the scoring of the Suite with that handful of instruments.

I have a tentative criticism – I sometimes felt (in both pieces) that the music was at times rather <u>static</u> (it is hard to explain what I mean), and I think it may be that there is a lack of progressiveness in your bass: I don't mean that it always stays on one note (which is a habit a lot of people, often including me, have, I think –) but that sometimes you play about over one note – & then on another – but that the bass itself doesn't seem to <u>progress</u>: which somehow makes the music stand still. I may be quite wrong about this, though; & it's very hard to put what I feel into words.

[. . .]

I must see you soon. I've been taking a very quiet & virtuous week this week – as I felt rather rotten last weekend, & thought I'd better be careful! But shall doubtless be coming to London again soon. The Agrippa parts were unexpectedly long to do, & I have put <u>endless</u> cues in them, as the entries are rather difficult, and I want to make it as easy as possible. That concert ought to be rather fun.

The two-violin pieces <u>are</u> going to be done at the Internat. Fest (or Freak Fest, as Uncle Ralph <u>will</u> call it –) I heard a few days ago. It's not till <u>September</u> – a very long way off: I think we'll <u>have</u> to go, though it's fearfully expensive: Carlsbad's in Czechoslovakia, so no doubt the Prague people will all be there.

All best love from
Betty

At the Macnaghten–Lemare concert on 4 February 1935, both Maconchy and Williams had works performed by a small orchestra conducted by Iris Lemare: Maconchy's Great Agrippa (or the Inky Boys) *(1933), a ballet for five dancers after* Struwwelpeter, *scored for 14 instruments and percussion, was given its first performance, and Williams's* Suite for chamber orchestra *was given its first concert performance. As the third new work, Elisabeth Lutyens's* The Dying of Tanneguy du Bois *for tenor, strings, and horns, was also by a woman composer, the concert received significant press attention.*

37) 11 February 1935

c/o Mrs Dawson, Shrubbery Farm, Old Romney, Kent
Feb. 11th

Dearest Grace.

I would <u>love</u> to see you – but alas! I'm not at Chart Corner. & shan't be home till the 24th [. . .] The notices have been <u>beastly</u>, haven't they? J.A.W. is a swine![6] The Times is the only passable one. There was one in the Referee (by Constant Lambert) yesterday – [(]not about the suite as he went before the interval –) but <u>not</u> nice about Agrippa – & I thought he liked it![7] I <u>am</u> so glad you like it – & I feel pretty satisfied myself – but I've been scolded all round! Uncle Ralph said at Steuart's[8] party (I'm sorry you didn't feel up to coming, it was rather fun –) when I asked him why he didn't like it 'it's not worthy of you' etc – and I've had a letter from him, saying the same thing, (as nicely as he can!) I've had the Suite in my head a lot – I do think it's <u>very</u> good – & several hearings make it better. I don't believe 'suite' is the right name for it – as it half-unconsciously implies a series of contrasted movements in contrasted moods I think – and they <u>aren't</u> contrasted in that way – (which I think is <u>good</u> – I mean they definitely make a 'whole' of a unified character, the way they are – but I'm not sure that 'suite' doesn't make one expect something different. Would 'concertino' perhaps have been better??)

I'm v. glad you're sending up things this month to the B.B.C. – (including the 'suite' of course?) I don't seem to have <u>anything</u> to send – (unless I send the old piano concerto again, & say Harriet[9] would play it –) I want to keep Agrippa to try ballet people with. No – Karen[10] is very different from Agrippa – more 'lyrical'. I awfully want you to see it. It will be <u>lovely</u> if there's any chance of seeing you – but it is horribly expensive.

Oh – Donald Tovey is going to do 'the Land' on the 28th – that's fun, isn't it? I heard a few days ago.[11] [. . .]

Best love from
Betty

---

6 J. A. Westrup, a well-known music critic, wrote: 'Miss Maconchy's music . . . is pert and lively. She seems at times, however, to have mistaken emphasis for vigour, and the thematic material is rather thin, a weakness which the ingenious scoring did not quite conceal. Grace Williams's Suite for chamber orchestra suffered from a garrulous monotony. Even a good idea can become tedious if it is repeated too often, and the ideas in this work were not particularly good'; 'Women Composers: Elizabeth Maconchy's New Work', *The Daily Telegraph* (4 February 1935).
7 Constant Lambert, a composer, writer, and conductor, wrote: 'It is a pity that in this work [Maconchy] should revert to the conventionally spiky and short-winded manner of post-War ballet music'; 'Women Composers Are So Forceful', *Sunday Referee* (10 February 1935).
8 Tenor Steuart Wilson had sung the solo part in the Lutyens piece.
9 Harriet Cohen.
10 Karen is the main character in *Little Red Shoes*. See Letter 40.
11 Maconchy's *The Land* was performed at the Reid Orchestral Concerts in Edinburgh on 28 February 1935 by the Reid Symphony Orchestra, conducted by Donald Tovey.

38) [After 11 February 1935]

51 Warwick Road
S.W.5.

Dearest Betty

Thanks so much for asking me to come down to Maureen's. I'd love to but I think I'd better not a) because isn't Maureen's baby nearly due? – in which case – well – & b) I think perhaps I'd better save my pennies because I'm going to take an unfurnished room before the end of this term, buy new spring clothes & go to Vienna for Easter; rather a lot of expense; but I can do it fairly comfortably if I'm careful. It will be lovely having my own furniture – I'll get everything from Heal's, I think.

– So may I come down to the cottage later on in the term? Or would you come & see me when you come up to London?

Now – about Agrippa. I am completely baffled by the press. – & Uncle Ralph too. I don't think any of them really heard it – I mean heard right into it – or they would have grasped that apart from the brilliance of the scoring, the work is so full of invention – & all so spontaneous & alive as though you must have been brimming over with inspiration when you wrote it: & those tunes I declare are pure Betty.

To anyone who knows your works well it ought to be quite obvious that the substance of Agrippa comes from the same source as all the other Maconchy works. Dolly thinks so too OF COURSE – & Anne – & Betty Lutyens (though she doesn't count so much – oh dear, I did find her thing embarrassing.)

Now Uncle Ralph is a dear, we all know, but he's got a great bee in his bonnet about one thing – he always turns his deaf ear to works which are brilliantly effective. Think of what he said about 'Sacre'! – & even worse things about 'Wozzeck'[12]

I know they are far removed from his own particular genre & perhaps it is only natural that they mean little to him. He is rhythmically so far removed from them. – & I think perhaps he is rhythmically very far removed from Agrippa!! that is probably what upset him. He couldn't really have heard it as music or he wouldn't have said he so much preferred the Overture because musically I find the Overture & Agrippa have a lot in common. I feel Agrippa scores over the Overture inasmuch as there is so much more invention & inspiration in the orchestration.

I love the stuff of the Overture & it is scored more or less successfully, but now that I've heard Agrippa I can't help feeling that you might have made a still better job of the Overture score. Benjamin says so too.[13] You mustn't bother your head any more, my girl, about writing safe scores. It doesn't become

---

12 Stravinsky's ballet *Le sacre du printemps* (1913) and Berg's opera *Wozzeck* (1922).
13 Benjamin Britten.

you. Besides it isn't necessary: your difficult things always come off best. And forget all that Gordon ever preached about doubling! Gordon's scoring is smug and dull.[14] – Another little thing I felt about the Overture was that at times there is perhaps too much counterpoint. I know it's hard cutting things out especially when every part seems vital – but counterpoint can thicken a score more than anything else.

The great fault of Uncle Ralph's scores is, to my mind, that there is too much thematic material going on at the same time & that so often the rhythmic balance is all wrong & sounds muddled. This sort of thing – [musical notation][15] (No this isn't genuine R.V.W. but I'm too lazy to look for my score of the Pastoral to give you genuine examples)[16] – interesting to look at but annoying to hear. They just don't match when played simultaneously – it's quite as bad as having wrong notes in a chord (I mean <u>real</u> wrong notes)

The amazing thing about the Schönbergians is that however complicated their rhythmic patterns are, they always hang together & fit.

Poor Uncle Ralph – I hate having to say that there's anything wrong with him – but he does bring it on himself when he says such things about a work like Agrippa.

– I'm sorry I missed Lambert's notice & very surprised to hear it wasn't good. Oh blast them all. I can't tell you how relieved I felt when I saw Lambert disappearing during the interval. <u>What</u> did he say about the Lutyens I wonder!

I haven't much sympathy with B. Lutyens. She's got something up her sleeve, I dare say, but oh it's so carelessly done: that sort of harum-scarum attitude towards composing shouldn't be allowed.

Do come & see me soon
Love from
Grace
[. . .]

Maconchy's Two Motets for double chorus (1931) was performed at a BBC Concert of Contemporary Music on 15 March 1935, sung by the Wireless Chorus conducted by Leslie Woodgate, and broadcast on the National Programme. Also given at the concert was the first public performance of Bernard van Dieren's Symphony No. 1 for soloists, chorus, and orchestra. Maconchy continued to work on the music for her ballet Little Red Shoes *(1935).*[17]

---

14 Gordon Jacob taught orchestration at the RCM.
15 Ex. Pl.4.1. Grace Williams, imitation of Vaughan Williams.
16 Vaughan Williams's *A Pastoral Symphony* (1922), later called Symphony No. 3.
17 See Letter 14.

39) 9 March 1935

Chart Corner
Seal Chart, Kent
Seal 106
March 9th

Dearest Grace

I'm longing to see your new abode: is it nice? I'm sure you've got nice exciting furniture. I've been meaning to write – but things seem to have been a bit hectic. I was in Edinburgh last week for 'The Land' – & had a lovely time. I must tell you about it when we meet. Tovey was very nice – (a comic man) – he knows everything that has ever been written, backwards – & has the most <u>miraculous</u> library of scores. He is a complete romantic in tastes really – but genuinely interested in new stuff. He took <u>heaps</u> of trouble over 'The Land' – & the orchestra were fearfully nice (quite good) & the University music students all came to the rehearsals simply oozing excitement: much the nicest students I've ever met – (can you imagine music students at R.C.M. ever being excited about anything??) He wants to do the piano concerto – & play it himself. (Do you think Harriet[18] will yield up the piano part??)

Maureen had a son on Wednesday (weighing 8 ½ lbs –) & she is getting on very well – also the baby. It is grand, isn't it? Mummy will be enchanted at having a grandson, after her own series of daughters!

The B.B.C. are doing the motets at the Contemp. Concert on Friday. <u>Can</u> you come? I haven't heard them yet – I'm going to a rehearsal on Monday. Wonder how they'll do them. There is a first performance of a Van Dieren choral symphony – hope they won't have to spend all their time on that!

[. . .] I'm going on with the 'Red Shoes' – but first being with Maureen for 3 weeks & then in Edinburgh I didn't do any work (except a piano arrangement of the Red Shoes) for a <u>month</u>. I seem to have got through nothing this winter.

Much best love from
Betty

Both Maconchy and Williams travelled to the continent in late summer 1935, Maconchy returning to Prague to attend the ISCM Festival at which her Prelude, Interlude and Fugue for two violins was performed. Back at home, Maconchy's sister Sheila, who continued to suffer from tuberculosis, came to stay.

---

18 Harriet Cohen.

40) 10 October 1935

Chart Corner, Seal Chart, Kent
Seal 106
October 10th

Dearest Grace

It is <u>too</u> tantalizing that you were at Salzburg when we were – I can hardly believe that you were at Figaro[19] the same night as us – as we walked about in the intervals, too. It would have been so lovely to have met you there, I do <u>wish</u> we had. We didn't see Fidelio,[20] alas, as we had to go on to Prague.

The festival was marvellous – and we enjoyed ourselves <u>a lot</u>.

[. . .] [I] haven't done anything much, as Sheila came to stay with us a few days after we got back, – & got badly ill – and has been in bed for 3 weeks, poor child. We think she's really getting better now though –

Are you writing anything? I've been writing nothing, & seem to have done nothing but copy scores for ages! loathsome job.

Let's meet soon for a 'good talk'

Best love Betty

On 20 March 1936, the BBC scheduled a broadcast of Maconchy's Piano Concerto (1928, rev. 1929–30), with Harriet Cohen (piano) and the BBC Orchestra, conducted by Adrian Boult.

41) [Before 20 March 1936]

Chart Corner, Seal Chart, Kent
Seal 106

Dearest Grace

I've written to the B.B.C. to ask for cards of admission for 'myself and four friends' for the Piano Concerto next Friday – can you be one? It will be just six years and a day since we heard it together in Prague – I'd love you to be there if you can come. It's 7.30 to 8.30 – perhaps you could have a bite with us somewhere afterwards? I've had two more goes at it with Harriet – she will do it pretty well, I think – but she doesn't learn quickly and I wish she could play octaves.

Best love
Betty

---

19 Mozart's opera *Le nozze di Figaro.*
20 Beethoven's opera, *Fidelio.*

I.5 Letters 42–49 (June 1937–Summer 1939)

Letters in this section are intermittent, often with months passing between those that survive. There is also a gap of nearly a year between the last letter in the previous section and the next surviving letter, written after 22 February 1937. In that time, several of Maconchy's works had received important performances, such as the first broadcast of *Great Agrippa* (15 April 1936), or her Piano Concerto performed by Harriet Cohen at a Prom (2 September 1936) and at a Reid Orchestral Concert (3 December 1936). Her Second String Quartet was first performed at a Lemare concert on 1 February 1937 by the Brosa Quartet.

Other significant work premiered or composed during this period included Maconchy's Viola Concerto and her Third String Quartet, while she started work on her Fourth Quartet. Williams's work included her orchestral suite, *Four Illustrations for the Legend of Rhiannon* (1939, rev. 1940), commissioned by the BBC Welsh Orchestra. On 5 August 1938, she conducted the London Philharmonic Orchestra in the première of *Variations: Breuddwyd Dafydd Rhys* (c. 1934) at Cardiff.[1] She also continued her demanding job as a school teacher.

Until Williams's planned trip to Vienna in 1939, neither woman mentions the threatening situation in Europe. Their correspondence continues to focus on works, performances, health concerns, and their family lives and friends.

The Brosa Quartet performed Maconchy's Second String Quartet again at the 1937 ISCM Festival in Paris on 26 June, and soon afterwards, on 4 July, broadcast it on the BBC National Programme. Maconchy and Billy attended the festival, as did Dorrie Gow; highlights included Sándor Veress's Second String Quartet (1937). Gow's Oboe Quintet (1936) was performed at an LCMC concert by the Lawrence Turner Quartet with Terence MacDonagh.

---

1 Graeme Cotterill, 'Music in the Blood & Poetry in the Soul? National Identity in the Life and Music of Grace Williams', PhD (University of Wales, Bangor, 2012), 9.

42) 28 June 1937 – postcard

[Maconchy to Williams]

[postmark: 28 June 1937]

<u>Monday</u>. We got back from Paris this morning, and I found a p.c. from you here – written a long time ago but our forwarding arrangements were rather inefficient & it didn't get sent on. Many thanks now! Paris was fine – it was awfully nice Dorrie being there. The quartet went fairly well, I think – the Brosa's play it pretty well now. (They are broadcasting it <u>next Sunday</u> – round about five – I don't know the exact time – that Sunday chamber concert there generally is about then) We had a <u>heavenly</u> fortnight in Touraine, with the car, before the Paris festival – then drove it up to Dieppe yesterday, & home from Newhaven to-day. I'd love to come and see you next time I'm up, if it suits you – may I send a p.c. or ring up? Haven't made any plans yet. France <u>is</u> a lovely country, isn't it? Yes, I <u>do</u> like Dorrie's oboe 5tet enormously. I thought the best work at the Fest. was a 4tet by Veress – Hungarian. Best love Betty.

43) [On or just after 4 July 1937]

98, Redcliffe Gdns, SW10

Dearest Betty,

I've just heard the quartet. It's as I thought; a fine work. A wonderful opening – everything up to the first break is magnificent & <u>all</u> the (2nd) slow mvt. is A++++. Next in order of preference come the second, the last & the first (excluding the opening, of course.) I think practically all the last mvt. is fine; the only place where it seemed a bit held up was in the fairly long piano passage towards the end; & the bit that came after it wasn't <u>quite</u> progressive enough – but the conclusion was again magnificent.

I expect I'm all wrong about the 1st mvt because everyone else seems to think it the best. Of course I think it's good; but to me it just isn't musically or structurally as interesting as the others; it's got a fine rhythmic power, but it hasn't got for me the sort of inner drive of the third mvt. <u>All</u> this slow mvt. has the stamp of a meisterwerk; really big stuff. The second is grand, too – just right.

It was marvellous being able to hear it at last.

[. . .]

– Must return to my marking – 140 scripts to do before next Sunday; it's not so bad at the start but I know that before the end of the week I shall be feeling very sorry for myself.

Wish you could drop in sometime the week after that.

Once more – it's a <u>splendid</u> work

Love Grace

One small thing about your quartet – I've just remembered it – during the effective pizz. passage in the last mvt. is the melodic arco line loud enough? I should have liked it marked up a little.

Later that year, on 3 December 1937, Maconchy's The Land *(1929), a work in four parts, was broadcast on the BBC National Programme by the BBC Orchestra, conducted by Iris Lemare. Maconchy had been discussing her new Viola Concerto (1937) with the BBC since June 1937. In July, the work was accepted for broadcast in a BBC Concert of Contemporary Music on 4 March 1938, with Bernard Shore as soloist and Constant Lambert conducting.*[2]

44) 2 January 1938

Chart Corner, Seal Chart, Kent
Seal 106
Sunday, Jan 2nd 1938

Dearest Grace,

That is the first time I've written 1938 – : I hope it will be a <u>very</u> good year for you. I am so distressed to hear your mother has been so ill – I do hope she's really better? and to hear that you've been ill yourself – did you get laid up like before? Are you all right again, too? I hope you're not doing too much, looking after the family. It was awfully nice of you to send me the measuring tape, – an inspired present, as I never manage to have one. Perhaps you had seen me trying to measure yards of stuff with a ruler? Thank you so much.

It was grand getting your letter, too. I don't know what to think about the Land, really: I think perhaps the first piece just <u>is</u> rather long & dreary – the performance <u>could</u> have been more sensitive, but I don't think it was only that: also I think the addition of accents would perhaps give it more punch – but even that couldn't really make much difference. (Incidentally, I find nowadays I am getting into a habit of putting an accent on nearly every note – in an effort to secure more attack!) The performance of the 2nd one <u>wasn't</u> very good – & also it was considerably worse through the microphone than in the studio – (I went to the control room & listened a lot of the time & 'David'[3] . . . was extremely nice & helpful, so I shouldn't think it was <u>his</u> fault. He took a lot of trouble:) actually I quite like no. 2. I think it's the best one – & <u>can</u> sound all right. I've never thought much of 3 & 4, & always think 4 only half comes off – 3 does come off, more or less, I think, but isn't very interesting.

Well, well, – sometimes I think all my music is a bit dry & dull.

---

2 BBC WAC EM1, 2 June and 6 July 1937.
3 A BBC engineer.

Alas – Sophie[4] sent back all the songs, yours & mine – saying she'd decided she wanted to do only brand new songs: she hopes to do yours on some other occasion, she said. She asked me to do a new one for her – which I have, a funny one, which I'd like to show you.[5]

I've begun doing my viola concerto with Bernard Shore – the BBC made a really prize muddle & although they'd fixed it up with me & told me it was fixed with him in August & have had it in their published programmes etc he had never been asked to play it! & only heard by accident about 10 days ago. He was in an awful fuss about it & has made me change all the difficult bits. The admirable Mr Percy Rowe[6] had put all the bits we've now changed as cues into the parts – so they have all to be changed too! Hell.

Do let's meet soon when you get back to London. I do hope the luck will turn for you & your family – it is dreadful that you lost your dog & your car. I hope the sea-air will set you up before you come back to London

Much love from
Betty.

Later that year, on Tuesday, 4 October 1938, Maconchy's String Quartet no. 3 (1938) in one movement was given its first performance by its dedicatees, the New Hungarian String Quartet, at a London Contemporary Music Centre concert at the Cowdray Hall. That performance was broadcast as a BBC Concert of Contemporary Music on the BBC National Programme the following Friday, 7 October. The broadcast also included Luigi Dallapiccola's Divertimento in quatro esercizi *for soprano, flute, oboe clarinet, viola, and cello. By this time, Maconchy was writing frequently to Kenneth Wright, Assistant Director of Music at the BBC, about scores under consideration for broadcast.*[7]

45) 9 October 1938 – postcard

98, Redcliffe Gdns, S.W.10
[postmark: 9 Oct 1938]

Dearest Betty,

This is just to say that a second hearing confirmed my impression that Quartet no.3 is one of your best works if not the best. Apart from its being the real stuff of music, & making a lovely sound, it is your most mature work (Dorrie agrees with me, too) & is really first-rate quartet writing. I am terribly grateful to you for letting me hear it on Tuesday as well. It is grand when a modern work gives one the same sort of wholesome complete feeling that one gets from listening

---

4 Soprano Sophie Wyss.
5 *How Samson bore away the gates of Gaza*, a 'scena' for soprano and piano, setting a poem by Nicholas Vachel Lindsay. Wyss gave the first performance at a London Contemporary Music Center Concert at Cowdray Hall on 8 February 1938.
6 Copyist of the parts.
7 See letters from the late 1930s in BBC WAC EM 1.

to Mozart or any of the others . . . But oh what a rare experience! I just couldn't bear any of the other works (except the DellaPiccolo which was rather nice.)
Love Grace

46) [Probably 11] October 1938

Chart Corner, Seal Chart, Kent
Seal 106
Tuesday

Dearest Grace

It <u>was</u> nice of you to write after Friday – and I'm so frightfully glad that you like the 4tet. That has given me more pleasure than <u>anything</u>, because I mind tremendously what you think and value your criticism more than anybody's. I'd been awfully uncertain whether I liked it before-hand, but I did like it when I heard it. I think perhaps it's a bit too much on <u>one main theme</u>, or at any rate that I must try & guard against making a habit of hammering away too much at one theme . . . Well, I want to talk to you about that & heaps of other things – but I don't see how I <u>can</u> get up to see you tomorrow. [. . .] But I never seem to see more than a minute of you – & I want to hear heaps of things – about the conducting particularly. <u>Do</u> go on conducting, I think you must be just right for it. Are you plying Kenneth Wright with scores – N.B. I believe he is now making a 'tour of the Regions' (Belfast etc – will he go to Wales again, perhaps?) but presumably he won't be away very long. His secretary, (Miss Evans) would be able to tell you.

I've had hell over the quintuplets in the 4tet – I wrote ‖c ♩. ♪♩. ♪♩♪♪♪♪♪ ♩. ♪|♩. ♪♪♪♪♪♪ | etc & then decided at the rehearsal on Tues morning that ‖c♩. ♪♩. ♪|₈♪♪♪♪♪|c♩. ♪♩. ♪|₈♪♪♪♪♪|[8] etc was right. I spent the weekend altering 2 scores and a set of parts (it meant re-copying practically <u>half</u>!) – – now I'm in doubt again. [. . .]

Very much love – Billy sends his love too
Betty.

The following year, despite coping with poor health, something that was to continue throughout the war years, Williams worked on and completed her orchestral suite, Four Illustrations for the Legend of Rhiannon *(1939, rev. 1940).*[9] *Maconchy was pregnant with her first child.*

---

8 Exx. Pl.5.1a and 5.1b. Elizabeth Maconchy, String Quartet no. 2 (1937), excerpts.
9 In January 1939, Williams was commissioned to write an orchestral suite for the BBC Welsh Orchestra for 20 guineas. The performance was postponed until autumn 1939; although the war

56 Part I. Letters 1–49 (1927–Summer 1939)

47) [Before 24 October 1939]

Chart Corner
Saturday

Dearest Grace.

I am so <u>very</u> glad that you got that good report from the specialist – thank you so much for writing to tell me. I know of <u>lots</u> of cases of badly taken X-ray photos, which had led to wrong opinions (– both ways – sometimes saying someone is 'cured now' when they aren't, as they did with Sheila at one moment.) That is grand. But <u>do</u> be careful of yourself, even so; try & get a good holiday, & if you don't feel <u>really</u> well at the end of it you ought to take some 'sick-leave' and get well: it's too dangerous to get 'below oneself' like that. But it's tremendous to have achieved the Meisterwerk & scored it & all in such a short time. I'm longing to hear it. You will let me know the date, if I don't see you – ? I find I never read the Radio Times properly because I get fascinated by the strip advertisements.

I'm feeling fine. Do tell Dorrie about the baby – (but she hates them, doesn't she?) I think the 'news' will have to be general soon! I didn't mean to be unduly secretive – but felt it rather premature when I saw you.

Go on with the Halibut Oil etc & try to get fat.

Best love Betty

[. . .]

Maconchy had written nine short piano pieces, collected into a suite published as Country Town *(1939), was struggling with a work for piano and orchestra, eventually titled* Dialogue *(1939–41), and had begun work on her Fourth String Quartet (1939–43).*

48) [Around June] 1939

Chart Corner, Seal Chart, Kent
Seal 106
Thursday

Dearest Grace

Here are my short pieces – for what they're worth. It is awfully good of you to bother about them, & it is such an excellent suggestion to ask the piano teacher at your school to try them out. Thank you <u>so</u> much. Billy had some more ideas about names (for the pieces – not the baby!): I don't know what you'll think of them. He thought the mixture of concrete & abstract names I had was perhaps a mistake, & that

then intervened, Williams received payment. See BBC WAC GW1, correspondence from 1939. See also Letter 50 and 52.

concrete were better.[10] You'll see your suggestions incorporated – very gratefully! The march is certainly more in its place here than where it came from.

It was lovely seeing you & Rhiannon. It is a grand work – I am most awfully glad to have heard it. It is bloody about this year's Proms. It is bound to be a winner when it has been heard once – though – : it ought to be really effective orchestrally as well as being good music.

You were awfully helpful about my problems – I think probably it had better be a new movement altogether for the last one of the piano & orch. piece. I'm hoping for Dorrie's advice too [...]. I've completely re-written the 4tet movement – using a good deal of the material (& a good deal of new) & making it into a Scherzo! Better I think. – Well – we must meet again soon, it's lovely when you can come down here. I hope you're going ahead with the choral work?[11]

Much love from Betty.

Williams went beyond having a local piano teacher test out Maconchy's Country Town; *she played them to her classes and constructed a report from their responses. Maconchy continued to work on* Dialogue, *while Williams still considered making a trip to Vienna, despite the declining political situation.*

49) [Before end of Summer Term] 1939

Chart Corner
Friday

Dearest Grace

I am absolutely fascinated by the report of the pieces – so is Billy. They are frightfully interesting & instructive as regards my pieces, & also as regards children's reactions to music in general. I'd like to keep them as valuable musical-psychological evidence – unless you want them back? We laughed & laughed over some of them! The younger children's ones are of course much the most amusing & the most interesting, they are so direct & spontaneous – I love 'the cross mother telling her daughter to no good' – it just catches the sort of nagging feeling of that piece ('the quarrel') – 'Happy men in a Coal Mine' is wonderful; lots of the suggestions of names seem to me to be excellent & all most apt – all the frog ones are good, & the kangaroos & 'clumping elephants' for the 1st piece, & heaps more. The small ones certainly seem to have liked them: as well as what you say about older children liking more emotional music (with which I agree) it also seems to show that young children have no difficulty in understanding modern music – no more, I mean, than other music (I've thought

---

10 The pieces are titled: 1. The Fair; 2. The Beggar; 3. The Quarrel; 4. Lament; 5. The Knifegrinder; 6. The Singer; 7. Bells; 8. The Recruit; 9. Goodnight.
11 Probably *Gogonedawg arglwydd* ('Praise the Lord Eternal') for chorus and orchestra, completed in June 1939.

this for some time): but this doesn't apply to the German children – which is interesting – I think the 'romantic music' culture which only soaks later into children here (& which I think causes the later difficulty in understanding modern music) must be almost born in them. I thought their reports touching, with their dislike of 'hard and loud' music!

[. . .]

You must be half-dead by now with all you've had to do. Hope all the end-of-term things will go very well. & that you'll have a very good holiday. I think it's very brave of you if you go to Vienna – (you must be discreet!) & it will be frightfully interesting to hear what you think of it: but don't go if the outlook gets much blacker, will you?

I'm very glad I've scrapped the last movement of the Piano & Orch. piece – Dorrie agreed with you about it. By the time she came I disliked it so much I felt it was quite indecent to play it to her! I'm on the way with another – a 'Burlesque' I think – which at present I like much better.

I had a letter this morning saying 'I hope your child won't be a Tenor' – Lord, – think of it! it hadn't occurred to me before –

Much love and heaps & heaps of thanks Betty.

Part II
Letters 50–93
(October 1939–April 1949)

Figure PII.1 Grace Williams, date unknown.

II.1　Letters 50–64
(October 1939–June 1942)

On 3 September 1939, Neville Chamberlain declared that Britain was at war with Germany. Maconchy flew to Dublin to give birth to her first child, Anna, born on 24 October. Both women were to move around frequently due to the war, trying to avoid the threat of German bombing and facing various war-time shortages and obligations which encroached on time they would otherwise have spent composing.

As usual, the two women's letters discuss their work, friends, and family – including the death in November 1940 of Maconchy's mother in Switzerland, where she had been with her daughter Sheila who, like Maconchy, had developed TB. Much of Williams's side of the correspondence in this period has not survived.

Concert life changed considerably during the war, but despite last-minute cancellations and postponements, such as the première of Maconchy's *Dialogue* for piano and orchestra (1939–41) at the Proms, both women continued to receive performances of their music.

During this period of nearly three years, Maconchy finished her Fourth String Quartet (1939–43), a ballet, *Puck Fair* (1940), and a *Dies irae* for contralto solo, chorus, and orchestra (1940–41) and was working on a *Divertimento* (originally called Serenade) for cello and piano (1941–3) and a work eventually entitled Theme and Variations for string orchestra (1942–3). Williams finished her *Fantasia on Welsh Nursery Tunes* for orchestra (1940), her Piano Concerto (1940–41, rev. 1942–3) – later called *Sinfonia concertante* – and started on a symphonic work inspired by Owen Glendower, eventually entitled *Symphonic Impressions* (1943).

With Kenneth Wright's assistance,[1] *Williams's* Four Illustrations on the Legend of Rhiannon *was first performed in a Home Service broadcast by the BBC Symphony Orchestra conducted by Welsh conductor Idris Lewis*[2] *on 24 October 1939 – the same afternoon that Maconchy's daughter, Anna, was born in Dublin. Williams*

1　See BBC WAC GW2, September – October 1939.
2　Idris Lewis was Director of Music for BBC Wales, 1936–1952.

had been evacuated with the Camden School for Girls to Uppingham in Rutland at the outbreak of war.

50) 26 October 1939

E. V. LeFanu, 26 Upper Pembroke St, Dublin
Thursday October 26th '39.

Dearest Grace

Just to say I do hope Rhiannon went well? And that you are pleased with it? I feel sure it must sound <u>fine</u> from having seen the score. I do wish I could have heard it – but Anna chose almost that moment to arrive! (6.15 on Tuesday) which she did with the maximum speed and absolute minimum of discomfort. She is really rather a pet, tremendously fat, (she weighed 9lbs 6ozs) & her face is so like a ripe red apple that one can't really tell what she'll be like later on. She is behaving admirably & I feel really <u>marvellous</u> – wouldn't mind having another one to-morrow. You were right about it being a daughter! Curiously enough from the instant I came into the nursing [home] I <u>knew</u> it was going to be a daughter – though earlier I had rather expected & hoped for a son. I don't mind a bit now! The only fly in the ointment is that Billy isn't here to enjoy it all. But he hopes to get over for a bit soon. – This is being a very odd war – and I regret having flown over here as there have been no raids yet, & I might have had Anna at home.

<u>Do</u> write & tell me how Rhiannon went, please. I hope you got the parts done & corrected all right? Nice to have a week at home, and a spell off from your co-evacuees. (I write to Uppingham as I expect you're back there.) Best love to Dorrie if you're writing (Maureen sent her a postcard to announce Anna's arrival) & heaps of love to yourself

Betty

I'm to read a paper to the Music Club here on 'Modern Music' in Feb. or March. I'd like ideas, please.

Correspondence was apparently interrupted as motherhood and war-time teaching duties intervened. In 1940 Williams was evacuated with the Camden School for Girls to new quarters in Grantham, and that summer, her Elegy *for string orchestra (1936, rev. 1940) was broadcast in its revised version on Sunday, 25 August 1940, on the BBC Home Service by the BBC Orchestra, under the direction of BBC staff conductor Clarence Raybould. Maconchy's* Dialogue *for piano and orchestra (1939–41) was announced for the 1940 Proms, to be performed by Clifford Curzon and the BBC Symphony Orchestra, with Henry J. Wood conducting; however, as she later wrote, 'the [air] raids came a week too soon'[3] and the latter part of the 1940 Prom season was cancelled. Meanwhile, she continued*

---

3 Maconchy, letter to Julian Herbage of the BBC, BBC WAC EM2, 22 October 1941.

to work on her ballet in five scenes, Puck Fair *(1940), for performance in Dublin by the Irish Ballet Club, and her Fourth String Quartet (1939–43).*

51) 17 August 1940

Chart Corner, Seal Chart, Kent
August 17th '40

Dearest Grace

Your postcard came this morning – & your grand long letter – how long ago? I don't like to think. Please forgive me for not answering it with an equally long one <u>ages</u> ago. It was lovely to hear from you – it came on the morning I was evacuating Nurse & Anna down to Devonshire & life since has seemed a bit of a rush – but all the same I have no real excuse except procrastination for not answering it.

We joined Anna in Devonshire – near Tiverton – for a fortnight's holiday & it was lovely – (we got back nearly a fortnight ago) She is with some cousins of John Christie's, (Lucie's husband) [. . .] they took us for one heavenly picnic to Exmoor & we looked across the channel to a miraculously beautiful Wales, blue hills & golden fields & cliffs & beaches, & thought of you, on the other side. With a sufficiently powerful telescope we could have seen you on the beach at Barry I am sure! I wish we could have flown across – I would love to see you & have a long talk. It will be splendid to hear your Elegy on the 25th. How strong-minded of you to rewrite & rescore it. You must be working pretty hard. And you seem to have worked very hard at Rhiannon. <u>I</u> didn't think it needed re-writing – & didn't realise it was full of 'faked – counterpoint'? Is that really true? But I agree that it is <u>always</u> good for one to work at counterpoint, & always results in making one freer afterwards. And I agree that perhaps you have sometimes rather lost sight of counterpoint – & this will probably have been very good for you. But don't please pull all your music to pieces – but start writing some more.

[. . .]

My Prom is on Thursday Sept. 26th. It would be <u>lovely</u> if you could come. Heavenly to see you: and I'd love your views on the work, although I think you might think it a very bad one – I don't know what I think of it at present – We had a run-through rehearsal last week – most unexpected, & I had a job getting the parts ready in time. It also came as a surprise at very short notice for Clifford Curzon. But he is excellent – most intelligent, & extremely nice & easy to work with. I did it with him twice last week with 2 pianos. The orchestra read it very <u>very</u> badly – it is scored much more for wind than strings, & the wind seemed pretty weak. I <u>longed</u> to conduct, too – as Henry is so awful about tempi etc – altogether it was rather agonising –: & it is <u>so</u> hard to tell exactly what is bad playing & what bad scoring at a quick first run-through like that. However it <u>has</u> enabled me to alter the balance in various places – smallish things, & that's useful.

I <u>am</u> glad that you have been feeling so much better – and also that your new quarters are so much nicer & that you have time to work – I've also done some work this summer – chiefly a ballet for the people in Dublin (who are enterprising though rather bad) & am now trying to get going on a quartet. I don't find the war makes it impossible to work (and I'm very glad you don't either) – but I don't get as much time as I want to. I haven't got Poldi (she is in Surrey – not interned) – & just have a daily woman in the morning & back for a bit in the evening – & I've felt it my duty to make a lot of jam & so on, & work hard at growing vegetables & am even keeping a few hens! I quite enjoy all this housewifery – but it <u>does</u> take time.

We are thinking of having Anna home again – because the feeling that whatever happens it is better to be all together is getting stronger. We are surprisingly quiet here: even the last few days, though we've had a good many warnings & some fighting quite close (and a bomber brought down 2 miles away) – there has been nothing alarming – & no bombs close.

You must be having a far less peaceful time – in fact it must be horrid. I'm glad you get some bathing in spite of it. I haven't had a swim for 2 years!

[. . .]

Much best love from us both

Betty.

Yes – you <u>must</u> see Anna before long. It is hard to describe her – she is getting more interesting & intelligent all the time. She is <u>very</u> large, has <u>bright</u> blue eyes & very fair curly hair & a lovely skin with pink cheeks & brown limbs.

52) 26 August 1940

Chart Corner, Seal Chart, Kent
August 26th

Dearest Grace.

Billy and I thought the Elegy was <u>beautiful</u> yesterday. I think it is a lovely work, & one of your best. It makes a beautiful sound and is really fine music. I hope you were pleased with the performance, or did Raybould take it too slow? I thought it was lovely at that pace, (& not 'morbid') We both were very indignant at their putting it at such an unearthly hour instead of at a proper time – & having an announcer who treated the programme as if it was intended only for congenital idiots. Does Ogilvy[4] think he will get 'the man in the street' to listen to serious music by introducing it with facetious & half-baked remarks? They always did it a bit & now are worse than ever. However, that is by the way. What matters is that they did the Elegy & that it is really good.

. . . I'm writing to wailing syrens & zooming planes. However we've not had anything much here since yesterday week, really. We are hoping to get Anna back quite soon, if things don't get worse.

---

4 Frederick Ogilvie was BBC Director General from 1938 to 1942.

I heard yesterday that the Blech quartet[5] are doing my third quartet at the National Gallery on Sept. 4th, which is nice. I wonder what the Nat. Gallery audience will think of it! not much, I expect.[6]

We had our tenth wedding day on Friday – isn't it extraordinary? And this week it will be ten years since 'the Land' at the Proms. It has gone so quickly – & yet in a way it seems a long time, & such a lot has happened. Much best love & congratulations

Betty.

Over the Christmas holidays, Williams found time to work on her Piano Concerto (1940–41), after she had triumphed as opera director for the school's Christmas production of Hänsel und Gretel, *presumably in Humperdinck's version. When domestic chores allowed, Maconchy worked on a setting of the* Dies irae *for contralto solo, chorus, and orchestra* (1940–41).

53) 10 January 1941

Chart Corner, Seal Chart, Kent
Seal 106
January 10th '41

Dearest Grace

I have a letter to thank you for, as well as the very nice Xmas presents you sent Anna & me. It was lovely to hear from you – & to know that you are at home now and working at your piano concerto: I hope you are getting lots done & that it's going well? I'm sorry you didn't get home till after Xmas. You must have been kept pretty busy at school. I am glad your Hänsel & Gretel went so well, it is splendid that you have started on opera production, & I hope you will do a lot more. I can imagine how well you would do it. I'd love to have seen H&G. It must have been fascinating for you to do, & grand that they threw themselves into it so.

[...] [Anna] is extraordinarily interesting now – I must say a child's development is marvellous and awfully engrossing. [. . .] I had A. for a fortnight at Xmas [. . .], & found I was pretty busy, as I only have a daily maid for part of the day now. – I don't get a great deal of time for working with one thing & another – Anna & nanny sleep downstairs in the dining-room where my piano is, for one thing: & as you know I'm too dependent on it! But I work in the afternoons, & get

---

5 The Blech Quartet, with Harry Blech and David Martin (violins), Frederick Riddle (viola), and Willem de Mont (cello), had been formed in 1933.
6 Although Maconchy's String Quartet no. 3 was planned for performance at a National Gallery Concert on 4 September 1940, an air raid disrupted proceedings and another quartet was substituted. See 'Borodin and the Sirens', *The Times* (5 September 1940). The popular concerts held at the National Gallery and organised by pianist Myra Hess were a notable feature of London's war-time life. See www.nationalgallery.org.uk/paintings/history/the-myra-hess-concerts/.

on quite a lot. I'm doing a setting of the Dies Irae for chorus & orchestra – I mean it to be in memory of my Mother. I don't think that I told you that she died at Arosa in November – she wasn't ill for long, which was a mercy really: she got hardening of the arteries of the brain, rather like having a stroke. We could not get out & be with her, as it's impossible to go to Switzerland now & felt terribly cut off & helpless. Sheila is alone there now of course – but seems pretty well, better than she has been for some time, I think. It was a great shock to us, & I feel terribly sad that she never saw Anna.

I had a letter a few days ago from Dorrie – it must be rather bleak & cut off from everything where they are, I fear. But then everyone is cut-off from everyone else now-a-days. I would so love to be able to see you & have a good talk! I have not stirred from here even to London for ages: but it is possible that we may have to move from here, as they want to evacuate Billy's library to the country if they can get a suitable place for about 50,000 books & ourselves & his assistant & secretary.

We are at present in correspondence over 2 castles! one in Shropshire & one in Worcestershire. I must admit I am a little appalled at the idea of starting wartime housekeeping in a castle after this easy little house. [. . .]

Best love always
from Betty
[. . .]

By the following October, Maconchy and her family had relocated from Kent to Downton Castle in Shropshire, accompanying Billy, who moved there with the library of the Royal College of Surgeons. Williams was still in Grantham, and had by this time met Zen Sliwinski (possibly Sliwinskius), a Polish refugee, who was working in a factory there. Williams met Zen when she and her friend and colleague, Joan Woodhead, were asked to teach English to some of the Polish community. She 'immediately seemed to feel an affinity with him' and 'admired his intelligence'. They remained very close throughout the war, although after the war he emigrated to South Africa.[7]

On 29 October 1941, the first performance of one of Williams's most popular works, the Fantasia on Welsh Nursery Tunes *(1940) was given in a BBC broadcast, played by the BBC Northern Orchestra conducted by Eric Fogg.*[8] *Shortly afterwards, her recently completed Piano Concerto (1940–41) was submitted to the BBC, and the Welsh conductor Idris Lewis sent it on to Bedford, since Adrian Boult had promised to look at it.*[9]

---

7 Letter from Williams's sister Marian Evans to Malcolm Boyd, 19 January 1979, quoting a letter from Joan Woodhead to Evans.
8 The BBC Reading Panel reports were lukewarm, agreeing that it was 'well done' but 'very slight'; nevertheless, the work was scheduled for broadcast, as, in Kenneth Wright's words, 'we do wish to encourage the creation of Welsh orchestral music [and] this is the first thing of its kind (I believe) in Welsh musical literature' (BBC WAC GW2, 7 October 1941).
9 BBC WAC GW2, 3 November 1941.

54) 27 October 1941

October 27th '41

Dearest Grace.

[. . .] It will be <u>lovely</u> to hear your Welsh Nursery Rhymes fantasy on Wed. What a ghastly time you must have had over the parts [. . .] Very glad that Boult is going to see your Piano Concerto. Please keep me informed as to what happens. It will be fine if they do it. It certainly is pretty difficult to get any performances now. I don't expect ever to get any B.B.C. performances as Julian Herbage (who loathes me) apparently controls the programmes now & K.A.W. does Overseas music.[10] (Sophie broadcast 'Samson' to S. America in the Summer)[11]

I went down to Dorking to see Uncle Ralph [. . .], & was rather shocked to find how much older & almost 'fallen away' he looked. He spends his time on committees, fire-watching, digging potatoes etc – I remonstrated but he said he felt he must 'do what he could to help' & then any time he had got left he felt he could use for his own work. I'm sure he's wrong, but if he has made up his mind there is no changing it. He talked away cheerfully a lot of the time, But I thought he was restless & not himself. He seemed to like the 'Dies Irae' I took to show him. I'd like you to see it – but feel it's rather wrong to encroach on your free time. So I won't send it unless you can genuinely say you have time for it.

This is only a note & not a real answer to your long letter which I loved getting. I think your Zen sounds nice & attractive as well as original. Much love from, Billy & me. Betty

55) [Shortly after 29 October] 1941 – postcard

Billy & I listened to your Welsh Fantasia & enjoyed it <u>immensely</u>. It is absolutely excellent – brilliantly scored, lovely tunes & <u>most</u> effective. It certainly ought to be played everywhere & I hope plenty of conductors heard it. You seem to have been able to use the Welsh tunes like the best of the Russians did, or Bartok with Hungarian tunes – I mean adopting them into your own modern idiom without any incongruity, & without any of the awful earnestness of the English folk-school. My only criticism is to wonder (very tentatively) if the slow movement is a little too long for the shape of the piece? But's [*sic*] it's only a suggestion & a second hearing may show it's a wrong one. Let me know if you were pleased, & when it will be done again. Also any news of the Pf. Concerto. Best love & congratulations from Betty & Billy.

---

10 When Kenneth Wright became the BBC Overseas Music Director in December 1940, Julian Herbage, a programmer in the Music Department since 1927, took over as the Assistant Music Director.

11 Wright's influence in overseas broadcasts led to Sophie Wyss performing Maconchy's *How Samson bore away the gates of Gaza* for voice and piano in a Latin American broadcast in summer 1941.

A month later, Maconchy had finished her Dies irae *(1940–41) and sent it to Williams for comments, along with a Serenade for cello and piano, an early version of her* Divertimento *(1941–3). She resumed work on her Fourth String Quartet (1939–43). On 1 December 1941, Williams's overture* Hen Walia *(1930) was broadcast by the BBC Orchestra conducted by Idris Lewis on the BBC Forces Programme.*

56) 20 November 1941

Downton Castle, Ludlow, Salop
November 20th '41

Dearest Grace.

I am taking you at your word & sending the Dies Irae to you, and also a rather negligible piece for 'Cello with piano accomp. Is it worth scoring for chamber orch. do you think? The piano part is an unpianistic one as it wasn't originally intended to be for piano. I might improve it perhaps – ? as I am thinking of sending it to William Pleeth the cellist, I met him & Margaret Good (his pianist) by chance when I went to London & he asked me if I had anything for 'cello & piano & to send him something if I did write it. So tell me what you think.

Uncle Ralph made a couple of suggestions about the end of the 'Dies Irae'. [. . .] I haven't tackled scoring yet & don't feel very self-confident about it. I wish I had your scoring skill. I don't agree that your scoring of the Nursery rhymes fantasia was 'sheerest conventional' because it not only came off but sounded fresh & alive and individual all the time & the scoring seemed to be part of the tune & to derive from it – as the best orchestration always must I think, & the Gordon Jacob kind doesn't – I mean it begins at the wrong end of the stick.

Is it 10.50 a.m. or p.m. on Dec 1st that Hen Walia is coming off? I'm looking forward to it. . .

Yes, B & I heard Les Illuminations & thought them superb – they are much the best things of his I've heard (I haven't heard the violin concerto, & want to) & seem to me to be very good indeed. (Sophie sang them beautifully, I thought) The Walton concerto we also thought disappointing at a first hearing & more so at the second.[12]

I mustn't write more as I want to do up this parcel for Anna & Nanny to post. I'm working at a string quartet now. I did one movement of it 2½ years ago when Anna was on the way but have never been able to go on with it successfully till now, when I seem to have got going again.

Very much best love from
Betty.
[. . .]

---

12 Britten's *Les Illuminations*, Op. 18, sung by soprano Sophie Wyss (no further details could be traced). Walton's Violin Concerto was given its first UK performance on 1 November 1941 in a Royal Philharmonic Society concert at the Royal Albert Hall.

By December 1941, Williams's school had moved to Stamford in Lincolnshire. However, she went home to Barry for Christmas, which gave her time to put together very detailed comments about Maconchy's Dies irae and Serenade.[13] Williams's interest in Polish culture, sparked by her friendship with Zen, led to her to make orchestral arrangements of Polish folk tunes, in addition to arranging traditional Welsh songs.

57) 26 December 1941

9, Old Village Road, Barry, Glamorgan
Boxing Day

Dearest Betty,

Very many thanks for the handkerchief – a most unexpected & welcome present these days!

At last I have had time to play & replay the Dies Irae & to jot down a few impressions – to which I don't at all expect you to give wholehearted approval – some of them you will probably – & rightly – think quite wrong. Others, you may decide may have something in them, & may suggest a compromise. After reading through what I have written I feel I've been far too dictatorial – & I do apologise. All these years of school-teaching must have left their mark & I find again & again that if I'm asked to give advice of this kind I am too apt to overstep the mark – so please forgive me. All that I enclose in pencil is in the nature of criticism. It looks a lot – but it isn't really & do please remember that everything that I have not criticised I like tremendously – it is a very fine work – strong with a strong & austere beauty – & I am overwhelmed by the sheer creativeness of it. [. . .]

I am very glad to hear about the new str. 4tet. Please may I see a sketch sometime? It is good to know that you are working so well. I must try & get something new written. All I have done lately is a simple S.S.A. arrangement of a Welsh folk song for a Welsh Madame & her girl singers who wrote & asked for something.[14] Then I got quite worked up about arranging Polish Songs & Dances (which Zen has whistled to me) for orchestra. I had planned quite a lot of the scoring but suddenly realised that I'll never get them played unless I could guarantee that there was no copyright attached to them. Zen has no idea how old they are & so far none of his friends can help but he is still enquiring. Isn't copyright a curse. So I am rather held up because I don't want to waste a lot of time on them if there is to be no market for them.

The Welsh programmes seem to have gone off the air as suddenly as they came on! I saw Idris Lewis in December & he was extremely vague about future plans.

---

13 Only part of Williams's extensive commentary on *Dies irae* and none of her commentary on the Serenade are included here.
14 Unidentified, but perhaps 'Dacw 'nghariad i iawr yn y berllan' ('See my love in the orchard yonder') for SSA chorus, later published by University of Wales Press (1960).

Someone called Elizabeth Poston who belongs to the B.B.C. Overseas Dept. recommended the Fantasia for Overseas Programmes & I've had to send the score to Arthur Bliss.[15] Love to you all from Grace.

[...]

Williams's Fantasia on Welsh Nursery Tunes *(1940) was given its second broadcast on the BBC Home Service on 1 January 1942 by the BBC Orchestra, conducted by Mansel Thomas.*[16] *Meanwhile, Maconchy finally neared completion of her Fourth String Quartet (1939–43) and continued thinking about the Serenade for cello and piano (1941–3).*

58) 6 January 1942

Downton Castle, Ludlow, Salop
January 6th '42

Dearest Grace

I listened to the Fantasia the other night again, & loved it as much as the first time. This time the slow part didn't strike me as too long – (it seemed to hang about a little the first time, but not this) but yet I don't think you had altered it? or had you? It's a beautiful little work – & it's very good it's having 2 performances straight away – which gives it a good start, & will lead to heaps of others, I'm sure.

[...]

Well, my dear I have a lot to thank you for. First your enchanting Xmas present of the 'Hunting of the Snark'[17] which B. & I are very fond of, & have enjoyed very much – the pictures are fine.

And then thank you more than I can say for all the time & trouble you have spent on the 'Dies Irae' – I really am enormously grateful & feel rather guilty that you have spent your time on it. It is an enormous help to have this detailed criticism of it, and all your points are very helpful & interesting (even when I disagree.) Most of them I do agree with, & am adopting, & your pencilled suggestions for making these alterations are fine.

I am very glad you like the work as a whole, & reassured, – as I have found it very hard to see it dispassionately & sometimes think it good, sometimes bad.

[...]

[...]

---

15 Composer Elizabeth Poston worked as a music programmer in the BBC's European Service during the war. Composer Arthur Bliss had taken over from Boult as BBC Director of Music in March 1941, while Boult continued as Chief Conductor.
16 Composer and conductor Mansel Thomas had been music assistant at BBC Wales and deputy conductor of the BBC Welsh Orchestra since 1936.
17 Lewis Carroll, *The Hunting of the Snark* (1876), possibly the edition published in 1941 with illustrations by Mervyn Peake.

I really must get down to scoring it. I haven't been able to screw myself up to it, up till now. I have so much less time for working than I used to, that I want to spend what I have in writing music instead of scoring, & still less copying!

I have just finished a new string quartet. I wrote the last movement 2½ years ago – & started working on it again this autumn, & have done the scherzo, 1st mvt. & slow movement, in that order. I feel rather pleased with it at the moment – the period of reaction sets in later, doesn't it? I always remember Uncle Ralph saying 'when one has just finished a work one thinks not only that it is the best work one has ever written – but that it is the best work anyone has ever written'.

Your title suggestions for the pieces of the Serenade are excellent – I like 1. Preamble 2. Scaramouch 4. Vigil & 5. Farrago (a good word) or Masquerade. I'm not sure which. Marionettes is a good idea for No. 3 – but I really mean it to be a clock – with its tick-tick & it strikes nine in the middle – is this too onomatopoeic? (no idea how to spell it) Yes – no 1. is decidedly Spanish & no. 2 Russe. If I'd had an eye to the main chance no 1. should have been American! It's all a very slight affair – but I'll send it to Pleeth, as you say you think it's worth it.

I do hope you are having a good holiday – which usually means doing some work! How is Zen? & have you had any further news of the Piano Concerto? – do tell me when you do.

Two annoying things have happened since I started writing this letter. A letter from Anne saying they are to play at the Nat. Gallery on the 13th & are going to play my 2nd quartet – which I'd like to hear both before & at the concert.[18] Ten minutes later a wire came from Nanny to say her young man (who has been expected home for months, after 3 years) has arrived in England – & of course it's a longstanding promise that she goes home for her holiday when he arrives! So I can't possible get away next week. [. . .] Then came a parcel of the records of my 2nd quartet made by the Brosa's (now disbanded, as you know) returned to me by the B.B.C. by rail & all 3 records broken. I'd lent them for extracts to be used in a series of broadcasts (for America) by a man called Edward Lockspeiser – & specially asked them to keep the records till I could get someone to call for them. Aren't they fools? it's so unnecessary, & I valued those records.[19]

[. . .] Well, I must stop – Very much best love and many very real thanks for your great help – you know how much I value your opinion and help, always.

Your loving
Betty

I suppose you have not got a rough score, or sketch of the Piano Concerto? I'd love to see it if & when you had one available now or later. [. . .]

---

18 Maconchy's Second String Quartet was performed at the National Gallery Concerts on 13 January 1942.
19 Maconchy had hired the Brosa Quartet and paid for this private recording, issued by Memphis Recording Company as a single copy. The BBC offered to make a replacement recording from an afternoon broadcast by the Salon Orchestra Quartet, and Maconchy gratefully accepted (BBC WAC EM2, January–February 1942); see Letter 62. Musicologist Edward Lockspeiser worked for BBC Overseas Music during the war.

72   Part II. Letters 50–93 (October 1939–April 1949)

59) 25 January 1942

15, Ryhall Road, Stamford, Lincs
January 25th '42

Dearest Betty,

Here is the piano score of the concerto – I am so sorry to have been so long in answering your letter; I just couldn't face the packing! – but now since I've had to pack up something else & send it off I think I am quite equal to coping with a bit more string & sealing wax.

[. . .]

Now for the Serenade. This poor work was sadly neglected by me at first. Whenever I had time to play your M.S.S. I always began with the Dies Irae & then never had time for the other. But now I feel I do know something about it. Yes, it is an attractive work – perhaps I don't think it quite as attractive as other works of yours in a similar vein – but I'd much prefer to hear this than most other things by contemporary composers – so – It ought to make a good sound & cellists should welcome it. I have practically nothing to suggest – everything is quite as it ought to be as far as I can see – [. . .]

All the best to the three of you for 1942. Thank you so much for Anna's snapshot. She is a dear – very like you, Betty, in appearance. She looks very aware of things for such a small child.

Love from Grace

Did I tell you that I went to Bedford for my last broadcast[20] – a miserable experience – the orchestra were more automaton-like than ever & Raybould came into the rehearsal & didn't (apparently) listen to a note but just gossiped to whoever was near him. That orchestra always makes me feel like a poor forlorn orphan. By the way, Idris Lewis asked about my Piano Concerto & I was told that it had automatically been sent to the Reading Committee. [. . .]

60) [Late January or early February 1942] – postcard

[Maconchy to Williams]

Downton Castle, Ludlow, Salop.
Tuesday morning.

I think you ought to submit your Piano Concerto to Henry Wood – I heard 2 days ago (from Mr Hinrichsen)[21] that H.J.W. was asking to see new works for 1942 Proms – so he evidently is going to do new works this time.[22] (I wrote to ask if he would do my Dialogue this time, which the blitz stopped in 1940 – & have just had a wire to say he will, which is good.) I don't expect you'll want to take

---

20   By January 1942, the BBC Symphony Orchestra had been evacuated to Bedford.
21   Maconchy's publisher, Max Hinrichsen.
22   No new works were included in the 1941 Promenade Concerts, which were not run by the BBC.

your score away from the B.B.C.: so would you like me to send the Piano score I have either to you, or to him direct? If so, send me a wire & I'll send it at once – (though I should be very sorry to part with it, as I don't know it nearly well enough yet. I like the slow movement particularly & the last also very much – at present I don't like the 1st so much – I haven't got hold of it properly yet. It is a real Concerto, the piano writing splendid all through. Elizabeth Poston is a mysterious character I thought she'd disappeared! She was one of Warlock's satellites & later pursued André[23] – she was loathed by Anne as you may imagine – & I disliked her too. Funny her turning up at the BBC. Best love, in haste, Betty.

61) 18 February 1942

February 18th 42

Dearest Grace

I wrote to Henry[24] – & have just had this p.c. from him. So do send him a score – (if you haven't already) I think the best to send of the 3 you suggest would be the Song of Mary – as he is always absolutely determined to have a first performance (& counts a broadcast as being the same as a public performance, i.e. won't do something that has already been broadcast.)[25] It's an idiotic idea, but still. Also the 'Song of Mary' is a more out-of-the-way combination than most – (soprano & orchestra –) which might be a help. But I think I should tell him about your piano concerto & the other things, as well. He might not do 2 piano concertos by women composers! (though mine isn't really a concerto at all, but still –) but I think he'd mind less about that than about this 1st perf. business, which he is as bad as anyone about.

Well, very best of luck to you; I do hope he'll do a work – as he so clearly ought to. Send him the score at once!

Forgive great haste

Best love

Betty

Yes – the one who wore the hats was Elizabeth Poston.

I should ask the advice of someone at the B.B.C. (why not Kenneth Wright – who is at Broadcasting House as Overseas Music Director – no doubt you know this) about the Polish songs & dances & the question of copyright. I believe it would be perfectly all right & that any Polish lawyer or such like would say waive the copyright & have the good propaganda for Polish tunes.[26]

---

23 Composer Peter Warlock (pseudonym of Philip Heseltine) had a devoted following before his sudden death in 1930. Violinist André Mangeot had taught Anne Macnaghten.
24 Henry J. Wood.
25 Williams's *Song of Mary* (1939, rev. 1940) for soprano and orchestra had not yet been performed.
26 Williams followed all Maconchy's advice, writing to Wood on 24 February, arranging for the BBC to forward the Piano Concerto to him, and corresponding with Wright soon after about the copyright question (BBC WAC GW2, February 1942).

62) 22 March 1942

March 22nd '42

Dearest Grace.

I hope I haven't kept your Concerto too long – I have really enjoyed having it & playing it. I still like the 1st movement the least of the three – it seems to lack contrast rather (– in the music itself – no doubt there is plenty of contrast in the scoring.) But the piano writing is masterly, here & all through – <u>real</u> concerto writing. I like the slow movement very much, as I told you. One bit I think falls below the rest – at Letter C [. . .] for about 6 bars – I feel it a little academic & uninteresting – not so 'inevitable' as the rest. The last movement I have grown to like more & more (– & I expect you are right that it is the best.) It 'grows' finely & has very good contrasts & I like the subject matter very much. [. . .] It's a fine work, and I do hope the BBC will do it –.

Have you heard anything from H. J. W.[27] yet? I'm longing to hear. I'm sending my new str. quartet for you to see as you said you'd like to see it.[28] But please don't spend time on it – I'd love to know what you feel about it after looking or playing through it – but I do feel that you must spend your time on your own work – & feel a bit selfish any how to be sending it!

The four movements have a few thematic links as you'll see. I don't know if that's a good thing or not – but it seems to happen. [. . .] Does it hang together as a whole. Billy says he feels movements 2 3 & 4 do, but that no 1 seems to stand apart from the others. Do you approve of the 3rd movement leading into the 4th? I know on practical grounds it is sometimes a mistake – but feel it wants to here

My 2nd quartet is being played by the BBC on April 10th by Jean Pougnet and other members of the 'Salon Orchestra (!)' – including Riddle & Pini, – all good players, but I haven't heard them as a quartet. [. . .]

What news of Dorrie? has she left London? I haven't been able to get to London – & don't see much prospect of it. My local maid has just joined the NAAFIs[29] so will be leaving in a couple of weeks – & Nanny is being married, probably in June, perhaps sooner. I don't know what I'll do about my Prom! I'm sure I shall get another maid – the only local possibility is a rather unwilling girl of 15 for the mornings. So I shall have to become more of a hausfrau than ever – . . . [. . .]

Very best love Betty

In a missing letter and postcard, Williams sent advice about Maconchy's String Quartet no. 4 (1939–43). Meanwhile, both Maconchy and Williams had embarked on large-scale orchestral works; Williams began a symphony on the subject of fourteenth-century Welsh leader and rebel hero Owen Glendower,[30] while Maconchy started on a work for string orchestra.

---

27 Henry J. Wood.
28 Maconchy's String Quartet no. 4 (1939–43).
29 Navy, Army and Air Force Institutes
30 In Welsh, Owain Glyndŵr, but anglicised as Owen Glendower.

Figure PII.1.1 Elizabeth Maconchy, autograph letter, 18 April 1942. (Letter 63)

63) 18 April 1942

Downton Castle, Ludlow, Salop
Saturday April 18th '42

Dearest Grace –

I'm sorry to have been such an age answering your letter (with the quartet) & your p.c. I seem to have been rushed with one thing or another – & have been incorporating some of your advice in the new quartet & altering the parts to match, before writing . . . Thank you so very much for your excellent advice about the quartet – & for having spent so much time & trouble on it. I am <u>very</u> glad to have your opinion: it is the greatest help when one is working quite in isolation It's so <u>awfully</u> hard to get an objective view of one's own work I think, don't you? (– at least until some time after it is written) & I sometimes feel that my standards & judgement may have become warped & that I may be writing something quite worthless. I'm <u>very</u> glad you like the new quartet. Your two major suggestions I have adopted – i.e. a cut in the 1st movement where that longish tune is repeated. You are absolutely right about this – I haven't made such a big cut as you suggested – but I think it achieves its object. The other is in the last mvt. The

section which you (& Billy) find 'sticks out' from the rest. I always knew it did! but liked it & was loath to cut it out. Now, however, I have changed the <u>inner</u> parts as you suggested – & it <u>does</u> seem to make a difference & to weld it in with the rest, without spoiling the theme itself. I've done this sort of thing – [music example] [31] it makes the rhythm less <u>bald</u>, too

[. . .] I must go & get fruit juice for Anna . . . Nanny is at home for a long weekend, & Billy in Ireland for 10 days, so I am holding the fort here. It is miraculous weather – I am writing on the verandah while Anna plays with a bowl of water & brings me innumerable little tin cups of 'tea', refilling them from a little tea pot. – – She turned up then with a nasty scratch on her hand, which had to be attended to, & is now asleep in the pram.

I have adopted some of your smaller suggestions (for instance for more of a splash in the last bar of all) but not others, which as you say are really a matter of individual taste, & I can only 'hear' them my way. I had no idea there was so much of that tri-tone progression in the slow movement – I'm sorry it grates on your ear so much! It just doesn't on mine – I feel it is right, there. I hope I haven't got an obsession for it? as one does sometimes for a chord or an interval or progression. . .

Yes – it <u>was</u> a good & intelligent performance of No 2. the other day. I'm glad you heard it & liked it. I still like it, & think it is probably the best thing I've written. [. . .]

I agree in liking the idea of Bliss as musical director.[32] I think he will be quite good – & sympathetic to such as us.

I do hope K. A. W.[33] will be able to prove your Polish tunes non-copyright. I can see your suite of them becoming <u>the</u> Anglo-Polish piece – think of all the occasions it could be played on, & the performing fees! K. A. W.'s musical advice is comic – but he has a good heart at bottom, as they say, hasn't he?

[. . .]

---

31 Exx. PII.1.2a and 1.2b. Elizabeth Maconchy, String Quartet no. 2 (1937), excerpts.
32 See Letter 57, fn 120.
33 Kenneth Wright. See Letters 57 and 61.

I'm most interested to hear about your new work – Symphony or Owen Glendower (Billy & I have been reading Henry IV & the other Falstaff plays during the last few months – we have become tremendous Shakespeare readers – & read all the tragedies, & some of the comedies & historical plays this winter. He <u>is</u> good beyond anything – isn't he?)[34] – I wonder which it will be? & if you've finished the mvt. yet? Symphony No 1. <u>would</u> be an event. – I have embarked on a Symphony for Strings – at least I think that's what it will be: but have only done part of one rather peculiar movement do far. It's rather like yours – I don't know how long it's going on, or how the form is going to work out! We must both have got bitten by the same bug.

Did I tell you Ina Boyle is scoring my ballet 'Puck Fair' for a performance in Dublin? (as time is short & posts to here rather impossible – so I couldn't do it myself) It is very noble of her – & she <u>says</u> she is enjoying it.[35]

I'm surprised you liked the song Sophie sang.[36] The words are by Sheila Wingfield a friend of B's & mine who is rather a good poet, I think. I didn't think Sophie sang it very well – there ought to be a big contrast between the <u>cold</u> colour (for the Northern balcony) at the beginning & end, & the warm Southern colour in the middle. [. . .]

I hope you're having a good holiday in this superb weather. I rather expect you're bathing? I haven't tried the Teme yet this year.

Much best love always from Betty

My 12 hens are laying magnificently & I have one sitting – the chicks are due to hatch any day

[. . .]

Later that summer, on 21 June, Williams's Fantasia on Welsh Nursery Tunes *(1940) was included in a concert from the Empire Theatre in Cardiff, broadcast on the Home Service and performed by the BBC Symphony Orchestra, conducted by Adrian Boult. Other works in the all-Welsh programme were by Joseph Morgan and Arwel Hughes. The Prom performance of Maconchy's* Dialogue *for piano and orchestra (1939–41) was finally rescheduled, to be given at the Royal Albert Hall on 16 July 1942 by pianist Clifford Curzon and the London Philharmonic Orchestra, conducted by Basil Cameron.*

64) 29 June 1942

Downton Castle, Ludlow, Salop
June 29th '42

Dearest Grace

Very many thanks for your letter – & many apologies for being such an age in answering. [. . .]

---

34 Owen Glendower appears as a character in Shakespeare, *Henry IV Part I*.
35 Boyle's orchestrated version of Maconchy's *Puck Fair* was performed at the Cork Opera House by the Cork Ballet Group on 10 May 1948.
36 Sophie Wyss sang Maconchy's song, 'The Disillusion' (1941). It is possible that this refers to the first performance, a broadcast on 7 January 1942.

I am awfully disappointed about the Proms – I'd seen the programme. I do wish H J W[37] had done a work of yours (– & I think he's an old idiot not to.) I imagine it was on account of practical considerations, not musical grounds – : I thought when you said he'd told you he would 'decide definitely later' or something like that he must have liked your works but didn't know how the programmes were going to work out.

Well, having sent to him once, do send again, won't you? (loathsome business though it is) as I'm sure it would be worth it.

B. & I heard your Fantasia from Cardiff – I like it better each time & so does B. I do think it's a good work. It seemed an excellent performance, I thought & our reception was better than usual, so we heard it really well. So I'm VERY glad you didn't refuse to let them do it: the other works were certainly bad – but it would have been a shame to miss the performance with Boult & the BBC Orch. and also it is a very good thing to show the world that there is a good Welsh composer (it's not your fault if the others were bad!) I hope it will bring lots more performances too, as a lot of people must have heard it.

How fine to do the Bartered Bride – it is lovely – & it will be all the better for having the less good bits cut out.[38]

I wish I could hear it. And I also wish I could hear your Piano Concerto – I wonder if there would be any chance of it, when they do it. How mean of them only to promise a try-over for it: they really are pigs. I think you are right to hear it at all costs – i.e. the cost of the parts, which is great in money & effort: but then it will have many performances, so that the parts will be done once for all.[39]

[. . .]

I have been having weeks of soul-destroying work altering the parts of my 'Dialogue' – as I thought the scoring was too thin & altered some of it: – it meant re-copying some of the parts, & sticking pages & half-pages all over the others – & then at the last moment I found they needed 5 extra parts and were having an unexpected rehearsal last Friday.

I'd only just got back from London & Hertfordshire where I'd been with my aunt when I heard this – so had to copy frantically & take the parts up last Thursday. Basil Cameron is conducting – quite careful & competent, I think – better than HJW anyway. Clifford Curzon says he is often difficult & puts everyone's backs up – but luckily we got him in a good frame of mind, & for a run-through the rehearsal went very well. The alterations I made in the score were well worth it, & there is nothing I want to change, I think. The only things I perhaps regret is that I have no full tutti – the whole thing is rather in chamber-music style – & it might have been a good thing to have one longish

---

37 Henry J. Wood.
38 Williams apparently directed a performance of Smetana's comic opera, *The Bartered Bride*, at Camden Girls' School.
39 When no Prom materialised for Williams's Piano Concerto (1940–41), the BBC offered her a playthrough of it, for which she prepared the performance materials at her own expense; it took place on 30 September 1942. See Letter 65.

fully-scored bit – however, I haven't, & can't alter that for this performance any how.

Clifford Curzon is excellent. It was so odd being at the Albert Hall![40] I'm having the L.P.O. with Pougnet leading. I expect you've heard they are disbanding the Salon Orchestra at Evesham?[41] A good thing, in my opinion – as they were employing about 20 superb players to play nothing but rubbish. But it's a pity from my own point of view as Pougnet – Jenkins – Riddle – & Pini were all in it, & were such a good quartet – & as I think I told you they wanted to do my new quartet, & perhaps the earlier ones. Now Pougnet has gone to lead the L.P.O. & the other three are 'going to Liverpool' – (I wonder if it will be to lead the strings in the orchestra there, or what?) so the quartet has come to an end.

I was only in London for one whole day, but enjoyed it so much I could hardly bring myself to return here! I went to the B&H concert in the evening & heard part of 'Pierrot Lunaire,' (I was late) & then 'Façade' in the original version, with Constant Lambert 'speaking' it:[42] he was unbelievably good. I must stop. All best love Betty.

Sheila has been very ill since January, and I don't think there is very much chance of her getting better, now. She isn't strong enough to have another operation. It is awful to be able to do nothing for her.[43]

---

40 The Prom seasons were held at the Royal Albert Hall after the bombing of Queen's Hall in May 1941.
41 The BBC's Salon Orchestra, based at Evesham in Worcestershire from 1939 to 1942, played light music in mostly studio broadcasts.
42 The Boosey & Hawkes Concert, given at the Aeolian Hall on 26 June 1942, included Schoenberg's *Pierrot lunaire* and Walton's *Façade*, with composer and conductor Constant Lambert performing the spoken text.
43 Maconchy's sister Sheila was living in Switzerland, being treated for tuberculosis.

II.2 Letters 65–81
(January 1943–December 1944)

The war continued and Maconchy felt more and more isolated in Ludlow, far from friends and colleagues and the increasing burden of domestic duties encroaching on time for composition. She also grew increasingly frustrated with her publisher, Hinrichsen. Williams faced her own frustrations, especially with an inadequate broadcast of her *Fantasia on Welsh Nursery Tunes* for orchestra (1940).

During this two-year period, the two friends gave each other detailed criticism of and encouragement about various works, such as Maconchy's Theme and Variations for string orchestra (1942–3) or Williams's symphonic work about Owen Glendower, *Symphonic Impressions* (1943, rev. 1952). Williams performed Maconchy's choral work about the Battle of Stalingrad, *The Voice of the City* (Jacqueline Morris) for female chorus and piano (1943), with pupils from her school, and finished her *Sea Sketches* for string orchestra (1944).

In the final stages of the war, Williams returned to London and Maconchy moved to Essex.

Following the BBC play-through of Williams's Piano Concerto, she revised the work, retitling it Sinfonia concertante *(1940–41, rev. 1942–3); it was then accepted for broadcast on 7 January 1943 in an orchestral concert of Welsh music, conducted by Clarence Raybould. The soloist was pianist Margaret Good. Meanwhile, Maconchy had completed her Theme and Variations for string orchestra (1942–3).*

65) 10 January 1943

Downton Castle, Ludlow, Salop
January 10th '43

Dearest Grace

It was lovely hearing your Piano Concerto – it is a very fine work. It is very impressive Billy & I both felt – on a <u>big scale</u>, which is kept up all the way through, with no 'let-downs' – most effective & assured throughout & the piano writing really concerto-esque. It is a great achievement. I am sure it ought now to be played a lot – I would love to hear it in the flesh – our old wireless is so inadequate – though we did get a pretty good idea of it, but one inevitably misses a lot. Musically I thought the 1st mvt. did lack variety a bit – though I didn't feel it nearly as strongly as when I saw the piano arrangement – in fact only slightly. I didn't feel this in the 2nd & 3rd mvts., which are fine. The cut of some of your phrases (& harmony) is definitely romantic – which rather surprised me, somehow – I think because it was rather new in you – (isn't it?) Do please let me know what you felt about the performance, and everything. I thought Margaret Good was absolutely excellent, as far as I could judge. I feel sure you must have felt that everything came off & that things that misfired before were due to lack of rehearsal? One small detail – I felt I wanted the last mvt. to begin with a definite accent of some sort – ♪[1] chord or something – I thought the strings sounded a little scrappy starting off & that the beginning wasn't quite defined enough.

I do hope you are feeling all right & that your tummy has quite recovered? You must have had a very nasty time with it. Do you think now it really was gastric 'flu & nothing else?

I have finished my String Variations & am making a tidy copy to send to Henry Wood – when I've done that (he wants scores now, Hinrichsen says)[2] I'd love to send you the pencil score. – I hope you're sending him something?

We had a very nice Xmas en famille – Nanny was at home, so I was pretty busy cooking & everything.

I must stop as this is due to go to the post with Anna & Nanny.

I think you ought to feel pleased & proud of the Concerto – it's a jolly good work
Best love
Betty
[. . .]

66) [11] January 1943 – postcard[3]

[Maconchy to Williams]

p.s. to my letter of yesterday

I heard from Margaret Good this morning (I have been corresponding with her about that Serenade for 'Cello & Piano which I wrote for her & William Pleeth[4] – which the ever-exasperating Hinrichsen has been trying to give away to another 'cellist!. .) and she says 'Did you hear Grace Williams' Concerto the other night? I thought it was an extremely good work and enjoyed playing it immensely'.

Best love Betty

---

1 Ex. PII.2.1. Grace Williams, *Sinfonia concertante* (1940–41, rev. 1942–3), excerpt.
2 According to Maconchy's publisher, Max Hinrichsen, Wood was considering potential scores for the next summer's Proms season.
3 The postmark date is 13 January 1943.
4 See Letter 56.

A few months later, Williams's symphonic work based on the life of Owen Glendower[5] *had reached a stage at which she sought Maconchy's advice about the slow movement.*

67) 14 March 1943

Downton Castle, Ludlow, Salop
March 14th '43

Dearest Grace

I am ashamed not to have written sooner – I have loved having this mvt. of Owen – (& hope for more later) and have enjoyed it very much. – My time is horribly full, or I would have written sooner – as I lost Nanny a month ago – I can't remember if I told you she was going? – so I have the cooking, house & Anna & all the extra things like shopping to cope with! However, I have the help of a very nice girl of 14 who is very good & is here from 8.30 to 5.30 & takes Anna out in the afternoons – & all is going well. Anna is good and happy & life not too arduous.

Well – enough of domesticity. I really rather enjoy it all, or most of it – and it is lonely just being ourselves with Anna – but of course my working time is all too short.

I like this slow mvt. of Owen very much – I like the main idea and the way the theme grows, and also the way the <u>intensity</u> of treatment grows up to the climax. I like your triplet theme (particularly in the trumpet) & the way it combines with others. I also like the scoring very much – it seems to me to fit the musical idea like a glove – or rather to be part of it, as good scoring should. I like its simplicity – nothing inessential or for effect only.

[. . .][6]

This is a very inadequate appreciation & criticism I think. You are such a good & clearheaded critic yourself – and I am rather a muddle-headed one, I fear – like Uncle Ralph and inclined like him to get only a 'general impression' – in this case a very good one. I think he often is a muddle-headed (& sometimes a wrong-headed one) – & particularly when he <u>writes</u> (he never ought to be allowed to write publicly about music I always think – he says some dreadful things!) when we were learning from him he often said things that were very illuminating I think (though he was never quick) – it was easier to understand what he really meant, verbally. His real merit as a teacher I'm sure was that he somehow inspired (for want of a better word) one to write better music than one would otherwise have done – & that this is a lasting influence. Don't you think so? Also he imparted unconsciously a very high ideal for a composer – I mean I know that we – and I think any worthy pupil of his – would be <u>unable</u> to write for cheap effect or

---

5 See Letter 63.
6 Detailed criticism follows.

against one's better instincts, or to 'write down'. Of course he had a lot of defects as a teacher too, I think – chiefly perhaps his attitude towards brilliance – which he always thinks is pernicious I'm afraid – & being scared of anyone acquiring a brilliant technique.

– Well, I'm sending you my Variations for String Orchestra – but I don't want you to spend too much time on them – quite honestly & seriously. I would very much like your opinion of them – but don't really spend your precious working time on them – H.J.W.[7] said a work for strings wasn't suitable for the Proms. Because of the Albert Hall being what it is![8] Hinrichsen sent the score to the BBC reading committee last month.[9] I don't know if anything will ever come of that. – Did you know that Steuart Wilson is back in England as 'European Music Supervisor' at the B.B.C.? (Bush House, Aldwych). I saw him for a few minutes (when I made a dash to London last month before Nanny left) & he wants to do a lot of British chamber music for the European programmes. Do write to him or send him something. I am having some things done on the Latin American service (unfortunately I have no way of hearing it!) Norman Fraser who does the programmes has taken a liking to my music it seems.[10] He liked the Viola Sonata (very surprising) which was done in Dec. & did my new Cello piece a few days ago – & my new 4tet is to be done on April 19th by the Blech 4tet.[11] I must try and make a dash to London to hear them rehearse it, I think. Have you ever sent him anything? [. . .]

Now about the Variations. I had forgotten that my pencil score is so untidy & I hope it won't be too tiresome to read. I have been playing them through & I still like it as a whole. My favourites are VARS IV, IX and X, & the return of the Theme. I want to know if you think this return musically–emotionally right? (very important that it should be) and do you approve of the slow serious end instead of a slap-up finale? will it be effective? [. . .]

[. . .]

I must stop – please send more of Owen when you can. I am very keen to see it. Best love – Betty

Have you had the same marvellous weather as us? Sun every day.

---

7 Henry J. Wood.
8 The cavernous Royal Albert Hall was known as an acoustical nightmare.
9 Maconchy's publisher Max Hinrichsen sent the score to the BBC Reading Panel, which had to approve scores by all but a few composers, deemed above panel approval, before they could be considered for broadcast. This work was assessed by Gordon Jacob, John Ireland, and Benjamin Dale. Their reports were negative, reflecting the BBC's conservative attitude to progressive compositional trends during the war. BBC WAC R27/603 Music General/Music Reports 1928–54, March–April 1943.
10 Composer, pianist, and writer on music Norman Fraser worked for the BBC from 1936 to 1943.
11 Maconchy's Viola Sonata (1937–8) was broadcast to the Latin American Service by Lena Wood (viola) and Tom Bromley (piano) overnight on 16/17 December 1942; the Serenade for cello and piano (1941–43) was given by Sela Trau (cello) and John Wills (piano) on 10/11 March 1943; and the String Quartet no. 4 was performed live from the Paris Cinema by the Blech Quartet on 19/20 April 1943.

84   Part II. Letters 50–93 (October 1939–April 1949)

Having thought in detail about Maconchy's Theme and Variations for string orchestra (1942–3), Williams finished the first movement of her Owen Glendower symphony, which she sent to Maconchy for comments.

68) [Before 25 April 1943]

15, Ryhall Road, Stamford

Dearest Betty,

I am returning your variations – with an immense amount of gratitude – again I got the same stimulating feeling when I played & read them & I do think them a fine set – splendidly thought out & they are closely knit together & make the work a complete whole – no interludes or side-lines as you so often get in variations. It sticks to the point from the start & the point has much strength & can stand any amount of repetition. I like the work tremendously. As for criticism, for once I am almost completely tongue-tied. It all seems quite right to me as it is. I have played it through many times & only one place trips me up slightly [. . .][12]

Of course the quiet end is right – for such a theme it must be so – & this kind of quiet ending after so much building up is always much more effective than a final flourish.

I don't know whether this is at all coherent – it is now 11.50 p.m. & I suppose I ought to stop & go to bed. I meant to get this written before but end of term has been as usual – & I've had more than the usual packing to do because we are now almost definitely returning to London in September & I am clearing away as much as possible now.

I am enclosing the 1st mvt. of 'Owen'. Would you mind keeping it until after May 5th (i.e. when I return here)? Don't spend too much time on it but what you said about the slow mvt. was so helpful. This is the 'warrior' movement. Or do you think that the whole idea of basing it on O. Glendower is too far-fetched & had I better call it plain Symph. No. 1?

I want to score the scherzo during the holidays & revise the piano sinf: con:[13] & knit for a nephew or niece due in May & make a summer dress. Perhaps I shan't do any of these things because my mother isn't too well & can't get any kind of domestic help, everyone is much too busy & well paid in the factories.

Please forgive this scrappy letter. I did mean to get it done earlier in the day – but I'll write again soon & reply more fully to your lovely long letter.

All best wishes for Easter

Love to you all

– Grace

At last, Maconchy heard Williams's Four Illustrations for the Legend of Rhiannon *(1939, rev. 1940) – broadcast by the BBC Northern Orchestra, conducted by*

---

12 Detailed discussion of work follows.
13 The *Sinfonia concertante* for piano and orchestra (1940–41, rev. 1942–3).

Mansel Thomas, on the BBC Home Service in the afternoon of 27 May 1943. In the meantime, Maconchy was working on The Voice of the City *for female chorus and piano (1943), a lament for the fall of Stalingrad, setting words by Jacqueline Morris, a pupil at Hengoed Girls' School in South Wales.*

69) 28 May 1943

Downton Castle, Ludlow
Friday morning

Dearest Grace – Thank you so much for sending a p.c., I wouldn't have missed Rhiannon for anything, & one so often has a blind spot for what one particularly wants to hear in the Radio Times!

It is a GRAND work & I enjoyed it very much indeed. It ought to be played everywhere – it is really good. It makes my blood boil to think of poor old Arnold Bax's milk-&-watery tone-poems being played, instead of this. But you are getting a lot played now, & will get more & more.

I think it suits you having a subject that suggests, (without in the least inducing programme music –) : it makes your imagination very fertile – It is very successful here & in what I've seen so far of Owen. The scoring is brilliant & quite excellent throughout, I thought.

I miss a lot of fine points on our old wireless of course. I felt the need of more strings – how many have they? (the string tone of the Northern Orch. is always very thin, I notice.) Your trumpet writing as usual was lovely – the theme at opening of Mvt. 2 superb. I like the pizz-chord theme later in the Mvt. very much – a lovely detail of scoring. I think I like Mvt. 3 the best – beautiful opening theme & lovely all through. It's a very good example of a quiet mood successfully sustained throughout a movement – the 'nursery rhyme' opening of No. 4 is charming – a very good movement. But I didn't quite expect the end when it came. Does this movement quite balance the work as whole – or do you need a bigger emotional climax somewhere? the work is on a big scale. That is my only criticism of a very good work indeed.

[. . .]

I expect in many ways, if not all, you'll be glad to get back to London? I envy you the prospect of hearing some music. But I feel sure Hitler will try some smashing raids on London when we start invading Europe. It seems the obvious thing for him to do. So I feel sorry your school is going back –

No time for more – must cook the lunch. I'm just setting a poem by a Welsh schoolgirl of 15 (a very good poem, too) about Stalingrad – for the W.M.A.[14] – as a sort of modest 'cantata' suitable for school-singing! I'm rather enjoying it.

Anna flourishes – rides a tricycle & in general is growing up fast.

Best love & many congratulations on Rhiannon
Betty

---

14 Workers' Music Association, founded 1936.

86   Part II. Letters 50–93 (October 1939–April 1949)

70) 2 June 1943

Downton
June 2nd

Forgive haste!

Dearest Grace – I'm sorry you felt dejected about Rhiannon. I didn't at all get the impression of a poor performance – considering it was the Northern Orch. which is never very good – & enjoyed it tremendously, as I told you. You are quite wrong to think it's 'not much of a work'. I'm sending back 1st Mvt. of Owen now, & shall be very glad to have the sketches & pencil score later on when you go home.

I enclose a few rather scattered notes I made on the 1st Mvt. for what they are worth.[15]

I forget if I wrote earlier to say I certainly think you ought to call it a <u>Symphony</u> (not a symphonic poem –) but to keep the Owen Glendower name & the suggestions it affords, which I like very much. But it <u>is</u> a real symphony & will need to be listened to as such. Best love Betty.

In this letter, responding to a broadcast of a Maconchy string quartet, presumably No. 4, performed by the Blech Quartet,[16] Williams gives unusual insight into her living circumstances during the war.

71) 7 June 1943

Stamford
June 7th

Dearest Betty,

The quartet came over very clearly on my set & listening it to it was one of the most satisfying experiences I've had for ages & ages. It is <u>all</u> first-rate music & finely wrought & it has apart from its beauty a fulsomeness & wholesomeness which is a very rare & precious thing these days. I was left with a feeling of a really full-toned lyricism & fine strong melodic lines. If they found it difficult to learn (you told me that they did) they certainly didn't sound as if they had anything to struggle with; it all sounded rightly played & rightly understood – if anything might have been better it was that they might have let rip with the rhythm a little more – there was a slight cautiousness with the rhythm here & there & a bigger rhythmic flow would have made it a pretty perfect performance. Perhaps I've got a bee in my bonnet over rhythm – I feel that only the really A++ people

---

15 The enclosed notes are too detailed to include here.
16 No domestic BBC broadcast of a Maconchy string quartet could be traced on 6 or 7 June in any year during the war.

have an A++ sense of rhythm. It oughtn't to be so – but I feel it is so. (I never can understand why there is only one Toscanini[17] in the world. There ought to be dozens – if not hundreds.) That was why I was so depressed at my Rhiannon broadcast. I felt that it was all mechanical & meaningless & the slow tempo of the slow mvt. too lugubrious for words. But perhaps I listened with a jaded ear – because the other few comments I've heard were good. I was terribly glad that you liked it as a work in spite of the Northern Orchestra's luke-warm playing. But I don't think it is good as a whole – only the bits I told you I liked. The last mvt. suffered most of all at the broadcast because there are several changes of tempo – the conductor got them all wrong & so it all sounded unbalanced & out of gear. I don't like the music of this movement any more. – The tune at the beginning is a Welsh tune (& not cribbed from Sibelius No 2[18] as all the orchestral players seemed to think) & one tires of it easily – The slow mvt. tune is also a traditional tune; & somehow, this doesn't have anything like the appeal which it had for me when I wrote the movement. However – I wish I could hear your quartet & all your other quartets very very often – it is music which, once you get to know it, is fine music & lastingly fine.

Do let me see the Stalingrad work sometime. Perhaps I can use it – if the Headmistress approves! – We sang some Soviet songs last term & as soon as we had finished she told the school that the music was very impressive but she didn't at all approve of the words – (& I must say that I myself didn't swallow them whole!). I have just finished spring cleaning this place in readiness for our removal on or about the 19th. I was thrilled to read in the News Chronicle some weeks ago that what I had always hoped would one day be invented already exists – in America. It is a contraption which you have fixed in your house, which absorbs all the dirt & purifies the air. The cost is at present, £75 – they didn't make it clear as to whether one per house would do or whether you have to have one in every room. However, reading about it cheered me up tremendously.

We are definitely returning to London in September – can't hold out here any longer because our numbers get less & less. I agree that there will probably be very heavy blitzes on London. We had a meeting at our London school at the end of last term & it depressed me very much – the dirty drab streets, the dark school building & the realisation that I should spend hours every week in buses & tubes made me realise with a shock that I didn't at all want to return to all those things. I never loved London – except for a few years when I was very young – & haven't wanted to stay there at all since we left it. At the same time I don't want to stay in Stamford for the rest of my life!! Nevertheless, the country has won me over far more than I ever thought it would, & being out in the open so much is good, & I shall never weary of riding a bicycle. What I really want, & have always wanted, is to live near the sea, & if I find I hate London when I get back, I'll break away & try & get a job near home. Zen finds the prospect of my departure rather

---

17 Conductor Arturo Toscanini.
18 Sibelius's Symphony No. 2 in D major, Op. 43 (1902).

bleak & we were disappointed last week because he lost his appeal for a transfer to London. For ages he has pointed out to them that he would be of far more use to the war effort if they transferred him to an air craft-productions factory because he has a specialist's qualifications for such work. But his present factory – which makes guns – is privately owned & won't release him. Isn't it stupid! One hears again & again of cases like his.

I am terribly grateful to you for your comments on O.G. mvt. I.[19] & shall go over very carefully all the pages which you queried. About its form – Betty I really don't know – this movement shaped itself, somehow: one thing grew from another & yet somehow it fulfilled what I wanted – i.e. a first section of fire & brimstone & pageantry – then a middle section (the tune you liked & all that goes with it) of remoteness & reflection, & then a short recapitulation snatching at the feeling of the opening, but never bursting forth on it & gradually giving out: rather like old Owen himself, in fact. I don't feel that it matters having a short recapitulation in the first movement. Yet I am undecided about this movement's shape: & wonder whether there is too much material in it & not enough of it developed. Is that what you felt too? That is why I hesitated to call the work a Symphony – & felt that Symphonic Impression, though an awful mouthful, would be more appropriate.

[...] I am really getting on with things this term. My partner has already left for London & is teaching at our Tutorial classes – & I find that I am much more free to get on with my job now that I am alone. She is a frightfully nice person & was very considerate when we shared this flat & we both went our own way – but we always gossiped at meal times etc. etc. & I never got a really long stretch on my own. So I've decided not to join with her in London, nice as she is. This term things are ideal (except for the cleaning & moving). I get a lot done during the week & Zen comes at week-ends. You are marvellous to be able to stick to your job in the way you do, & carry on a family. There are very very few who could do it.

I heard from Dorrie last week, & sent her a card about your broadcast in case you hadn't told her. I doubt whether she heard it, though, because she has a rotten wireless. Eleanor's mother died some months ago, & the house is let so D. & E. have to stay at a club when they go to London. One good thing about my return to London will be that I shall see you all from time to time, I hope, though I still shan't see Anna, I suppose, until the war is over. [...]

My love to you all, Grace.

I wish they'd publish some of the European programmes in the Radio Times.

In summer 1943, Williams's school relocated from Stamford back to London, though she spent much of the summer at home in Barry. On Saturday, 3 July 1943, a BBC Home Service broadcast devoted to 'British Women Composers', performed by the BBC Scottish Orchestra conducted by Guy Warrack, included both Maconchy's ballet Great Agrippa (or The Inky Boys) *(1933) and Williams's* Fantasia on Welsh Nursery Tunes *(1940).*

---

19 The first movement of Williams's symphonic work inspired by Owen Glendower.

72) 6 July 1943

July 6th '43

Dearest Grace

Many thanks for your p.c. this morning – very nice of you to send it. The only part of Sat's concert I enjoyed was your piece! Which I thought sounded very nice indeed despite a rather unfinished performance. I thought poor Agrippa sounded too awful – all the tempi too slow & some very bad omissions indeed – in at least 3 places no tune once trumpet, once piano & I forget the other one – it included the 2 most definite tunes in the whole piece. [. . .] However, it's not worth bothering about, as it's not a good work, I fear – & doesn't stand up to concert performance, though (at the right tempo) it might make a ballet. [. . .]

I see you are at a new address, so must have accomplished your move, & you must have had a busy time. I hope you are settled now & comfortable?

I've been meaning to thank you for your very nice letter about my quartet.[20] I can't tell you how glad I was to get it, or what an encouragement it was, & how cheered I am that you like it. Because I'd put a great deal into the quartet – & it's a work I really mind about – & I was feeling rather flat about it. The performance, though quite good in a way – left out so much that I wanted! I mean I wanted lots of gaiety (& quicker tempi) in the Scherzo & last movement – & lots more fire everywhere – & as you said, I wanted them to let it rip with the rhythm. The slow movement they played well & I thought it sounded the best. The others I thought sounded rather all the same & rather cold & careful & grim & earnest – not impassioned as I felt them. So I felt it was all a bit of a failure & that what I'd put into the work didn't somehow sound in the music – Then all together I got your splendid letter & very nice ones from Uncle Ralph & Ina Boyle – so I was immensely cheered & encouraged & still am. Thank you so much. [. . .]

Forgive me writing so much about myself . . . I listened to Uncle Ralph's new Symphony[21] (I'm sorry you weren't going to be able to hear it) & I think it is very beautiful in a quiet way. There is nothing new in it – & very little incident or even outstanding material – quiet contrapuntal texture throughout – the kind of music that is in 'Shepherds of the Delectable Mountains' & parts of Job[22] – rather as if he was ruminating over the bits of his own music that he likes best. It certainly has his own kind of beauty in it, that no-one else gets. I had a horrid feeling that it may be a kind of epilogue to his work: – but he is an unexpected person, and might take a new lease of life & produce something quite new after the war But I rather think not this time. I'm looking forward very much to further instalments of Owen when you get home. How sad & disappointing that Zen can't transfer to London. We all flourish. Best love Betty.

I believe the end of July is closing date for sending in for next year's I.S.C.M. Festival (where?) to Mrs Hart, c/o/ Chester's. Do send.

---

20 Presumably Quartet No. 4 (1939–53). See Letter 71.
21 Vaughan Williams's Symphony No. 5 in D major (1938–43).
22 Vaughan Williams's opera *The Shepherds of the Delectable Mountains* (1921) and his masque for dancing, *Job* (1931).

The W.M.A. are going to publish my Stalingrad 'cantata'[23] – (it's not really one) – so I'll let you have it when it appears – I haven't kept a copy as I simply hadn't time to make one.

Several months later, after the summer holidays, Maconchy resumed contact with Williams, having just begun her Violin Sonata (1943–4).

73) 6 September 1943

at Fenn Farm, Great Henny, near Sudbury, Suffolk
Sept 6th '43

Dearest Grace

Anna and I are staying here with Maureen, who has bought this farm (it is very nice) we've been here nearly a fortnight & go home on Thursday. [. . .]

I hope you've had a good holiday? Getting to Anglesey with Zen must have been lovely. How funny your dashing through Ludlow – you couldn't have seen our (hideous) chateau as it's 6 miles from Ludlow – but may have seen our 3 beautiful hills, west of Ludlow, which stand up across the Terne from us, and which I've become very fond of. I shall miss them when we go – but apart from the beautiful country we shall love getting back when the time comes.

You must be in London now looking for somewhere to live – I fear it won't be easy to find it & I hope you will not have too difficult a time & will find what you like.[24]

Did you do lots of work in the holidays? I haven't thought of music for this fortnight – not because I do too much at home, far from it. I get horribly little time – but because it's nice to get a break & change from everything, & I feel restored & ready to go back now.

I'm trying to make a clean break with Hinrichsen[25] – he's dithering & trying to avoid the issue & I don't know yet if he'll let me off. I can't stand his hopeless muddles etc any longer. He's done me much more harm than good.

I've tentatively started a Violin Sonata – but don't know if it will be any good. I get depressed about my work pretty often – & feel that I'm drying up. Or is it lack of stimulus, – lack of time – hearing no music – & will it come back? but sometimes I feel it's lack of new ideas with advancing age, which is depressing. However in general I feel happy & satisfied with life, & the war prospect seems better, if one can say that with wholesale murder going on. Best love Betty

The following summer, Williams's Fantasia on Welsh Nursery Tunes *(1940) received another BBC Home Service broadcast, on 5 June 1944, performed by the BBC Orchestra, conducted by Idris Lewis. Maconchy's Suite for orchestra from the ballet* Puck Fair *(1943) had been selected for presentation in the Golden*

---

23 *The Voice of the City* was published by the Workers' Music Association in 1943.
24 Williams moved to her new address, 30 Willow Road, Hampstead, on 13 September 1943.
25 Max Hinrichsen, Maconchy's publisher.

Jubilee season of Promenade Concerts in 1944.[26] *Meanwhile, she had finished her Violin Sonata (1943–4) and, at the request of the Workers' Music Association, was preparing an orchestral accompaniment to* The Voice of the City, *a work that Grace was rehearsing with her girls' choir at Camden School for Girls.*

74) 7 June 1944

June 7th 44

Dearest Grace.

It was grand getting your letter – : also grand hearing your Nursery Rhymes Suite again, which I love, & enjoyed very much indeed on Monday. It is a lovely & very successful work. (No feeling at all of the slow part being too long this time, I thought – perhaps because of better playing? Probably before the playing not being good enough was what gave this impression.) This work really is in the orchestral repertoire as they call it – now, isn't it?

Yes, I do wish they'd put my Prom. date earlier, so that you'd have been in London & we could have gone together. I haven't heard a word yet as to whether they are going to broadcast it.

[. . .]

I think the last, or almost the last time we met was when you played me the choral setting of the Welsh poems which you say the B.B.C. are going to do.[27] I'm awfully glad to hear that – in spite of the sweat over parts – as the BBC singers really are good.

Can't you suggest that they get the vocal parts duplicated (they must have one of those duplicating things.) I really would if I were you – & I think they'd probably do it for the vocal parts, as long as you provide the orchestral ones (for a good big hire fee!) [. . .]

[. . .]

I'm so glad you have a niece. Is your sister pleased with her? It must keep her very busy.[28]

[. . .]

I have at last finished my Violin Sonata – & want to show or send it to you. Sometimes I like it, sometimes not. It's taken a year! I'm now making a tidy copy. I haven't embarked on anything new, as correcting the parts of Puck Fair, & scoring 'Stalingrad' for strings (& trpts & percussion) by request of the W.M.A. has taken all my available time lately. Also Maureen has been here for a bit, which was lovely – (her Richard has just gone to school.) I've felt less depressed lately about writing music – & hoping something good may come after the war – (which seems to be moving bloodily on to its last stage now.) You wrote me such a very nice and heartening letter, which helped to cheer me a lot. I still have it on my table to answer!

---

26 See Letter 79.
27 In May 1944, Williams was told that her *Gogonedawg arglwydd* ('Hymn of Praise') for chorus and orchestra (1944) had been passed by the BBC Reading Panel (BBC WAC GW2, 15 May 1944).
28 Williams's sister Marian Evans gave birth to her daughter Eryl.

But have never succeeded. But thank you very much for your good counsel & the nice things you said. [. . .]

Much best love from Betty

My solicitors are still trying to cope with Hinrichsen[29]

I wrote the music of Puck Fair during the 1940 blitz. but only scored it this autumn.

75) 21 June 1944

June 21st '44

Dearest Grace

Many thanks for your letter this morning – it was very good of you to write. Of course I'm coming – (I haven't heard a proper bomb since 1940 so shall be very out of practice, but what matter.)[30] It's grand that you can come to the rehearsal on Sunday: I want you there very much. My own ears become numb at rehearsal & you will be an enormous help.

Good that 'Stalingrad' will be earlier on Friday, we can then have a nice long evening. I'll bring my violin sonata: & want to hear a lot of yours. [. . .]

It must be hell spending the day in the school shelter & I hope you've been able to get them above ground again. It's good you can sleep all right: I hope none come close to you.

In great haste –
best love
Betty.

On 29 June 1944, the Promenade Concerts were suspended, due to the dangerous conditions in London with continued flying bomb attacks; nevertheless, Proms rehearsals – including that of Maconchy's Puck Fair *Suite on Sunday, 2 July – took place as planned, in the hope that the season could be resumed. Maconchy and Williams met up in London a couple of days before to go through Maconchy's cantata and Williams's new suite for string orchestra,* Sea Sketches *(1944), before joining Dorothy Gow in Bedford in order to hear the Proms rehearsal.*

76) 3 July 1944

In the train, Monday
11 o'clock

Dearest Grace.

I've just got into the train at Paddington – pretty crowded platform etc but I'm very lucky in a comfortable seat, so can take the chance to write to you. I do

---

29 Maconchy's solicitors were extricating her from her publishing agreement with Max Hinrichsen.
30 In mid-June 1944, the Germans began a particularly vicious late stand, attacking London with V-1 flying bombs, known as 'Doodlebugs'.

HOPE you & Dorrie got the bus all right – I hope & believe you'd have come back if you hadn't – but I'm afraid the rush and anxiety outweigh the cup of tea! [. . .]

I do think it was noble of you & Dorrie to make such efforts to come to the rehearsal – I can't tell you how nice it was to have you there: it made all the difference to what would have been a lonely affair otherwise. It was <u>lovely</u> being with you in London; I enjoyed seeing you so very much & would like to go on talking for days & days more. You were frightfully good to me – giving me your bed & your rations! & everything else. It was grand hearing 'Stalingrad' and lovely to hear it so well sung by such nice fresh and enthusiastic girls. I was awfully impressed [by] them – & they made me feel it's quite a nice piece in its own way. I felt as sung by them it was quite moving.

It's disappointing about the Proms – but I don't feel I mind much because I was pleased by the rehearsal. I found I couldn't make <u>any</u> independent judgment of it as a piece of music (– less than usual –) but it seemed to come off as I meant it to, & the sound was I think everywhere what I intended. [. . .]

[. . .] I hope your 'Heat Wave' will conclude as well as it began in the unsuitable weather. I liked the Suite very much indeed; & the string writing looks excellent. I think you ought to try & <u>meet</u> & talk to Jacques or Boyd Neel[31] – it is so much more likely to produce results than writing. I should send it to the BBC as well – but it means an extra copy as they are so slow, doesn't it?[32]

It will be nice to see Billy & Anna again this evening – I'm sure he'll have fixed up where to stay tomorrow, but will tell him of your noble offer.

There is a very attractive little girl of about 2½ in the carriage & a less attractive dog who is asleep on my feet at present.

Well – I hope those beastly bombs will keep far from you. Do let me know how you get on & thank you a thousand times. Love Betty

77) [After 3 July 1944]

30, Willow Road, N.W.3.

Dearest Betty,

At last I have a moment to spare – – I liked 'Puck Fair' quite 100% & have absolutely nothing to suggest in the way of improving it. It seemed to me to be just right as it stood (just that one scrap of timps. which I would delete). [. . .]

I can't tell you how relieved I was to hear that you were departing from London unscathed – & I'm pretty sure that you must have heaved a sigh of relief when Billy returned from his trip to this dangerous city.

But things seem to be getting better – today not so good – but we had a quiet week-end which meant a lot. There was a crash on the Heath[33] at breakfast time last

---

31 Reginald Jacques and Boyd Neel were well-known conductors of their own string orchestras.
32 Williams sent it to the BBC Reading Panel in March 1945, and it was passed for broadcasting a few months later (BBC WAC GW2, 23 March and 19 June 1945).
33 Hampstead Heath.

Wednesday – you remember the walk up from the bus? All those houses facing the heath lost their windows & some were badly blasted – the blast extended as far as our corner of Willow Road so we had a very lucky escape – the only window of ours which went was a well-protected basement window! It was a nasty jolt for this vicinity, though fortunately no one was killed & all injuries were minor.

We are <u>not</u> nervous wrecks yet, & things could be much worse even though one is sometimes inclined to look back on pre-flying-bomb London as a sort of Elysium.

The Head told us this afternoon that we'd finish the academic (!) term on Friday week, & would probably keep the school open for another week, with a few staff on duty each day. After that, holidays until the second week of September. I haven't grasped it yet. Meanwhile singing classes are in full swing – the Head says it is good for their morale, & so I have the whole school in two divisions every morning, & am free in the afternoon. Not too bad. By the way, the Stalingrad Quartet[34] were very thrilled at meeting you & I think it did them a lot of good to have such an experience during their examinations & bombs ordeal.

[. . .]

Tell Anna that her lettuces were beauties – this is no exaggeration – they really were, & kept fresh & crisp until the last leaf had been eaten. I still have one egg left & can't bear to part with it.

So – I must have some tea & then get on with the scoring of my final sea piece[35] – yes, at last I've finished the sketch of it & shan't be long before I've scored it & copied it out. When London is a safe place again I'm going to ask you to lend me your Vln. Sonata – but not now!

Love
Grace

78) 11 July 1944 – postcard[36]

[Maconchy to Williams]

Downton, July 11th

Just a p.c. to tell you two things. First, Anna & I had lunch with Benjamin Britten in Ludlow on Friday (– he has been staying with Lancing School people & Jasper Rooper[37] brought him by to meet us.) He was very nice, – couldn't have been nicer – & particularly asked if I'd seen you & wanted your address & tel. no, which I gave him. (He was going to Suffolk on Monday so may not be in London for a bit.) The other thing is – Billy says DO sleep in a shelter. He stayed with Nick

---

34 Williams's pupils who had sung Maconchy's 'Stalingrad cantata' to her.
35 'Calm Sea in Summer', the fifth movement of Williams's *Sea Sketches* for string orchestra (1944).
36 The card is postmarked 12 July 1944.
37 Composer Jasper Rooper was music master at Lancing College where Britten's partner Peter Pears had gone to school.

Bagenal in Percy Street while he was in London & found he always does now, & so accompanied him to a very comfortable shelter, where he says you have a perfectly quiet night, as you don't hear the things so sleep all right and feel perfectly safe. Do do it: this was a shelter in the basement of a house in Bedford Square. Are there similar ones near you? I'm sure you can find one. Much best love Betty

B. took a dust-sheet (to lay over bunk) pillow & rugs, in a bundle!

Although most of the 1944 Proms were not performed in concert in London, due to the devastating effects of flying bombs, some of the concerts were broadcast from Bedford, including Maconchy's Puck Fair *Suite, which was heard on the BBC General Forces Programme on Saturday, 5 August, performed by the BBC Symphony Orchestra, conducted by Adrian Boult.*

79) 6 August 1944

9, Old Village Road, Barry, Glamorgan
August 6th

Dearest Betty,

In a way I was sorry that you had asked for a report – because all I wanted to do was to sit back & enjoy it – What I really wanted was two performances, one to listen to with the critic's ear, & then to hear it again, & relax: because it is very pleasant & very attractive music. The score is excellent & all was very clear. I now feel that I know this music quite well, understand its temperament, & know just what I'd do with an orchestra if I were conducting it (i.e. assuming that I'd had a conductor's training.) I'd sing that music to them & make them feel it under their skin – it oughtn't to be a difficult job because it is all so singable & alive. You must feel just as I feel about this awful business of conductors. Boult is at least conscientious, & nice enough, & efficient up to a point but he doesn't ever begin to be an artist. Knowing the score is just not enough – they should know the whole temperament of the music – & it seems to me that 80% of conductors in this country never get anywhere near a true understanding of modern works. The majority of them don't even bother to know the score. How many contemporary composers are ever consulted by conductors before a first performance? Perhaps a few, but only a very few. Yet I am sure that a really first-rate conductor would want to meet the composer before the first rehearsal & listen to the composer either playing or singing (or both) the score again & again until the music is familiar. Beecham,[38] I believe, would do this (though he'd get someone else, not the composer, to do the playing.)

Please, this is not by way of saying that the performance wasn't good – it was quite good as first performances of new works go in this country nowadays – but,

---

38 Conductor Thomas Beecham.

having listened with a very alert ear, I couldn't help feeling that the music deserved a much more understanding & human performance [. . .].

[. . .][39] By the way, I felt so angry after the last performance of my little innocent Nursery Rhymes work[40] that I felt like withdrawing it & not allowing anyone else to touch it – but of course I lacked courage & did nothing; & so it still rests with Goodwin & Tabb[41] & anyone else who wants to maul it may do so on payment of the usual fees.

[. . .] I must say I am glad to be here & now that the weather is so grand, all my good resolutions of looking for a holiday job are vanishing. I fully intended doing canteening [*sic*][42] or something of that nature. However, there is enough to do in the house (mother hasn't any help at all) & Marian & baby (now a pretty thing & quite bonny & strong) are here. We are not at all overworked, but there is always something to do if you look for it. We do get down to the beach of course & are having some lovely bathes. I have done all the strings parts of my Welsh Chorus & shan't be long finishing the rest of the parts. Miss Duncan seems to be taking a long time over the photographing of the chorus parts – I rang her up before I left London & she said very vaguely that she had done nothing about them yet.[43]

My Sea Sketches are finished – Noon on a Summer's Day[44] seemed to fare very well during the heavy-clouds & fly-bombs period.

Zen comes here next Friday for a week – he doesn't complain about being in London, but he seems to be looking forward to coming here. His home-town Rseszow has just been liberated.

All the very best to you all for a very nice August.

Will you venture to Maureen's?

Love

Grace.

80) 26 September 1944

September 26th 44

Dearest Grace

I'm writing to your home because I don't know if you are back in London, or what has happened about your school? I hope very much that if you are back in

---

39 Detailed comments about *Puck Fair* follow.
40 *Fantasia on Welsh Nursery Tunes* for orchestra (1940).
41 The work's publishers.
42 Possibly working in a canteen is meant here.
43 In summer 1944, Williams corresponded with Miss L. A. Duncan of the BBC about the preparation of the parts for her *Gogonedawg arglwydd* ('Hymn of Praise') for chorus and orchestra (1944) (BBC WAC GW2, summer 1944).
44 The final movement of Williams's *Sea Sketches* for string orchestra (1944), which was eventually titled 'Calm Sea in Summer'.

London you are all right? There seem very few f-bombs, but what about these rockets, of which I've only heard one account so far? but which must be appalling.

I have never yet written to you since Puck Fair & to thank you for your very nice letter: but so much has happened since then requiring endless writing & taking all one's time I seem scarcely to have had time to think – (and have done no work since then) Just as I was leaving for Bedford (& Puck Fair of which more anon) we heard that Chart Corner had been hit by a flying-bomb and was a complete ruin. It was almost a direct hit – the thing came down where the garden-hut used to be – & apparently there is very little left of the house – part of one wall is all that is left standing, & the stairs. The sheds etc & garden have 'disappeared' – and the trees very broken & so on. We are very sad about it – as we both feel it so much a part of ourselves & our lives. Of course we are very lucky not to have been there – and our tenants had mercifully evacuated (they lost their furniture.) We hoped at first it might have been possible to re-build it – but it seems past rebuilding – so we had to set to work to find another house. So we started trying to get something – there is almost nothing to be had! Then we went for a long holiday to the Pembrokeshire coast – between Tenby & Pendine [. . .]. I hadn't seen the sea for 5 years, & it was Anna's first time. She loved it & we had a grand time, though it was cold & windy a great part of the time.

While we were there Maureen telephoned to say she'd seen a house in Essex for us & liked it very much – so Anna & I went off to her direct from Amroth & Billy joined us there – & he & I saw the house – had it vetted by a builder – & 2 days later bought it by auction! (a terrible experience I thought.) That was a week ago to-day – to this minute, in fact. We like the house very much – and I think we are lucky to have got it: it was horrid feeling we hadn't a home to go to. It has a very nice friendly feeling – a mixture of dates, with a pretty Georgian face looking down the garden – good sunny rooms and a nice feeling of space. It faces south & west – & the garden is full of good things – lovely fruit & shrubs & roses etc.

[. . .]

. . . It's Wednesday now, & your postcard has come this morning, saying that you are back in London again.

Did you find Zen all right? & your flat undamaged? I do hope all will be quiet for you now. No – I didn't indeed find your letter about Puck Fair too critical – it was very stimulating & helpful. What you say about conductors & new works is only too painfully true – & this business of only doing new works on sufferance & then skimping them is very depressing. Given these conditions I was on the whole pleased with the performance & felt that Boult's conscientiousness is worth a lot for a first performance – BUT – and what a big but – how different a performance one could make it oneself. Will one ever get a really good performance of anything without being a conductor?

I was very encouraged that you like P-F (and even more so that you liked my Violin Sonata – which is much more recent music, & I feel more my real music) and I think P-F is perhaps a fairly successful small work – by no means a remarkable one.

I was rather depressed by Uncle Ralph's views of it! He said he liked some of it straight away but was 'baffled' – 'the atmosphere does not seem clear at present – I do not know whether you want it to be gay or sinister – it seems rather to fall between two stools.' He thought the last piece – (the Tinkers) too short – with which I rather agree – & the 'Evening' one 'not worthy of the rest in distinction of style' – which is true & a deserved rebuke.

But I don't feel it is <u>wrong</u> to be gay in one piece & sinister in another – do you? & why 'baffling'?

Actually Higgin's [sic] central idea in the ballet was that the Tinkers should be sinister & the country-people normal & happy & the contrast of the two elements was important – & this seems to have come off all right in the ballet.[45] But I think Uncle R. may mean that the two <u>styles</u> are incompatible, & I mix them. Anyway he seems to have found it unsatisfactory in some way, I'm afraid. It made me feel that perhaps it is suited to a ballet but <u>not</u> as a piece of straight music of the concert hall? I wonder.

[...]

Well – I could go on writing pages more without saying half the things I want to! The only thing is to meet again as soon as possible. We hope we shall be moving before very long – we don't know when yet, it depends on the RCS[46] and transport: as soon as we get to Wickham Lodge (that's the new house – at Wickham Bishops, 4 miles from Witham – 40 from London) you must come & stay with us, which will be lovely.

What have you done about your String Suite?[47] What are you writing now?

Did you have a good holiday? & Zen a good week with you? tell me all this & lots more – meantime much love always from
Betty
[...]

81) 20 December 1944

December 20th '44

Dearest Grace

A very happy Christmas to you & every good thing in 1945, my dear. I have been waiting to send you a line of Xmas wishes till I had a snapshot of Anna to send you – [...]

[...]

---

45 The ballet's libretto was by Irish poet Frederick Robert Higgins. The action focuses on an episode at the annual Puck Fair: 'Tinkers are carousing on the fairground in sight of the historic Puck Goat. Farmers enter, and are horrified when one of their company dances with her lover, the Fiery Tinker' (programme note for the ballet's performance at the Opera House, Cork, 10 May 1948).
46 Royal College of Surgeons, Billy's employer.
47 *Sea Sketches* for string orchestra (1944). The first performance of this work was to be given on 31 March 1947 by the BBC Welsh Orchestra conducted by Mansel Thomas. See Cotterill, 'Music in the Blood', 50.

I'm terribly distressed that you got ill again, it is sickening.[48] It is excellent that sleep & diet got you right pretty quickly – but enough rest & the right food is difficult to achieve when doing a job. I hope you'll be able to have a real rest at Xmas? But I know that's not easy either without domestic help – & you'll be longing to work at your own stuff – but I hope will be strong-minded & rest instead. Will Zen get down, I wonder?

When is your choral work being done?[49] When it is you'll just send a card won't you? [. . .]

We saw in today's paper that Uncle Ralph has given Leith Hill Place to the Nation. (He is marvellous, isn't he? We saw that his brother died lately – & it came to him then.)[50]

I must stop and will write a proper letter after Xmas – there seems little time at present!

Very much love always from

Betty.

---

48 At the end of 1944, Williams spent two weeks in hospital with exhaustion. See Rhiannon Matthias, *Lutyens, Maconchy, Williams and Twentieth-Century British Music: A Blest Trio of Sirens* (Farnham: Ashgate, 2012), 143–4.

49 Williams's *Gogonedawg arglwydd* ('Hymn of Praise') for chorus and orchestra (1944) was broadcast on 16 February 1945 on the Home Service, performed by the BBC Chorus and Orchestra, conducted by Leslie Woodgate (BBC WAC GW2, 26 Feb 1945).

50 Vaughan Williams inherited Leith Hill Place on the death of his brother Hervey, and donated the house and estate lands to the National Trust. See Ursula Vaughan Williams, *RVW* (Oxford: Clarendon Press, 1964), 258–9.

II.3   Letters 82–85
(May 1945–January 1947)

VE (Victory in Europe) Day was celebrated on 8 May 1945, marking the Allies' acceptance of the German armed forces' unconditional surrender. In 1946, Williams, who had been seriously ill, left her job at Camden School for Girls and started working for the BBC.

Surviving letters from this period are sporadic – three from Maconchy and just one from Williams – although they convey a clear sense of Maconchy's frustrations, with critics, performers, and even with her own music.

Maconchy's sister, Sheila, died on 28 May 1945 in Switzerland, where she had been for several years in an attempt to cure her tuberculosis.

After a five-month hiatus, Maconchy resumed correspondence just a few days after VE Day – though, curiously, there is little reflection on the end of the war. Instead, her focus is on their respective bouts with poor health, and also with several recent and upcoming performances. Her Violin Sonata (1943) was performed twice in a week by Maria Lidka (violin) and Antony Hopkins (piano): on 3 May 1943 at the Cowdray Hall, in a London Contemporary Music Centre concert, and on 8 May at the Wigmore Hall, in a Gerald Cooper Concert. Moreover, Maconchy and their mutual friend, the Irish composer Ina Boyle, were both looking forward to Irish broadcasts of their works.

82) 12 May 1945

Wickham Lodge, Wickham Bishops, Essex
Wickham Bishops 350
May 12th '45

Dearest Grace

I'm so awfully sorry you have been bad again – it is miserable. I do hope you're beginning to feel fairly fit again? But do for goodness sake do what your very sensible-sounding doctor tells you & don't dream of getting back to London & work again. I'm perfectly certain that you ought to have a term off & then the summer holidays, so as to give you a good long time for <u>real</u> recovery. It's perfectly true that you make lightening recoveries – but that's because of your extra ration of spirit & vitality, & the thing doesn't have time to get really cured & comes up again when you are tired, & overworked, as you were last term which is a shame. I feel this doctor must be right about it's being an ulcer, – when you've had haemorrhages. It must be. [. . .]

Forgive me not writing sooner but I waited till after hearing my sonata to report to you . . . And now this week has got completely disintegrated by VE Day to begin with! & also because my well-behaved tummy has been giving me trouble. [. . .] Anyway I got to both my concerts. The Wigmore Hall one – unluckily came on VE Day itself, but they decided to go on with the concert – there was a small audience but very enthusiastic – more so than the Cowdray Hall one. Maria Lidka is a beautiful player & she & Anthony Hopkins both played it very well, & it really got a very good performance. It was so nice hearing good players rehearse one's stuff again – I greatly enjoyed the rehearsals – but don't now feel, after two performances, absolutely satisfied with the work. I just can't quite make up my mind about it. In a way I feel it's good – or is it second-rate? – – I feel more than ever about the world of music and music critics – 'plus ça change plus c'est la meme chose' – & hate them all.

Howes,[1] in the Times, wrote so grudgingly & sneeringly about the concert as a whole (though he was decent about me – saying 'the themes were somehow memorable' & it was 'real music, a vehicle for emotion not an experiment in sound') and Ralph Hill writing in the Daily Mail & Liverpool Post was more sneering & unpleasant still about the whole thing – & said my Sonata 'started in the grand manner' but 'petered out into the grandiose & trivial'. I think that's an unfair criticism of anything I've written – & naturally don't attach much weight to his opinion – but the attitude is discouraging to say the least.

The nicest thing about the L.C.M.C. was the people we saw – & I do wish you'd been one of them. Uncle Ralph was there, I thought far better, and more his old self than the last time I'd seen him (which was ages ago.) He seemed genuinely to like the sonata – partly on the grounds of its having some of the sort of tunes that I'd 'used to write when I was about sixteen' – which made me say I'd take them out! But actually I don't think it's strictly true. Dorrie & Eleanor were there too, & Anne & a few others.

[. . .]

[. . .] I wonder if you heard Ina's Donne setting with string 4tet?[2] It was broadcast on the afternoon of May 3rd & unluckily coincided with my concert so I couldn't hear it. She & I are each having an orchestral broadcast concert from Dublin in an 'Irish composers' series. Mine's on July 16th, & we are all going to Ireland early in July. We'd planned to take Anna this summer, as Billy's father is 87½ & mayn't live much longer. It will be lovely to be in Ireland again.

---

1 Frank Howes.
2 Ina Boyle's *Think then my soul* (John Donne) for tenor and string quartet (1938).

102   *Part II. Letters 50–93 (October 1939–April 1949)*

We are very happy here. It's just a bit far from London – & a long day for Billy. But apart from that it suits us very well & we're getting very fond of house & garden. [. . .]

Isn't it hard to realise that the war's over? I haven't taken it in yet. One's got so horribly used to it! There were a good many V-bombs & rockets here at first, & one almost expects them still!

I do hope you'll have the luck you deserve from the Proms committee. I had not got anything new to send & didn't think it any good sending an old work. Do send a card to say if they are going to do your Sinfonia Concertante[3]?

Anna has started going to school – for the mornings only – at Witham. She goes by bus with some other children – & is enjoying it. It's grand to have other children for her at last. It <u>will</u> be fun to introduce you to each other! Billy & I find her a great handful, but she has got lots of character.

I must really stop . . . Very much love my dear – & I do hope you are getting on very well? Send a line when you can Your loving
Betty.

The next surviving letter dates from nine months later, prompted by the possibility of the two composers meeting up in London once Williams resettled there after recovering from her illness.

83) 2 February 1946

Wickham Lodge, Wickham Bishops, Essex
Wickham Bishops 350
February 2nd

Dearest Grace

How are you? and are you back in London? & what happened about the Cardiff job? and when are we going to meet? I was up in London this week & shall be again this coming week having electrical treatment for headaches as I told you I was going to [. . .] but unfortunately I've got to meet Frederic Thurston for whom I wrote the Clarinet Concertino, this coming week (he says it's 'much too difficult! ' – aren't soloists awful –) I was to have met him last Tuesday & he muddled the day – thinking it was Wed. & wrecked my plans.

If I have to go for another treatment the following week (Feb 11th onwards) I wonder if we might meet then? [. . .] I want to show you the 2 mvts. I've done of my Symphony, & very much to see Owen.

We have really decided, though reluctantly, to sell this house & come to live in London. The trains have got worse instead of better – & Billy has no life at either end – & it really isn't good enough for him. I think it would in the end make him ill again too. I really never can get up to hear any music either – or not often: so we

---

3 Williams's *Sinfonia concertante* for piano and orchestra (1940–41, rev. 1942–3).

think it's the best thing to do, though I can't help being very sorry. I love this, & it's splendid for Anna. Well – we want to find a house at <u>Hampstead or Highgate</u> – with a garden (absolutely essential) & not too large or impossible to run. <u>Do</u> tell me if you see or hear of anything you think might be suitable. It would be really angelic if you will. We could pay up to £4,000 or £4,500 if necessary. [. . .]

All best love, & hoping to see you soon
Your loving
Betty

The following month, Maconchy's family were still looking for a house in north London, and Maconchy and Williams had exchanged scores. Maconchy had looked over Williams's Symphonic Impressions, *the title of which was still uncertain,*[4] *making interesting comments about Bartok's Concerto for Orchestra (1943), given the many comparisons made about her style in relation to Bartok's.*

84) 12 March 1946

Wickham Lodge, Wickham Bishops, Essex
Wickham Bishops 350
March 12th '46

Dearest Grace

Many thanks for your letter – please forgive a hasty scrap in reply, to go with Owen. (Don't alter that trumpet tune in Mvt. 1 unless you're <u>convinced</u> that it's better than the wind on the tune.) It <u>is</u> difficult to decide about the title. I think I incline to calling it Symph. Imp. 'Owen Glendower', with the 4 movements named – but without the actual 'quotes' – as you say. I think it's a pity to scrap the O.G. connection – though it completely stands on its own feet as a Symphony in any case. Thank you very much for copying out the notice about the ISCM Festival[5] – which I hadn't seen. I think I'll send – Clarinet Concertino, Variations for Strings, St. Quartet No 4 & Violin Sonata. Nothing orchestral – but Puck Fair isn't suitable. Things <u>don't have</u> to be unperformed, I'm sure. So do send your Piano Sinfonia & Welsh Chorus & Song of Mary – too.

No – the prison-like house would not do if it is large & the garden very small. I'm coming rather reluctantly to the conclusion that the 'garden suburb' has the most suitable houses at our price. Perhaps when (& if) I have several suitable ones to see I might come & spend a night with you? & we'd have the evening together.

I decided last week that I would scrap my symphony.[6] It was after hearing the Bartok – although I don't think the Bartok a completely satisfactory work at all – yet I felt it was alive and original & full of vitality – & that mine was still-born &

---

4 See letter 71.
5 The ISCM Festival in 1946 took place in London.
6 Maconchy had been working on her Symphony since 1945.

dull. – However, I've now had new ideas about it (transferring all the slow part of the 1st Mvt. to the slow Mvt – & having a new 2nd half to the 1st mvt & so on) so I'll give it one more chance, – though I'll probably be right to scrap it in the end.

Yes – the last Mvt. of the Bartok is magnificent – the real thing – & some of the slow and no 4. I feel rather as you do about the rest. (No 2 irritated me more than No 1!) [. . .][7]

Nine months pass before the next surviving letter, during which Williams had left her job at Camden School for Girls, and on 2 September 1946 began to work for BBC Schools Broadcasts in London. This full-time job, 'writing radio scripts, arranging music, and visiting schools',[8] only lasted for a few months, due to continued illness. Despite all this turmoil, Williams wrote to Maconchy, inspired by a BBC Third Programme broadcast on 20 January 1947 of Maconchy's Fourth String Quartet (1939–42), performed by the Philharmonia Quartet.

85) 23 January 1947

9. Old Village Road, Barry, Glamorgan
Jan 23rd 1947

Dearest Betty,

It was indeed a joy to hear Quartet No. 4. – a splendid work & I thought a splendid performance apart from the first movement which was rather mechanical at the first performance, though better at the second. I thought I only had got right under the skin of the other movements.

I feel the quartet grows in interest & strength as it progresses. I liked the slow movement <u>immensely</u> – though you might remember my saying when I saw the score that I thought it might sound rather down & dark – but no – it's right.

The last movement is <u>fine</u>.

[. . .]

My mother has had her operation & everything is <u>very</u> satisfactory – the whole thing removed & no roots elsewhere . . . She is marvellously cheerful & comfortable & delighted with the hospital & staff. It's a great relief. Thank the Lord we've found a woman to work for us for two mornings a week. She squints & is called Victoria & talks & talks & talks. However – we are thankful for the smallest mercies these days. With love & heartiest congratulations – Grace

[. . .]

---

7 The end of this letter is missing.
8 Malcolm Boyd, *Grace Williams, Composers of Wales*, vol. 4 (Cardiff: University of Wales Press, 1980), 29.

II.4 Letters 86–90 (October 1947–June 1948)

Maconchy's second child, Nicola, was born on 28 April 1947, although no letters between the two friends have survived from this time. Maconchy's family had abandoned the idea of a move to London and were still at Wickham Lodge in Essex. During this eight-month period, Maconchy heard several of her works performed, including her Concertino for clarinet and string orchestra (1945), finished her Symphony (1945–8), and started work on a Fifth String Quartet (1948–9).

On 25 February 1947, Williams had made the permanent move back a self-contained flat in her parents' house in Barry, Wales, where she was to make her living as a free-lance composer, arranger, and writer.

Maconchy responded to a missing letter from Williams prompted by a BBC Third Programme broadcast on 7 October 1947, showcasing her chamber music in a British Contemporary Music series. The concert included the Fourth String Quartet, played by the Zorian String Quartet, and the scena, How Samson bore away the gates of Gaza *(1937), performed by Sophie Wyss (soprano) and Josephine Lee (piano). In the meantime, Maconchy continued work on her Symphony (1945–8).*

86) 12 October 1947

Wickham Lodge, Wickham Bishops, Essex
Wickham Bishops 350
October 12th '47

Dearest Grace

It was grand to get your letter & to know that you heard last Tues concert and liked it. I was more pleased with the 4tet than with Samson – I liked the feeling that the Zorian's[1] put into it & thought they played it well altogether (& will

---

1 The Zorian String Quartet, consisting of Olive Zorian and Marjorie Lavers (violins), Winifred Copperwheat (viola) and Norina Seminor (cello), was active from 1942 to 1949.

play it better if there is another chance of their doing it – they want to get more confidence I think – they weren't 'in full sail' as you say.) [. . .]

No – Sophie hasn't got the dramatic power that Samson demands. She's at her best in French folk-song etc (& I fully agree about her lack of musical intelligence! Nice as she is –) I've never yet felt satisfied with Samson – I like it when I play it & yet (so far) it has never seemed to be successful in performance, to me. (It's true it has only been sung by Sophie & a fairly good baritone in Dublin) I got up to London for the broadcast, as my Nanny is still here – & may be for a week or so more. (My concertino is to be done on Nov. 2nd with Thurston & Antony Bernard:[2] I shan't have the nanny then so don't quite know what to do with Nicola – but I feel I must hear it – –)

[. . .] I wonder what will happen about your Sea Sketches and the Riddick Strings:[3] quite right of you to testify & I hope it will take effect. The 3rd programme people do seem much readier to take other people's suggestions – even to invite them – than the rest of the B.B.C.

Fancy it being Uncle Ralph's 75th birthday tomorrow! – Are you sending anything up for the Amsterdam Festival?[4] The things have to be in by Nov. 30th.

I THINK I have got the music of the Symphony finished at last. Unless I decide to scrap it in the next day or two I will send you the piano-score of the whole thing. You will condemn it if necessary, won't you? I really can't judge it at all

Very best love – Betty.

[. . .]

87) 27 November 1947 – postcard

Barry
27.11.47

Betty At last I'm getting down to the Symphony & at last I realise what a treasure has been lying in my cupboard for the last few weeks. Frankly – in the few minutes I could snatch away from all the work for juveniles that I'd been doing[5] – at first I couldn't make head or tail of it – my head was stuffed with 'children's' tunes & – it was too much for me.

---

2 The Concertino for clarinet and string orchestra (1945) was to be given its first UK performance as a broadcast on the BBC Third Programme on 2 November 1947, performed by Frederick Thurston and the London Chamber Orchestra, conducted by Anthony Bernard. The previous June, Thurston and Bernard had given the work's first performance at the ISCM Festival in Copenhagen.
3 Williams had been in correspondence with Eric Warr, Music Programme Organiser for the BBC Third Programme, concerning her *Sea Sketches* for string orchestra (1944); in September, he had passed the score to conductor Kathleen Riddick to see if she might wish to programme them (BBC WAC GW2, 11 August, 25 September 1947).
4 The ISCM Festival in 1948 would take place in Amsterdam.
5 Throughout this period, Williams was involved in free-lance work for the BBC, writing scripts and music for Schools Broadcasts, as well as scores for Features programmes (see Malcolm Boyd, *Grace Williams, Composers of Wales*, vol. 4 (Cardiff: University of Wales Press, 1980), 29–30).

BUT since Tuesday evening I've been more or less free, and – I've grown up again. I'm working backwards – why I don't know – but that's how it happened – perhaps because, by the time I'd broken the new ground of movements 1 2 & 3 I was much more receptive when I arrived at 4. However I really have got hold of 4 & it is to my way of thinking probably better than anything you've written – & that's saying a mighty lot. It is a <u>fine</u> movement in every way – strong & clear, & it sings. I've a pretty good grip of the Scherzo, too, – in bits – I haven't assembled it all together yet, but it will come. It's an original scherzo – a bit like Busoni's Rondo Arlechinesco[6] (– a fine work) which is purely accidental – & in a way a good thing just as it is a good thing to feel the influence of Bartók in the symph. as a whole. I wish Bartók & you had met. You should have. I've the feeling he'd have been delighted with this symphony. Now – for some more. – Grace

I come to London for ten days labour on the 7th of December – to prepare music for Easter & Summer Term scripts. Then – goodbye to schools! [. . .]

88) 5 December 1947

9, Old Village Road, Barry, Glamorgan
Dec 5th 1947

Dearest Betty,

I am sending the Symphony & Dialogue under separate cover[7] – with many many thanks to you for letting me have them for such a long time.

The symphony really is in every way a magnum opus. The only criticism I have to offer is that perhaps the first mvt. is too reiterative – but I don't know – it's all full of music & wd. be lovely to listen to – in fact the whole work wd. be lovely to listen to – I feel it's all rhapsodical & would like to suggest your calling it a Sinfonia rapsodica (e.g. <u>if</u> rapsodica is the adjective from rapsodia??) At any rate I've suggested rapsodica for the slow mvt. You see the whole work has sweeping flowing tunes, in fact, I feel the whole texture is a rhapsody on symphonic lines.

I still feel the best of all is IV – which is as it should be – an absolutely <u>heavenly</u> ending it has.

The score of the scherzo: when I first saw it I thought it didn't look very creative or inspired scoring – rather a lot of doubling – it wasn't intrinsically orchestral.

However – I soon saw I was wrong. This music doesn't need the usual tricks – it is creative enough in itself & this is the right kind of scoring for it. I remembered Uncle R. once telling me that when he first looked at a Wagner score he was very unimpressed by it as scoring – then of course realised that it was absolutely right for Wagner & couldn't have been done in any other way.

[. . .] Now Betty get on with the scoring . . . We need a work like this <u>very badly</u>. I'm all for calling barren contemporary music 'hairshirt' stuff (I believe Charles

---

6 Ferruccio Busoni's *Rondo Arlecchinesco*, Op. 46, for orchestra with tenor (1915).
7 The scores to Maconchy's Symphony (1945–8) and *Dialogue* for piano and orchestra (1939–41).

Stuart first used the name)[8] & those who <u>can</u> write <u>music</u> in contemporary idiom <u>must</u> get a hearing.

It has made me feel an adult again – having your Symphony to look at. Not only the married are slaves of children, believe me! – And now I have to view things with the child-mind again for the next few weeks & finish up my schools scripting. I never get a moment for anything else but 'schools' work these days – every day is filled to the brim. It is nice work – yes – but it does shut out the rest of the world. [. . .]

You have written a fine work. Now score it.

Love from

Grace

89) 5–10 February 1948

Wickham Lodge, Wickham Bishops, Essex
Feb 5th 48

Dearest Grace I hardly dare to write to you because you must think me such an ungrateful pig – I don't like to think of it. I have been trying – yes really trying, that isn't a figure of speech, to write to you ever since Xmas – first to thank you <u>very</u> much for your presents to Anna & Nicola. They both love them – Anna has enjoyed the Tale of Tombo[9] very much (has just re-read it while in bed) & I wish you could see Nicola & the dear little boat in the bath together! She kicks & splashes so violently that it would sink any less gallant & buoyant craft! She is grand, & great fun, & I do enjoy her a great deal. BUT there is scarcely time to breathe! [. . .]

Well – you may imagine I was delighted and enthralled by your letter about the Symphony. I am more pleased than I can say that you like it – it's most heartening: one just <u>can't</u> tell (for some time anyway) if one's own work has any value, & I've put all my work for the last 2½ years into this. I finished the quartet mvt. I was working at before embarking on the score: it will be the Scherzo of what I hope one day will be Quartet No 5 – rather a serious Scherzo: I'll hope to have a really light-hearted finale to off-set it, I think. I should much like to send you the Scherzo but I feel you have already spent far too much of your time over the Symphony.

You do know how much I value it, & how VERY helpful it is. I have now scored most of the 1st Mvt – only a dozen more pages to do. I try to let nothing prevent me from doing it from 9 p.m. till about 11 on the weekday evenings (when B. is in London) & have therefore got on with it solidly though rather slowly. I am enjoying it enormously – but I fear perhaps it is rather a dull score in the classical style. I think you are only too right about the Scherzo score being unenterprising & too much doubling etc. [. . .]

[. . .]

---

8 Charles Stuart Boswell translated 'from the Irish text' a description of a hair-shirt in *An Irish Precursor of Dante* (London: David Nutt, 1908).
9 Ada Harrison, *The Tale of Tombo* (J. Fairston, 1940).

Section II.4. Letters 86–90 (October 1947–June 1948)

Yes – the slow Mvt. is rhapsodical – but I don't feel that the whole symphony is, really. Or not to the extent to justify calling it a 'Sinfonia rapsodica' – ('rapsodica' is right for the slow movt. as you suggest – if that is the word – –.) Coming back to it – I like the slow mvt. less. I hope I shall get more enthusiastic about it again when I score it. (It's Feb. 10th now, by the way – & I've only 2 more pages of Mvt. 1 to do – –) I'm glad you like the last – I can't tell you all the vicissitudes & postponements & agonising delays it went through (from outside causes): I was in despair of making it a 'whole' & a sort of summing up – but in the end it seemed to work out. I rather like the very end too. Very glad you do.

It's fun to be really scoring it at last, & I'm enjoying it. Anna got back to school yesterday, & is well & happy.

The chief excitement of the last few days has been that Peggy (the nursery-maid) smoked a cigarette in bed, went to sleep & set her bed on fire! It smouldered for over an hour, apparently, but she woke when it burst into flames, & I smelt it at the same moment. A mercy she wasn't burnt. The bed clothes are the only casualties. She remained perfectly calm, which was satisfactory & seemed to be more scared of what I'd say than of the fire!

Is there any more news of your Symphony since that wretched try through?[10]

[. . .] I had a letter from a man called Hartmann[11] in Munich a few days ago, saying they'd like to do a work of mine at the '48/49 series of chamber concerts (connected with the Munich Opera House – 'Musica Viva', I think) preferably a str. quartet. So I'll send them No. 4.

I have no other performances in view – except I think Puck Fair ballet (with orchestra) in CORK! In May.[12] Billy Anna & I plan to go to Ireland in July – leaving Nicola & Peggy with Maureen. I hope it will materialise – it would be heavenly.

I must stop as it's late & I'm sleepy & barely writing sense, I expect.

Much love, & gratitude for your help and encouragement.

Your loving Betty

[. . .]

The next surviving letter dates from four months later, prompted by Williams's music for Dark Island, *a poem for radio by Henry Treece,*[13] *first broadcast on 11 June 1948. In mid-1948, Williams also completed a score for the film* Blue Scar, *which was eventually recorded in November of that year. Such incidental music projects wore into Williams's creative reserves, causing her 'for some time to regard herself as retired from composing'.*[14] *Nevertheless, she began to think about writing a one-act opera.*

---

10 Williams's *Symphonic Impressions* (1943) was rehearsed by Adrian Boult and the BBC Symphony Orchestra on 10 November 1947 at the BBC Maida Vale studios.
11 Composer Karl Amadeus Hartmann, organiser of the post-war Musica Viva concert series in Munich.
12 Maconchy's ballet *Puck Fair* was to be staged by the Cork Ballet Group, choreographed by Joan Denise Moriarty, and performed on 10 May 1948 at the Cork Opera House, in a version for small orchestra played by the Cork Symphony Orchestra, conducted by Aloys Fleischmann.
13 Henry Treece was a British writer. *The Dark Island* radio play remained unpublished.
14 Boyd, *Grace Williams*, 29.

90) 21 June 1948

Wickham Lodge
June 21st

Dearest Grace

It was lovely to get your good letter, & very nice of you to write. Billy & I both liked your Dark Island Music very much indeed – and thought it exactly right in its function of heightening the emotional effect of the poem, and giving the right atmosphere & feeling – as well as being lovely as music pur sang.[15]

The first perf. I was a good deal involved with the children & couldn't hear it all – the 2nd time I did. I liked the poem (though not <u>nearly</u> as much as the music) – B. didn't much! You are of course absurdly modest to say you have a 'flair for the dramatic' because it's a hundred times more than that. (I long to hear your film which will be brilliant, I know – though I am sure there are a lot of depressing things about writing music for films as you and Uncle Ralph say!) <u>Do</u> go ahead with your idea for a one-act opera – when you have the opportunity. [. . .]

I hope you won't have to kill yourself scoring your film when you get the timings & can go ahead. It's a shame you can't bask on the beach meanwhile – the weather is <u>vile</u>. [. . .]

Jack Thurston is to do my Clarinet Concertino at Hampton Court, & I hope to be able to go.[16] But the silly ass didn't tell me about it or ask for the score & parts for the Jacques Orch. till the last moment – so that they have had no preliminary rehearsal & all are agreed that it can't be done with one – ! So I don't quite know what will happen. Possibly they won't be able to do it. [. . .]

[. . .]

I thought Uncle R. very well when I was there. Did you? You haven't even told me what you think of the new symphony?[17] I think it very fine indeed – (though not flawless) I will <u>certainly</u> ask him if I can apply to the Carnegie Fund (I <u>have</u> heard of it – but I wouldn't have thought of it) for help in getting the parts of my Symph. copied: it is bound to be a huge expense: & I expect you're right that one ought to get them done <u>before</u> trying for a performance. What a shame you couldn't have tried them for Owen Glendower (could you ask them retrospectively, I wonder? –) When is the recording of O.G. to be?[18] Will one be able to buy the records in the ordinary commercial way? I hope so. – – I must get Nicola ready to go out & must stop.

Best love always Betty.

---

15 French phrase: 'pure bloodedly'.
16 In summer 1948, Frederick (Jack) Thurston once again performed Maconchy's Concertino for clarinet and string orchestra (1945) with Reginald Jacques (conductor) and his string orchestra.
17 Vaughan Williams's Symphony No. 6 in E minor (1946–7) was first performed and broadcast by Adrian Boult and the BBC Symphony Orchestra on 21 April 1948.
18 No evidence of this recording of Williams's *Symphonic Impressions* (1943) has been traced.

II.5 Letters 91–93
(February 1949–April 1949)

Maconchy's growing stature in the late 1940s can be seen in her election to the committee for the London Contemporary Music Centre. This brief three-month period saw the first performance of Maconchy's Fifth String Quartet (1948–9) while music by Williams for film and radio continued to be broadcast.

Continuing a conversation in a letter from Williams that has not survived, Maconchy wrote of doubts about her compositional approach and the problematic conditions in which she was working. Despite her uncertainties, Maconchy's recent string quartet, No. 5 (1948–9), had recently won the first Edwin Evans Memorial Prize.

91) 16 February 1949

Wickham Lodge, Wickham Bishops, Essex
Wickham Bishops 350
Feb. 16th 49

Dearest Grace

I'm in the train – going to see two possible schools for Anna (St Mary's, Calne, where the Christie children[1] are & one at Wincanton – both awfully far away – –)[2] so have a chance to answer your letter.

First, thank you very much for writing about Quartet No. 4. I think you are right in what you say – & suggested in the summer – that I too often 'control my themes instead of letting them control me'. It's my worst weakness, I believe. It may be an inherent weakness – i.e. a lack of sufficient powers of invention, not a sufficient flow of musical ideas – making too little musical material go to [sic] far by dint of intellectual effort. If this is so – as I fear is very probable! – nothing can be done about it, my music will die a speedy & natural death – which is the natural &

---

1 Jane and Catherine, the daughters of Billy's sister Lucie and her husband John Traill Christie.
2 They eventually chose to send Anna to boarding school at St Mary's Calne in Wiltshire, but not until 1951.

proper thing. It might possibly (as I hope) be a symptom of the way I have to work – I mean having to break off (– for days, & often weeks or even months) just when one feels underway with a movement & one's material has taken a hold of one's imagination. One has to start again in cold blood & <u>consciously</u> take hold of the material again – & though all may go ahead again after a bit, one doesn't get into the <u>same</u> musical–emotional condition. Also, I lack the stimulus of performances & of hearing other music – of just having orchestral sound in the flesh. Of course too much of this may be nearly as bad as too little – but there must be <u>some</u> musical stimulus: you know the way something suddenly sets one's musical imagination alight . . . If these practical conditions of work account, or partly account for the condition, they may improve (I'm always hoping for that!) though perhaps not till the children are nearly grown-up, & then I'll be too old. (One is very unlikely to improve with age like Uncle Ralph – in fact I feel at times getting a bit worn out already!)

That's more than enough about me! But I'd like to send you my new quartet No. 5 (I've had the score photographed, so have five or six copies). I'd like to know what you think of it. I don't know yet if it's any good – but I think perhaps there's rather more <u>freedom</u> than in the 4th: I hope without losing the sense of cohesion (it has won the Edwin Evans memorial prize – & will be done in April at the L.C.M.C. by the Hurwitz Quartet[3] – do you know their playing? I don't – they do a good deal of new work, I believe.) I've been put on the L.C.M.C. committee & went to a meeting yesterday – the first I've been to. I fear Edward Clark is mostly words, words, words. Humphrey Searle, the sec. I like & Ben Frankel was practical & obviously has a very good brain.[4]

To return – you say 'with the great music of the past once they had got hold of a theme they did let it in a great measure get hold of them – & sweep them along; and at the same time they kept criticising the process & rejecting anything that went off the rails'. I think that's a <u>very good</u> description of the process of writing music – & I couldn't agree more; – I think probably that happens whenever great music is written. (I wonder if you think perhaps rather too much of the kind of 'musical sweep-along' of the nineteenth century? The same process went on with Bach & Mozart (– Don Giovanni – not perhaps all Mozart,) & surely <u>all</u> the best music of the past: and their sense of continuous (musical & emotional) growth is not inferior to the nineteenth century – though different, & perhaps more in tune with our own. I think we are a bit too close to the great romantics <u>&</u> the break-away from them, to take them as a model.)

About conditions for composers here and in USSR I don't know what to think. It's baffling & unsatisfactory in both places (& no grounds for complacency here, certainly.) I don't know enough of the facts about a composer's conditions in

---

3 Maconchy was the first recipient of a prize for chamber music awarded in memory Edwin Evans, the late *Daily Mail* music critic. In addition to £25, the quartet received a first performance. The Hurwitz String Quartet was founded and led by Emanuel Hurwitz.
4 Edward Clark was then LCMC Chairman, and the board included composers Humphrey Searle (secretary) and Benjamin Frankel.

USSR (or America or elsewhere) & indeed I'm so isolated (a bad ivory-tower case) that I don't really know about them here.

– Now, what are you writing? I've done nothing since the completion of the 4tet (as I've been making scores & parts which has taken all my time). I may embark on a setting – perhaps for voice & 4tet – of a poem by Kenneth Gee: he wrote the Sonnets from which I took my Sonnet Sequence – & has sent me four new poems.[5] [. . .][6]

As part of the Edwin Evans Memorial Prize, Maconchy's String Quartet no. 5 was given its first performance by the Hurwitz String Quartet on 5 April 1949 at the RBA Galleries in London, under the auspices of the London Contemporary Music Centre, and was simultaneously broadcast by the BBC Third Programme. The programme included works by Bernard Stevens and Darius Milhaud. Meanwhile, in March and April 1949, Williams worked on incidental music for the radio fantasy Rataplan *by Henry Treece, based on a sixteenth-century French poem.*

92) 5 April 1949

9, Old Village Road, Barry, Glamorgan

Dearest Betty

I write before the applause has finished – it's grand to hear a manly voice shout 'encore' & I wish we could have an encore, & many encores of the slow mvt which is perfectly beautiful & about the best thing you've done. I think perhaps the scherzo is your best scherzo too – a grand movement.

The last movement I want to hear again before I know what I think of it. – They seemed to have mastered it well enough & it was rhythmically <u>very</u> attractive – but it didn't have the clarity of the other mvts at first hearing. As for mvt I – a lovely opening – but for me it stopped <u>growing</u> after the first allegro cut in – it was all lovely as music but there wasn't anything like the <u>soundness</u> of invention here as there was in the 2nd & 3rd mvts – at least that's how I felt it at first hearing. 2nd & 3rd grew perfectly . . . Musically the work is <u>beautiful</u> all through – <u>the slow mvt most beautiful</u>. May I have a score after May 1st to browse over? Until May 1st I must make a big effort to try to get Rataplan finished. It is very hard & an awful lot to do in a short time . . . Henry Treece has supplied a fine libretto (most of which will be <u>spoken</u> over music – not sung – though of course there will be some singing.) . . . Are you & Billy doing something about the Arts Council Opera Scheme?[7] I'm over the first fence & if I decide to carry on must submit a

---

5 Maconchy had worked on *Sonnet Sequence* in 1946–7, setting Kenneth Gee's poems for soprano and chamber orchestra. The new work, *A Winter's Tale* for soprano and string quartet, was composed in February and March 1949.
6 The end of this letter is missing.
7 The Arts Council of Great Britain had launched an opera competition with the aim of commissioning operas for the 1951 Festival of Britain.

story & one scene of libretto by end of June. It's all rather a gamble I feel – – but H. Treece is again willing to collaborate & I've found an excellent story – Welsh – 1830 (time of Chartist Riots).[8] No time to think of it until Rataplan is off my hands.

I liked the Bernard Stevens songs very much – but oh the Milhaud. All my congratulations – & Love –

Grace

P.S. [. . .] Had to be in London for a few days last week & stayed at Dorrie's. I now like her 4tet a lot – it was a revelation hearing her play it.[9] At rock bottom she is very sure of what she is doing – if <u>only</u> she cd. get some big incentive to go at it . . . I daren't begin another page but there is so much to say. . .

P.P.S. Reading it through I find this an awful letter – in no way expressing how I really felt about the quartet. – perhaps it's because when one has found a thing so lovely & satisfying one is too inarticulate to express one's feelings. G.

Kathleen Merritt and her string orchestra broadcast Williams's Sea Sketches *for string orchestra (1944) on the BBC Home Service on 15 April 1949. The work is in five movements: 'High Wind', 'Sailing Song', 'Channel Sirens', 'Breakers', and 'Calm Sea in Summer'.*

93) 24 April 1949

Wickham Lodge, Wickham Bishops, Essex
Wickham Bishops 350
April 24th 49

Dearest Grace

We were (all three) thrilled by your Sea Sketches – I think they are quite excellent, & most brilliantly effective – lovely sound – and extraordinarily varied & evocative: B. & I liked the Sirens best, I think – & thought it very beautiful. I was greatly impressed by the string writing – which made the Merritt Orchestra seem a large & impressive body (which I don't think it is?) everything was effective in just the right way, without <u>sounding</u> technically difficult or the least like 'tricks' – which seems to me to be the test of really good writing: all grateful & genuinely string-music. I haven't any criticism – except a very tentative suggestion that the last is perhaps a little too long for its material? but I'm not at all sure. One does want a good long stretch of that quiet music for the beauty of the calm string tone to make its full effect – & with very beautiful playing it probably isn't too much. – I'd no idea the Merritt Orch. were so good – but I suspect your skill makes them

---

8 Williams submitted a proposal for a three-act opera, *Dic Penderyn*, to a libretto by Henry Treece, which was declined. See Rhiannon Mathias, *Lutyens, Maconchy, Williams and Twentieth-Century British Music: A Blest Trio of Sirens* (Farnham: Ashgate, 2012), 147–8.
9 Dorothy Gow's String Quartet in one movement (1947).

Section II.5. Letters 91–93 (February 1949–April 1949)

sound better than they usually do! I liked her very much – (but never heard them rehearse or play my piece owing to Nicola's advent.)[10]

I do hope you are getting on fast with Rataplan & may have it finished? – I don't know how you've managed in the time. Dorrie & Eleanor were enthusiastic about what you played them, I saw them at the L.C.M.C. concert. We saw a review of your 'Blue Scar'[11] – (very short and of course nothing about the music) – was it a sort of private showing? & what is happening about it? & were you pleased? – No – B & I aren't doing anything about the Arts Council thing: we both have an itch to write an opera – but feel we haven't the skill & experience – real practical experience, one needs. – I think it would be good for me to do something of the sort – or I shall become too shut up in my ivory tower.

I am very pleased that you like the new 4tet – most of it. I haven't quite made up my mind about it yet. I only heard one rehearsal – chaotic – then the performance which was much better than I'd expected – but I think it can actually sound a good bit better all through: & I believe it will after a bit, as the 4th has – each performance has seemed to get nearer to one's original 'conception' – even though played by a different quartet each time. – I agree entirely – the scherzo & Slow Mvts. of the new one are all right – my doubts are about the same things as yours – so I fear they have some foundation – i.e. the allegro part of the 1st Mvt – though I think the latter part of the allegro (where the Lento themes are used in the allegro tempo) is all right – & that the 2nd half of the mvt. does grow. It's the first half of the allegro that I feel un-sure about it. And I have a kind of general uneasiness about the last Mvt. It is very difficult – more than the other Mvts which I don't think can be called really difficult – & I feel it will all be much clearer as it becomes more familiar – & I find it is very hard to judge it till then. – Meantime Lengnick's are going to publish it – I wrote to them out of the blue – feeling I must make some effort about a publisher – & they were very nice. (They may possibly do the 4th Quartet as well – which would be nice.)[12] I have re-written the last page of the last Mvt – which will now be more effective I think – & am making some very small changes – but I don't think I can make any major changes in a hurry – I should have to spend a long time in rewriting the 1st Mvt. if I was going to change it – I know – but don't quite like it going into print when I'm not quite certain about it. On the other hand, I don't think I'd better hold up the publication when I'm making a start with Lengnick's . . . B. has had 10 days holiday in this glorious weather & we have bathed 3 times & all enjoyed ourselves a lot. A. & N. both flourishing. All best love & good luck with Rataplan.

Your loving Betty

[. . .]

---

10 Maconchy's song cycle *Sonnet Sequence* (1946–7) had received its first performance by Joan Cross (soprano) and the Kathleen Merritt Orchestra at a Gerald Cooper Concert on 29 April 1947, the day after Nicola's birth.
11 The film for which Williams had composed the music in 1948; see Letter 90.
12 Alfred Lengnick & Co. published the Fourth and Fifth Quartets in 1950.

Part III
Letters 94–146
(November 1949–December 1959)

Figure PIII.1 Elizabeth Maconchy and family, 1955. L to R: Nicola, Maconchy, Anna, William LeFanu.

III.1 Letters 94–104
(November 1949–July 1950)

During this seven-month period, both women were very involved in looking after their respective families and households – Maconchy with her husband and two young children and Williams with her elderly parents and helping look after her sister's young daughter, Eryl.

Williams continued to undertake much work for BBC Wales, including writing music and scripts for children's programmes, and was very involved in the politics of that institution. She encouraged Maconchy to write orchestral work for the BBC Welsh Orchestra. In January 1950, she also began teaching part-time at the recently established College of Music and Drama in Cardiff.[1] Maconchy joined the Composers' Guild and continued to serve on the executive committee of the London Contemporary Music Centre.

Both women heard performances of their symphonic works, Maconchy's Symphony (1945–8) and Williams's *Symphonic Impressions* (1943, rev. 1952). Williams also heard her Violin Concerto (1950) while Maconchy began her Sixth String Quartet (1950).

In the latter months of 1949, Maconchy was composing a Concertino for piano and string orchestra and revising A Winter's Tale *for soprano and string quartet (1949). Williams was working on her Violin Concerto (1950) and looked forward to a first performance of it alongside her* Symphonic Impressions *(1943), which Maconchy still affectionately referred to as 'Owen', in a broadcast on the Welsh Home Service on 30 March 1950.*

94) 11 November 1949

Wickham Lodge, Wickham Bishops, Essex
November 11th 49

Dearest Grace

There does not seem to have been a moment in which to answer your splendidly crowded postcard – until to-day when I have had to take a day in bed with a

---

1 See Malcolm Boyd, *Grace Williams, Composers of Wales*, vol. 4 (Cardiff: University of Wales Press, 1980), 32.

nasty cold on the chest & temperature: and Nanny now is succumbing to the same germ – so I shall have to be up & doing tomorrow & must seize the opportunity at once! Even with this Biro pen which I can hardly write with – Our day in London together was *grand* – it is lovely when we can meet again for long enough to talk properly. Next time you are in London, try to come here for a week-end – will you? *please* (And you must see Niccy again soon – she is heavenly now)

At the moment I imagine you must be pretty busy with the Violin Concerto – ? I am very glad to hear of that and about Owen – which is splendid. With the Augmented Orchestra rehearsing under your eye (& conductor and players knowing you & your music) you ought to get to a good performance. I'd love to come down & hear it – do tell me when you know dates & details – & say if this might be possible?

The business with the Arts Council in Cardiff made me boil! Sickeningly stupid. Why oh! why haven't they given you the opera commission? (Possibly their 'advisers' think anything so large as an opera unsuitable for women??) It was strong-minded of you to refuse to write the Festival Overture & quite right to take the strong line.[2]

[. . .]

I've been working at my Concertino for Piano & Strings – have finished the music & done most of the score of the 1st Mvt. I think I'll send it in for the I.S.C.M. Festival (Brussels, June 23rd to July 1st) – it has to go in by Dec. 1st. Are you going to send up something?

I've enjoyed doing the Concertino – though I really can't tell yet if it's any good. (Terrible yells from Niccy downstairs – she must have hurt herself – Anna is with her & has now brought her to Nanny – – and all seems well again.) I seem to find it much harder to make up my mind about my own music – and also, I think, other people's – than I used to: and also to decide with certainty about the ordinary things of life: is it just increasing old age? & partly perhaps because one gets too tolerant & sees all sides of the question too easily?

I've made quite a few alterations to the 'Winter's Tale' on the lines of your suggestions – I suddenly found it quite easy to introduce some coloratura – no, that's not the right word – can't think of it – anyway some of the same sort of thematic material as the strings have in the Allegro – with the voice part – it seemed to come naturally and I think is a great improvement – & came from your suggestion. I'd like to send it for you to see sometime – perhaps the voice & piano copy – as I think I shall get hold of the score again from the L.C.M.C. & make the alterations in it & send it up to try for the I.S.C.M. Fest. as well.

I've done nothing with the Symphony & have no performances in view – the Hurwitz say they hope for a broadcast of the new Quartet 'soon' – but I wish they'd hurry up.[3]

The Composer's [*sic*] Guild (whom I have just joined at last) asked me to be on the Executive committee for next year – : I'd like to be – but I can't take on

---

2 Williams's proposed opera had been rejected by the Arts Council; see Letter 92. Presumably the Arts Council decided to soften the blow by offering her a commission for a Festival Overture.
3 The Hurwitz String Quartet next broadcast the String Quartet no. 5 (1948–9) on 15 April 1950.

another committee & ought to go on for another year on L.C.M.C. if they ask me – I said if they thought of asking me again in a year's time I hoped I'd be able to accept. [. . .] All best love Betty

Williams's children's programme, The Merry Minstrel,[4] *was given a repeat broadcast on the BBC Home Service on 18 January 1950, the day before the next letter from Maconchy was written. Williams looked forward to being the guest speaker on Women's Hour on 30 January, discussing the use of Welsh folk songs in her compositions. Maconchy's Symphony (1945–8) was to be given its first performance in a high-profile LCMC–BBC studio concert on 27 April 1950 by the BBC Symphony Orchestra, conducted by Adrian Boult; Maconchy's work replaced Peter Racine Fricker's Symphony No. 2 (1950–51) in this Third Programme broadcast.*

95) 19 January 1950

Wickham Lodge
January 19th '50

Dearest Grace

Never has a letter been so badly overdue – I haven't yet said thank you for the extra-pretty handkerchief you sent me at Christmas (– the only one I got, so you can imagine me blowing with it continuously throughout 1950!) – it's nice to have something pretty & useful at the same time. I have twice taken notepaper & envelope & your letter to answer to London with a view to writing to you in the train (which seems to be the only chance) – & both times came back with the letter unwritten. The second time was yesterday – when I went up to hear the MacGibbon Quartet[5] rehearse my 5th (which they play at Bristol University on the 25th) – they are very enthusiastic – & intelligent (though not really 1st class solo players) – & will do it pretty well, I think. And also to go to Lengnick's with my Symphony score – because they have – three cheers – taken it on![6] [. . .] I missed your Merry Minstrels, by having to go to London which was sickening – I haven't heard it yet – & really thought I should this time – but had to fit in with the MacGibbons. . . (who incidentally said my 5th Quartet was not difficult – & would like to learn the 4th as well!) Anna & Nanny, who heard it, give a most enthusiastic account of the Merry M.

I'm very pleased about the Symphony – it's to be April 27th, with Boult (& 4 rehearsals.) It was just a stroke of luck – because the Fricker Symphony (which won that Koussevitsky prize for the under 35 composers) was to be done at the joint L.C.M.C – B.B.C concert in April –, but it fell through as Cheltenham are

---

4 'In this very young persons' guide to the orchestra the minstrel . . . demonstrates his skill on every orchestral instrument' (Boyd, *Grace Williams*, 30).
5 The MacGibbon Quartet was led by violinist Margot MacGibbon.
6 Maconchy's Symphony was published by Alfred Lengnick, but was subsequently withdrawn.

also doing it & they INSIST on a 1st performance – so they decided to do my Symphony instead – a great piece of luck for me. . [. . .]

It is marvellous that you have finished the piano score of the Vln. Concerto – very quick work. And what a mercy you score quickly too – as you have only 2 or 3 weeks – it sounds rather desperate. Can you work at it un-interrupted? (I presume you've done your script for Jan. 30th – I must hear that!) Are you pleased with the Concerto? Have you got the date of your concert with Owen & the Concerto fixed yet?[7] – I do want to come & hear it, if I may? [. . .]

When is the Kathleen Merritt Orch. doing your Suite? & what has happened about your Songs which you were sending up for 3rd programme?[8]

The 3rd Prog. are going to do my 4th & 5th Quartets fairly soon. Date & players are in course of negotiation[9] . . . (the 5th has been sent up to the Internat. Jury for this year's ISCM Fest – but probably won't get any further)

[. . .] I've done a Concertino for piano & strings – but have done nothing with it yet – I suppose I ought to 'approach' Boyd Neel who is almost un-approachable, – or perhaps better to send it to Kathleen Merritt? I've half-given the 1st performance (if there is one!) to Margaret Kitchin – do you know her playing?

I also just started a sixth Quartet!! before Xmas – but haven't been able to look at it since. I don't know if it will ever come to anything. I shall never write another Symphony, I'm sure – & shall no doubt be even more sure when I've heard the first.

We are all well – long may it last. [. . .]

I hope your household are all right now? & that you are being able to work consecutively. All best love always, Betty.

Maconchy wrote soon after she travelled to Cardiff to attend the rehearsals and performances of Mansel Thomas conducting Williams's Violin Concerto (1949), with soloist Granville Jones, and Symphonic Impressions *(1943), broadcast on the BBC Welsh Home Service on 30 March 1950. The experience inspired her to consider sending Thomas an orchestral work for him to perform with his orchestra.*

96) 2 April 1950

Wickham Lodge
Sunday April 2nd, 50

Dearest Grace

I have been thinking a lot about your two works – I feel they are both really good works, & I found them very satisfying. The Concerto certainly completely

---

7   See Letter 96.
8   In December 1949, Williams sent to the BBC two songs, 'Fairground' and 'Flight', which she had set in 1949 for tenor and piano, writing: 'I have not yet figured in the Third Programme except as composer of music for Features Department'. Williams also offered her Suite for string orchestra (1949), drawn from her score to *The Dark Island* and written for the Kathleen Merritt String Orchestra, who had offered to perform it (BBC GW2, 5 and 21 December 1949).
9   See Letter 97.

so – you are right in thinking it is the best work you have done, I think – its form as well as its music is satisfying, & it is a real Concerto with really exciting & rewarding stuff for the soloist without detriment to the music. I think that's almost unique in modern Concertos – almost always the music suffers at the expense of virtuoso writing – or else there is no genuine virtuoso writing in it (as of course there ought to be in a Concerto – & players rightly don't like it if there isn't. . .) I think it will go straight ahead & get properly into the 'repertory': what are you going to do about it first? Consult Ken[10] about the 'Proms'? You ought to send it up for 3rd Programme, too, as soon as possible (but the Proms is more urgent.) Is Granville Jones in a position to suggest it for the 3rd Prog?

I think the Symph. Impressions is a very fine work too. (By the way, I still feel it is a Symphony – & could well have been called one.) I do like the Scherzo & last Mvt. best – the scherzo is splendid – & comes off beautifully (the end is marvellous) & there is grand music in the last – (particularly all the opening part & the last part, I thought). But that doesn't mean I don't like the 2 first movements – I do. The trumpet-tune-part of the 1st is one of the best things in the work, I think – & lots more fine writing. I think the 2nd movement perhaps is musically less interesting than the others – but it's hard to say – as it needs beautiful tone etc – & didn't get as much rehearsal as the others. (Of course it all needed more.) [. . .] I think it is a fine and intellectual work (in spite of what you say about not being intellectual!) & am very proud to have it dedicated to me.

I am glad I was able to come & I enjoyed it all tremendously – I'm awfully glad I heard all the rehearsal. I laugh whenever I think of the cor anglais' face! he would make a superb episode in a French film – & in the intervals of the action one would hear him practising his little bits – as we did.

[. . .] I've got out my Puck Fair & looked at it – but I don't think the music is good enough – it seemed very bad going back to it again. It would be better to write something new for the Welsh orch. – though of course it will take longer. I had them in view when I started the Concertino for piano last summer, & then it turned out to be for strings only.

[. . .] Goodbye – my best thanks for all your hospitality & goodness to me
Lots of love Your loving
Betty.
[. . .]

In April 1950, the BBC Third Programme featured three Maconchy works in studio broadcasts: the Fourth String Quartet by the Blech Quartet (5 April); the Fifth String Quartet by the Hurwitz Quartet (15 April); and, in conjunction with the London Contemporary Music Centre, her Symphony (1945–8) by the BBC Symphony Orchestra, conducted by Adrian Boult (27 April). Williams described various responses to the broadcast on 30 March of her Violin Concerto (1949) and Symphonic Impressions *(1943); she was busy proofreading the score of her*

---

10 Kenneth Wright.

Sea Sketches *for string orchestra (1944), which her copyist had hand-copied onto transparencies, the way that composers then prepared scores for duplication.*

97) 6 April 1950

9, Old Village Road, Barry, Glamorgan
April 6th 1950

Dearest Betty,

It was lovely hearing the 4th again – & a fine start to the Maconchy Festival!

The Blech were good – though I can't ever forget the Philharmonia performance which drew <u>all</u> the music out of it[11] – that was something the Blech didn't always do.

It's a <u>dark</u> quartet – the most nocturnal thing you've done. The 5th I feel is much lighter – do you feel it that way?

(By the way there was a strange muttering at one point which I swear came from someone in the studio – You didn't by any chance have Uncle R. in tow. . . ??)

I'm longing to hear the 5th again, & hope the Hurwitz excell [*sic*] themselves.

I wonder how you have reacted to Harold Rutland, feminologist, in next week's R.T.[12] It would serve him right if not a single angry amazon swooped down on him – but instead, a host of <u>men</u> who happen to care about our music.

But it's too much to hope for. And yet – I rather think men outnumber women in the few fans we have. – a curious thought – but I have found that my <u>women</u> supporters have nearly all come from the profession – whereas quite a few of the men are laymen – Oh dear I'm becoming Rutlandish! & had better stop this speculation.

It was lovely having you here for my broadcast – I am terribly grateful to you for coming. – it was somehow essential for me to have the opinion of someone like you.

Marian (who heard well at Basingstoke after all) in her usual effortless way managed to hit the right nails on the head – agreed with you that slow mvt. of Owen was weakest part – wandered about without getting anywhere (though she, too, suspected lack of rehearsal.)

I don't like the middle music of this mvt. – didn't <u>really</u> like it too much in the old days – I think it <u>is</u> descriptive (if played properly) of the 'pleasing heaviness – – twixt wake & sleep'[13] – but whereas there is a wonderful beauty in the way Shakespeare describes this state – there just isn't any beauty in my music (except that I think the opening theme <u>cd</u>. make a lovely <u>sound</u>.)

---

11 Broadcast on the BBC Third Programme on 20 January 1947; see Letter 85.
12 Pianist and composer Harold Rutland worked at the BBC from 1941 to 1956.
13 Quoting Glendower in Shakespeare's *Henry IV Part I*: 'And she will sing the song that pleaseth you / And on your eyelids crown the god of sleep. / Charming your blood with pleasing heaviness, / Making such difference 'twixt wake and sleep / As is the difference betwixt day and night / The hour before the heavenly-harness'd team / Begins his golden progress in the east' (Act III, scene i).

Section III.1. Letters 94–104 (November 1949–July 1950)

What to do about Owen I don't know – yet – must relax a bit after I've finished correcting Sea Sketches transparencies (the copyist is going to have some heartbreaks when he sees my corrections.)

And goodness knows what I can do with the Concerto. Not a word from anyone at B.B.C. Cardiff – nor from Ken Wright or P. Crossley Holland. The recording was done at Cardiff & I'm sure Idris Lewis won't send it to London. Also, Mansel told me that Idris & Steuart W. are great pals.[14]

My only hope is that Mansel, if he gets the Headship, will do something for it. BUT, I've realised that M. hasn't actually told me he likes either work.

He gets very enthusiastic about my Fantasias[15] & things – but now I come to think of it he doesn't say too much about my big things.

[. . .]

Another Welsh musician (an old one) got lost in the symph. & blamed the B.B.C. for lack of explanatory notes – & Henry Treece was thoroughly bewildered & found idiom & texture completely different from concerto & all the things of mine he knows – (all written in last few years.)

I must say his reactions to the concerto are rather unique – here's a bit of what he says of 2nd mvt. 'sudden swirls of strings, sometimes a suspension of force, even of terror – then a glorious panache! Almost a romantic male arrogance! – – ' (I wish he'd fling that one at H. Rutland!) The last mvt. reminded him of the muttering murmuring undertones of a nightmare wood.

Well – I don't know – to me it was just music.

[. . .]

Now – about Puck Fair – I liked it all when I heard it though can't remember it well enough to say whether it would all be suitable for a Music Hour programme but one piece – I think you called it Romance [–] was beautiful & it was not at all an obscure beauty – & it might well become a really well known short piece. How long does it take? If you feel it is too short could you perhaps extend it? By all means write something new for Welsh Orchestra & when they have done it send it to Midland – same size orchestra – because Third Programme Mr Lowe (whom you know) now becomes Head of Midland Music. DO begin, though, with the Romance, either as part of Puck Fair, or as a separate short piece.[16]

If all goes well I'd love to come to you for the week-end 21st–23rd. Thank you so much – & then spend the following few days in London seeing about jobs

---

14 Williams considers different contacts at the BBC: Kenneth Wright (Music Department), Peter Crossley-Holland (Home Service), Idris Lewis (BBC Wales), Mansel Thomas (Principal Conductor of the BBC Welsh Orchestra), and Steuart Wilson (BBC Head of Music, 1948–9). Williams is aware that Thomas was likely to become Head of Music, BBC Wales, an appointment that was made later that year.

15 Williams's *Fantasia on Welsh Nursery Tunes* (1940).

16 Maconchy arranged for chamber orchestra Two Dances from *Puck Fair* (1950), including 'Lovers' Meeting' and 'Tinker's Curse'. Mansel Thomas and the BBC Welsh Orchestra gave its first performance on the BBC Home Service on 30 September 1950. John Lowe was then a music programmer for the BBC Third Programme.

(H.M.V. education records asked me to call when I next went to London) & if it's possible come to one of your rehearsals & of course the performance of symphony.

Best love to you all

Grace

[...]

98) 16 April 1950

9, Old Village Road, Barry, Glamorgan
Sunday April 16th 1950

Dearest Betty,

I hope many many musicians & music lovers heard your fifth last night because they would have got what they so very seldom get from contemporary works – a real musical & emotional & intellectual satisfaction. The slow movement is for me the best & most mature thing you've done. In a way it's too good a work for a fleeting thing like radio – it's maddening to have it moving away from one – one wants to keep it & hear it again & again. I really am longing to have a score – & then if only I could have records – for a work like this (as I found with the Bartok concerto)[17] they are essential.

You must have felt as I did that the Hurwitz didn't always get at the root of the music (except the slow mvt. which I thought they played most beautifully) but that didn't prevent the music getting across their performance. Very good music can get across a performance that isn't absolutely first rate – but it has to be very good.

In many ways I thought their playing & understanding was very good indeed (it was only here & there that they fell short.)

[...]

[...] I'll come on Wednesday morning & if you've managed to get a ticket for the Wed. rehearsal I'll be at Maidà Vale at 2.15.[18]

Eryl has now written me an irresistible letter – – 'wil it be worm inof to bathe?' (I think she had help with the last word!)

So I'll stay with her until Wednesday – there is no one else to take her to the beach [...]

The day after your symphony broadcast – the Friday – I am invited to have lunch with Ken Wright & H. Murrill – all very hush hush – to discuss Welsh Radio. Ken got them to send to Cardiff for the records of the concerto – so now I think they'll get a hearing – though whether they'll win approval I don't know. Steuart is retiring – & Murrill taking over.[19]

---

17 Bartók, Violin Concerto No. 2 (1937–8).
18 Williams was to attend the rehearsal of Maconchy's Symphony, at the BBC Maida Vale studio on Wednesday, 26 April 1950.
19 Williams names several BBC contacts: Kenneth Wright (Music Department), Herbert Murrill (new Head of Music), Steuart Wilson (former Head of Music, 1948–9). Williams was invited to lunch after having written extensively to Wright (see BBC WAC GW3, 12 April 1950).

If you have notices of your broadcasts could you bring them & show them to me? The papers we take (News Chronicle, Listener – Observer – & local rags –) are not to be depended on for reporting on contemporary music. The Listener man is usually infuriating anyway. (He praised Mervyn Roberts' sonata for imagination, musicianship & God knows what)[20]

All very best wishes & many thanks for asking for rehearsal tickets for me. I'm longing to come to London

Love
Grace

99) 19 April 1950

Wickham Lodge. Wickham Bishops, Essex
Wickham Bishops 350
April 19th '50

Dearest Grace

It was lovely to get your letter – I can't tell you how glad I am that you liked the quartet so much. I was very pleased by the performance – which for once came near what one intended – I suppose one never gets the PERFECT performance – but this was really very good & I thought they were beginning to be familiar enough with the music for the natural intrinsic expressiveness of the phrase to show itself – the sort of expressiveness that every good player puts unconsciously into all classical & familiar music – (dictated by the shape of the phrase itself) but which one simply doesn't get when the music is unfamiliar to them –

[. . .] I didn't know Steuart is retiring. From a purely selfish point of view I'm sorry Murrill succeeds him as I think he dislikes my stuff! – Ken is splendid – so glad he's sent for your records & I hope great things will come of it – as they should.

We shall all listen to Petrouchka with attention to-day. We couldn't hear Blue Scar & the polka yesterday[21] – as we went to Kent for the day (over the Tilbury – Gravesend ferry) to see the Darwins & had a glimpse of Chart Corner (– just rebuilt) – for the first time.[22] It seemed very queer. [. . .]

[. . .]
All best love Betty.
[. . .]

---

20 Welsh composer (William Henry) Mervyn Roberts.
21 Stravinsky's ballet *Petrushka* (1910–11). Williams's orchestral works *Mountain Sequence* from the *Blue Scar* film score and *Polish Polka* (1948) were broadcast on the BBC Light Programme on 18 April 1950.
22 Maconchy's house on Seal Chart, Kent, which had been bombed in 1944 (see Letter 83).

100) 1 May 1950

9, Old Village Road, Barry, Glamorgan
May 1st 1950

Dearest Betty,

I've still got the Symphony running thro' my head – it followed me all thro' London traffic – & it's still haunting me but I must get rid of it today because I have some teaching to do! (I am laden with B.Mus. students again this term –). I hope you felt <u>well</u> satisfied after the performance – my parents send their congratulations (the only criticism my father made was that we are <u>both</u> a bit too preoccupied by major & minor triads in juxtaposition – well Uncle R. started that & I can't see that it's a failing but something irresistible)

Mansel rang up – was very impressed & wanted your address so I hope he writes to you. (He's got the Headship – doesn't know yet – Ken told me. He was the only possible choice – but it's a sad loss to the orchestra.)[23]

[. . .] Did Gerald C. (when I'm feeling not very nice I now call him (to myself) Gerald Cocksure) write to you?[24] He liked the 4th quartet <u>very</u> much – was mystified in some ways by 5th which he found harder to grasp at first hearing – & I doubt whether he heard the symph – was back at Brighton where reception is awful.

Well – I do feel that comments like these from <u>sensitive</u> listeners are worth far more than what the professional critics write or don't write. . . <u>In the end</u> the reaction of the public <u>always</u> wins through – though at the moment it doesn't help when Martin Cooper (who really dislikes all contemp. music according to Dorrie) says his silly little bit.[25]

[. . .] Alas Ken didn't listen – had to be listening to Beromunster at the time.[26] Murrill (as I might have guessed) didn't turn up – had forgotten to put it in his diary & got fixed up with someone else. Ken was very nice – talked mostly about his baby Jonathan – but said they had <u>at last</u> realised what a wretch Idris Lewis was (Mansel had his salary docked because of I.L.'s very bad report to Head Office on his conducting – – really Betty it is a wicked world.)

A propos of my concerto I must send score to panel & they will <u>make</u> I.L. send the records.

<u>10.30 p.m.</u> I got interrupted – B.B.C. rang up to ask me to go in this morning to listen to some records for scripts – so I've been all day in Cardiff.

---

23 Kenneth Wright of the BBC Music Department told Williams that Mansel Thomas was to be promoted to Head of Music, BBC Wales, from his former position as Conductor of the BBC Welsh Orchestra.
24 Several letters from composer Gerald Cockshott, a private Vaughan Williams pupil, to Williams have survived.
25 Martin Cooper, music critic for the *Daily Telegraph* 1950–1976.
26 Beromünster, a town in Switzerland. Williams was to have had lunch with Kenneth Wright and Herbert Murrill, Head of Music, on 28 April 1950 (see Letter 98). She and Wright discussed, among other things, Idris Lewis of BBC Wales.

Section III.1. Letters 94–104 (November 1949–July 1950) 129

My composition pupil couldn't hear the symph. – – was laden with school work at beginning of term – but I used your 5th 4tet score (for which many many thanks) to illustrate thoroughly concentrated organic writing during his lesson and for one of my Mus. Bac.s (I got so tired of the dull examination B.Mus. exercises – & thought I'd whip out your score & try it on him – & it really brought the lesson to life.)

The only criticism I have to offer of 4tet & symph. isn't really criticism at all – it's just something I haven't fully grasped – the build-up of each mvt. I feel it's much easier to grasp in 4tet (except first mvt.) than in symph. – in fact I feel as composition the scherzo & especially the last mvt. of 4tet are the best things you've done. And the slow mvt. the loveliest. In the first mvt of 4tet and [first mvt.] of symph. I'd like a much longer Introduction section – they can both stand a much longer build up. – it's all so good & satisfying we want more of it – it's big music & wants space. But the creativeness of the music in both works is superb and the counterpoint. I feel the same mystification about Bartók's form. I love the Vln. concerto[27] – yet I can't feel the formal growth is inevitable. – – at the same time I realise (& am more mystified) that the same is true of lots of late Beethoven – those later quartets are chopping & changing tempo & themes all the time – – I give it up – if YOU feel that your form is absolutely right & inevitable then it is so – I'm sure that's the true test.

I wonder how soon you'll hear the recording – & wonder if you'll feel as I did when I listened to mine – cool & detached & ready to pounce on everything that didn't come off as I'd wanted it to. I wonder whether you ought to add lots more expression marks to symph – whether they might have been able to interpret it more quickly if you had – – the 4tet is very carefully marked – – & orchestral players aren't nearly so good at sensing interpretation as good chamber music players are (neither are some conductors!)

Did you see Sophie Wyss at your concert? She liked your symph. very much – (incidentally she's been slimming or something & looked so girlish – & attractive that I hardly recognised her.)

I wonder how poor Uncle Ralph heard it – I hope as well as he possibly could – & felt proud – & will try to influence A.B.[28] to put it into a concert programme soon. You might hint to your Mr D. of Lengnick's[29] that he might try to get Kubelik interested. (Sargent I fear will be deadly to contemporaries – except that he occasionally does some Britten.)[30]

Well now it's midnight (in the middle of these last pages I've re-read your 4tet yet again – once I start there's no stopping.)

Why don't you & Billy have a night out to celebrate? Have you seen the Lady's Not for Burning? – It's delightful – so is Ring Round the Moon[31] which I saw on

---

27 Bartók Violin Concerto No. 2 (1937–8).
28 Conductor Adrian Boult.
29 Bernard de Nevers ran the publishing company, Alfred Lengnick.
30 Conductors Rafael Kubelik and Malcolm Sargent.
31 *The Lady's Not for Burning* (1948) a play by Christopher Fry. *Ring Round the Moon: A Charade with Music* (1950), first produced at the Globe Theatre in 1950, is an adaptation by Fry of Jean Anouilh, *L'invitation au chateau* (1947).

Sat. matinée (before catching 5.55 from Paddington). I called in to see Dorrie & Eleanor Saturday morning. E. is up & about & very cheerful – it is impossible to believe she is so ill. Dorrie has bought a television set with her burglary insurance & I'm sure it's really meant for Eleanor.

Now – to bed – & tomorrow I begin tackling in real earnest a heap of jobs that have accumulated – most of them rather dull – but unexacting

Best Love – Grace

[. . .]

101) 7 May 1950

Wickham Lodge, Wickham Bishops, Essex
Wickham Bishops 350
May 7th '50

Dearest Grace

It was lovely to get your good letter – & very heartening – one feels flat after an 'occasion', & probably nothing more will be heard of the Symphony. I did however get some satisfaction in listening to it myself – & it is very nice to know that some other people did too. Thank you very much for the nice things you say – & for letting me know some favourable opinions – (I haven't otherwise heard very many! Howes[32] criticism & the silly Telegraph one are the only ones I've seen so far – Mr de Nevers may collect others . . . I had a very nice letter from Dorrie, & Anne said that when she got home she found Arnold (her husband – a cellist –) in a state of great excitement (having listened-in) – saying it was 'the best Symphony he'd ever heard'!! – From Uncle Ralph I've had just a line – saying 'the Symphony was fine the other night. I will write again when I can collect my thoughts about it' – but I haven't had his 'collected thoughts' yet! – Mansel Thomas wrote a very nice letter – very good of him to write.)

The records are quite good – but it is funny listening to it again in very cold blood (because the excitement of the performance is of course lacking in the records.) I felt completely detached, like you. I've ordered a set for myself – not too costly – so one day I should play them to you. [. . .]

I'm going to score two pieces from Puck Fair & send them to Mansel Thomas – that Romance one you suggested – and a quick one that I rather like. They are short – but I think just long enough (I've extended them both a bit, and made them more complete than they were in the ballet.)

[. . .]

I feel sleepy & stupid – partly the effect of a wonderful summer day, perhaps, (& stewing over the Symphony parts!) It was lovely having you there for the Symphony – and a very great help. Do try to come here next time you're up – which I hope may be soon. Much best love, your loving Betty

---

32 Frank Howes, chief music critic of the *Times*.

My love to your Father & Mother. How much more to the point what he says (about major and minor triads in juxtaposition) is than what the professional critics say!

102) 12 May 1950

9, Old Village Road, Barry, Glamorgan
May 12th

Dearest Betty

This must be just a note as I'm trying to get four scripts off to the typist by Monday (& only 2 1/2 done so far – & teaching to do this afternoon). But in case you haven't seen the Listener criticism here it is – just another case of backing the wrong horse.

Other comments: Bernard Stevens[33] wrote (about Budapest) & said he found the symph. disappointing after the 4tets which he thought excellent – <u>but</u> he suspected the symph. hadn't been properly rehearsed. [. . .] You will I'm sure have heard from Ina by now & as she must have told you what she told me her impressions are I think very valuable – <u>especially</u> as she had <u>not</u> been at the rehearsals as we had – it was someone knowing the score – & hearing it played for the <u>first</u> time. – & think it's pretty conclusive that the interpretation did not give radio listeners anything like the full meaning of your music. Certain listeners with uncommon sensitivity <u>cd.</u> read their <u>own</u> interpretation with the music – unfortunately critics are not of that ilk. The only thing in Ina's letter which surprises me is that she blamed the players & not Boult – but it was <u>absolutely his</u> shortcoming & no one else's.

The symph. <u>must</u> have a second performance under another conductor. If Kubelik is an impossibility what about Barbirolli?[34]

[. . .]

[. . .] I've loads to do – three folk songs to arr. & orch. – Twelve Welsh airs to write harp accomps. for – & the Peter Pears songs – & all these scripts – but nothing very hard (also I have to write a 'Piano Concerto' lasting 2 to 3 mins!! based on the folk dance tune 'The Shoemaker' – for a Schools Programme.)[35]

I'm giving a broadcast in Welsh Children's Hour on the 25th about writing music for a film – with 'Blue Scar' illustrations played by BBC Welsh Orch.

<u>I'm so glad</u> you are doing something for Mansel (He doesn't take over until the Autumn.) If you'd like me to look over the score before you have parts copied I'd

---

33 Composer Bernard Stevens.
34 Conductors Rafael Kubelik and John Barbirolli.
35 Three folk songs (broadcast Summer 1950) included 'Bill Bones' Hornpipe', 'Out in the Garden', and 'The Derby Ram'; Williams arranged *Three Traditional Ballads* for tenor, flute, oboe, and string quartet: 'Sweet Primroses', 'The Lass of Swansea Town', and 'Fair Lisa', which Peter Pears first performed on 14 November 1950; and the *Variations on a Swedish Tune: The Shoemaker* for piano and orchestra (1950) was first broadcast in the *Rhythm and Melody* Schools programme on 6 July 1950.

be delighted to – I know pretty well what those players can tackle – I do advise you for these pieces to make them as <u>orchestrally effective</u> as possible – spotlight the tunes in such a way that even nitwitted critics will hear them & say 'What lovely music'. [. . .]

Love

Grace

P.S. Perhaps I'm too conscious of an audience when I score . . . I think – the result of years of teaching – when I had to consider everything I said as it wd. be interpreted by a child! A teacher goes all out to find the most effective & simplest means of registering impressions & driving them home. One can easily overdo it if one applies it to the <u>actual substance</u> of music – but it isn't a bad thing to do when <u>orchestrating</u>. G.

103) [Late June] 1950

9, Old Village Road, Barry, Glamorgan

Dearest Betty,

Two nice things – one you probably know about – G. Cockshott wrote to say your symphony had a brief but enthusiastic notice in the June Musical Times[36] [. . .].

2. K. Merritt took my advice & kept badgering B.B.C. to let her have Third Prog. dates – to do new works & now Leonard Isaacs (is he the new Third Head of Music?) has rung her up to say she is to have dates in the Autumn – programmes to be chosen by her & Peter C-Holland.[37] She tells me that you & I figured largely in the programmes she submitted. –

Now – your scores – I love the Romance & Tinker's C. <u>ought</u> to be very effective[38] but is a devil to score as the intervals don't lie well on strings – it wd. actually sound fine on two pianos – but it <u>will</u> score if you take a deal of trouble over it [. . .]

I've given some suggestions. . . & what about getting a score of say, Dukas' Apprent sorcier?[39] I feel in a way presumptuous for hacking your score about in this way – but – well all the time you've been writing chamber music I've been doing orchestration – especially for these <u>small</u> orchestras. I wdn't say we were quits because I cdn't write a bar of a quartet whereas you <u>can</u> score – but just need to get into practice again – & it will soon become <u>creative in itself.</u>

I'm sure it wd. be worth your while to get these two pieces as well scored as possible – & get them into the small orchestra (there's B'ham too) repertoire. It's

---

36 Colin Mason, 'London Contemporary Music Centre', *Musical Times* 91 (June 1950), 235.
37 Kathleen Merritt, conductor of her own orchestra; Leonard Isaacs, BBC Third Programme Music Organiser 1950–1954, replacing John Lowe; Peter Crossley-Holland, BBC Home Service.
38 Two Dances from *Puck Fair* (1950).
39 Paul Dukas, *The Sorcerer's Apprentice* (1897).

what everyone is doing. You must come down again for their Cardiff broadcast. M. will see that they get done – & he probably won't take over the Headship until the autumn.

[...]

Love Grace

It is wonderful hearing the Ring again[40] – alas I have to miss Twilight. Not the best of performances – but the best of music. I don't mean best of all music – but sometimes I'm sure it's as good as anything . . . except Tristan.

[...]

104) 2 July 1950

Wickham Lodge, Wickham Bishops, Essex
Wickham Bishops 350
Sunday July 2nd '50

Dearest Grace –

I am so ashamed that I haven't written a line since I had your letter & my score with all your brilliant & illuminating ideas – a week ago yesterday. But oh! for the time to write you the long letter I've written more than once in my head. (We are swamped with fruit – red currants, black currants, gooseberries, loganberries & raspberries, raspberries, raspberries to be picked & made into jam & bottled. – and all ripe at once, as well as the famous local strawberries . . . and as Nanny goes on a fortnight's holiday tomorrow I've been trying to get it done this week – as I'll have N. all the time now – – I've done nearly 40lbs of jam & 36 bottles of fruit. – Well, I've pretty well got the score into its new and immensely improved shape – & must now make a fair copy – or two, I suppose, one to send to Mansel – & one to 'submit' to de Nevers & get the parts done from. . .[41]

My dear, I've learnt a great deal from what you say & suggest – & I could & should love to have a great deal more from you. I realise only too well how dull & unenterprising my scoring is – & how seldom 'creative'. I suffer very much from never having had any working experience of any orchestra – & I'm fumbling & un-sure in consequence. (I don't think really though I have a 'feeling' for it. I write my orchestral music from the wrong end – as it were – as abstract music, instead of hearing it in the first place as pure orchestral sound –. And then I set to and score it very clumsily (– not unlike Uncle Ralph's method! But his music somehow carries the day). You've got a real imaginative command of it all – and I can't tell you how grateful I am for all your advice & the time & trouble you've taken. If these pieces come off it will be entirely due to you! ('Maconchy – arr.

---

40 While in London in June 1950, Williams attended Wagner's *Ring* cycle at the Royal Opera House, Covent Garden. She also attended two performances of *Tristan und Isolde*.

41 Two Dances from *Puck Fair* (1950), one score to be sent to conductor Mansel Thomas and the other to her publisher, Bernard de Nevers of Alfred Lengnick.

Williams' – or perhaps 're-arr. Williams') I see how I really hadn't faced the problem of getting the 2-piano idiom in Tinker's Curse (I wrote the original Puck Fair ballet for 2 pianos – & kept a piano in the orchestra when I scored the Suite as there was a good deal of pianistic stuff like this) . . . re-laid out for strings. Your solution is ingenious & obviously right. I've adopted nearly all your suggestions for both pieces as they stand – (some slightly modified in the 'Romance' – <u>what am</u> I to call it??) yes – I ought to have more violin lessons – I never reached the stage of being able to try things out, though even the little I did helped a lot with string writing. I'd like some lessons on the harp, too, & in the percussion department, where I'm particularly gauche. (I wish I could have a few years or even months to myself to learn in; I often think what much better use I could have made of 6 years at the College – but one doesn't know what to make for, coming at it out of the blue)

[. . .]

I've had very little time at my new quartet[42] – but have done 2 movements now & part of the slow movement. It will work out longer & rather bigger than the others, I think. . .

[. . .]

How did Merry Minstrel go in Manchester?[43] I do hope now you are having your 'easy time' – & that it really is? – We are going to Ireland for nearly a fortnight from about August 31st with the car – taking Anna but leaving Niccy here with Nanny & a friend to help her . . . It will be 20 years since B. & I were married on Aug. 23rd (and 20 since 'The Land' was played on Aug 30th!! Well, well.) I should <u>love</u> to come down if Mansel does my pieces. That would be really nice – Best love & 1000 very inadequate thanks Betty.

[. . .]

---

42 String Quartet no. 6 (1950).
43 An abbreviated version of Williams's *Merry Minstrel* had been performed in a children's broadcast from Manchester on 27 June 1950.

III.2   Letters 105–113 (December 1950–November 1952)

Over the next two years, Williams continued to make her living through various 'jobs', such as writing music for film and arranging folk songs for radio broadcasts. Both women continued to have their large-scale works performed on various BBC radio stations. New music by Maconchy that premiered during this period included her *Nocturne* for orchestra (1950–51) and her String Quartet no. 6 (1950–51).

Always intensely self-critical, Williams had a 'Day of Destruction' on 10 May 1951. She wrote in her diary: '[I] examined all my music manuscripts and destroyed nearly all which I considered not worth performing'.[1]

On 13 December 1950, in a broadcast on the Third Programme, Williams's suite The Dark Island *for string orchestra (1949) was first performed by the Kathleen Merritt Orchestra, the music drawn from incidental music she had written for the Henry Treece radio play of that name.*

105) 14 December 1950

Wickham Lodge, Wickham Bishops, Essex
Wickham Bishops 350
Thurs. December 14th '50

Dearest Grace. Reception here was good last night and I was <u>electrified</u> by the Dark Island pieces – these were immensely assured & effective (I couldn't help smiling to think you'd said they sounded 'amateurish' at the 1st rehearsal – they couldn't be less so) and I liked them very much. I particularly like the opening & closing ones, with their dark colour & sombre feeling – (exactly rightly scored) – & the March came off superbly, I thought. I liked the Barcarolle too – but my <u>only</u> criticism is that I thought it a bit too long: I wanted either something different to happen somewhere – or else the piece to be a little shorter. But I may be quite wrong, on one hearing. I do wish I'd

---

[1] Malcolm Boyd, *Grace Williams, Composers of Wales*, vol. 4 (Cardiff: University of Wales Press, 1980), 33.

136 Part III. Letters 94–146 (November 1949–December 1959)

been able to hear the rehearsal as well. They must have worked to very good effect yesterday morning. What were your own reactions? & other people's? (Anna liked your pieces very much. B. wasn't back to hear them unfortunately – [)]
[. . .]
I expect you are speeding back in the train? I wish you were here. (I've just remembered my Puck Fair pieces – hope I shan't forget to listen at the right moment!)[2]
[. . .]
Funny coincidence, on Tues night when we got home – – (rather chilly after an unheated train & drive from Chelmsford! I've had beastly neuralgia ever since. . .) . . . after hearing Kathleen Merritt rehearse in the afternoon & seeing Iris in the morning, I found a letter out of the blue from Kathleen Riddick![3] Wanting to do a work of mine at a S.W.M. Fest of Britain Concert – for which they've engaged her str. orch. I've suggested my Variations or else the new Piano Concertino:[4] [. . .] I also said, if she didn't know them already, I thought she would like to see your Sea Sketches & that the O.U.P. are publishing them. (Are they soon to be out? please let me know when.)[5]
I must get lunch – so mustn't go on I hope you were as pleased as I was with your Dark Island – and that we shall both hear it again soon.
Best love Your loving
Betty
Please give my love to both your parents.

Maconchy's Piano Concertino (1949) was given its first performance by Margaret Kitchin (piano), Kathleen Merritt, and her orchestra as a Third Programme broadcast on 21 February 1951. Williams was working hard on professional commissions, music for BBC Schools Broadcasts, and a score for a documentary film, for the Welsh Committee of the Festival of Britain.

106) 25 February 1951

9, Old Village Road, Barry, Glamorgan
added by hand: 30 Willow Road, NW3, Hampstead

Dearest Betty
Forgive me for not writing at once about the Concertino – I've been desperately busy until this morning. It's fine – but my first impression was that although it

---

2 Maconchy's Two Dances from *Puck Fair* (1950) were given a second broadcast on the BBC Light Programme on 14 December 1950.
3 Three conductors, Kathleen Merritt, Iris Lemare, and Kathleen Riddick.
4 Kathleen Merritt gave the first performance of the Piano Concertino (1949) in February 1951, while the first UK concert performance of the Theme and Variations for string orchestra (1942–3) was given by Kathleen Riddick with her string orchestra at a Society of Women Musicians' concert at Queen Mary Hall, London, on 27 June 1951.
5 Williams's *Sea Sketches* (1944) were published by Oxford University Press in 1951.

began in concertino style it became more & more serious & large-scale in character & should have been a full length concerto.

There is the usual lovely music – the slow mvt. – sombre this time rather than lyrical – but I had a feeling that it cd. have come out of its shell & expanded more – perhaps when you were writing it you were too conscious of keeping it within the confines of a concertino mvt? The last mvt. was brilliant at the start – & concertino brilliance (tho' it cd. also have been concerto [brilliance]) – not typically you, this start though it soon enough became Maconchy music – a fine movement. [. . .]

[. . .]

I'd started orchestrating a 58 page score (school broadcasts)[6] on Sunday & knew I had to have it finished by Thursday. (They cdn't get orchestra fixed – & Easter is early this year – so I had half the usual time for the job.) I posted it off at mid-day on Thursday – went off to Cardiff to do my Friday teaching on Thursday aft. & evening – then yesterday I came up to London to see a short film I'm to write music for about 18 mins. orchestral music & they want it recorded at end of March. It's a Festival of Britain (Welsh Committee) film about Wales. Not bad – it might have been awful – story (written by the wrong Welshman) full of Welsh clichés – no human – stock-in-trade emotion – but it's been saved by the director, a young Jew who has just had an Academy Award for another documentary recently released.[7]

Muir Matheson[8] insisted on having me – though the Welsh committee wanted anyone but me (they are more or less the same lot as the Welsh Arts' Council Committee).

Funnily enough the producer,[9] who thought he'd better have a Welsh musician's opinion too hit on writing to the Head of Music at B.B.C. Cardiff – Mansel – & M. wrote back at once & said only one Welsh composer cd. do the job – me. So here I am – still tired & without a clue as regards the music I'm going to write. Muir has 'flu so I have to wait for discussions with him until he's better. Meanwhile I'll be haunting the cutting room & studying the film under the movieola.

Must ring & find out how Dorrie is. She was spared a major op. & the obstruction was quite harmless.

I am terribly sorry you've had such a rotten time – with 'flu & more domestic difficulties – but hope things are easier now & you are getting on with the Nocturne score.[10] (I'd just settled down to my Mezzo songs – 'The Galleons of Aeneas'[11] when all these jobs came along.)

---

6 Williams arranged five folk songs of different nationalities for an Easter 1951 broadcast. See Boyd, *Grace Williams*, 94.
7 The 38-minute documentary film *David*, directed and scripted by Paul Dickson, is available on the BFL website: http://player.bfi.org.uk/film/watch-david-1951/. The other, prize-winning documentary by Dickson was *The Undefeated* (1950).
8 Muir Matheson was an influential Scottish film composer.
9 James Carr.
10 Maconchy's *Nocturne* for orchestra (1950–51).
11 Untraced.

138   Part III. Letters 94–146 (November 1949–December 1959)

I feel my opinions on music are apt to be <u>very unreliable indeed</u>. You know all I said & wrote about 'Ullyssees'[12] – well I heard the broadcast of 10 days ago – & realised I'd been wrong – the second time it sounded <u>quite different</u> to my ears – clear-cut & luminous – & (I blush to confess it) a fine piece of impressionism (though not in any way great <u>creative</u> music.)

I felt so conscience-stricken that I wrote off to Edward Clark & asked him to let M. S. know that I humbly recanted.[13]

E. C. replied that <u>of course</u> M. S. wouldn't have heard what my opinion had been since our reports were strictly private!!! – well – that hurt my poor conscience more & more – especially as L.C.M.C. has made me an honorary member – what a fraud! Yet I know I didn't [*sic*] going over your 4tet[14] & they'll know, too, when they hear it! It was the most personal, creative work sent in. All best love

Grace

[…]

It was seven months before the next surviving letter, prompted by a broadcast of 'Music from Wales' on 25 September 1951 from St John's Church, Cardiff, which included Williams's Song of Mary *(1939–40), sung by Dorothy Bond with the BBC Welsh Orchestra, conducted by Arwel Hughes.*

107) 26 September 1951

Wickham Lodge, Wickham Bishops, Essex
Wickham Bishops 350
Wednesday

Dearest Grace

Billy & I both heard your Song of Mary last night, as he got back just in time. It is lovely – we both thought it was <u>very</u> beautiful. It is 'all of a piece' in the best sense – real continuity & lovely long lines – & has breadth & serenity. I thought she sang it very well, with the right feeling of upliftedness – were you pleased? I couldn't really judge if the orchestral playing was all it should be?

But it sounded lovely, we thought. I couldn't hear Dan Jones' piece as I was hurrying Niccy to bed in time to hear yours! – & lost interest in the Arwel Hughes pretty quickly![15] I was sorry not to hear the other.

[…]

I am projecting a Symphony for Strings – when I can get to work again. Kathleen Cooper is playing my Concertino (with a small section of Antony

---

12 Mátyás Seiber's cantata *Ulysses* for tenor, chorus, and orchestra (1947).
13 Edward Clark, Chairman of the London Contemporary Music Centre, for whom Williams had written an assessment of Seiber's cantata.
14 Maconchy's String Quartet no. 6 (1950).
15 The programme also included Daniel Jones's *Cloud Messenger* for orchestra (1944) and Arwel Hughes's *Gweddi* ('Prayer') for soprano, chorus, and string orchestra (1944).

Bernard's strings) at Wigmore Hall on Oct. 2nd (next Tues.)[16] But I fear you won't be in London? Nanny is coming back for a night, so that I can go.

Much very best love: I hope this is not too incoherent – Niccy is rather demanding of my attention – though otherwise angelic! Betty.

Five months later, on 19 February 1952, Williams's Violin Concerto (1950) was broadcast on the BBC Home Service. The work was performed by Granville Jones (violin) with the BBC Northern Orchestra, conducted by Clarence Raybould. A week before, on 12 February, at the Mercury Theatre, London, Maconchy's Duo: Theme and Variations *for violin and cello (1951) was first performed by its dedicatees, Anne Macnaghten and her husband, Arnold Ashby; a few days before that, on 8 February, Maconchy gave a talk introducing her Sixth String Quartet before the MacGibbon Quartet played it twice in a concert at the Institute of Contemporary Arts, London, having played it also on 3 February, for the Oxford Ladies' Musical Society.*

108) 19 February 1952

Wickham Lodge, Wickham Bishops, Essex
Wickham Bishops 350
Feb. 19th 52

Dearest Grace

I heard your Violin Concerto beautifully this afternoon – it seemed to me a very good & eloquent performance – & there were lovely orchestral sounds (esp. the harp) but that was to your credit even more than to the orchestra's! (I do hope you were able to be there?) Everything sounded completely assured & very <u>mature</u>.

The parts I like <u>best</u> are the part of the 1st Mvt. from just before the Cadenza up to the end of the movement. The latter [*sic*] part of the slow movement & the link (excellent) to the last movement – & the whole of the last mvt. It's an <u>extremely</u> good movement. I think my only criticism would be that there is not quite enough contrast between the 1st & 2nd movements – when the slow mvt. starts one doesn't immediately get the refreshing feeling one needs when one starts a new movement, I think: (just as one doesn't in the slow mvt. of my Symphony, which is somehow too like in <u>feeling</u> to the 1st.) But it all did sound fine – grand violin writing, too. Do tell me your feelings about the performance & what Raybould said etc – that is, when you have a breather – after the film rush is over.[17] You must be pretty worn out – I fear – though I <u>hope</u> not so much as over the last film, as you managed to get more time for it? I'm longing to hear more about it.

---

16 Maconchy's Piano Concertino (1949), performed by Kathleen Cooper with the London Chamber Orchestra, conducted by Anthony Bernard.

17 On 28 January 1952, Williams had begun working on a film score for *A Story of Achievement*, a documentary directed by Paul Dickson about the development of margarine.

[...] I'm working at my Str. Symphony – haven't got very far yet, as I scrapped a lot I'd written – & have also rather accidentally started a work (perhaps a Serenade in several short movements –) for bassoon & strings.[18]

Anne & Arnold played my Duo at the Mercury Theatre last week – they really played it remarkably well – & it sounded rather nice.

The MacGibbons played my No. 6. <u>badly</u> at the I.C.A. – but better the 2nd time after the Interval, though not really good: it was better at Oxford. I sweated like anything in preparing my talk – & learnt it by heart! As I didn't want to have to read it. I never thought my memory would hold out – but it somehow did – for about 15 minutes! Uncle Ralph came, which was awfully nice of him, & liked the quartet.

Best love, & many very real congratulation on the Vn. Concerto – Your loving Betty

Williams's response, giving her thoughts about the Violin Concerto performance, was prompted by a broadcast of Maconchy's Sixth String Quartet on the BBC Third Programme, performed by the MacGibbon Quartet, led by Margot MacGibbon.

109) 14 March 1952

9, Old Village Road, Barry, Glamorgan
March 14th 1952

Dearest Betty,

I listened last night & felt as I always feel when I listen to your quartets – a real musical fulfilment. I feel this is your best quartet from the point of view of <u>composition</u>. Musically it is very like No 5 in its themes – but not <u>too</u> like it in the overall impression. Whether I shall love it as <u>music</u> as much as No 5 I can't tell yet ... maybe I shall. If so I shall love it <u>very</u> much.

[...]

I am now going to relax for a day or so – & read your quartet.

Then I must start on another film. The last was a success & John Hollingsworth, who conducted, was very impressed & said I must do lots more ... And now already he wants me to do one – 40 minutes – & <u>perhaps</u> I'll have to do it in 3 weeks. I've told him exactly how I feel & he's trying to have recording put off till beginning of May.[19] – I don't know yet whether he has succeeded. I daren't turn it down – it is in a way my salvation, but it is exacting work. No let-up at all – just composing & scoring all day until midnight – & later of course if I have to do it in 3 weeks.

---

18 Maconchy's Symphony for double string orchestra (1952–3) and Concertino for bassoon and string orchestra (1952).

19 A 40-minute documentary film, *Fawley Achievement* (1951), directed by Geoffrey Gurrin about the building of the new Esso refinery at Fawley, near Southampton. The music was recorded on 19 May 1952.

I took every minute of 3 weeks for the last – 22 minutes. The new one is about the new oil refinery near Brighton. Anything less inspiring I can't imagine – but margarine proved surprisingly interesting so I hope for the best.

Thank you so much for listening to my Vln. Concerto. I've never been so long in replying – but felt I wanted to write a longish letter to you – & there hasn't been time until now. I felt the performance was lovely – Granville at his best. The only thing is that the slow mvt. will never sound the way I want it to – contemplative & serene (therefore different from mvt. I) until they know it well. It is apt to sound dull if taken gently & slowly when players don't really know it – so tendency is for conductor to whip up tempo.

I feel there is too much soaring for solo vln. (Uncle R. said 'too many arabesques & no tune' – I don't think he liked it much) & I'm going to revise solo part of slow mvt. – actually I <u>heard</u> a revised version when I was last in London – walking through an underground subway – & feel I know what to do.)

Criticism from friends seemed to point to its being too easy on the ear.

[. . .]

I'm sorry you may have to lose Yvonne[20] – these domestic trials are more than 999 out of 1000 women composer would put up with – I mean they'd just give up trying to compose. Yet you manage to write fine works in spite of it all.

[. . .] I'd love a week or so with nothing much to do. Have only just finished my B.B.C. jobs. Mansel is a big disappointment. The orchestra now call him 'Big Head' & say he is a changed man. Luckily I've had a break in other directions. No sign of the Directorship being advertised – & now if I can come to some understanding with John Hollingsworth about having enough time for film-writing – I think I shall be happier sticking to free-lancing. J.H. is an extraordinary kind young man – Betty Lutyens had told me that before I worked with him.

[. . .]

'Billy Budd' had a <u>great</u> success in Cardiff:[21] an unsophisticated audience was completely held by it – & I heard people saying things like 'Well it's all full of discords but it's wonderful' – 'It's all strange & unusual – but somehow it's all <u>clear</u>'. I love the work. A friend of mine – not particularly musical – but sensitive – thought it was full of compassion. I agree. The ballad before the hanging is for me unbearably moving. It's something I can't understand – that Britten is understood so much better by laymen than by the profession. For me he is first & foremost a musician's composer – yet hardly any musician has a kind word for him these days.

Must stop & take the grocer's order & go to post – All best love

Grace

[. . .]

Williams had two broadcasts within a few days in April 1952: her Symphonic Impressions *(1943) was aired on 15 April on the BBC Home Service, played by*

---

20 Nicola's nanny.
21 Britten's opera *Billy Budd* (1951).

the BBC Scottish Orchestra, conducted by Clarence Raybould, and two of her Sea Sketches *were broadcast on 18 April on the Light Programme, performed by the BBC Welsh Orchestra, conducted by Arwel Hughes.*

110) 19 April 1952

Wickham Lodge
Saturday April 19th 52

Dearest Grace

At last a snatched moment to write to you. I got both the broadcasts well. It was lovely hearing Owen[22] again – & it made the impression of a very fine work – I felt it was very good indeed.

I couldn't spot where you'd made your cuts – but they must have been just right, as it certainly does not seem too long (except just possibly in the very last bit of all – which I love – which psychologically I thought perhaps went on a shade too long? But I'm not sure – it all deserves better quality playing than it had, & this would make this final passage sound richer in quality, & then probably it would be exactly the right length.) I think it is a beautiful & most effective score – & want to hear it played by a really first-class orchestra. – I longed for front-rank playing [in] the Sea Sketches too – especially 'Breakers'. But I enjoyed them enormously – they are lovely – (Why didn't he do them all?)

[. . .]

My Nocturne is going to be done on May 13th at the B.B.C. – L.C.M.C. Concert[23] – (contrary to my expectation!) fortunately Lengnick have taken it on so they are getting the parts done (I shall have to give them all the Hire fee & all the performing fee from the 1st perf. though!) – as time is hard to come by at the moment. [. . .] Anna is in very good form – she came with Sophie & Billy & me to Ipswich for the day when my Yeats settings were done & enjoyed it all![24] Sophie was grand & carried through the rather odd performance (with one amateur Horn & a terrible amateur clarinet! but a good Harpist) wonderfully well. The choir are good, but hadn't really had enough rehearsal. Armstrong Gibbs[25] was there & wrote a most frightfully nice letter afterwards, which was nice.

[. . .]

All best love my dear – & many congratulations on the Symph. Impressions – Your loving
Betty

---

22 Maconchy continued to refer to Williams's *Symphonic Impressions* as 'Owen' after Owen Glendower.
23 Maconchy's *Nocturne* for orchestra (1950–51) was given a studio broadcast on 13 May 1952 on the BBC Third Programme by the Royal Philharmonic Orchestra, conducted by John Pritchard. It was published by Alfred Lengnick in 1952.
24 Maconchy's *Six Settings of Poems by W.B. Yeats* (1951) were tried out at Christchurch School, Ipswich, on 5 April 1952 by Sophie Wyss (soprano), the Northgateon Singers, and instrumental players (clarinet, harp, and two horns), conducted by Peter Burges.
25 Composer Cecil Armstrong Gibbs.

Williams responded by describing the process that had led to the Symphonic Impressions *performance in Glasgow.*

111) 21 April 1952 – postcard

[Williams to Maconchy]

[postmark: 21 Apr 1952]

Many thanks for lovely letter. I went to Glasgow – I think they did all they cd. in one rehearsal – Raybould worked v. hard & all said they needed two days (at least) – all very nice about it. The end of last mvt. is too long – the one bit I forgot to cut. Originally it was too short so I repeated a couple of pages & now more pages need rewriting. The scoring is in many ways ungrateful to players & if I wrote it today it wd. be very different.

Raybould very friendly & interested in dedication to you whom he admires so I told him about your symph. & he said 'Where can I get hold of it?' so I told him – – & I wonder if it wd. be wise for Lengnick's to ring him up & remind him – ... Then I said 'Why don't you be original & do something no one has ever done – a programme of works by women composers' – & he thought it an excellent idea & said 'Who shall we have?' so I went thro' the list & when I got to E – L –[26] he said 'You must excuse me if I exclude her' – I put in a plea but I'm afraid he won't. I really think he will put it to the B.B.C. – – Also I have asked M. Whewell[27] if we can hear something of yours in the Tuesday series ... but it looks as though they are only doing works passed by panel in last 20 years & never performed (in Home Service or Third). Delighted about Nocturne. If a miracle happens (but it won't) & I finish my oil score in time I'll come to it and stay up for Anne's concert on 15th & film recording on 19th. I begin scoring today; all very dull, but I have been fortified by two things

(a) Uncle R.'s saying that in film music you can make anything mean anything
(b) Leonardo wd. have been interested.

[...] Love G.

112) 14 May 1952 – postcard

[Williams to Maconchy]

[postmark: 14 May 1952]

Nocturne is most lovely – & quite your best <u>score</u> – everything translucent & perfect for the words. You must do more programme works. Only criticism is that it seemed to hang fire <u>a bit</u> towards end just before the pizzicatos – but perhaps it was the performance. But altogether lovely & most moving.

---

26 Elisabeth Lutyens.
27 Michael Whewell, organiser of the BBC Home Service Tuesday afternoon concert series.

Have just finished – pretty exhausted – still loads to do checking parts & testing the very complicated – & mathematical – order of recording, involving several 'reprise' sections. – J. Hollingsworth[28] simply said 'Repeat as much as you can it will save rehearsal time' – easier said than done when it comes to measuring it up with the film!

However – – –

Recording on Monday then I must stay up for a few days & help the Editor fit it to film. Will you by any chance be in London on Tuesday or Wednesday?

Thank you again for the beautiful Nocturne. I told J.H. to listen to it – hope he did.

Six months later, Williams immediately responded to the first broadcast of Maconchy's Third String Quartet, performed on 24 November 1952 on the BBC Third Programme by the Hungarian Quartet.

113) 24 November 1952

9, Old Village Road, Barry, Glamorgan
November 24th 11 p.m.

Dearest Betty –

Lovely to hear your No 3 again – I shall never forget the thrill I had when I first heard it & when I spotted it in the Radio Times last week end I took out the score again & played it & felt all I felt before – that it was a real contemporary romantic lyrical work. I thought the Hungarian were very good – especially the viola – the only thing that surprised me was the crisp way they played the pizz. chords – rather too dry in sound quality for my liking. What did you feel? And tonight I wondered whether there were too many glisses. . . (just a minor point). Otherwise it made lovely listening.

[. . .]

I was delighted to get a long letter from Ina about your Irish performances & I hope you'll go often now, it will be a godsend if they give you regular performances – & you can fly there in no time. I dare say the Irish trip is responsible for your great spurt of work – things work that way!

I wish I could hear your Duo next Tuesday[29] – instead I shall be helping to welcome Kabalevsky[30] & a Bass & a violinist to Cardiff. The Soviet Friendship Society got them to come & have asked me to preside! – – but I've talked them out of that.

---

28 Conductor John Hollingsworth.
29 Maconchy's *Duo: Theme and Variations* for violin and cello, was performed by Anne Macnaghten (violin) and Arnold Ashby (cello) at a Society for the Promotion of New Music concert on 2 December 1952.
30 Soviet composer Dmitry Kabalevsky.

The strangest thing happened last night – Anne rang up & asked if I'd be prepared to go to Vienna as British delegate at a Musicians Organisation of Peace gathering – Dec 12–17. I was so stunned & so delighted at the prospect of seeing Vienna again that I didn't have the courage to refuse point blank though I put all my cards on the table . . . Of course after sleeping on it I realised I had none of the very necessary qualifications – ability to speak & think in public, thorough knowledge of international affairs etc. etc. – so early today I sent her a telegram 'Reflection clinches my incompetence'. A pity, she can't go – or Lady Mayer.[31] Apparently there's a snag about most of the male possibilities (near Communist & what not) – but <u>why</u> they chose me I can't think. – it struck me as being rather like Albert Herring[32] in reverse – a politically pure & unspotted G. W.!! (but they didn't know about Kabalevsky!) Forgive me for joking about what is a very very serious subject (especially now that Foster Dulles ascends to power in U.S.A.)[33] & I do hope they get the right person to go to Vienna.

Have you seen or heard from Dorrie? I am worried – a few weeks ago I had a short note – she was obviously stunned by Eleanor's death (which was very sudden) – & ended the note by saying that she & Nelly would be leaving Holland Avenue before or just after Christmas '& thank goodness Nelly has her flat to go to'. Nothing about herself – I guessed things were bad (especially if she has to part with Nelly) & wrote at once & asked what I could do & had Eleanor perhaps not made a will & was she left high & dry? No answer – perhaps I shouldn't have asked such direct questions but it does look as though something is seriously wrong. I had hoped that she would link up with her brother Colin who is now a widower (& well-off I think.)[34]

I'd hoped to be in London to ring her up – but so far there hasn't been anything to go for & now I don't want to be disturbed for a bit because I have a chance of doing some real composing . . . I'd struck a bad barren patch – had got so used to doing 'jobs' that when I found I was free to write what I liked I felt lost without the props & ideas the 'jobs' had provided. It was awful – struggling & scrapping & switching from one thing to another. Then last week I thought I'd found what I wanted – something (perhaps a serenade) for Two harps & orchestra[35] – & I got started in real earnest & the old feeling of being full of it returned – Then of course the inevitable happened – I got caught up in nightmares of pedalling (when I first

---

31 Soprano and biographer Dorothy Moulton Mayer, wife of philanthropist Sir Robert Mayer, who supported music and sponsored concerts for children.
32 Britten's opera hero, who is crowned King of the May, because that year no girls in the village are pure and virginal enough to be suited for selection as Queen.
33 The American election in November 1952 resulted in Dwight D. Eisenhower becoming president, and he was to appoint John Foster Dulles, known for his aggressive stance against communism, as his Secretary of State.
34 From 1929 (until at least 1965), Dorothy Gow lived with Colin and Helen Morrisson ('Nelly') who were probably servants. From the mid-1930s, the household was joined by Gow's partner Eleanor Ramsbotham.
35 Unidentified.

wrote I was determined not to think about pedalling – but just write what I felt wd. sound good on harps) – & now I don't know how to solve it all – I <u>can</u> divide it up between the 2 harps so that the pedalling is possible <u>but</u> the 2 players would have to be more or less identical in tone – strength & sensitivity – & I had hoped it wd. be for Sidonie & Marie G.[36] & of course S. is far better than M. (& far better than anyone!) – Anyway I've now got interrupted. Cardiff wants to use lots of my carol-arrangements for schools in a Xmas Eve programme <u>but</u> they are not having a school choir – instead Mgt. Ritchie & René Soames[37] – & everything is too low & for Sop & Alto – & I have to re-do the voice parts & copy reams & reams.

How I envy you pouring it out – what is it? – I long to see some scores of yours – so many things you've written lately that I've neither seen nor heard. In the New Year we must meet or perhaps you can lend me scores as you used to?

I hope & pray now that I don't get a film until I've really had a chance to settle down to real composing. I can afford to lay off for a month or two – <u>but</u> if I get asked to do a film I daren't refuse.

The only thing I'm proud of is that I've done <u>loads</u> of revision of old scores – a great weight off my mind.

And I've written lots of scripts (the great standby if I dry up as a composer!)

It is now midnight so I'd better leave off – How are Billy & the children? How you can cope with all the Christmas preparations & compose I don't know – but it will be good to have Anna home. I get quite frightened by the prospect of Christmas – the Cardiff shops are teeming with people already.

with love
Grace
[. . .]

---

36 Sidonie and Marie Goossens, distinguished harpists and sisters.
37 Soprano Margaret Ritche and tenor René Soames.

III.3 Letters 114–122
(March 1953–March 1955)

During this two-year period, both women's music received many broadcasts on BBC radio, but there were hierarchies of broadcast, with evening performances on the Third Programme more prestigious than daytime performances on the Home Service or Light Programme. Getting works passed by the BBC Reading Panel continued to be a significant issue.

Maconchy received first performances of a number of works, including the prize-winning overture *Proud Thames* (1952), her Bassoon Concertino (1952) and her Symphony for double string orchestra (1952–3). In 1955, the BBC broadcast a series of all six of her string quartets, with an introductory talk given by Williams. Maconchy started work on her Seventh String Quartet (1955).

In 1953 Williams bought her first television set, although neither woman yet owned a tape recorder or a record player. After a period of concentrating her composing on 'jobs', Williams returned to writing concert works, notably with her orchestral *Penillion* (1955).

Maconchy and her husband sold their houses in Essex and in Ireland, moving to Shottesbrook in Boreham, Essex.

On 27 February 1953, Maconchy's Concertino for piano and string orchestra (1949) was given another broadcast on the BBC Third Programme, performed by pianist Margaret Good with Kathleen Merritt and her string orchestra. Her new Bassoon Concertino was to be broadcast on the Third Programme on 24 March, performed by Gwydion Brooke with the Goldsbrough Orchestra, conducted by Edric Cundell, while Williams anticipated a Light Programme broadcast of her Sea Sketches *on 26 March, performed by the BBC Northern Orchestra, conducted by John Hopkins.*

114) [?1] March 1953 – postcard

[Williams to Maconchy]

[postmark: [?1] Mar 1953]

I like the Concertino very much indeed – just feel as I felt before that it is <u>concerto</u> music rather than concertino. I feel slow mvt. is completely satisfying – & lovely – as it is – but there is so much fine material in last mvt. that needs to expand & develop more. First mvt. seems to me rather too reiterative & doesn't travel enough . . . Bt slow mvt. is lovely. A very good performance [. . .]

On 26th B.B.C. Northern are doing Sea Sketches in Light – Midday. Also earlier that morning my usual Schools Folksong arrangements will be done (11 a.m.[)][1] This term I've had to do a nice Irish tune ('Her hair was like the beaten gold'.)

I don't think I'll ever get promoted to an evening performance. They are all H.S. or Light[2] & at times when no one really listens. The only consolation is that they pay!

Did you hear Gertler broadcast the Bartók Sonata for unaccompanied violin?[3] A fine work & surely the most violinistic ever written – wonderfully written for the instruments – a curious contrast to the Berg vln concerto which Gertler had played a few days earlier. The mood of the Berg is marvellous – it mesmerises me in such a way that I couldn't tell afterwards whether the music was organic or improvisatory if I hadn't read that it was all highly organic. . .

I read somewhere that it was fiendishly difficult & ungrateful to play, but how true that is I don't know.

[. . .].

Love G Love to Niccy.

In late July 1953, it was announced that Maconchy had won the London County Council competition prize of £150 for a Coronation Overture with her Proud Thames *(1952).*

115) 27 July 1953 – postcard

[Maconchy to Williams]

Monday July 27th

Just to say that they have just rung up from Festival Hall to say I've won the L. C. C. Overture Competition! . . . Performance to be with L.P.O – & Adrian Boult in Oct. or Dec. & 'presentation' made at the concert. . . (£150 wasn't it? – I've lost my original particulars!) Hurray! Glad the young things don't have it every time. . .

We go to Ireland on 10th Aug. – Have not sold this house yet – but have sold the Irish one,[4] but are having this last holiday there

Best love B

I called it 'Proud Thames' in the end – Billy's idea

---

1 Williams had arranged and orchestrated songs for the *Rhythm and Melody* Schools programme on the BBC Home Service.
2 BBC Home Service or Light Programme.
3 On 28 January 1953, violinist André Gertler had given a concert broadcast of Alban Berg's Violin Concerto (1935). On 30 January, he gave a broadcast recital which included Bartók's Sonata for Solo Violin (1944).
4 This house, Ballymorris in Enniskerry, Co Wicklow, had been left to Billy LeFanu by his uncle, Victor LeFanu.

As part of the competition's prize, Maconchy's Proud Thames *was to be given its first performance in a BBC Symphony Concert on 14 October 1953, at the Royal Festival Hall, London; it was to be performed by the BBC Symphony Orchestra, conducted by Malcolm Sargent, and broadcast on the BBC Home Service.*

116) [After 29 July] 1953

9, Old Village Road, Barry, Glamorgan

Dearest Betty,

At last I can follow up my telegram (have been a copying machine for several days) & say what I feel – that at last a competition has proved worth-while – & for once a prize-winner will go streets ahead of the commissioned composer (I haven't heard a note of Proud Thames – except the theme – but know it will more than make up to L.C.C. for what they lost on Orb & Sceptre.[5]) but we must feel sorry for Walton – an awful thing to lose one's grasp so utterly & irretrievably – & he was so good when he was young. I long to hear it & hope it will be round about October 17th – because on that day my old Merry Minstrel is being done at a children's morning concert at F.H.[6] by Philharmonia conducted by Ernest Read, who wanted parts to try it out at a Summer School & since there were 6 extra strings to be done I had to sit down & copy 60 pages more or less non-stop.

M.M. is quite my worst (performable) work & I do indeed envy you having Proud Thames done at F.H. – but it's a nice kind of envy – I don't think a true musician can ever be unpleasantly envious or jealous of a <u>good</u> composer, he is too grateful for the good composer's music.

What does make me feel awful is when benefits & commissions are bestowed on inferior composers & I feel if only I had their chances I could in my small way do better things than they do (Wales – thanks to Mansel [–] has now downgraded me & I get nothing except a few broadcasts from Arwel Hughes[7] ... [)] Last week a D.Mus. was allowed to broadcast a talk on Welsh composers – & referred to the creative genius of Arwel H. the versatile genius of Mansel T. & the collossal [*sic*] advent of Daniel J.[8] I was referred to simply as composer of Fantasia on Welsh Nursery Rhymes which he called felicitous, & he said my technique was improving.

Part of me says I oughtn't to mind – but the other half tells me it is quite natural to mind very much & fight for recognition of what I know are my best things.

Forgive me for mentioning all this but I have no musical friends here – except young Alun Hoddinott who has recently married a very nice Welsh girl & I go to see them fairly often & talk music for hours. I <u>believe</u> he's going to be

---

5 In fact, William Walton's coronation march, *Orb and Sceptre* (1952–3), had been commissioned by the Arts Council of Great Britain.
6 The Royal Festival Hall, London.
7 Welsh composer and conductor Arwel Hughes worked in the Music Department of BBC Wales.
8 Mansel Thomas and Daniel Jones.

good – an astonishing grasp of <u>compositions</u> for one so young (23) & an excellent orchestrator. It is pretty cerebral music – & he isn't at all a poetic type – something a bit insensitive about him (worships Bach but can't see what people find in Mozart). But he is nice.

I am sorry you have had to sell Ballymorris – & Ina will be heartbroken (<u>please</u> give her my love & greetings when you see her) – & I'm sorry you are having difficulty in selling Wickham Lodge – it has suddenly become difficult to sell houses – so many in this town take <u>months</u> to sell.

Have a good holiday & forget all your troubles.

I had three weeks alone when my parents were at Marian's (& did some work – also finished the spring-cleaning) – & now they are back, also M. & Eryl (my brother in law is in America for a few months) – a full house – but I mean to get to the end of my jobs which have been interrupted by so many things. I still have four scripts to write (lovely work – <u>no</u> drudgery – just pure pleasure & thank goodness it is well paid – nothing else I do these days seems to pay anything like as well.)

I'm not having a holiday this year – frankly I don't mind – I bought a television set for my mother (fulfilling a rash promise made when I was doing films!) & find to my surprise that I am more than interested in it. The Proms tele-broadcast was a <u>revelation</u> – excellently done – it not only analysed the orchestration but the <u>very texture</u> of the music – cameras followed the <u>counterpoint</u>. Musicians have <u>always</u> been able to do that – but just think what it is going to do for <u>audiences</u> of the future. Audiences will hear all the things composers long for them to hear. All the inner voices!

Love & all congratulations once again – Grace

[. . .]

Williams travelled to London to attend the concert on 14 October 1953 at the Royal Festival Hall, at which Maconchy received her prize for her overture Proud Thames, *which received its first performance. A few days later, in the same hall, Maconchy and Nicola joined Williams at the performance of her* Merry Minstrel *at an Ernest Read Children's Concert.*

117) 18 October 1953

Wickham Lodge
Sunday, Oct 18th 53

Dearest Grace – It was lovely coming up yesterday – Niccy enjoyed the concert tremendously (– she has talked a lot about the different instruments: the double-bass was her favourite! & after that the drums –) it was a <u>marvellous</u> idea of yours that I should bring her. I wish we could have stayed on & lunched together: there was lots more to talk about.

I was immensely impressed by Merry Minstrel – I think it is absolutely first-rate: has <u>good</u> (as well as very attractive) music in it, & comes off perfectly in every way. My foremost feeling as I listened was sheer enjoyment (– as a grown-up, at the same time as feeling how much the children were enjoying it as children.) You've achieved a wonderful balance between story, music, & a lesson in the orchestra: (which never obtrudes, – the lesson I mean) It should be done far & wide – [. . .]

We've been listening to Gotterdammerung most of the evening[9] – How marvellous it is. (B. & I think that very late in life we are becoming Wagner-fans, – it's been coming on gradually lately. It was lovely hearing Flagstad in the Liebestod[10] . . .)

I'm going to have a shot at making Proud Thames a little longer – but only a little, I think [. . .].

I've had some nice letters. I haven't heard from Ina yet – but expect I shall. I don't think I told you that Mr Howgill (the new Controller of Music)[11] went out of his way to be friendly on Wed. & muttered about my not having to bother about the Panel – which I think means they have taken me off the Panel: that would be very nice. I'm getting de Nevers to make sure.

I must go to bed – Well, it is nice that you & I made our first appearance at the Festival Hall in the same week. Here's to many more for both of us!

[. . .] Best love always
Betty

Ten months later, on 30 July 1954, Williams wrote following Maconchy's next major performance and broadcast: the Bassoon Concertino (1952) was performed in a Promenade Concert at the Royal Albert Hall, London, by Gwydion Brooke with the BBC Symphony Orchestra, conducted by Malcolm Sargent.

118) 31 July 1954

<u>Barry</u>
July 31st 1954

Dearest Betty

I like the concertino much better last night than at first hearing – when I'm alone with my radio I can concentrate! (& can't at concerts any more – not in the same way).

The slow movement is for me far better than the first – & the end of the slow as lovely as anything you've written. Melodically it's a very fine movement – harmonically too (but perhaps a bit too static? –). The last movement is fine – just one place where I feel a cut might help – before the cadenza & there is a place where I felt the mvt. was going to end – then it began repeating itself (losing a bit

---

9 *Götterdämmerung*, the fourth and final opera in Wagner's cycle, *Der Ring des Nibelungen*.
10 At the same concert at which Maconchy received her prize, soprano Kirsten Flagstad sang her farewell concert appearance, with the *Liebestod* from Wagner's *Tristan und Isolde*.
11 Richard Howgill took over as BBC Controller of Music in Autumn 1953.

of strength, I thought) & I thought – 'this is a long finish – surprising for Betty' – – then it didn't end – but went on leading to cadenza. Apart from that everything was splendid.

There were some lovely high notes from the bassoon! And quite unique to have so much lyrical music written for that instrument – no wonder Gwydion B. was grateful to you for writing it.

It must have been wonderful facing that young audience & hearing the applause. I think you've won over Sargent & I hope he'll now turn to your other scores – & do the Symphony – & perhaps he'll do the new Strings Symph.

All my congratulations & best wishes to you all for holidays.

Love Grace

P.S. The Welsh Youth Orch. has several raw recruits this year & I'm afraid they'll make my scherzo sound as though it were written by a madwoman![12] But bless them, they like it & go around whistling & humming it. It is marked allegro barbaro e segreto & I realize now that the 'barbaro' should be reserved for professionals! Their concert tour starts tonight, & I have to be brave & go to their second concert (in Cardiff) tomorrow. The rehearsals were very worthwhile – but hearing it in the middle of a concert performance in presence of an audience doesn't bear thinking about! G.

[. . .]

Williams's Seven Scenes for Young Listeners (1954) *was given its first performance on 9 August 1954 in a* Children's Hour *broadcast on the BBC Home Service, by the BBC Welsh Orchestra, conducted by Rae Jenkins.*

119) 11 August 1954

Shottesbrook, Boreham, Chelmsford
Boreham 286
August 11th 54

Dearest Grace

Your 'seven scenes' are lovely! I listened with Anna & Nicola on Monday & we all enjoyed them very much. They are full of vitality & rhythm & incident & all the things that are right for children's music, & good in their own right, (apart from children) too. [. . .] N. took me to task for looking 'severe' while your pieces were played! I think she thought such happy music should produce a happy expression – I was evidently fiercely concentrating! [. . .]

Many thanks for your letter about the Bassoon Concertino (– & your suggestions re-last Mvt. . . [. . .] It was a v. good performance. Gwydion is marvellous – & does what one wants musically without having to be told, apart from his actual

---

12 The Welsh Youth Orchestra played the Scherzo from Williams's *Symphonic Impressions* (1943).

playing which seems to me very remarkable – especially the high notes. Sargent took lots of trouble and was in a very good frame of mind & liked the work; & there was plenty of time at the rehearsals & the orchestra seemed to like it, too. So altogether it was a good evening. I had a new frock! Silvery-grey-blue – & felt nice in it.
[. . .]
I heard yesterday that the B.B.C. – I.C.A are going to do my new Symphony for Double Stn Orch. on Nov. 30th, which is good news.[13]

Must stop – it's late. [. . .]

Forgive such a stupid letter. When do you go to Scotland? Very best love Betty.

I've had a very good press. All good (except a nasty piece in the Daily Mail!) & some long & intelligent ones.

A few months later, on 1 November 1954, Maconchy attended the first Macnaghten Concert of the season in the Great Drawing Room of the Arts Council in London, with her String Quartet no. 4, played by the Macnaghten Quartet, and two of Williams's songs: 'Flight' (Laurence Whistler) (1949, rev. 1953) and the first performance of 'To Death' (Caroline Southey) (1953), sung by tenor Wilfred Brown, accompanied by Eiluned Davies.

120) 6 November 1954

Shottesbrook, Boreham, Chelmsford
November 6th 54

Dearest Grace,

[. . .]

I'd hoped very much to see you on Monday at Anne's 1st concert – & I wish you'd heard the very good performance (& very enthusiastic reception) of your 2 songs. I thought the Caroline Southey setting lovely – a beautiful sustained line, very dignified & just right for the words – a very fine song. Flight is a splendid song too – very effective & it made a fine impression – though I didn't like it quite so much musically – as the other, which made a very deep impression. I expect you saw the nice notice in Tuesday's Times? I believe it was Howes[14] – I didn't see him – & I think he arrived after they'd played my quartet: which they really played very well & with real understanding – which goes a long way to a really good performance! (Eric Blom[15] was there – so there should be a notice tomorrow)
[. . .][16]

---

13 Maconchy's Symphony for double string orchestra (1952–3) was first performed (and broadcast on the BBC Third Programme) at the BBC–ICA concert on 30 November 1954, by the Royal Philharmonic Orchestra, conducted by Walter Goehr.
14 Frank Howes was chief music critic of the *Times*.
15 Music critic for the *Observer*.
16 The end of this letter is missing.

Part III. Letters 94–146 (November 1949–December 1959)

The next surviving letter dates from several months later. On 13 February, Williams gave a talk introducing a series of Third Programme broadcasts of the six Maconchy quartets to date. The next day, her Three Nocturnes *for two pianos (1953) received their first broadcast on the Third, performed by Joan and Valerie Trimble, and on 15 February, the quartet series was launched with Maconchy's First String Quartet (1933), performed by the Allegri String Quartet.*

121) 16 February 1955

Shottesbrook, Boreham, Chelmsford
Wednesday morning

Dearest Grace,

Immense excitement at 7.15 a.m. this morning when Billy brought up (he always gets up first) a parcel from <u>Fortnum & Mason</u>: – undoing it quickly dispelled the headache, backache, cough, pain & feeling sick which Nicola had woken up with – (this unfortunately happens rather often on school-mornings & I'm always having to decide what's real & what a wishful-thinking of the imagination) & opening the little yellow-pot of honey for breakfast completed the cure. I am as pleased as she is with them – the honey is ambrosial & the whole thing the most attractive ensemble I've ever seen. The six little pots (B. says they are the 6 quartets) will be <u>heavenly</u> for spring flowers: we chose the yellow first for aconites and snowdrops, as we have a few out now & more coming, & I shall have them always in use (when we have enjoyed the different tastes of the honey –) as one can always find enough flowers for such darling little pots. My dear, it was sweet of you to send it – & I can't tell you how delighted we all were! It joined on, as it were, to the excellent perf. of No. 1 (nearly as fresh and clear as the 1st pot of honey!) last night, which sent us to bed feeling very happy.

I hope you've got back safely & not worn out? & that you feel well-satisfied (as everyone else does) with the success of your labours? Especially I hope the Nocturnes went very well with the Trimbles? I was again in the train & couldn't hear them – sickening: I've never heard them. [. . .]

[. . .]

Anne rang up last night – she'll be letting you know about the Variations.[17] Alan R. had worked out a scheme – rather ingeniously I thought – I'm not quite sure of it all – but you and I are as below –

---

17 Friends of Vaughan Williams were planning a collective work, *Diabelleries*, variations on 'Where's my little basket gone?', for performance in a Macnaghten Concert on 16 May 1955. According to the scheme outlined here, Variation 4 was to be by Gerald Finzi, and Variation 7 by Patrick Hadley or Alan Rawsthorne. In the end, the movements were by Vaughan Williams, Ferguson, Bush, Rawsthorne, Lutyens, Maconchy, Finzi, Williams, and Jacob; see British Library Add. ms. 59809.

Theme recollected by Uncle R.
Variations   i Moderato – Howard Ferguson
                ii Allegro molto – Alan Bush
                iii Adagio – Betty Lutyens
                iv Pastoral – Finzi
                v Passionate – Me
                vi Grazioso – Grace
                vii Paddy Hadley or Alan R – –
                vii Intense – Dorrie
Finale   Gordon Jacob.
Quite a good scheme I think – & it ought to be rather fun. [. . .]

I like the sound of the idea of your new work very much – the improvisation over the foundation tune – I can't remember your Welsh word? It sounds a most promising form – & new as an instrumental one.[18]

I mustn't go on – – When is your next broadcast?

Well – I can't begin to say how grateful I am for your excellent talk (& all the work & preparation that went into it.) I am very lucky to have this series – & supremely so in having had you to talk about the quartets. It has given just the best possible start to the thing – & I feel the good performance of No 1. last night (even though it is a youthful work & all that) is carrying on the good start you made

Very best love – hope we can meet again soon

Betty

One of the Allegri 4tet said 'Did you study at the Royal College at the same time as Dr Vaughan Williams?'!!

The series of Maconchy string quartet broadcasts on the Third Programme continued in February and March 1955,[19] but in the meantime Maconchy continued to work on her new quartet, No. 7.

122) 29 March 1955

                                    Shottesbrook, Boreham
                                      March 29th 55

Dearest Grace – Lovely to hear from you – & very nice of you to write with all the work you have in hand: (splendid that 3 of the 'Penillion' were done – good luck to the fourth. It's a beastly feeling to have time at one's heels, & I think very

---

[18] Williams was writing *Penillion* (1955) for the National Youth Orchestra of Wales to perform at the 1955 Edinburgh Festival. 'The title refers to the ancient Welsh practice of *penillion* singing, in which a traditional tune on the harp is repeated as an accompaniment to newly improvised counterpoints by the singer' (Malcolm Boyd, *Grace Williams, Composers of Wales*, vol. 4 (Cardiff: University of Wales Press, 1980), 38.

[19] No. 2 was performed by the Martin String Quartet on 24 February 1955, No. 3 by the MacGibbon String Quartet on 2 March, No. 4 by the New London Quartet on 7 March, No. 5 by the Aeolian Quartet on 14 March, and No. 6 by the MacGibbon String Quartet on 22 March.

inhibiting – & probably why nothing particular seems to come: – but by now I hope it has? I didn't realise it was a work on such a big scale . . .)

I'm very glad you've been pleased with the quartets as a whole – & in particular with 5 & 6. [. . .] I've had private L.P. records made by a man called Troutbeck – very good, I think – I haven't got them yet, as he got pneumonia in the middle (– but got someone else to record 5 & 6 on his apparatus) so I shall have them, which will be nice.[20] [. . .]

It has been a grand experience for me – the rehearsals have been tremendously interesting & I've enjoyed them very much. All the players have been really keen & co-operative & very nice to work with (also v. enthusiastic). No. 2 was a bad performance!

The comments I've had (though not a great many) have been v. nice. Uncle Ralph has been very enthusiastic, & taken such a lot of trouble about hearing them. There was a short but v. nice bit in the Listener after No 5. – I hope there may be more comments elsewhere. Apparently Scott Goddard[21] rang up to ask the MacGibbons how he could hear No. 6. (as he couldn't listen to the broadcast) as he had heard them all & 'been very much moved by them'. I only hope some more performances will follow!

I haven't had any spade work on-hand, so when not rehearsing the quartets (or having 'flu or having N. at home – she's had 2 spells with bad colds – one awful one for over a fortnight) I've been getting on with No 7. – & after more scrapping I think I've really got it. I've done 1st mvt – rather fierce & rather short – : light prestissimo Scherzo (I hope not too empty – for once I've tried to be effective & pretty easy to play: I'm tired of strained, nerve-racked players coping with my Scherzo's!), I've only done part of the slow movement – it's not exactly a reposeful one, (but there is to be a reposeful slow end to last mvt –) then a pizzicato mvt – a sort of 2nd Scherzo – then last – which I think should be pretty effective – I'm still at it. (5 mvts. in all). I think my finales are my worst mvts. on the whole. No. 1 is all right on its small scale – I loathe last mvt. of No 2. – no 3 hasn't got one. No 4 finale is the best, I think – No. 5 too difficult to bring off for a finale, I think – this is the first time it has come off. No 6. the last mvt. is the weakest & I don't much like it . . . Sorry for going on so about the 4tets, but I've been 'living in' them & trying to see them as a whole (I've learnt a lot I think) & it's very helpful to write to you about them as you know them as no-one else does now.

[. . .]

[. . .] Oh! The variation.[22] I end in G. major – plain G. major – quietly: having started 'con passione' (as ordered) in B major/minor. . .

Getting in to L'pool St.

Goodbye

Betty

---

20 The recordings of four of these BBC performances survive at the British Library Sound Archives: No. 1 (1CDR0015504 BD4 NSA), No. 3 (1CDR0015504 BD5 NSA), No. 5 (1CDR0016000 BD01 NSA), No. 6 (1CDR0016000 BD02 NSA).
21 Scott Goddard, chief music critic of the *News Chronicle*.
22 See Letter 121.

III.4 Letters 123–136 (February 1956–August 1958)

There are large gaps in the correspondence from this two-and-a-half-year period, one which saw the deaths of Williams's father, William Williams (20 June 1957) and of Ralph Vaughan Williams (26 August 1958).

As so often at this time, the two women regret lack of performances of their music, and the inadequate performances their music did receive. They also discuss contemporary music by young composers, publishers' terms, and the politics of music institutions such as the Composers' Guild of Great Britain and the ISCM.

During this period, Williams wrote her Second Symphony (1956, rev. 1976), commissioned by the Welsh Committee of the Arts Council of Great Britain and premiered at the Swansea Festival, as well as *Six Poems by Gerard Manley Hopkins* for contralto and string sextet (1958), commissioned by the Cheltenham Festival. Often down-hearted about the reception of her instrumental music, Maconchy worked on her one-act opera *The Sofa* (1956–7) and, although not discussed at this point in these letters, her second one-act opera *The Three Strangers* (1957–9) to her own libretto, after Thomas Hardy.

In a letter, written nearly a year after the previous surviving letter, Maconchy outlines the terms of contracts for pieces she had published with Alfred Lengnick & Co., comparing them to a contract she had had with Oxford University Press in the 1930s.

123) 4 February 1956

Shottesbrook, Boreham, Chelmsford
Boreham 286
February 4th 56

Dearest Grace

I've looked up my contracts with Lengnick (& discovered that I have by no means got copies of all of them! But they are all the same, I am sure) & <u>everything</u> seems to be divided equally, 50–50: Mechanical Fees, Hire Fees, and Performing Fees.

Bernard de N.[1] says he 'doesn't have a Hire Library' – & regards all works, whether printed or not, as published works. In some cases he has provided all the orchestral material – in fact always where a new work is concerned – in other cases, when I've already got the material, I've handed it over to him – : but either way the hire fee is divided 50–50.

I've been looking up an old Hire Library agreement with the O.U.P. (dated 1937 & now at an end) & their terms then seem much more generous to the composer – i.e. 'should the Composer provide the score & parts, proceeds from hire shall be divided 60% to the composer & 40% to the Publisher.' P.R.S.[2] fees divided 2 thirds to the composer & 1 3rd to the publisher.

'Royalties for the sale of gramophone records or other mechanical reproductions . . . 60% to the composer, 40% to the Publisher'

Now it all seems to be the other way! I do feel you'd be justified in asking for 50% Mechanical Fees, at least. And when you are providing them with 2 scores & all the material, I don't feel you are getting much in return. Of course with the O.U.P., I think you do get much more publicity than for instance, with Lengnick (where I feel one gets very little benefit indeed from handing over a work with all the orchestral material: I did this with de Nevers this autumn, with my Dialogue & Theme & Variations for str. orch. – but only on the condition that he prints my 1st & 2nd Quartets – which he is to do this year – –)

[. . .]

Daren't embark on a long letter – Nicola's school has been closed this week as half the staff have 'flu, the previous week she was at home with a cold! So I haven't had much consecutive time. I've finished the music (but not yet the score) of a Double Concerto for Oboe Bassoon & Strings for Gwydion Brooke & Evelyn Rothwell – but much too late to try for Cheltenham[3] this year!! Very best love B.

My unlucky Symph. for Double Str. Orch. was to have been done by Maurice Miles & R.P.O. in March – but the Concert has been cancelled! Aeolian are to do my No 5. at a Thursday Concert on March 15th.[4]

Have you seen there is an Internat. Contest for Women Composers (got up by the Nat. Council of Women of U.S.A.) for a choral work – a capella or with piano – not more than 6 mins. Closing date Sept. 1st [. . .]

Maconchy's Divertimento *for cello and piano (1941–3) was broadcast by Florence Hooton (cello) and Ross Pratt (piano) on the BBC Third Programme on 4 February 1956, prompting an immediate response from Williams. At this time, Williams was hard at work on her Second Symphony (1956, rev. 1976).*

---

1 Bernard de Nevers, director of Alfred Lengnick & Co.
2 The Performing Right Society, which collects and pays royalties to members when music in copyright is performed in public.
3 The annual Cheltenham Festival.
4 See Letter 125.

124) 6 February 1956

9, Old Village Road, Barry, Glamorgan
February 6th 1956

Dearest Betty,

Why is it that all these years have gone by – & no performances of the Divertimento? – which, as well as being finely written, is so <u>immediately attractive</u> that I'm sure every 'cellist in Britain would play it if copies were available. [...]

[...] It was most kind of you to write in such detail about contracts. I have written today to ask A.F.[5] to reconsider that clause. If 33 1/3% is their hard & fast rule I'll accept – but I have pointed out to him again that I have given him all the material he is likely to need – & transparencies make duplicating a much cheaper business. [...]
[...]

I heard from Dan Jones that Fricker & Searle[6] were bowled over by the look of Hoddinott's Symphony & consider him a genius.[7] [...] Dan's comment on what he calls the Hoddinottwins (have you heard it?) is that it is a nocturne in so far as Night must Fall if you stick your head in a basinful of glue & keep it there long enough. A callous comment, but saner than the comments of those who praise it. I was left guessing after the first hearing – but now that I've heard it several times I know it is nothing but a web of superimposed seconds – there are hardly any other intervals in it – each part moving lugubriously. If it is impressive it is so in a murky nightmarish way. But one never knows what will happen to a young composer. – I had always thought I. Hamilton[8] was no good at all – was sorry for him having so much played in his youth for I was sure he'd never stay the cause. And now his violin concerto has proved me wrong. It was written in memory of his father – has nothing remarkable in it as far as themes go – but the cumulative effect is poignant in rather the same way as the Berg – (yet not having the same musical worth of course – it's hard to express what I mean – but I hope you get a chance of hearing it if you didn't last week.)

The Malcolm Arnold Second Symphony I heard again last week – a most remarkable work – not a true symphony – but so spontaneously inspired & so original in treatment & of course tremendously effective – & all neurotic & very highly strung. His smaller works are often good for nothing but these two symphonies are for me <u>very</u> interesting.

Naturally I'm concentrating on symphonies at the moment – have at last got down to mine – just finished the sketch of the scherzo, & started the slow movement. I have been in despair over it – thought I was past it & ought to give up the commission – then I did get going on the scherzo – it's rather ugly – & it

---

5 Alan Frank of Oxford University Press.
6 Composers Peter Racine Fricker and Humphrey Searle.
7 Alun Hoddinott, Symphony no. 1, Op. 7 (1954–5).
8 Composer Iain Hamilton.

never possessed me as I used to get possessed by what I was writing & was this autumn when writing smaller things – I put in a lot of real plodding – it came spontaneously only in spurts – then a full stop for a while. Now I've finished the sketch I think it adds up quite logically & sounds alive even if it is a bit of an ugly duckling.

Anyway, thank heaven I have something to score – I can get on with that during blank moments. Which are bound to descend when I'm writing the rest. I know what I want for the finale – but still haven't a clue for the first movement.

[. . .]

Must go to bed. It's 11.30 now & will be midnight before I switch off the light.

[. . .]

Love Grace

[. . .]

As Maconchy travelled to London to attend the final rehearsal and performance of her Fifth String Quartet, broadcast on 15 March 1956 by the Aeolian Quartet in a BBC Thursday Concert on the Home Service,[9] she responded to a missing letter from Williams, written sometime after 1 March.

125) 15 March 1956

Shottesbrook.
March 15th 56

Dearest Grace,

I'm in the train going up to rehearse with the Aeolian 4tet (who play my No 5. Tonight – I hope you'll hear it & let me have a report – it's immensely helpful: I hope I don't rely too much on you!) [. . .]

However – it was lovely getting your letter. I wish I'd heard your 3rd Nocturne on that Sunday[10] – I hadn't spotted it in the Radio Times, alas!

I want <u>very much</u> to hear your Penillion (on Ap. 16th)[11] – & am very glad there will be a chance then – though I'm sorry if you preferred the Sinfonia Concertante, which is a lovely work. But I've been wanting very much to hear the Penillion.

I hope by now you've been able to get back to the Symphony? & that it is 'going on' well? You must have a great deal to do, with your parents not growing any younger. [. . .]

---

9 Forerunner to the prestigious Thursday Invitation Concerts of the 1960s, when William Glock was BBC Controller of Music.
10 Williams's 'Masque' from *Three Nocturnes* was broadcast on 1 March 1956 on the BBC Home Service, performed by Joyce Allen and Maisie Balch (pianos).
11 The date of the *Penillion* broadcast was in fact 19 April. See Letter 126.

We both feel so infuriated at Martin Cooper getting this Welsh boy to write about you for the Musical Times.[12] The only point of getting a Welshman would be if he really knew your music (& Arwel Hughes would have been a good choice, as he does) but this seems indefensible. When does it appear? it is maddening, though.

[. . .] Thank you for writing about the Duo[13] – I didn't know you hadn't heard it before. As you realised it wasn't a good performance – they had to get it up much too quickly (that was the B.B.C.'s fault) – so un-necessary, because they are good players & nice people & wanted to do it well, & enthusiastic – but they barely knew it – (thank goodness I had one rehearsal with them, the day before) & there was no inevitability or conviction about the perf. – apart from errors – they were out once or twice. (Yes Anne & Arnold[14] really understand it & play it v. well)

Friday now. The performance last night was pretty good – really that sounds grudging – when they'd worked very hard at it, & one must be grateful for a performance that isn't actually bad – – & as things go, this was good: but how one does long for a really good one!

The best performance I've had in many years was my Dialogue in November (the Str. Variations in Oct, v. good too.)[15] but the Dialogue is much easier & more straight forward of course – – All the same it shouldn't be so difficult to play my 4tets now, I feel. [. . .]

I'll send you my Duo – & Sho-heen-sho (an Irish folksong arrangement)
Best love always Betty

The following month, Maconchy responded to the Third Programme broadcast on Thursday, 19 April 1956, of Williams's orchestral work Penillion, *performed by the London Symphony Orchestra, conducted by Maurice Miles. The programme of Welsh works also included Daniel Jones's Symphony No. 4 'In Memoriam Dylan Thomas' (1954).*

126) 22 April 1956

Shottesbrook
Sunday April 22nd 56

Dearest Grace

I failed to ring you up (as I meant to after the broadcast on Thursday) & only now succeed in getting pen to paper . . . I'm so sorry. I loved the Penillion – I felt

---

12 Martin Cooper, editor of *The Musical Times*, had commissioned a feature on Williams: A. F. Leighton Thomas, 'Grace Williams', *Musical Times* 97 (May 1956), 240–3.
13 Maconchy's *Duo: Theme and Variations* for violin and cello was given its first broadcast on 1 March 1956 on the BBC Third Programme, performed by Jan Sedivka (violin) and Sela Trau (cello).
14 Anne Macnaghten (violin) and Arnold Ashby (cello).
15 The *Dialogue* for piano and orchestra (1940–41) received its first broadcast on the BBC Third Programme on 8 November 1955, performed by Robin Wood (piano) with the Royal Philharmonic Orchestra, conducted by Maurice Miles. The Theme and Variations for string orchestra (1942–3) was broadcast on the Third on 10 October 1955, performed by Kathleen Riddick and her string orchestra.

it was very much 'you', – & that it was an inspired idea to develop the traditional form in the way you did & that your treatment of it was completely successful. I can see, too (what you had told me) that it is necessarily a <u>limiting</u> form & that you couldn't stretch it any further than you have done. I think you got wonderful variety of treatment & feeling into it. The only thing that struck me as having been rather hampering in using the form was in tonality – that each piece stayed around one tonal centre more than it otherwise would with you. [. . .]

[. . .]

I was impressed by the Daniel Jones – I thought it was a very fine work – (& <u>ever so much</u> better in every way than No. 2 (or 3) which is the only other one I'd heard.) I must confess to places here & there where I was a little bored (– not enough variety I think), but apart from that I felt moved & interested by it.

I had a letter from Ina yesterday having just 'heard & liked' your Penillion. She's coming over for a few days in June – Kennedy Scott had fixed (definitely) to do a new motet of hers at an Oriana Concert – & now the wretched man has written to say it hasn't proved satisfactory – & he's not doing it after all: he's going to do a 'Hebridean Hymn' of hers – an old work – instead.[16] It is sickening & so disappointing for Ina – & it's so impossible for her to get things done.

[. . .] I <u>must</u> go to bed – B. went ages ago! Please forgive a late & stupid letter.
Always your loving
Betty.
[. . .]

Nearly a year later, as Maconchy approached her 50th birthday on 19 March 1957, Williams wrote immediately after a Third Programme broadcast on 10 March of Maconchy's Symphony for double string orchestra (1952–3), as well as Bernard Stevens's Ricercar and Arthur Bliss's Music for Strings, performed by the London Symphony Orchestra, conducted by Maurice Miles.

127) 10 March 1957

9, Old Village Road, Barry, Glamorgan
March 10th 1957

Dearest Betty,

I've just heard your Strings Symphony & feel convinced that it is your best orchestral work – it's worth growing older if one can write mature music of such quality – deep & vital – & serious in a way that is more <u>profoundly</u> serious than one's early work can ever be. (So take heart as you approach the 19th! How much worse it would be if you were a singer!) [. . .]

---

16 English organist and choral conductor Charles Kennedy Scott was founder of the Oriana Choir. Ina Boyle's recent motet *The spacious firmament on high* (1955) was replaced by one of her *Gaelic Hymns* (1923–4).

[. . .] You are right to feel dejected at lack of performances – & wrong, too, because the all important thing is that you have composed all these truly original & fine works & there must come a time (I'm sure it will come suddenly) when they will be recognized for what they are worth. So do go ahead with your opera – it is sad that you are dropping 'Life's a Dream'[17] – it seemed right for your music. 'The Sofa' sounds a very good idea but is it right for you? Perhaps it is – you must tell me more about it – is it lyrical – & serious – as well as amusing?

Sad about Cheltenham. Me too – but that was inevitable.[18] My Symph. came back the same day as my Songs for America[19] (The competition was won by a Lucie Vellére of Belgium who set Claudel's 'Air de Syrinx'.) The unsuccessful received a very nice & informative circular letter: 'many excellent compositions – from 184 contestants – from 32 countries'. & it ended 'we would appreciate further word of your publications or performances or any recordings of same'. The National Council of Women of the U.S.A. appears to be much more enterprising than our own women's guilds.

My symphony is to be done at the Swansea Festival in October by the Hallé & George Weldon.[20] The Festival Committee feared it would be hard to persuade them to do it – but G. W. saw the score & rang up to say he thought they could do it without much extra rehearsal (he was glad I'd bowed the strings – & marked in all harp & timp. changes & so on –) – he seemed to like the look of it. [. . .]

[. . .]

[. . .] I wish I could look forward to & be eager for performances – as I used to be; but something has happened to me. I now rather dread them & feel it would be so much less nerve-racking if there weren't any more & I could just retire. But, like you, I don't want to stop writing – & am longing for this symph. to be out of the way so that I can start something new – but NOT another symph. (& yet – I don't know – there have been moments when I've felt that if I started another one right now it would be much better than the one I've just finished!)

An awful thing has happened about Proms . . . I had a letter from Alan Frank[21] a few weeks ago to say that he was trying to get my Nursery Tunes Fantasia into this year's programmes. It made me feel really desperately sad . . . a first Prom. at my age – & that old work. I did manage to write to him & suggest that perhaps it was more suitable for the B.B.C. Light Music Festival – the Press would receive it more favourably there than at Proms. (where of course they wd. damn it without mercy) – & suggested the Sea Sketches instead (also published by them.)

---

17 In 1957, Maconchy prepared a synopsis for an opera, based on the Spanish playwright Pedro Calderón de la Barca's seventeenth-century drama of this title, but never took the idea any further.
18 Maconchy and Williams had both submitted works for that year's Cheltenham Festival, which were apparently not selected. At that time, Cheltenham was the leading festival for the presentation of new British orchestral works.
19 It is not clear which songs are referred to here. About the competition, see Letter 123.
20 See Letter 130.
21 Of Oxford University Press.

164   Part III. Letters 94–146 (November 1949–December 1959)

Then I swallowed my pride & saw Mansel Thomas – who got on to Maurice Johnstone,[22] who said the Fantasia was practically fixed . . . but they talked it over & M.J. agreed that Fantasia was not the best choice – & then remembered he'd heard my 'Penillion' & liked it. . . & promised to square Alan F. & put the 'Penillion' in instead. It's in O.U.P. Hire Library so I hope A.F. won't be too put out – but somehow I think he will be pretty furious. I've not heard a word officially so it's quite possible that between everything I've been dropped – & quite honestly I can't make myself care one way or the other. The thought of facing a Proms. audience makes me feel faint – so if nothing comes of it it will be quite a relief.[23] If it is to be done then I'll have to do something about 1st mvt –
Love Grace
[. . .]

The following month, on 22 May 1957, Maconchy's String Trio (1956) was given its first performance in a Third Programme broadcast by the London String Trio, along with chamber works by Reginald Smith Brindle, Ann Hamerton, Iain Hamilton, and Arnold Cooke's Nocturnes *for soprano, horn, and piano.*

128) 23 May 1957

9, Old Village Road, Barry

Dearest Betty,

It's a thrilling work! Heavenly slow movement – I almost feel it's your best! And last mvt. very exciting & attractive & full of vital music. The first mvt. is good Maconchy – but I wouldn't perhaps call it vintage M. as the rest certainly is.

It was such an experience listening to it. I'd been spring cleaning my room since 7 a.m. & was just finishing up washing paint around & cleaning the windows when the concert began & I'm afraid the early items didn't really steal my mind from the windows. But I did lend my ears to the Cooke songs which I thought were very good [. . .]

Then your Trio – for which I sat down to listen! – & suddenly felt physically relaxed – & mentally too – but clean – & hearing everything – it was such a joy to be able to love contemporary music again – had been feeling I'd got completely estranged after trying my best over the tintinnabulations of Boulez & co.[24] Must stop – because today I begin on my kitchen. [. . .]

Thank you so very much for the pleasure you gave me yesterday.
Love Grace
[. . .]

P.S. Maurice Johnstone says I'm to have first consideration for Proms. next year!

---

22 Then BBC Head of Music Programmes.
23 *Penillion* was not given at the 1957 Proms, but was instead performed in the 1958 Proms season.
24 Avant-garde composer Pierre Boulez.

129) 30 May 1957

Shottesbrook, Boreham
May 30th 57

Dearest Grace.

It was very nice of you to write, & even more so to like my Trio & I was really grateful for your letter. I hope you're right that there is some merit in the Trio – though I can't really see it – there are just a handful of things in it that I feel are worthwhile.

I've had such a revulsion against almost everything I've written. I'd decided before hearing it that the Trio wasn't much good – then when I heard it I almost came to like it – but I've gone back to the other opinion now! I don't think I shall write any more serious chamber music – nobody wants to play the large quantity I've written anyway! And what one goes through in writing it nearly kills one: & then if one doesn't like it oneself even in the end – well, it's surely better not to do it.

I've been going ahead with my frivolous opera – because I do still feel I must write something – & I think perhaps of its kind of music it's not bad – (though I expect it would all be considered 'vieux jeu' –) & I've enjoyed it so far: I think the story (mine!) is good – but, though it is fun doing it with Ursula V-W as librettist[25] – it is impossible to get her to write the kind of thing I really want. She has a nice flair for light verse & is most inclined to be co-operative – but there are too many words – not always telling & to the point – or good to sing – or in the enough variety of mood & so on. I think the only thing is to do a libretto oneself. I continue to search for a serious one. . .

I think your treatment over the Proms is monstrous. [. . .]

[. . .] Very best love & thanks B.

The next surviving letter is four months later, when Maconchy wrote after the first performance of Williams's Symphony No. 2, performed by the Hallé Orchestra, conducted by George Weldon, at the Swansea Festival on 8 October 1957, and broadcast on BBC Wales. Maconchy had difficulty picking up the transmission at her Essex home.

130) 10 October 1957

Shottesbrook, Boreham, Chelmsford
Boreham 286
October 10th 57

Dearest Grace –

I sat on the floor with my ear glued to the Radio – but with horribly little result. I just got a little here & there – several little bits of No 1 – nothing of No. 2. – one

---

25 Ursula Vaughan Williams was the librettist, adapting a play by Crébillon *fils*, for Maconchy's opera *The Sofa*.

or two bits of the Scherzo & only one passage of the Finale – with all the time a rising & falling background of sound like the waves breaking on the beach at Barry! (but almost no other interference.) What I did hear sounded really exciting – a most alive and thrilling sound, both orchestrally & musically – & I simply long to hear more. I heard principally brass of course, (beautifully written for –) upper register of strings sometimes – & surprisingly, harp! I do hope Arwel Hughes will be able to do it, so that it's broadcast on the Home Service? I feel sure he'll contrive to get all the extras needed. I am sure, despite the awful time you had at rehearsal & the lack of time, & no doubt deputies at the perf. – that it was a great success? but I wish you could have had an intelligent & co-operative conductor & more rehearsal & have proper justice done to it. Do you suppose George Weldon & Walter Goehr[26] are strong anti-feminists? (there is plenty of anti-feminism these days.) B. & I felt very indignant when we heard about your Sunday rehearsal. Blast the beastly man – it is sickening being at the mercy of conductors. – – [. . .] A. went off to Oxford this morning[27] – a lot of things to be got ready for her – & last night she & B. & I went to the Phil. Concert for Uncle Ralph & the party afterwards – wh. was great fun.[28] We got to bed at 2.30! [. . .] Very best love & hoping to see you B.

A month later, Maconchy congratulated Williams on a BBC commission for the Cheltenham Festival. Williams chose to write a song cycle, Six Poems by Gerard Manley Hopkins *for contralto and string sextet (1958), exploring works of a poet whom Maconchy had also set on a number of occasions. Meanwhile, Maconchy was working hard to finish her comic opera* The Sofa *(1956–7).*

131) 10 November 1957

Shottesbrook, Boreham, Chelmsford
November 10th 57

Dearest Grace

I am absolutely delighted to hear about the Cheltenham commission – that is lovely – something really nice, & richly deserved: & especially good that you have been asked to do exactly the thing you want to (that is when a commission really is worthwhile, & produces a good work.) I do hope you'll set Gerard Manley Hopkins – who I admire more & more, I think he is a wonderful poet. [. . .]
[. . .]
I was awfully sorry not to see you last week (& so sorry I haven't written sooner as of course I meant to!) – I'd looked forward so much to seeing you, & had promised myself to go – but then when I heard from the New Opera Group people

---

26 Walter Goehr had conducted the first performance of Maconchy's Symphony for double string orchestra. See Letter 119.
27 To begin her studies at St Hilda's College.
28 A Royal Philharmonic Society concert to celebrate Vaughan Williams's 85th birthday at the Royal Festival Hall, London.

that they were at the final point of deciding on their next season's programme and that Leon Lovett, their conductor [...] was going to Germany in a week – & could I send 'the Sofa' as soon as possible ... well, I just had to stick to it. I couldn't in fact get it finished in time – (I have now just got to the end, or within 1 minute of it!) so had to send it unfinished (with about 5 mins to go) & in a pencil-draft, not a very impressive way to send it! I now await the result – I don't think it's very likely they'll do it, really – but it would be great fun. I think a smallish & sophisticated University production would be the right thing for it.

I must say it has been enormous fun doing it & I think I've written myself in to the medium a bit in doing it. It is entirely frivolous – with a Polka & a Galop as well as a Waltz – all suggested by the Ball going on in an adjoining Ballroom – whence the Chorus come in in couples. I would like beyond anything to be able to show it to you, & go through it with you: but I feel it's a lot to ask you. [...] I want to revise it all now, in the light of the thing as a whole – & perhaps cut some of the early part – & I think it wants a short overture. I don't want to start scoring till I've got the music just so – if possible. For practical reasons I fear it ought to be scored for a v. small orchestra: I suppose single ww. 2 horns, 1 trpt, percussion, harp and strings, is all it's safe to count on. I should dearly like some brass, though! [...] I want very much to find the skeleton-story for a serious one now – that would perhaps make a partner for 'The Sofa'. It's a big undertaking isn't it? – even a short one like the Sofa, which is 45 mins (without an overture) – so a partner would need to be nearly twice as long.

[...]

My No 7. Quartet was to have been done (at last!) this month by the Aeolian – but was postponed (owing to 'higher planning'!) till the New Year sometime. They are to prerecord it on Dec 20th.

[...]

My love to your Mother, & lots to you, Betty.

After postponements stretching back several years, Maconchy's Seventh String Quartet finally received its first performance on 8 January 1958 in a Third Programme studio broadcast by the Aeolian Quartet (pre-recorded on 20 December 1957).

132) 10 January 1958

9, Old Village Road, Barry
January 10th 1957[29]

Dearest Betty,

Yes, No 7 is a fine quartet too, & I felt it was at its best in the two scherzos & the slow movement – particularly Scherzo No 1 [...]. Naturally since it was a first hearing I can't be too sure, but there seemed to me to be more new trends in

---

29 Williams dated the letter 10 January 1957, but meant 1958.

these movements than in the first & last, having a certain kinship with the String Trio – & the song 'Come away, Death'[30]. The last movement ended when I wasn't expecting it to – but, on reflection, I thought the end was convincing – but it did make a rather short last movement – & I rather expected a Finale after a 2nd scherzo to be more expansive – it began & developed so well – then – all too soon perhaps? – it was over. But that's my only query – except that I still – ponder about the pull of C major – is it your strength? – or is it a sort of powerful magnet you can't help returning to? – but you did resist it in mvts 2, 3 & 4 (by the way I'm calling Scherzo I mvt 2 – is that right? All that preceded it sounded as though it were a complete 1st mvt.)

I hope to hear tape recordings of No 7 & the String Trio when next I come to visit you – which I hope will be sometime in the spring. And I look forward to hearing 'The Sofa'. Any news from The New Opera Group? I do hope they'll do it. You'd never guess what I'm writing at the moment – : a piano piece for the left hand! Eiluned Davies has fractured her right arm & is asking Welsh composers to rally to her aid & help her prepare a Welsh broadcast of left-hand music. Well, it's the sort of request we can't refuse. Strangely enough, now I've got started on it, I'm amazed at the eloquence of my left-hand [. . .]. As soon as this piece is finished (it is, practically) I'm returning to my Gerard Manley Hopkins. I'm longing to get on with it. 'Peace' is nearly completed & I'm well away with 'No worst, there is none'. Did I tell you I want them sung by Helen Watts?[31] I hope they can get her because I hear her singing them as I compose. It's just the kind of voice for the poems – rather ascetic – but having warmth too –

In the end I felt absolutely sure that I wanted a string sextet to accompany (2 vlns, 2 vlas, 2 cellos). I think for most of the time the 1st cello will be above 2nd viola. It is a very sonorous ensemble – & it's questionable whether all the words will come through – but in that respect (at any rate for broadcasting purposes) a contralto is a better bet than a soprano (high soprano words are the most difficult for the microphone to pick up).

It was strange – I couldn't find any case for a wind instrument. – not even an oboe – the only possible one I felt was a Cor Anglais & in the end I decided I didn't want that either.

[. . .] Best love, & many thanks for the pretty handkerchief – – Grace

P.S. I've had two afternoons off this week – at sales! – at the two big shops in Cardiff. Highly successful – my reductions amount to over £8. At last I've found the curtain material I want – it's lovely (& was reduced by 7/= per yard). I also found a nice hat & blouse (combined reduction £3.17!) Am so rejuvenated by these two expeditions & feel as though I've had a holiday.

[. . .] P.S. What I've written about No 7 sounds awfully inadequate & can't in any way express the extremely satisfying experience I got from listening to it. It was a great joy to feel so alive & so inside music. I long to hear it again. G.

---

30 From *Four Shakespeare Songs* for voice and piano (1956, 1965).
31 Helen Watts, Welsh contralto.

133) 28 January 1958

Shottesbrook
January 28th 58

Dearest Grace

It was nice of you to write – & an answer is much overdue. You know that I value your opinion very much indeed, & rely on your criticisms – & I am really glad that you liked No. 7 – I have had such changes & revulsions of feeling about it, for so long. On the whole after hearing it, I think I am fairly pleased with it (& after all, glad I wrote it!) but there are certain things I'm not quite sure about yet. I feel, like you, that the last movement is a bit too short – (the main part, before the slow coda, which I feel is right –). I had thought that the 1st mvt. might be scrappy with the alternations of fast & slower tempo – but I now feel it is right. Watson Forbes[32] thought the slow movement (which he liked v. much) a little too long: & I've been wondering very much about this. Did you think this? Please tell me if so – which would encourage me to cut it a little. I've had some v. nice letters about it – (especially from Wellesz & Alan Rawsthorne, both of whose views I value.) & this week (not last) the Listener had a most startlingly handsome review of it – which was nice. . . [. . .]

[. . .]

I could do v. little work in the (now much prolonged!) Xmas vacation – but since term started I have been doing my vocal score, with proper piano arrangement, of 'The Sofa'. – now almost complete. I haven't embarked yet on the full-score in the hope of a promised performance – so that I can know just what to score it for! But perhaps that's too much to wish for – –

I'm very glad you have been getting on with the Hopkins poems. . . & I like the idea of a str. sextet & Helen Watts to sing them, very much . . . I hadn't heard that Eiluned had broken her arm – I'm so sorry. [. . .] We had a dance here for Anna just after Xmas – which was great fun & seemed to go very well. But it was an upheaval; we danced in both the drawing-room & dining-room, with the doors off, & a loudspeaker through to the drawing-room –

You really will let me know when you see a chance of coming to London, and to stay here, won't you? I'm looking forward to it. Much best love B.

I saw the 1st perf. of the Carmelites[33] – but found the music terribly dull.

134) 20 February 1958

9, Old Village Road, Barry
20.2.58

Dearest Betty,

I must send off a reply to your long letter without any more delay – have been racing to get a vocal copy of my songs off to Helen Watts for her

---

32 Watson Forbes, Scottish violist who played in the Aeolian Quartet.
33 Poulenc's opera *Dialogues of the Carmelites* (1957).

comments before I score them in earnest – no, I didn't feel that your slow movement was too long – only that the Final was perhaps too short. I think I felt that the slow mvt. needed more true understanding from the players – perhaps that was what made No. 7 feel that way. All slow mvts. are too long if they are not truly felt.

I was delighted to read the Listener notice & only hope it was read by all critics as well as by thousands of Listeners readers & I hope it will encourage the B.B.C. to give a repeat performance soon. I've been thinking about the difficulty of rehearsing intricate tempi: naturally, new works with rhythms not easy to read are bound to suffer at first performances; until the players have got them more or less by heart they are bound to be anxious about accuracy – & that is what detracts more than anything from true interpretation: half the mind being on guard all the time. This is particularly applicable to your works – & I think it's responsible for a lot of adverse criticism of the new Tippett symphony.[34] It was the rhythm (unusual & fine, I thought) that kept the orchestra outside the work for the main part. They brought off the slow mvt. because it was easier. (I didn't think the outer movements were successful in form – too much metamorphosis of material in 1st without true development – but I was very taken with slow & scherzo.)

There are of course several modern composers of exciting rhythm which are easy to read! Britten – Stravinsky – & Bartok in his orchestral works (& something too in his chamber works there are an awful lot of regular patterns) & so first performances of their works lead critics to believe that they have a 'surer touch – firmer mastery' & so on – which isn't necessarily true.

Oh dear – time is racing on & I must dash out to the shops – mean to post this on the way – so here is my news in a nutshell: My songs are: 1. Pied Beauty 2. Peace 3. Spring & Fall 4. No worst there is none 5. Hurrahing in Harvest 6. The Windover. There have been many problems – but fascinating ones. I had wanted to swap 2 & 5, but Helen wanted 2. transposed down & it made the key sequence awkward. [. . .]

The biggest problem was that I found I was writing more for Mezzo than Contralto – but was sure Helen W. had the right voice & couldn't think of any Mezzo to equal her.

[. . .] Best love – Grace

Five months later, Maconchy was prompted to write directly having heard the first performance of Williams's Six Poems by Gerard Manley Hopkins *for contralto and string sextet (1958). It was given on 14 July 1958 at the Cheltenham Festival, and as a Third Programme broadcast, by Helen Watts (contralto), the Allegri String Quartet, Cecil Aronowitz (viola) and Terence Weil (cello). Maconchy had attended a rehearsal the Saturday before.*

---

34 Tippett's Symphony No. 2 was given its first performance on 5 February 1958.

135) 14 July 1958

Shottesbrook, Boreham, Chelmsford
July 14th '58

Dearest Grace

The songs are lovely – it was lovely having got to know them already so that I could really hear & enjoy them properly, as I did very acutely. She sang them most beautifully, I thought – & the sextet were very good indeed [. . .] They are beautiful & suggestive settings of the very beautiful, but difficult, words. My favourites are No. 1 which is a very fine song – No 2 & No 3 which in their different ways are both most lovely, & No 5, a beauty too. The sonnet is the hardest to get hold of, I think & the early part doesn't, to me, make such a definite impression – but the last 3rd or so from the quiet part to the end I thought beautiful – (both last Sat. & now –)

[. . .]

The vocal line is lovely all the way. – I think this is the best thing you've done. I do hope you were pleased – ? I think you ought to be – very. It sounded from the applause as if you'd had a great success – & you do deserve it. I wish I could have been there – did you see Uncle Ralph?

Now on to the Prom![35] It will be lovely to see you there... [. . .]

[. . .] Must stop – many, many congratulations for a lovely work.

Betty.

[. . .]

136) 29 August 1958

Shottesbrook, Boreham, Chelmsford
August 29th '58

Dearest Grace

Isn't it a stunning blow that Uncle Ralph's dead?[36] One knew of course that it must come sometime – but now that it has happened it seems a fearful blow & loss, & I feel the world isn't, & won't be, quite the same place again.

It was wonderful for him to go like that – & thank goodness he didn't 'decline' & was working up to the end. Ursula rang me up on Tuesday morning early, before we were up, to say he'd died early that morning: & that he'd had a normal & very happy day on Monday – but had been restless & couldn't sleep on Monday night – so they got the doctor to come & he gave him an injection – & that he died while

---

35 Williams's *Penillion* was presented at the Proms – her first Prom performance – on 13 August 1958 by the London Symphony Orchestra, conducted by Basil Cameron.

36 Vaughan Williams died on 26 August 1958, the night before he was to supervise the recording of his Ninth Symphony.

the doctor was there, – (he said it was a 'coronary thrombosis') One wouldn't wish it otherwise for him, any how.

I wonder if you could send me back 'The Sofa' piano score next week? Norman Tucker[37] wanted me to send it to him 'at the end of August or thereabouts' – [. . .] I've never written about your Penillion – which, as you know, I thought was lovely – genuine and sincere & personal music, as well as being assured & skilful. Best love always B.

---

37 Norman Tucker was the managerial head at Sadler's Wells Opera.

III.5 Letters 137–146
   (January 1959–December 1959)

In 1959 Maconchy, who had been involved with the Composers' Guild of Great Britain for several years, became the organisation's chair-elect, and Williams was invited onto the committee. Maconchy's daughter Anna, met her future husband, Francis.

Maconchy was preparing her opera *The Sofa* (1956–7) for performance, while finishing work on the vocal score of her opera *The Three Strangers* (1957–9) and starting work on a third one-act opera *The Departure* (1960–61), to a libretto by Anne Ridler. Williams started thinking about what was to become to her one-act opera, *The Parlour*. She was also writing a series of vocal and choral works, such as *Songs of Sleep* for soprano, alto flute, and harp (1959) and *All Seasons shall be Sweet* for soprano, women's SSA chorus, and orchestra or piano (1959).

In the new year, Williams prepared to work on the libretto of an opera, based on de Maupassant's short story 'En famille'. Meanwhile Maconchy planned to attend the rehearsal and first performance of her A Winter's Tale *for soprano and string quartet (1949), which April Cantelo (soprano) and the Amici String Quartet were giving in the BBC Third Programme on 21 January 1959 (pre-recorded on 19 January).*

137) [Before 19] January 1959

Shottesbrook, Boreham, Chelmsford
Monday

Dearest Grace

It was <u>lovely</u> seeing you, and I do wish it could have been for a bit longer – I hope you found all well? [. . .] You are going to be very busy with your film[1] – but I think you'll enjoy doing it. I hope it goes swimmingly – & that then you'll be able to get to 'En famille'. I'm thrilled to think of you writing an opera, as I've

---

1 Unidentified. It is unlikely that this film project materialised, as Williams did not mention it in her response (see Letter 138) or in her diary.

174   Part III. Letters 94–146 (November 1949–December1959)

always wanted you to. I'd <u>love</u> to see the libretto, if you could spare it for a few days.

This morning a parcel came from Fortnum's with the most <u>glorious</u> pot of honey – really, Grace it is very naughty of you to send it to us – it's the most lovely present. [. . .]

Ina went off with B. this morning. I am having a catch-up with household washing, letters, Guild affairs, accounts for income-tax etc: tomorrow I spend at the Guild office – (with a working committee in the afternoon after a morning with Topsy Levan[2] –) & go to a rehearsal with the Amici & April Cantelo in the evening.

On Wednesday I want to get down to my opera,[3] if possible, in the light of all the tremendously helpful things you said. <u>I can't tell you</u> what a lot it meant to me to go through it with you – (or how much I've wanted to, for a long time!) I think now I can go back to it with a much clearer idea of what needs to be done to it, & a good chance of being able to do it properly.

. . . when I played 'The Three Strangers'[4] to Ina yesterday I realised that a good deal must be done to it – too; – small things that will clarify it – & 'point' the words more, & make them more telling (and audible): as well as a bigger change to the later chorus-part. Thank you very, very much for your help & advice – I long to be able to hear these two one-acters some day – but seriously doubt if I shall. I have this very uncomfortable feeling (very frustrating sometimes, though not always) that the Zeitgeist has left us behind – & that however good our music may be (& I'm pretty sure that it's better than a lot of what the Zeitgeist is so engrossed with now!) it will just be left to be decently buried.

One doesn't seem able to stop writing it, though: and I suppose to do that would be the worst of all! Do you keep on hard, anyhow: & I intend to, too, as long as I can. I'm greatly encouraged that you liked the music of the opera.

[. . .] I mustn't go on
Much best love always
Your loving Betty

138) 22 January 1959

9, Old Village Road, Barry
Jan. 22-'59 10.45 p.m.

Dearest Betty,

I was thrilled with 'A Winter Tale' & thought it far better in vocal line than what I remember of the score you played to Dorrie & me – at Dorrie's – one

---

2 Topsy Levan was an administrator, secretary to the Society for the Promotion of New Music and the Composers' Guild in the 1950s.
3 *The Sofa* (1956–7).
4 A draft of Maconchy's second one-act opera, *The Three Strangers* (1957–58).

afternoon ten+ years ago; I think then you hadn't finished it (for all the spring section seemed new to me tonight) & although I liked the music immensely I felt then that the voice part was too static – & repetitive – but tonight it was flexible & adventurous & really thrilling. The music of the accompaniment is full of deep intuitive feeling & great imagination. The only criticism I have is that I still felt the rhythm of some of the words-setting was not quite natural – strings rhythm rather than true vocal rhythm – but that was only in one or two places near the beginning. The words didn't come over too well on Medium wave (alas we still haven't got Third Programme officially on V.H.F. It's due at any moment; – we can get it via some other station but not clearly enough to risk tonight). It's always a risk with the overtones of a string quartet (or sextet as I know to my cost!). Nevertheless, the clear résumé given before the performance made everything perfectly clear. I'm not sure that I like the string music of the concluding bars – or was it their playing? – it sounded rather too much like the surface of joyousness & not inner joy. This is very badly expressed by me – but what I wanted was something fuller, richer. The fioratura writing came off magnificently: I'm so glad you had April to sing it; she is a fine artist, no one quite like her in this country.

[. . .]

[. . .] You ask what is happening to me: time slips away & I have less & less to show for it. I have put in some hours, lately, of very concentrated work & they have produced one S.S.A. & piano part-song (for University of Wales Press . . . Welsh words, for which I had to write a translation).[5] It took me about three weeks to complete it & the snag is that they insist on my selling out – for 10 guineas – which is all they can afford, I know.

Now the slowness continues as I struggle with a few songs for Soprano (April, I hope), Harp and Bass Flute (or perhaps it will have to be a Clarinet – I haven't decided yet.) They are commissioned by a Welsh doctor who is engaged to a young & promising Welsh harpist. She doesn't know about the commission – he wants to spring a surprise on her – when they've finished – which is rather a pity because I'd love to consult her now about several things in the harp writing. It's taking me ages to write them – it's not that the music doesn't come spontaneously at first but that, having written it down I subject it to microscopic scrutiny & have 2nd – 3rd – 4th thoughts – which isn't right for songs. They are Songs of Sleep, one of them is Beaumont & Fletcher's 'Come sleep, & with thy sweet deceiving. . .' [. . .]

I've also set 'Sweet & Low'! no companion poem for 'Come sleep – ' but I chanced to see it as I searched for words – & lo, the music came into my ears & I couldn't resist it. It is, I think, an unusual setting![6]

[. . .]

---

5 Williams's *Yr Eos* ('The Nightingale') for SSA chorus and piano was composed in December 1958.
6 Williams's *Songs of Sleep* (1959) for soprano, alto flute, and harp were settings of 'Come, sleep' (Beaumont and Fletcher); 'The cypress curtain of the night' (Campion); and 'Sweet and Low' (Tennyson).

The house runs away with far too much time & energy – but there's no way out – the more domestics we have (we now have Mrs Ball for two mornings, Mrs Newnham for one, & Mattie, who comes for an hour on Sat. & Mon. to light the fire) & I do see how Parkinson's Law operates: the more we have, the more I seem to be involved. How nice it would be to have a Robot!

Mother is fairly well, but physically frail in many ways (her way of walking reminds me more & more of Uncle Ralph, though she's not yet as bad as he was). Old age is very pathetic & I hope to goodness I'm spared it; I've seen too much of its loneliness these last few years: (friends of my parents who are left with no one to look after them). [. . .]

It is now past midnight & I must go to bed.

It was a lovely experience listening to A Winter's Tale – something to think back on & to be immensely grateful for

with love
Grace

139) 28 January 1959

Shottesbrook, Boreham, Chelmsford
Boreham 286
January 28th 59

Dearest Grace.

It was a blessing to get your letter about 'A Winter's Tale'! I'd felt awfully uncertain about it beforehand (in particular about the Allegro parts) & felt I still couldn't judge it after the pre-recording: April Cantelo was wonderful, but the Quartet simply didn't know it – & I was listening to details & for all the things that could go wrong (– they actually played it far better than I expected.)

Then I heard the broadcast, & a record I had had made – and an <u>excellent</u> tape-recording made by a neighbour of ours who has just got a tape-recorder, & have gradually come to like it a good deal. But I still thought it might be against my better judgment & your letter was an enormous support. I'm glad you didn't like the end – what you say about it is exactly right – outward show of joy, rather than inner joy – & is exactly what I felt, too. I have re-written it, & have something <u>much</u> simpler & I think a good deal more satisfying. [. . .] How lucky I was to have April C. – she was wonderful at rehearsal with the quartet, too – so patient & tactful & so on. I felt she sang it just as I should, if I was a singer! (one doesn't often feel that.) Her words <u>were</u> beautifully clear – as the recordings show – in the studio.

I am delighted that your Hopkins songs are to be done in March, I hope it will be a live performance & look forward very much to seeing you, if so.

– I am most interested to hear about the songs for soprano, harp & bass flute (rather limiting? Perhaps you can make it optionally a clarinet?) & hope to hear April sing them. I laughed about them having to be kept secret so as to be a surprise! But a bore for you. – I'm sorry you are suffering from 2nd, 3rd, & 4th thoughts – one gets too critical, I think, & it depends to depress one. I'm in the train, on the way to hear 'Riders to the Sea'[7] at Sadlers Wells – (I like it very much indeed) hence worse scribble than usual. [. . .]

Arnold Ashby played the variations on a theme from Job which I wrote last year for Uncle Ralph's birthday, at Friday's Macnaghten concert. His playing has come on <u>tremendously</u> – & he played them splendidly. I didn't know they would come up so well – they were very well 'received', too! I didn't like the final fugue myself. I thought it gloomy to end with & it sounded so difficult – (rather inevitably): so I've written another variation (not a fugue) instead, which (at the moment) I like much better – with a theme that turns back on itself like 'the house that Jack built'.

[. . .] Did I tell you I've said I'll stand as 'Chairman-elect' of the Guild?[8] To be chairman a year from now – wh. means going on to the working committee now. I rather regret having said 'yes' as I know it will take so much time! But can't go back on it now & I think it is useful work

I'm so glad your Mother is happy & keeping pretty well. I wish you weren't so inevitably tied – and tired, too, I'm afraid.

We are getting in to L'pool St. & I must stop!

Very best love & real thanks

B.

Maconchy wrote some weeks later, on 9 March 1959, after hearing a BBC Third Programme repeat broadcast of Williams's Six Poems by Gerard Manley Hopkins *for contralto and string sextet (1958).*

140) 10 March 1959

Shottesbrook, Boreham, Chelmsford
Tuesday morning, 10.3.59

Dearest Grace

The Hopkins songs were <u>lovely</u> last night – it is a beautiful work & lovely to hear it again. I could hear every word (I had them in front of me, which of course makes a big difference) & felt that your setting of them was always right – & always <u>added something</u> to them, – illuminated them: (which is surely what a song ought to do? & often doesn't.)

[. . .]

[. . .] I finished the music (only) of <u>The Three Strangers</u> yesterday – or rather I got through to the end – I expect I shall have to re-write lots of it. It <u>has</u> been fun to do. I am to go & play it to Norman Tucker at S. Wells[9] about the end of April – but

---

7 Vaughan Williams's one-act opera, *Riders to the Sea* (1936).
8 Composers' Guild of Great Britain.
9 Sadler's Wells.

I don't suppose anything will come of that. I just want to try that first. Then I think we ought to try one of the University Opera clubs for it and/or the Sofa. The New Opera Co. are still keen to do it whenever they can – but I greatly doubt their survival, when they aren't in a position to put on any new productions – –

[. . .]

I mustn't go on – I wish I could see you. Very best love always B.

Would it be vandalism to extract one or two of the Hopkins songs, as separate songs with piano accompt? I feel that such a really beautiful song as 'Peace' ought to be heard <u>often</u> – much more often than it could ever be with str. 6tet.

Three months later, Williams wrote without delay to respond to the first performance of Maconchy's Concerto for oboe, bassoon, and string orchestra (1955–6) on 8 June 1959, broadcast on the BBC Third Programme by Evelyn Rothwell (oboe), Archie Camden (bassoon) and the Welbeck String Orchestra, conducted by Maurice Miles. Meanwhile, Williams had the opportunity for an opera commission from the Welsh Committee of the Arts Council as well as a commission from BBC Wales for a choral work.

141) 8 June 1959

9 Old Village Road, Barry
June 8th 1959

Dearest Betty,

I have just listened to the concerto & loved most of it: the slow movement was quite perfect, lovely music & all unfolding with great imagination & creativeness – and the whole movement having complete unity.

The finale was fine too, and if I hadn't been so bowled over by the slow mvt. I'd have been able to listen to it with complete concentration: as it was, the second movement held me enthralled long after it was over. Unfortunately, at first hearing, I was disappointed with the first movement. It began marvellously well & I did so want it to go on in that vein for much longer – for me it fell back into meditation far too soon & seemed to get static. Perhaps the performance didn't have enough grip? . . .

Yet the opening was so well played; (like manna after the poor Hamerton!)[10] and the vivace conversation between bassoon & oboe most exciting: they should have spread their wings – but not flown away.

But it is impertinent to judge like this after only one hearing.

Please forgive me if I am quite wrong – as indeed, I hope I am.

It is ages since we wrote to each other & I keep wondering how your operas[11] are faring. Is there any chance of performances? [. . .]

10 Other works on the programme included Ann Hamerton, *The Persian Flute* for contralto, flute, and string orchestra.
11 Maconchy's *The Sofa* and *The Three Strangers*.

I feel rather sad at the moment: at last I have a chance to write an opera – a one-act opera – and I think I'll have to turn it down. There isn't time – & I feel past it. The offer of a commission comes from the Welsh Committee of the Arts Council – with opportunity for performance by the Welsh National Opera. It was Daniel Jones who put the idea into their heads – he wanted to write an opera, & for some reason unknown to me included me in the proposition he put to them: 2 one act-operas, one by him & one by me. I have told them I feel I can't do it but they've said there's plenty of time to make up my mind it has first to be approved by the central committee . . . but unless I feel quite sure I can tackle it I can't bring myself to take public money. It's awful to have to confess that I wish I hadn't been offered this commission

Meanwhile I'm working at another choral suite for S.S.A. & strings (with perhaps a harp & one or two woodwind) This is a Welsh B.B.C. commission: it has to be finished by August 31st. I've been terribly slow getting started but at last it's on its way: & I've just found a poem (or rather, part of a poem) to start off with: Coleridge's Frost at Midnight – beginning with 'Dear Babe, that sleepest cradled by my side', & I'll take the title of the Suite, 'All Seasons Sweet' from the final stanza 'Therefore all seasons shall be sweet to thee'. I've already set 'When icicles hang by the wall' (during last week's lovely weather – but an owl in the gardens opposite was most helpful – round about midnight each night.)

I've also done 'I know a bank' – & got started on a long stanza for a winter from James Thomson's 'Seasons' It's difficult to find summer poems – all the heavenly poetry in Midsummer Night's Dream – but where else? One finds any amount of references to summer – often as a contrast to the poet's unhappiness [–] but it's like looking for a needle in a haystack to find a poem purely in praise of summer. If you have any suggestions I'll be most grateful for them.

When this is over I think I'm going to be asked to write a short orchestral work for the National Eisteddfod at Cardiff in August 1960.[12] So long as it's short I feel I can do it.

[. . .] I've been listening to the broadcasts of Reginald Smith Brindle's music and finding some of it (not all) rather enthralling. His guitar music in particular – & there was, I think, a chamber symphony which had real lyricism & wonderful clarity of sound. He spends part of his time now at Bangor University College – introducing B. Mus. students to serial technique – & earning money to support his Italian wife and children (who, I believe, are still in Italy.) Do write soon

With love to you all – Grace

P.S. If you feel equal to another one act opera what about 'The Lady of Shallott'?[13] Or, possibly, 'The Diary of Anne Frank' – could be adapted. Strangely enough this has an affinity with 'The L. of S.'. G.

---

12 No such work has been traced.
13 Tennyson's poem 'The Lady of Shallott' (1832).

142) 10 June 1959

Shottesbrook, Boreham, Chelmsford
June 10th 59

Dearest Grace

It was <u>lovely</u> to hear from you – & very good of you to write straight off about my Concerto: and thank you <u>very</u> much for sending your Shakespeare songs[14] – more about them anon – I'll write first about the Concerto, because my brain is seething with it. You are the <u>one</u> person who gives me criticism of my work which is really valuable, & I prize it enormously & place great reliance on it. And when your criticism coincides with my own doubts I know only too well that you are right – as in this case – (& it's not the first time!) First – I'm very glad you like the slow mvt. – I do feel that it 'grows' naturally & is a satisfying movement (to me, at any rate) – though what you say about it is far too good. I'd had some qualms about the last mvt. – but I <u>think</u> perhaps it's all right [. . .].

The first movement is the trouble. It didn't go smoothly when I wrote it & I scrapped & scrapped, with the result probably that I somehow lost its natural impetus & growth. As it stands I fear it has too many changes of mood (& tempo) & too much material not properly integrated. And playing it again to-day I felt that some of the material is rather second-rate – (though some of it I like.) I think when writing I felt that often I overwork my material – (getting a sort of intensity of feeling from it, by hammering away at it) & that I wanted to get away from that method a bit, & give freer rein to the imagination. But the result is not very happy!

I feel very undecided as to what to do about it – [. . .] a practical difficulty is that it is to be done at a Prom. on July 31st,[15] and whether to try & do it before then I really don't know! [. . .]

(Incidentally everyone seemed to like the Concerto very much – I've been the one with the doubts & reservations – ! it had a very nice notice in <u>The Times</u> yesterday – in which (isn't it typical) the only note of criticism is that 'the brooding slow mvt. was "static"!!['])

I feel dreadfully tempted to put a score (I have copies of the piano reduction – haven't had a full-score back yet – & have only a pencil one here. . .) into an envelope & send it to you, to see if you feel on seeing it, confirmed in your impressions – & think I ought to scrap it, or rewrite it instantly or wait till after the Prom. I am restrained by knowing how much too much you have to fill your time, already. [. . .]

Oh! dear, how difficult it is being a composer, isn't it? I wonder what you will decide about your commission for a one-act opera. My feeling is that if you feel

---

14 *Three Shakespearian Lyrics* for SSA chorus and piano (1959).
15 Maconchy's Concerto for oboe, bassoon, and string orchestra (1955–6) was given its first concert performance at a Promenade Concert on 31 July 1959, performed again by Evelyn Rothwell (oboe) and Archie Camden (bassoon).

a wish to write it you ought to at all costs. (I feel you might so much regret it, otherwise!) [...]

[...]

Thursday morning now. I've been having a go at your Three Shakespeare Lyrics – they are lovely – & sound as good as they look! I like all three very much & they make an excellent trio, with their well-contrasted ideas.

I do admire the most skilful way in which you give each of them something interesting to sing all the time (without ever being fussy) & they are beautiful without being too difficult. 'Sigh no more' seems to me to have a genuine madrigal-feeling – but up-to-date – not pastiche: Orpheus has lovely feeling – & 'Blow, blow' will make a fine sound – particularly the 'Heigh-ho the holly'-s: (difficult to achieve without men's voices –) The piano part is lovely to play – & lovely in sound, – & not too hard: (your piano accompts. always are fine)

[...]

The New Opera Co. performance of the Sofa at Sadlers Wells fell through (I felt sure it would! Though it was supposed to be definite – but one expects that in opera, I think –) They want to do it in a 'workshop production' in Nov or Dec[16] – but I think that would be without orchestra – so I don't feel committed to that if anything better offers. (I'd told them I would agree to a 'workshop production' with orchestra) though to see it on the stage even without orchestra would obviously be excellent experience which I need! I'm still at the stage of liking The Three Strangers a good deal – & hope sometime I'll be able to see it come to life . . . I'm just embarking (with Anne Ridler doing the words) on a very short tragic one – chiefly for a soprano – though not quite a solo-opera – to be less than ½ an hour. It's still in the very early stages – I'll tell you more when it's crystalising [sic] a bit.[17]

[. . .] Lots of very best love Betty My love to your Mother.

[. . .]

143) 14 June 1959

9 Old Village Road, Barry
June 14th 1959

Dearest Betty,

I think I've done rather a cruel thing – in criticizing a movement[18] fully scored & ready for performance – it is a dreadful undertaking revising, rescoring – scrapping band parts & having new ones copied – & you couldn't possibly do this before the Proms. performance.

---

16 See Letter 145.
17 *The Departure* (1960–61), a one-act opera to a libretto by Anne Ridler.
18 The first movement of Maconchy's Concerto for oboe, bassoon, and string orchestra; see Letters 141 and 142.

I didn't know it was being done at Proms. If I had I don't think I would have dared breathe a word of criticism. Basil Cameron is an irascible man – & it would be unwise to cross him so near the date of performance. <u>Later</u> – when you've heard it again – & heard more opinions – if you still feel the first movement needs revising you can do it then – in the autumn.

The piano score hasn't arrived – so I take it you are waiting to hear from me. I couldn't write before today because I've been dashing to Cardiff to act as outside assessor for Children's Hour auditions (lovely work – no preparation – & no revision when it's completed!) and now, a further complication: mother had another fall – last night as she was getting into bed – & is laid up today [. . .]

So, all in all, I wouldn't be able to do justice to the concerto if you sent it now – but later, after the Prom. (& by then I hope I'll have at least composed my choral suite)[19] it will be lovely to see it. Is the Prom. performance being broadcast? If so – could you let me have a piano score – however rough – just beforehand? – that would be ideal for me, to follow the score & hear it. I don't think I told you how much I loved the scoring for the solo instruments (& indeed the strings) particularly in the slow movement. As I was returning from Cardiff yesterday I suddenly remembered the heavenly high notes for the bassoon in the slow movt. – & lovely cadences.

[. . .]

If nothing else materialises with regard to 'The Sofa' you <u>must</u> let them do a workshop production whether it has orchestra or not. To hear it sung would be invaluable experience.

[. . .] With love Grace

[. . .]

Five months later, Maconchy wrote a semi-official letter inviting Williams to join the Council for the Composers' Guild of Great Britain. In a personal postscript, she hastily described upcoming performance opportunities.

144) [Before 22 November] 1959

The Composers' Guild of Great Britain
c/o Arts Council, 4 St James Square, London S.W.1

Dearest Grace.

Will you be willing to be nominated for the Council of the Guild? I proposed this, & Gerald Cockshott seconded, at the Executive Committee this afternoon – and it was unanimously supported. We all felt you should be on the Council. You would be proposed by the committee at the A.G.M.[20] – for endorsement by the membership.

---

19 Williams's *All Seasons Shall Be Sweet* for soprano, women's SSA chorus, and orchestra/piano.
20 Annual General Meeting.

As you know – there are no duties attached! You lend your name for the greater glory of the Guild (on the notepaper etc!) – and the minutes of the meetings are sent to you, & you are invited to Guild functions (such as parties for distinguished visiting composers), but there are no tiresome obligations – though ideas and suggestions are welcomed from members of the Council. You know all this already, I am sure. Please say yes!

Betty

How are you? & how is your Mother? Have you decided to accept the opera commission – and to adapt Ann Frank? Two nice things have happened to me in the last two days – The New Opera Co. are going to put on a single Sunday performance of The Sofa at Sadlers Wells (in a workshop production) on December 13th ... and Beecham is going to do my Nocturne at Festival Hall on Sunday November 22nd: (he has only taken that and a work by John Addison out of the twelve selected by the Guild – which is rather wretched – and awkward for me!)

145) 1 December 1959

Shottesbrook, Boreham, Chelmsford
Tuesday December 1st 59

Dearest Grace

Lovely to get your letter. It is grand that you can come to London – & how lovely that Schwarz is doing your Penillion at the Sunday Concert on Dec. 13th:[21] that is marvellous – the only fly being that I shan't be able to hear it (perhaps it will be repeated?) & how I shall miss having you at my dress rehearsal![22] I think I shall have to be all day at S. Wells on the Sunday – so don't see how I can hear Penillion at all – damn! I fear it is bound to be a bad performance of the Sofa – none of the soloists have any experience – & the hero is rather hopeless, I'm afraid: the 2 girls & the other man are better. The Chorus aren't nearly ready yet – & not as good as I hoped – nor is the conductor Keith Darlington – though a very nice lad. I shall hear the orchestra for the first time tomorrow – mostly Guildhall students – I gather they are very bad! The producer is good, though. So the prospect isn't bright: & I fear a bad performance & consequently bad notices may kill the poor Sofa straight off. But I can't withdraw it now – though I feel I shouldn't have let them do it in a 'workshop' production.

[...]

The Nocturne really had a pretty good performance – [...] Beecham gave me very little chance to have much say in the matter – kept me at a safe distance, & he is very deaf! I was able to say I wanted a slower tempo (which he acquiesced in) & not very much else. But he gave a good deal of time to it & took trouble, &

---

21 Rudolf Schwarz was then conductor of the BBC Symphony Orchestra.
22 The dress rehearsal and first performance of Maconchy's *The Sofa* was given at a New Opera Company workshop at Sadler's Wells Theatre, London, also on 13 December 1959.

conducted it as if he liked it. The audience were attentive (Mark Lubbock,[23] who was there, said 'amazingly attentive & concentrated listening') & rather enthusiastic – Beecham made me come and bow, & I had to come on a second time. He was very aloof all the time – : he's an amazing person – he has the orchestra in the hollow of his hand – & yet appears to do very little at rehearsal except let them play. The new Lady B.[24] seems terrified of him! I wish you'd been there.

[. . .]

I'm going to be on television tomorrow! For an interview in Weekly Magazine during 'Mainly for women'[25] apropos becoming chairman of the Guild. Rather alarming.

[. . .] Must go to bed – All best love always B

After Christmas 1959, Maconchy wrote in response to a missing letter from Williams about The Sofa.

146) 28 December 1959

Shottesbrook, Boreham, Chelmsford
December 28th 59

Dearest Grace

Very many thanks for your letter – it was lovely to get it: (I'd been looking forward very much to hearing from you about 'the Sofa') & for the exquisite little hanky you have sent me – & your card & good wishes to us all.

[. . .] When we returned home after the Sofa we had Anna's Francis (who was with her at Sadlers Wells) for a week, & had a 'young' dinner party for A., of 14 – then Christmas (8 for lunch, 13 for tea & 8 for supper) – now have my sister & her husband coming to stay (at any minute!) then a school-friend of N's & a supper-party for her age – & so on . . . Anyway, they are both well and happy . . . and I like a change of occupation & not having time to feel too flat.

I did feel pretty flat after the Sofa performance – & the previous week or two had been an absolute nightmare: the chorus were slow to get hold of it – and as soon as they began to improve a bit I heard the orchestra for the first time (or part of it – there were always less than half the players there together) & realised (no-one else did) that they were impossible. I did all I could to make the New Opera boys realise they couldn't put on something that was a travesty (feeling like Ethel Smyth!)[26] – and some pro. players were engaged – but it was all left to the last minute, & muddled in every kind of way . . . No good going into it all.

---

23 Mark Lubbock was a British conductor and composer of light music.
24 Shortly after the death of his second wife, the pianist Betty Humby, in 1959 Beecham married his former secretary, Shirley Hudson.
25 'Mainly for Women' was a strand of daytime television programming in the 1950s.
26 Ethel Smyth, English composer who was known for robust intervention during rehearsals of her works.

But of course apart from being at sixes & sevens a good deal of the time, & not being able to play p (except when they nearly all stopped! When it should have been f!) there was no assurance or conviction of <u>sparkle</u> in the playing – & that is what makes any new work get across to an audience, isn't it? more than anything . . . However – nothing can alter that now – but I fear it will make the difference between having & not having another performance ever!

[. . .] The soloists were <u>all</u> nice people – & I did enjoy some of the rehearsals & seeing the thing come alive & feeling that it <u>could</u> come off on the stage was thrilling – it was all a mixture of nightmare & thrill. But I fear all three of my one-acters are going to prove too difficult for University & similar opera-groups – who are the sort of people who might do them: the only alternative is Sadlers Wells proper, & I'm afraid they never will!

You didn't tell me your <u>final</u> decision about the opera for the Welsh Arts Council. I hope you were able to say 'yes' – & that you will have a chance to be able to get at it? (I feel sure they would let you have a longer time to do it in if you asked for it.) And did you decide in favour of Vernon Lee's story?[27] Which we thought sounded <u>splendid</u>.

Have you read 'Heirs & Rebels' – the letters between Uncle Ralph & Holst?[28] I'm finding them fascinating – those two <u>were</u> good for each other: I think Uncle Ralph badly lacked a critic-friend <u>of his own calibre</u> after Gussie died. Reading the letters made me wish we lived nearer to each other, & could meet & play & criticise & discuss as much as we liked. What a help & what fun it would be!

Mustn't write more –
Best love always
Betty
It WAS nice seeing you – brief glimpse though it was.

---

27 Vernon Lee's 'Dionea', in *Hauntings: Fantastic Stories* (London: Heinemann, 1890).
28 Ralph Vaughan Williams and Gustav Holst, *Heirs and Rebels: Letters Written to Each Other and Occasional Writings on Music* (Oxford: Oxford University Press, 1959).

Part IV
Letters 147–187 (August 1960–December 1965)

Figure PIV.1 Grace Williams and family, 1957, on the occasion of her father being granted Freedom of the Borough of Barry. Front row, L to R: Williams's sister Marian, her mother, her father, Williams, Williams's brother's wife Marjorie. Back row, L to R: Williams's brother Glyn, his sons, Marian's daughter Eryl, Marian's husband Glyn Evans.

IV.1 Letters 147–151
(August 1960–May 1961)

In this nine-month period, few letters survive from Williams. Maconchy's letters highlight the amount of time and energy she was spending as 'chairman' of the Composers' Guild of Great Britain. Both women's letters from this time also throw an interesting light on their responses to serialism and other avant-garde ways of creating music, including electronic music and 'chance-music'.

Williams spent much of her time and energy caring for her elderly mother, but when she could was working on her opera (eventually to be called *The Parlour*). Maconchy returned to writing instrumental music, including *Reflections* for oboe, clarinet, viola, and harp (1960–61), after work on her three operas.

Maconchy responded to a missing letter from Williams, after returning from Stratford, Ontario, where she had attended, on behalf of the Composers' Guild, the First International Composers' Conference, held in August 1960 during the annual Stratford Festival.

147) 29 August 1960

Shottesbrook, Boreham, Chelmsford
August 29th 60

Dearest Grace.

It was lovely to hear from you just before setting off for Canada – I've carried your letter about – to Canada & back – in the hope of answering it, but this is the first chance I've had! I'm now at the hairdresser's – preparatory to going to Greece! B. & I fly off on Thursday night & shall have a fortnight – won't it be heavenly [. . .] [Anna] & F[rancis] announced their engagement last month – but they won't be able to be married for a long time yet – as he has 2 more years at New College. They seem quite prepared to wait, though & are very happy – & B. & I like him very much [. . .] [Nicola] is growing up in every way; getting keen about playing the piano & has been writing some rather nice music! (though still rather at sea in writing it down)

[. . .]

Now I must tell you a bit about Canada which was a hectic time, with very numerous 'panel sessions', with papers, (good & indifferent) on a great variety of topics, in the mornings & afternoons, & concerts in the mornings, and the 3 Shakespeare Festival plays thrown in [. . .]. Iain Hamilton read a rather dogmatic paper on 'serial composition to-day' – but his piece was a good example of a 12-tone work & went well: a young S. American Aurelio de la Vega[1] read an even more dogmatic 12-tone paper – but a str. quartet of his was played at one of the sessions of tapes & I thought was really exciting & good – a real quartet with the excitement of a Bartók 4tet though arrived at by different methods. Krének[2] read a seemingly broader & less dogmatic paper on serialism – <u>but</u> when he played a new piano work of his own I thought that both in it and the accompanying programme note he had really gone over the borderline into madness – it was a work of 'total serialisation' & <u>everything</u> had gone (– rhythm, counterpoint, & of course harmony & melody & any sense of direction or form) & only cold calculation was left. I think everyone felt this! (though Iain H., for instance, was too guarded to say so)

The Russian work was an almost pre-Glinka tone-poem, & one or two others, including some of the Canadian works were rather backward-looking – & I must say none of them were at all interesting: – just one or two of the forward-looking ones (including one by Edgar Varèse[3] who is old now, but always has been interesting & uncompromising) seemed to me to be alive & to have genuine <u>musical</u> interest (as distinct from theoretical interest – there was plenty of that.)

There was quite a lot of electronic music & also of talk about it – & I was glad of the chance to hear it as one has heard so little here. But I found it depressing on the whole: I think no-one has gone near creating a work of art in it yet & only the two Italians, Berio (who was there) & Maderna,[4] seem to me to have begun to get any sort of form or discipline into it. . .

Well – it <u>is</u> a difficult time to be writing music. I feel that the heart has gone out of writing tonal music – & yet I'm sure strict 12-tone technique isn't the answer to the music of the future. I think perhaps it <u>has</u> done something in sweeping away tonality, or rather the accepted use of it: but what it has put in its place seems to me to be totally inadequate. I suppose someone with <u>real creative</u> genius will turn up soon & solve the problem almost without knowing it . . . I was very interested at your bringing up the question of improvisation in your letter to me: because that and 'chance-music' seem the exact opposite to the procedure of serialism, but presumably show that composers feel a sort of hunger for spontaneity. But why must they surrender it to the <u>performer</u>? It surely is the <u>composer's</u> birthright if anything is.

[. . .]

1 Cuban composer Aurelio de la Vega had settled in Los Angeles in 1959.
2 Viennese-born composer Ernst Krenek, who had lived in the USA since 1938.
3 Edgar Varèse, a French-born composer, had lived in the USA since 1915.
4 Luciano Berio and Bruno Maderna.

So glad you got your film finished & the recording went well.[5] I don't wonder you felt exhausted after it! Have you now been able to get on with your opera? I'm longing to hear more about it. Yes, do let's go to B.B.'s Midsummer Night at CG. together.[6]

I have actually got 2 commissions – (I, who never have any!) a nice one – from the C.B.S.O. under the Feeney Trust, for an orchestral work for the 1961–2 season[7] – more or less my own choice of what I do – (& a fee of £100): the other is an invitation (rather than a commission – as there is no fee) from William Glock to write a work for the next lot of Thursday Invitation Concerts.[8] (Very unexpected this – as I assumed he would invite only the young avant-garde –) It's fortunately to be short 12 to 15 mins – for March or April – & I rather dread it (I've said I'll do it) as I know I can't get much consecutive time till I stop being chairman of the C.G[9] in December – I've suggested doing something for ob. clar. harp & vla . . . So I'll be busy – as there is a good deal coming on in the Guild for the autumn.

I must stop, though I could go on for ages – Lots & lots of love – & do come & see us when you possibly can

Your loving Betty

Three months later, Maconchy wrote after having travelled again on behalf of the Composers' Guild, this time to the USSR, during which she had played a recording of Williams's Penillion *(1951) to Soviet musicians.*

148) 27 November 1960 – postcard

GERrard 7531
The Composer's Guild of Great Britain
5 Egmont House, 116 Shaftesbury Avenue, London W.1
Sunday November 27th 60

Dearest Grace – I'm home again after a wonderful time in the U.S.S.R. – I daren't begin to tell you about it (I will one day) but just must send a line to say what a success 'Penillion' had. We gave a 'recital' of about 7 recordings to a group of composers & critics (after presenting our collection of scores by 27 composers) – most were extracts, or 1 movement of a work – but we played 'Penillion' complete at the end – (A. Bush[10] & I didn't by any means agree on every thing but we did agree about the merits of your Penillion) and they really liked it, & many nice

---

5 Williams's score based on Welsh folk tunes for the British Transport Film, *A Letter for Wales* (1960), directed by Tony Thompson.
6 Benjamin Britten's opera, *A Midsummer Night's Dream*.
7 This was to be *Serenata concertante* for violin and orchestra (1962).
8 This was to be *Reflections* for oboe, clarinet, viola, and harp (1960–61). William Glock was the BBC Controller of Music.
9 Composers' Guild.
10 Composer Alan Bush accompanied Maconchy to the USSR.

things were said about it. Khachaturian and his wife (also a composer, & very nice)[11] both sent special messages to you to say how much they liked it . . . The friendliness and hospitality were overwhelming: we went to Leningrad for 2 days (& saw the Hermitage) & there was a radio concert in our honour – a banquet at the end & so on. Kabalevsky[12] met us & saw us off & was charming. I did a talk on British contemp. music for the Radio, with illustrations, lasting an hour – at ½ a day's notice! [. . .] All best love B.

On 5 January 1961, Maconchy's Piano Concerto (1928; rev. 1929–30) was broadcast on the BBC Third Programme, performed by Liza Fuchsova with the London Symphony Orchestra, conducted by Hugh Maguire.

149) 10 January 1961

9, Old Village Road, Barry
Jan. 10th 1961

Dearest Betty,

How wonderful to hear the Piano Concerto (I won't call it Concertino) again – & what memories it evoked – of those days at the College when I played the orchestral reduction on second piano & Prague . . . Oh dear, it is a long time ago, but the concerto hadn't aged at all: too many ideas in the 1st movement (but what spontaneous creative ideas they are!) perhaps, but the slow movement is quite perfect & very beautiful. This work had a profound & lasting effect on me when I was a student – & when I heard it last week I seemed to know it by heart. (The only thing I don't like now is the final chord of the finale. So right in 1928 – but now – it sounds left in mid-air)

[. . .]

I hope you all had a far better Christmas than we did. Alas, I got ill on Christmas Eve, of all unfortunate times, & if a wonderfully kind neighbour hadn't come to the rescue & cooked our duck along with her own bird I don't know what would have happened.

The doctor thought I had gastric 'flu but I think it was a sort of collapse which I'd been heading for all that week; Christmas preparations so soon after the day & night nursing was just too much. The outcome is that Mother has gone to Marian's – until the end of March!

[. . .] And now I'm alone; the peace & quiet is wonderful & the day twice as long. I keep looking at the clock, thinking it's noon, & find it's only half past ten. I feel a lot better – but am dieting very carefully & not taking any risks. Luckily I slept for hours & hours when I was laid up – & the pain across my shoulders has eased a lot so I'm finishing off letters & hoping to begin in real earnest on the

---

11 Soviet Armenian composer Aram Khachaturian and his wife Nina Makarova.
12 Soviet composer Dmitry Kabalevsky.

Section IV.1. Letters 147–151 (August 1960–May 1961)   193

final phase of the opera tomorrow. (This evening, perhaps) When it's too tiring to sit at the piano I'll begin a rough full score of what I've done. It will be a hermit's existence – locked front door – just what I want.

[. . .]

I also have a vocal score of 'Billy Budd'[13] which I've followed during the two recent broadcasts. How packed full of invention it is! I loved it when I saw it (twice) on the stage & it seemed simple & direct; but now I find it full of subtleties – all passing so swiftly as one listens – it would take an age to become really familiar with it. So long as works like this exist (& I include your own) one need not feel that the heart has gone out of tonality. And there's Shostakovich –.

I'm told that Britten himself is worried about the situation – but he needn't be. New developments must come – but needn't overthrow the old if one has true perspective. Yesterday I listened to a radio programme of bird-song records; there were some rare birds which sounded very like electronic music – & one which swooped down a sort of chromatic scale, chirping up thirds towards the end of the descent. Then there were two birds singing in unison – in a most complicated rhythm. I've always been tone deaf with regard to birds – but if I do concentrate – & ponder – well it's all very marvellous and mysterious. Must stop.

All best wishes for the new work – love Grace

[. . .]

150) 22 January 1961

Shottesbrook, Boreham, Chelmsford
January 22nd 1961

Dearest Grace

At last I can start a letter to you! I have such a lot to thank you for. It was LOVELY to get your letter about my old, old Concerto & I do appreciate it: & am more delighted than I can say that you still like it. (I was surprised to find I did, too! – a lot, – though with reservations.) It took me back to those early days at College, too, & to Prague, very vividly – (Liza Fuchsova who played it this time – I'd never met her before – said that poor Erwin Schulhoff who played it in Prague died in a concentration camp – Jirák, who conducted it, survived & is in Chicago – or possibly San Francisco, mainly teaching.) I agree in liking the slow movement best – & in thinking there are too many ideas in the 1st mvt [. . .]. Still it was nice to hear it again & to feel it is worthwhile: though with the inevitable accompanying thought '– if I wrote that when I was 20, what have I done with the time in between – ? & I'm 53 now.'

. . . I haven't thanked you yet for so nobly flying up to the A.G.M. of the Guild & it was lovely to see you, though so briefly: & for the nice, though quite

13 Benjamin Britten's opera *Billy Budd* (1951).

undeserved, things you said about my chairmanship: (thank goodness it has come to an end – though it was very interesting, I must say.) & for your charming Xmas hanky & good wishes. How awful your falling ill on Xmas Eve – I am so sorry. [. . .]
[. . .]

I have mercifully got a reprieve for my piece for the Thursday concert, till May 4th[14] [. . .] – – I also wrote to Anthony Lewis in Birmingham to ask if the 1962–3 season would suit them as well as the 61–2 season for my piece for them[15] – & that is all right: he wrote awfully nicely – : so I am frightfully lucky – I hate not to fulfil things up to time – but have really only been able to work in scraps this past year – and it is so very unsatisfactory – as you know. Also getting back to chamber-music and 'abstract' orchestral music after three years on the operas takes some time, I find – it's such a very different cup of tea.

I've still got a good deal of Guild work to do, particularly about the return visit of two Russian composers here & various other things [. . .]

I drove down to Aldeburgh about ten days ago & had lunch with Ben – & a long talk about the Guild & his reasons for distrusting any sort of 'Union' which could restrict the liberty of the composer or try to 'regulate' the process of composition in any way. I was able to convince him that the Guild does not do this nor ever will (or if it ever did begin to lean towards it, he would be justified in resigning & I should do the same –) & he has definitely said he'll join. I'm very pleased about this – it will make a real difference to the Guild – it really has been an awful handicap not having him. [. . .] He enquired very much for you straight away & wanted to know all that you were doing. He is writing a piece for cello & piano to play with Rostropovicz at the Aldeburgh Festival this summer[16] – & said he was having difficulty with it & having to write every bar about 15 times. He is also working at the big Requiem for the Coventry Festival[17] – (which is said to be going to be a huge work) We talked a good deal about serialism – & the whole situation that has arisen here. Rather surprisingly he likes Hans Keller[18] very much (who is the arch-priest of serialism here now, of course, & is apparently the big influence behind Glock. He seems to me to have set the line for all the younger critics, too – & they obediently toe it – –) Hans Keller does allow that Ben is the one composer who can write convincingly without being a serialist! – it's true – ; so that may partly account for it.

[. . .]

Much best love always your loving Betty – & love from Billy too.

14 The BBC commission, *Reflections* for oboe, clarinet, viola, and harp (1960–61), was in fact first performed at a Thursday Invitation Concert on 27 April 1961; see Letter 151.
15 The *Serenata concertante* for violin and orchestra (1962).
16 Britten's Sonata in C, Op. 65, for cello and piano, first performed by Mstislav Rostropovich (cello) and Britten (piano) at Aldeburgh, on 7 July 1961.
17 Britten's *War Requiem*, Op. 66, first performed at St Michael's Cathedral, Coventry, on 30 May 1962.
18 Hans Keller, an influential critic and writer about music, was then a BBC programme planner, working directly under William Glock.

Anna is enjoying her year's statistics course. She'll start in a job next September. She & Francis both flourish

Four months later, Maconchy wrote in response to a missing letter and postcard from Williams, both commenting on the first performance of Maconchy's Reflections *(1960–61) in a BBC Thursday Invitation Concert on 27 April 1961, played by members of the Melos Ensemble, including Peter Graeme (oboe), Gervase de Peyer (clarinet), Cecil Aronowitz (viola), and Osian Ellis (harp).*

151) 13 May 1961

Shottesbrook, Boreham, Chelmsford
May 13th 61

Dearest Grace –

It was so good of you to write – first a p.c. & then a letter, when you have so little time for anything. I must admit I was longing to hear from you – I am immensely glad you liked my Reflections – & in particular that you felt it was in some way different & 'exploring new ground' – I felt I was doing that when I was writing it – I worked very hard at it & scrapped & scrapped – & felt myself that, though the piece is on a very small scale, I had perhaps moved on a little (I don't feel so tied to tonality, for one thing.) I had felt I was in a rut a few years ago (already while writing 4tet No 7. & the string trio) – & by going right away from chamber music & doing the operas, hoped to come back to it fresh again. (I do think it is very stimulating and great fun to do something different – as opera is – haven't you felt this, too, while doing your opera?) It is different psychologically, too, to go on writing one's own kind of music in the teeth of the new school of thought, so to speak – isn't it? I feel it rather like the Roman Catholic Church waiting to catch one & enfold one to its bosom – and an obstinate refusal to give up my own freedom of choice & bow to the judgement of the Pope! But all the same, one doesn't remain un-affected by it in some ways – and that presumably is as it should be?

I felt while writing Reflections that I lacked a bass & I expect I should have made more use of the lower harp strings – I also felt the oboe stood out rather from the texture, & so found I couldn't give it as much to do as the other 3. The viola really has the lion's share (as usual!) [. . .]

[. . .]

I hope the Bournemouth S. O. did Penillion well?[19] I'm longing to hear it again – it is a good work. I missed a broadcast of your Sea Sketches by a few minutes the other day:[20] just had never looked at the R. Times – & then someone found it just too late. Maddening.

---

19 The Bournemouth Symphony Orchestra performed Williams's *Penillion* on 28 April 1961.
20 Williams's *Sea Sketches* was broadcast in the Basic Home Service on 14 April 1961, performed by the BBC Welsh Orchestra, conducted by Meredith Davies.

I'm delighted that you managed to finish the vocal score of your opera. I think when you consult your producer [. . .] you'll find you long to get on with the score & the whole thing will become very much alive – if only you can get the time, & feel able for it. I don't know how you manage. I am appalled by the idea of your taking a full-time lectureship[21] – & yet I realise what a struggle it is for you now. I wonder if after a bit Marian will be able to have your Mother again?[22] Which seems the one possibility of your getting a break.

– O, I feel the opera ought to be called En famille – every time. I think an adaptation should have its own title only if a really good one presents itself. [. . .]

[. . .]

I've been asked to go to Prague by Mr Dobias,[23] (President of the Czech Guild of Composers – who I met in Canada) – during the Spring Festival of Music – and am going for a week on May 25th! – it's 31 years since you & I were there together – & I'm afraid it is a very different place now.

[. . .]

I must not write more. Lots of best love – & my love to your mother please. I wish I could see you sometimes! Betty

---

21 Although Williams may have contemplated a full-time academic post at this time, she apparently did not take one on; Malcolm Boyd, *Grace Williams, Composers of Wales*, vol. 4 (Cardiff: University of Wales Press, 1980), 36–7.
22 Williams's sister Marian had looked after their 89-year-old mother from 6 January to 21 March 1961.
23 Czech composer Václav Dobiáš.

IV.2 Letters 152–162 (December 1961–February 1963)

During this period, several letters from Williams, whose mother died in June 1962, have not survived. Towards the end of the year, several events – such as performances of Britten's *War Requiem* (1961–2) and the première of Maconchy's opera *The Departure* (1961) – brought the friends together.

Maconchy continued to work on her *Serenata concertante* for violin and orchestra (1962) and started composing a Quintet for clarinet and strings (1963). She was frustrated by delays to a planned recording of her Fifth String Quartet (1948) and felt generally despondent about her work. Although no longer Chair of the Composers' Guild, she was still involved in activities such as serving on the BBC's Central Music Advisory Committee.

Both women hoped that Williams's opera to de Maupassant's story 'En famille' (eventually to be called *The Parlour*) would find a performance, and both were writing music for harpsichord. Williams started work on her Trumpet Concerto (1963), and performances of her music included the première of her *Processional* for orchestra (1963) at the Llandaff Festival.

On New Year's Eve 1961, Maconchy wrote when a snow-storm halted her usual activities.

152) 31 December 1961

Shottesbrook, Boreham, Chelmsford
Boreham 286
December 31st 1961

Dearest Grace

Thank you <u>very</u> much for your Christmas letter – and your perfectly lovely present of a record token for a 'family record'. This has evoked the greatest enthusiasm in the family – who greatly like your suggestion of George Malcolm playing the Chromatic Fantasy & Fugue & Italian Concerto.[1] [. . .]

---

1 The recording of harpsichordist and conductor George Malcolm that Williams recommended included J. S. Bach's *Chromatic Fantasy and Fugue*, BWV 903, and *Italian Concerto*, BWV 971

Now we are well snowed-up – I expect you are too? I do hope you can manage all right? [. . .]

We had a very pleasant Christmas – but without Anna, for the first time, as she was in Lincoln with Francis and his family. They are going to be married next summer, (Francis having squared the warden of the Theological College) – probably on 1st September – which is lovely, as they won't have very much longer to wait now. [. . .]

Nicola is getting more & more keen about music – & plays really rather nicely now – (much better than I ever expected she would.) She enjoys the G.C.E. music – but is taught Harmony from Kitson![2] – & has a flair for counterpoint. But I don't think she ought to think of going into the musical profession – I feel sure no-one ought to unless they are very outstanding indeed – don't you agree?

At last the recording of my No. 5 is coming off (sponsored by the British Council) & the Allegri are to record it this month[3] – –. It is now January 1st 1962 – a very happy & productive New Year to you. I hope we'll meet properly somehow this year – I often long to see you, but I know how impossible it is for you.

I'm going on slowly – (scrapping volumes) with my work for Birmingham:[4] & it is very nice to have that to do, & plenty of time for it. Did I tell you that Ricordi are publishing the children's cantata 'Christmas Morning'? (which I wrote for blessed relief while being chairman of the Guild.) [. . .]

I feel sure there will be a performance of En Famille before long – & am already greatly looking forward to it! I think it is marvellous that you have got it done – & feel sure it is absolutely first-rate . . . I see no prospect of performance of any of my three![5] What a lovely day-dream that some time we might have a double-bill of 'En Famille' & my short tragic one 'The Departure' – which would go together, I should think. Let's look forward to that one fine day.

Mustn't go on! The sun has just come out & it's like Switzerland outside the window. Our car is grounded in the garage – few trains running – telephone cut, but is back again [. . .] My love to [your mother] & lots to you always. Betty
[. . .]

Williams wrote a few weeks later, prompted by a BBC Third Programme broadcast on 16 January 1962 of Maconchy's Duo: Theme and Variations *for violin and cello, performed by Robert Masters (violin) and Muriel Taylor (cello).*

---

2 Charles Herbert Kitson, author of *Elementary Harmony*, 3 vols. (Oxford: Clarendon Press, 1920), had taught at the Royal College of Music when Maconchy was a student there.
3 Finally released in 1964 by the Allegri String Quartet, with the Walton String Quartet in A minor (ARGO mono RG329: stereo ZRG5329).
4 The *Serenata concertante* for violin and orchestra.
5 Maconchy's three one-act operas, *The Sofa* (1956–7), *The Three Strangers* (1957–8), and *The Departure* (1960–61).

153) 17 January 1962

9, Old Village Road, Barry, Glamorgan
January 1962

Dearest Betty,

It was grand to hear your Duo yesterday – & so well played, with real love & understanding of the music. I was glad to have a score to follow – & to read – & play – again afterwards. I love all the variations – but particularly 5, 7 (very beautiful) & 8. The only one which perhaps isn't quite as good in sound (i.e. on vln. & 'cello) as it is to read (or even played martellato on the piano with its dead accurate intonation) is 6. Yet it's a fine variation.

What a joy & relief to hear such music! I mark up my Radio Times dutifully each week but find less & less to interest me on the Third. The only good thing is that we are now having far more Britten. How can they say that tonality is dead when music like yours & Britten's & Shostakovich's – which is absolutely of our time & couldn't have been written at any other time – is here to prove that it still lives & has abundant fertility.

One is fascinated now & again by the experiment in Germany & Italy – by Berio last week[6] (but oh the monotony after a few minutes!) & they must be heard sometimes – but it's so unfair to let them monopolise the Thursday concerts.

Several young musicians I know have given up listening to the Thursday concerts – they say they are full of 'weirdy' stuff. One would only mind weirdy stuff if it gripped – but that's the snag – it doesn't.

It was lovely to have your letter & news. I can imagine how happy you'll be preparing for Anna's wedding & having her at home to help you plan. [. . .]

I've got to the age when I realize that in spite of having no religion myself (I can't go to church because I can't believe in an after life) I'm jolly glad all my forbears were religious – even those who were uneducated knew the New Testament by heart – & they had good standards & natural wisdom.

It's so good to hear that Nicola is turning more & more towards music. I don't think I do agree that one has to be very outstanding indeed to take it up professionally – unless of course you mean composing. If music is going to be N's first love then I think she ought to go ahead with it. There are all sorts of possibilities for a highly intelligent music specialist – musicology, script writing, translations (if her modern languages are good), criticism (!) – she might even find her way to Broadcasting House – I know she writes fluently – & if she loves music more than anything else she'll be far happier working at it than she would be in any other job . . . and she may suddenly develop into an exciting composer – you never know –.

[. . .]

---

6 The Thursday Invitation Concert broadcast on 11 January 1962 on the BBC Home Service, featured two pieces by Italian composer Luciano Berio: *Differences* for flute, clarinet, viola, cello, harp, and tape (1958–60) and *Circles* for voice, harp, and percussion (1960), setting words by e. e. cummings.

[. . .] I've just finished copying out my song for Croydon Schools Festival (a setting of a Homeric Hymn translated by Shelley)[7] [. . .] & now must begin at once to think of my Processional for Llandaff Festival.[8] It's to be played by the Liverpool Philharmonic – conductor Charles Groves.

I have not the slightest prospect of a performance of En Famille. Yes it wd be lovely if we could form a double bill. But . . . Best love Grace

[. . .]

154) 17 April 1962

Shottesbrook, Boreham, Chelmsford
April 17th 62

Dearest Grace

I have owed you a letter for so long that I hardly know where to begin! – but I think I'll begin by saying how tremendously warmed and pleased I was when you wrote (in January!) to say you'd enjoyed hearing my Duo & liked it still – – It had been recorded last Aug. or Sept. – & I hadn't heard a rehearsal: & liked the way they did it v. much, though I regretted not hearing them before the recording – it seems to induce players to be much freer & more <u>instinctive</u> in their playing when they have had the composer to encourage them to be – don't you agree? I always find that . . . But it was really nice of you to write – & oh! how one welcomes & needs encouragement.

Another thing I have been truly grateful for was what you wrote about Nicola: (ie that you 'don't think you do agree that one has to be very outstanding indeed to go into the profession' –) she is getting more & more keen about the piano, & I am astonished at how mature & musical her playing is – but she would not have the <u>toughness</u> for a concert-pianist I'm sure – even if she ever had the brilliant technique, which she probably won't achieve. [. . .]

Any prospects for <u>En Famille</u> yet? I <u>long</u> to hear it.

I've pretty well finished the music for my Birmingham work – but not started the full-score: I seem to work very slowly now, with endless discardings. I've turned it into a Serenata concertante for violin & orchestra – it began as something in the nature of a concerto grosso with a group of solo-instruments – but the solo violin got more & more important as I went along: now I have still to work some more concertante material for it into the 1st mvt. It has been v. nice to do, & I think I'll enjoy the score. [. . .]

I'm beginning to feel I might soon write another quartet – (mad as it seems when no-one plays the others.) [. . .]

I didn't tell you I had a crashing disappointment about the recording of my No 5 by the Allegri, – all fixed, and at the very end they hadn't got it up to scratch – or

---

7   Williams's *Hymn to the Earth* for unison voices and piano (1962).
8   Llandaff is a district in the north of Cardiff; the annual music Festival is held at Llandaff Cathedral.

the Walton which is to be the other side – & had to let the whole thing go. They have had too much work & hadn't allocated enough time – & it has to be a good performance! [. . .] I was much knocked down by that!⁹

How is your Mother? I'm afraid everything must continue to be frightfully difficult for you to manage. It would be most lovely to see you if ever there is a chance. You are marvellous in managing everything as you do. I won't ask for a letter, when you have no time at all – but would love one of those nice long postcards some time.

Best love always
Betty

*Two months later, Maconchy wrote in response to the news that Williams's mother had died on 4 June 1962, 'looking very beautiful and serene'.*¹⁰

155) 24 June 1962

Shottesbrook, Boreham, Chelmsford
June 24th 62

Dearest Grace

I am really sad to hear that your Mother is dead – I liked her so very much although I didn't know her well – & think of her & your father as one of the most likeable and worthwhile (if you know what I mean) couples I've ever known. You have been an absolutely marvellous daughter to both of them always: – it is terribly sad for the one who is left of a devoted couple when the first one dies – & you have made this last part of her life as happy as it could possibly have been. And she was splendid all the time, wasn't she? You will miss her terribly, of course – in every sort of way. You must be very tired after the long strain you've had for years – & I do hope as well as catching up on everything, (which I know you will do)! you will really give yourself a chance to build up physically. Do try to be kind & considerate to yourself for a bit! & relax & don't drive yourself too much. [. . .]

It was lovely to hear that you'd had such a good performance of your Processional – it must have been lovely hearing it in the Cathedral.¹¹ I wish I could have heard it too. We went to King Priam last week¹² – there are very good things about it – but very much the reverse, too. I feel he is writing the same kind of music, or rather, perhaps, keeping up the same kind of dramatic tension all the way through: there is no musical characterisation. There is also no substantial

---

9 The ARGO–British Council recording was eventually released in 1964. See Letter 152.
10 Williams, Diary, 4 June 1962.
11 Williams's *Processional* for orchestra (1962) was first performed on 18 June 1962 at Llandaff Cathedral during the Llandaff Festival by the Royal Liverpool Philharmonic Orchestra, conducted by Charles Groves.
12 Michael Tippett's opera *King Priam* at the Royal Opera House, Covent Garden, in London; see Letter 150.

lyrical element – all is declamation – & when two characters sing together (which they rarely do) it is just two people declaiming, not a real integrated ensemble And yet there is a lot that is worth-while. It was beautifully produced & fine to look at – (without that, it would have had no success at all, I think)
[. . .]

I've finished the music of my piece for the C.B.S.O. – which has turned into a Serenata Concertante for violin & orch. (I may have told you this) & done more than half the score. I've also made just a beginning on a Clarinet 5tet & a work for Harpsichord & wind ensemble[13] (which I suddenly felt I wanted to do, but must get hold of a harpsichord that I can play somewhere.) But I get brought up short very often by this awful feeling – what is the good of doing it? no-one wants to hear it & no-one is going to play it – it would be far better not to write at all. It is the lack of stimulation of performances that is worst I think: (aggravated by the numerous performances & commissions that a handful of serial composers get! – & not all good ones – & most of them writing too much, I suspect.) However it is very selfish of me to complain – I'm sorry. . .

Anna's wedding is on Sept 1st – & it should all be very nice, I think. [. . .] I am doing lots of dressmaking etc (which I enjoy) so have plenty to occupy me, which is a good thing.

Billy is well & happy – & how lucky I am to have him!

With best love always

Your loving Betty

Billy says he sends you his great sympathy with mine – we think of you a lot.

Maconchy wrote, replying to a missing letter from Williams, as soon as she could after Anna and Francis were married on 1 September 1962.

156) 30 September 1962

Shottesbrook, Boreham, Chelmsford
September 30th 62

Dearest Grace

It's a long time since I had your very nice letter – which I loved getting. I'm sorry not to have answered it much sooner, the difficulty being to get time to write a proper letter (I've had lots of short letters & notes to write, these get done!) It was so nice of you to write about the wedding – & to send Anna & Francis a telegram, which they loved getting. Yes – it was a lovely day here – wonderfully lucky – about the best Saturday of the summer, & it really was, I think, a very happy wedding. [. . .]

I have to go into Chelmsford hospital on Oct 14th for an operation next day – nothing bad – just getting hitched-up inside – but it means a fortnight in the hosp. & then going easy at home for another fortnight or so: a bore, but better to

---

13 The first work is Maconchy's Quintet for clarinet and strings (1962-3). No trace of the second work survives.

get it over. The only thing I have coming on at all is the recording of my No 5. by the Allegri on Nov 17th & 18th – I only hope they bring it off this time![14]

[. . .]

Sometime later on when N. has got a bit farther – I'd <u>love</u> you to have a session with her & see what you think about her & what she should do – – One thing has amused & pleased me: up till this summer her most sophisticated composition was a Mazurka – <u>very</u> much in the style of a simple Chopin mazurka! which she played at a school concert. Then she came with me to a concert of the I.S.C.M. festival at half term – & liked best Alexander Goehr's <u>Deluge</u>[15] (not a work I like very much) – & when her exams were over started on a setting of a D. H. Lawrence poem for sop. & alto in a <u>free atonal</u> style – very sensitive word setting (more so than the Deluge!) I hope she'll finish it – & if so, I'll show it to you.

[. . .]

I wonder what you & the Hallé principal trumpet have decided for you to write?[16] I'll be awfully interested to hear – – Am also v. interested that you have used harp & harpsichord in your Welsh song cycle.[17] What you say about harpsichord-writing (e.g. the shape of arpeggios so as to sustain the first note etc) is <u>fine</u> – I've never seen this said anywhere else – & certainly never thought of it. The work I'd just begun has come to nothing yet – as I've scrapped what I'd written! But still think I'd like to write for harpsichord & wind (& brass?) if some good ideas come. I haven't properly got to work yet since the long preparations for the wedding & holidays – & soon I must stop again. However it matters to no-one except myself if I never write another note! If I do get going again it will be on a clar. quintet, I think – (of which I've made a tentative beginning a little time ago.)

[. . .].

B. & I went to the Prinz von Homberg [sic] last week – interesting; but not really very satisfactory to me. We go to Lulu on Wed – if we can drive up as it's the day of the strike![18]

B. is going to Montreal for a couple of months in the spring – & we plan for me to join him there for a week or so in May & then go to U.S. together, to N.Y. (to the Löwenbachs)[19] & Washington (for a conference for B) Yale, & we hope California. Won't it be lovely? back about the end of June.

I really must STOP & go to bed – it will be lovely to see you before too long Much love
Your loving
Betty

---

14 See Letter 154.
15 Alexander Goehr's cantata *The Deluge* (1957–8).
16 Trumpeter Bram Gay, for whom Williams was to write her Trumpet Concerto (1962–3).
17 Williams's *Four Medieval Welsh Poems* for contralto, harp, and harpsichord (1962).
18 Hans Werner Henze's opera *Der Prinz von Homburg* (1958) at Sadler's Wells Theatre, London. Berg's opera *Lulu* (1935) was performed there in the same Hamburg State Opera season. There was a national train and rail strike on 3 October.
19 Critic Jan Lowenbach, whom Maconchy had known in Prague, and his wife. See Anna Beer, *Sounds and Sweet Airs: The Forgotten Women of Classical Music* (London: Oneworld, 2016), 312.

157) 25 October 1962

Private Ward
Chelmsford & Essex Hosp, London Rd, Chelmsford
October 25th 62

Dearest Grace

It was lovely to hear from you – & it will be even better to see you before too long . . . I was delighted with the nice <u>different</u> reading-matter – <u>House & Garden</u> which I've enjoyed a lot – (& will send on to Anna, who is of course immensely interested in everything to do with house and housefittings & studies everything she can) thank you <u>so</u> much for sending it to me: & I've had even more interest from the <u>Listener</u> article. I don't agree with everything he says – some of it I disagree with: But I <u>do</u> agree about the danger of seeing the 'end-product' all the time, – instead of making 'free decisions' on the way. I think this 'freedom of decision' is really the heart of the matter & that every real act of creation proceeds by it – & that often the 'decisions' take you somewhere quite unexpected – not where you meant to go: so that if you have started with an overall-plan you have to abandon it or modify it: but that through a mixture of conscious & unconscious processes the form shapes itself from the material. (That is the ideal – if the creative faculty goes on working all the time.) The alternative of a hard & fast prearranged formal scheme (however interesting & satisfying in itself) seems to me to inhibit the emergence of really creative ideas – as if the ideas that come up are the ones that fit neatly into the prearranged scheme but are somehow trammelled by it – born with pinioned wings & never soar. I find it frightfully hard to say exactly what I mean & this all sounds rather pompous – do you see what I'm getting at? I think the keeping of the end-product in view all the time has a lot to do with the overall effect of deadness & boredom of so many competent & well-organised works, (particularly serial ones) where the interest & symmetry of the formal scheme appears to be the composer's main concern & the <u>musical</u> interest of the material is low-quality (of course in words you can't define musical-interest or say what really makes one theme a good one & another just not. Obviously, to me, inspiration is at the back of it – but that is indefinable too)

Well – thank you for taking my mind off myself! I'm fearfully bored by being here & it hasn't alas, proved a rest-cure. The op. went very well & the unpleasantness from that was soon over – but since then not so good. [. . .]

[. . .] Did I tell you the New Opera Co. plan to do <u>The Departure</u>. For one Sunday perf. at Sadlers Wells on Dec. 16th but a <u>workshop</u> performance (with Catherine Wilson who was in the recent Albert Herring[20] & they say is v. good & can act as well as sing) <u>but</u> not a professional orchestra – the Guildhall student-orchestra suggested: but Alan Boustead (who is to conduct & is a good musician & sincere person) & I agree that it must not go ahead if they are entirely hopeless: I'm having to leave it to his decision. It's not at all an easy score and I really <u>mind</u> about this music. I probably ought to have said an unconditional 'No'!

[. . .] Best love always B.

---

20 Benjamin Britten's opera *Albert Herring* (1947).

158) 9 November 1962

> Shottesbrook, Boreham, Chelmsford
> Boreham 286
> Friday

Dearest Grace

Many thanks for a very nice letter – it was very good of you to write again . . . I've been home now for over a week – heaven to be at home again, – but not quite back to normal yet! as a few more things have cropped up & a few days ago I started having 'spasms of the bladder' (nearly as nasty as it sounds!) & had to put off going to London & the Allegri rehearsal yesterday. [. . .] Did I tell you (Yes! I did) that somehow money has been found by the New Opera Co. for a small pro. orch. for The Departure? [. . .] Haven't yet been able to go through the score with the conductor, producer or Catherine Wilson – I'm <u>delighted</u> to hear your good report of their Cenerentola.[21] In a way everything will depend on how well she gets it across as the whole dramatic burden really rests with her in The Departure. It's <u>grand</u> that you say you'll come up for it.

This is really meant to be a scrap to say that <u>of course</u> I'll be well enough for you to come here as planned on Dec 5th – I'm looking forward to it tremendously – & wouldn't miss it for worlds. On 6th Dec (which is the War Requiem Day)[22] I'm afraid I'll have to go to the B.B.C. C.M.A.C.[23] meeting – so sorry when it's a day you'll be here, but think I ought not to miss it as there are only 3 a year. [. . .]

[. . .][24]

Williams went to stay with Maconchy and her family on 5 and 6 December 1962, so they could together attend the performance of Britten's War Requiem, Op. 66, *at Westminster Abbey on 6 December 1962. She was also able to see a rehearsal of* The Departure.

159) 9 December 1962

> 9, Old Village Road, Barry
> December 9th 1962

My dear Betty & Billy,

Thank you so much for your kindness to me. I have come home feeling very happy – as though I've been given a very stimulating tonic. It was high time I got away & met my old friends again.

---

21 Catherine Wilson made her opera debut as a mezzo-soprano at Sadler's Wells in 1960, playing the title role in Rossini's *Cenerentola*.
22 See Letter 159.
23 BBC Central Music Advisory Committee.
24 The end of this letter is missing.

I'm sorry I had to rush off before yesterday's rehearsal ended – it was hard to tear myself away. I was becoming more & more impressed by Julia.[25] There was only one small thing I thought could be improved – I didn't hear Julia's first 'Mark'. In the score it's *mp* & she faithfully sang it *mp* & it didn't come across. If it's too late to alter the rhythm – bringing it after the chord – then just mark it up.

I wish the chorus would <u>travel along</u> the long sustained notes – keeping the tone alive. It's such a common fault in choral singing – & so important. As they sang yesterday those long notes were static & toneless. What you want really is to have boys instead of women in that chorus . . . but that's not possible in this production.

[. . .]

<u>Do</u> try to get round the conductor to let you into the first orchestra rehearsal. It is monstrous to keep you out.

With love & many thanks
Grace
[. . .]

Williams joined Maconchy's friends and family to hear the New Opera Company workshop on 16 December 1962, giving the first performance of Maconchy's one-act opera The Departure *(1960–61) at Sadler's Wells Theatre, London, conducted by Alan Bousted and with the principal role, Julia, sung by soprano Catherine Wilson.*

160) 19 December 1962

9, Old Village Road, Barry, Glamorgan
December 19th 1962

Dearest Betty,

It was a joy to hear lovely lyrical music flowing naturally from the voices in a modern opera – & from the orchestra, too. We all felt this – & were deeply moved by The Departure. Iris[26] said – 'This is a new Betty' – but I disagreed – it was very much the Betty we'd always known branching off into something new. Peter Pears was quite wrong about the libretto. It is most moving & singable.

It had to be Catherine Wilson singing Julia – it wasn't just chance – I really do believe there's a kind of magnetic force attracting the right person for the right part at times – just as when one is searching for words to set – or a theme for opera – the search may go on for some time, then the magnet intervenes & does the trick. [. . .]

[. . .]

---

25 Catherine Wilson was singing the principal role, Julia, in Maconchy's *The Departure*.
26 Conductor Iris Lemare.

I have no criticism of The Departure that's worth mentioning – none of the music – but if there is a weakness in the libretto it is that it doesn't develop towards the end & from a purely dramatic point of view perhaps there ought to be more tension. There is so much up to the point when she realises that she's dead – & after that less & less – but I didn't mind it that way. I was too absorbed by the music. Best love & wishes to you all Grace.
[. . .]

161) 30 December 1962

Shottesbrook, Boreham, Chelmsford
Boreham 286
December 30th 62

Dearest Grace
Thank you very much for the extra-pretty hanky, which it was lovely to get: but even more for your very nice letter, which I welcomed & appreciated more than I can possibly tell you. I felt rather empty & blank after The Departure performance (you know the feeling) but on the whole thought I had expressed something of what I wanted in it. I hadn't expected the hardboiled critics to like it, but all the same I was surprised by the beastliness of almost all the notices (Philip Hope-Wallace in the Guardian & F. Aprahamian in S. Times[27] were almost the only exceptions I've seen. . .), some, like The Times, really were offensive – & only interested in the breaking of the bed, & thankful to write about that & not to have to bother with the music.[28] Anyway I felt rather cast down by them – (I never used to care a straw!) 'wishy-washy music'. 'conventional ideas' – 'not an original idea' & so on. . .

So your letter, coming from you whose views I really respect was a great cheer, & did something to restore me! Yes – the dramatic tension does drop in the 2nd half: I wonder what I ought to do about that. I've been thinking about it, and will continue to.

Anyway – the notices will certainly have killed any chance of life The Departure had – so it will never be heard again & I'm glad to have heard it with Catherine Wilson, who was lovely (& I'm thankful most of the critics said nice things about her.) I really must keep off opera for the future! But not sorry to have done the 3 one-acters,[29] despite all.

---

27 Felix Aprahamian, critic of the *Sunday Times*.
28 'It was unfortunate that the bed broke when the lady in the blue négligé sat on it, for she was meant to be a newly dead disembodied spirit (after a motor crash) in the evening's other work, *The Departure*, by Elizabeth Maconchy (to Anne Ridler's libretto)'. 'Beggar's Opera in New Terms', *The Times* (17 December 1962), 5B.
29 Maconchy's *The Sofa*, *The Three Strangers*, and *The Departure*.

I'm now (– when I get an opportunity! at the moment it's mostly feeding 5 hungry people & trying to keep house & family warm) beginning to get hard down to my clarinet 5tet – which I've promised for July (& you know how slow I am) & want to be as good as I can make it – – I have done quite a lot of (smallish) alterations to the solo-part of my Birmingham piece[30] – esp. in the last mvt, on the lines you suggested – & may revise still further. You were most helpful – as you always are!

It <u>was</u> nice being able to see you properly at last again: & to hear & see 'En famille' – I've always wanted you to write a comic opera, as you know, & I think it is awfully good & <u>very</u> accomplished & assured: lyrical, too – & I particularly like the two girls – genuinely alive characters & <u>I like the variety</u> that you get into it each time they appear. I do hope that a definite performance for it will get fixed up – & that the Welsh Arts Council, having commissioned it, will bestir themselves over its performance.

It's lovely having Anna & Francis here, & we've had a good family Christmas. We all go frivolously to Beyond the Fringe[31] on Thursday – [. . .] B. & Nicola & I are going to <u>King Lear</u> – which seems to be a wonderful production, at the Aldwych,[32] next week – which will be fun. We are going to read it 'en famille' this evening! [. . .]

It <u>was</u> good of you to make the long trip to come & hear my opera – I hadn't a chance to say thank you properly – but I <u>did</u> appreciate it: & everything else. Much best love B.

Two letters from Williams haven't survived.

162) 12 February 1963

Shottesbrook, Boreham, Chelmsford
12th February 1963

Dearest Grace,

I have two lovely letters to thank you for – it was <u>very</u> good of you to write a comforting letter about The Departure – & I do value it: & then again about my 5th quartet. I'm so glad you heard it[33] [. . .]

I hope your house & weather problems are not being too ghastly? & that you can cope without exhausting yourself? It has been bad at times here – but we've

---

30 The *Serenata concertante* for violin and orchestra (1962).
31 A highly popular and satirical British comedy revue which played in London's West End in the early 1960s.
32 Shakespeare's *King Lear* at the Aldwych Theatre, London, in a production by Peter Brook.
33 Maconchy's String Quartet no. 5 was broadcast on the BBC Third Programme on 5 February 1963, performed by the English String Quartet.

learnt how to keep the pipes going gradually – & by using an awful lot of electric heaters & an Aladdin oil-stove. [. . .]

[. . .]

How is the vocal score of En famille? I don't think its <u>slight</u> connection with the Gianni Schicci[34] theme matters <u>at all</u> – it's so completely different.

[. . .]

---

34 Puccini's one-act comic opera *Gianni Schicchi* (1917–18) is about a rich man dying and his relatives faking a rewriting of his will, mainly to the benefit of Gianni Schicchi, the main schemer. Williams's *The Parlour*, adapted from de Maupassant's story, 'En famille', is about the death of a grandmother, and a couple switching the parlour furniture in order to defraud the woman's sister; however, it turns out that the grandmother was merely in a coma and heard the couple's scheming, resulting in her making a will in favour of the sister, cutting out the couple entirely.

IV.3 Letters 163–173
(July 1963–April 1964)

In this nine-month period, following her trip with Billy to Canada and the USA (see letter 156), Maconchy was busy with numerous commissions while her music had various performances and broadcasts, including the premières of her *Serenata concertante* for violin and orchestra (1962) and her Quintet for clarinet and strings (1963).

Williams was putting the finishing touches to her opera and continuing to work on her Trumpet Concerto (1963). Maconchy's daughter Anna gave birth to her first child, Christopher.

Maconchy wrote in response to the first broadcast on the BBC Home Service on 5 July 1963 of Williams's Songs of Sleep *(1959), performed by Anne Davies (soprano), Sebastian Bell (alto flute), and Ann Griffiths (harp).*

163) 6 July 1963

Shottesbrook, Boreham, Chelmsford
Boreham 286
6th July 63

Dearest Grace

Your <u>songs of sleep</u> were lovely last night – we both enjoyed and liked them very much indeed. The first is a beautiful song & the second even <u>more</u> beautiful – I thought it suffered a little from proximity to the first (not quite enough difference in tempo, character & tonal colour?) & had an idea that I'd rather like a <u>dream</u> song (not necessarily a nightmare – but it could be quicker & different) between them . . . The <u>Western Wind</u> one is lovely too – a lovely wide-ranging vocal line (the singer not <u>quite</u> happy with it we thought?) an unusual and beautiful setting of it. It was a joy hearing them. Many thanks for telling me – I couldn't alas! hear the folk-song programme as I was in London from v. early.[1]

---

1 Maconchy is possibly referring to a half-hour Welsh Schools programme, 'Rhymes and Song', on the BBC Welsh Home Service, in which Williams's folk songs arrangements were frequently performed.

The Reflections perf. at Aldeburgh was a beautiful one[2] – much the best to date (it was a morning concert – we left here for Aldeburgh at 7.30 a.m! only having got home from U.S.A at midday the day before! – – but perhaps will be broadcast later.) [. . .] I have come back to a lot of catching-up to do – & musical ideas seem to have started flowing – which they hadn't for some time! So I've rationed myself to this small sheet of paper: but I'm longing to tell you about the American trip, which was marvellous. Best love B

Williams wrote about the repeat broadcast of Maconchy's Duo: Theme and Variations *for violin and cello, on the BBC Third Programme on Friday, 12 July 1963, performed by Robert Masters (violin) and Muriel Taylor (cello).*

164) 13 July 1963

9, Old Village Road, Barry, Glamorgan
Barry 4776
July 13th 1963

Dearest Betty,

Thank you again & again for writing music. The Duo came over splendidly last night & one could get right at the heart of the music. Those players understood it & their playing of the slow variations was very moving. And how truly contemporary it was! A gt. relief after the Cheltenham disappointments (though in the Musgrave[3] I felt there was a poet trying to break through – but the shackles were too strong – the din became boring after a short while)

I'd hoped for something better from William Mathias, who can be very good & write music full of spontaneity & sounds which are far more original than they appear to be at casual hearing; but his Wind Quintet[4] – in spite of lots of original things which the critics missed – wasn't up to his usual standard.

[. . .]

Thank you for listening to my 'Songs of Sleep' & telling me what you thought. The second song shouldn't really sound like the first – but it needs a Lady Macbeth to bring it off, & a soprano of that type would hardly be right for 'Sweet & Low': I feel I've made a bad mistake in that respect & 'The Cypress Curtain of the Night' (terrifying poem) should belong to a different cycle.

[. . .]

---

2 Maconchy's *Reflections* for oboe, clarinet, viola, and harp (1960–61) was performed at the Aldeburgh Festival on 24 June 1963, by Janet Craxton (oboe), Thea King (clarinet), Margaret Major (viola), and Osian Ellis (harp).
3 Thea Musgrave's Sinfonia (1963), commissioned by the Cheltenham Festival, was first performed on 3 July 1963 by the BBC Northern Orchestra, conducted by Jascha Horenstein.
4 William Mathias's Wind Quintet, commissioned by the Festival, was first performed at a BBC Invitation Concert on 3 July 1963 by the Dennis Brain Wind Ensemble.

[. . .] So glad you are full of ideas & getting down to more & more writing. I wish my ideas flowed consistently – but they are so spasmodic these days – & now I must get some more of the trumpet work done[5] (did I tell you I'd done piano score of the slow movement & a Passacaglia? – I sent it to the Trumpeter & he said it was fine – but hinted he wanted more virtuoso writing in the other movements. [. . .]

Goodness knows when I'll come to London – when the house is ready & my jobs finished

with love Grace

I could write another comic opera – about the plasterer & his four apprentices who invaded the house one wet day to deal with a damp wall. The noise & mess were indescribable. [. . .]

[. . .]

165) 7 August 1963

Shottesbrook, Boreham, Chelmsford
August 7th 63

Dearest Grace

It was lovely to get your letter – & awfully nice of you to write about my <u>Duo</u> – : they <u>do</u> play it well – a very satisfying performance to <u>me</u> – & it is very nice of you to like it: It's only a small work, & 12 years old now!

[. . .]

America is beginning to feel rather far-away & unreal, & I hope it's good stimulating effects won't fade away too quickly . . . I got my short String 4tet[6] finished off & sent to Chappel[l]'s (who I hope will publish it – they want it for their educational side). [. . .]

[. . .] I like the idea of a comic opera about your plasterer & his 4 apprentices – – (who presumably had transistor sets and powerful voices of their own)? – perhaps a short TV opera?

[. . .]

My <u>Reflections</u> are to be done at a Thursday Invitation at Bangor on Oct 8th (Tuesday) I believe[7] – & the 1st perf. of the Violin Serenata with Manoug Parikian at Birmingham on Oct. 17th.[8] Anna's baby is due on Oct. 27th – & I'll go up to her for about a fortnight – but probably <u>after</u> it has been born

---

5 Williams's Trumpet Concerto (1962–3), composed for Bram Gay, principal trumpet of the Hallé Orchestra.
6 Maconchy's Sonatina for string quartet (1963).
7 The Invitation Concert from Powys Hall, Bangor, broadcast on 8 October 1963, did not include Maconchy's *Reflections* (1960–61).
8 See Letter 167.

We went to Monteverdi's Poppea at Glyndebourne and also at the Albert Hall![9] (with Nic) It is lovely – & was amazingly successful at the A. H.

[. . .] I must end off – this is a very scattered sort of letter I'm afraid . . . Promise to tell me when there is a chance of seeing you –

Much best love
Your loving B
[. . .]

166) 30 August 1963

Shottesbrook
30th August 63

Dearest Grace – – My letter is much overdue – : it has been lovely having your Songs of Sleep – & I wanted several good sessions with them, in peace (very difficult to achieve in the holidays!) before parting with them again. They are all three lovely songs – The Cypress Curtain of the Night is a beauty – (I particularly like your opening phrases for the voice: – & the growing emotional intensity – all the better and stronger for being restrained.) but both the others are lovely, too. [. . .] I'd love to hear a tremendous singer do them – esp. no. 2. (I thought the sound of the alto fl. lovely – though certainly a cor ang.[10] would be superb here) – and Sweet & Low is a lovely setting which should be in the repertoire of all good sopranos. I've loved getting to know them – thank you very much for letting me have them.

Sorry there is no likelihood of seeing you at Worcester – I hope your trumpeter's visit has been satisfactory & stimulating?[11] So glad you'd finished your first & slow mvts. & I hope you'll have fun with the last . . . The welcome flow of ideas I had when I returned from America. . . (& when alas! I had so many other things to do apart from music) has abated, I'm afraid. I only hope it may return when I get down to work again at the end of Sept. I have a good many small commissions in hand – though no great hurry over them – & still have a lot to do to my Clar. 5tet; I've scrapped such volumes on the way! [. . .]

[. . .]

I must get lunch – forgive a scrappy letter. Much best love B

Maconchy wrote in response to another missing letter, in which Williams sent good wishes for the first performance of Maconchy's Serenata concertante *for*

---

9 Monteverdi's opera *L'incoronazione di Poppea* (1643).
10 Alto flute and cor anglais.
11 Bram Gay, for whom Williams was writing her Trumpet Concerto (1962–3).

violin and orchestra (1962) on 17 October 1963 at the Town Hall, Birmingham, performed by Manoug Parikian (violin) and the City of Birmingham Symphony Orchestra, conducted by Hugo Rignold.

167) 27 October 1963

Shottesbrook, Boreham, Chelmsford
Boreham 286
27th October 1963

Dearest Grace.

You must think me a perfect pig not to have written sooner to thank you for your very nice pre-Birmingham letter. It was very heartening to have it – & <u>oh</u> how I longed to have you there for advice, criticism, reassurance etc! . . .

I waited to write till after the performance & I just don't seem to have drawn breath since then. I am in fact <u>very</u> busy with a tremendous lot to get through (the most pressing being to finish my Clar. 5tet, at last approaching conclusion I think – but there are a lot of things I'm supposed to be writing – –) before I go to Anna – the baby is due today – but naturally may not be punctual [. . .]

Well – Birmingham was rather an exciting experience on the whole – & I think the work is going to be worthwhile – which is the crucial thing & really the only thing that matters. I'm longing for you to hear it – & tell me: as there is no-one else I can really trust. [. . .] The 1st rehearsal in YMCA hall with a low ceiling was hell (on the Wed), impossible to hear anything except deafening brass: then the longish Thurs. morning rehearsal was amazingly better – in fact it <u>began</u> to feel as if everything might come off just right. The performance in the evening just wasn't quite so good as the morning – lots & lots of things went for nothing – & <u>little</u> things that went wrong made them feel insecure, I think. I doubted if it would 'get across' as a result – but it amazingly did – & the audience really seemed <u>very</u> enthusiastic which was nice. Manoug Parikian was <u>quite excellent</u> – & also entirely to be relied on the whole time: he played v. well at the performance (better he said, than at the rehearsal) which of course greatly helped its success; & it did sound as if the thing had plenty of vitality (orchestra as well) [. . .]. He would <u>like</u> a bit more to play! – & although it's <u>not</u> a concerto – I think it does need a bit more for him & I'm writing in some more – (which seems to come quite easily & I hope is not just facile) – to which I hope the O.U.P won't object too much. He wants some double stopping! (I really had given him none to speak of.) [. . .]

[. . .] I felt very low for a day or two after the perf. was over – wondering if it was really a good work or not. But anyway I've cheered up again whether it is or not! There have been good notices – a 'rave' one in Daily Mail! But probably they will be contradicted by the ones after the London perf. (The Times didn't have one)

Section IV.3. Letters 163–173 (July 1963–April 1964) 215

It is grand that you plan to come up for Dan Jones['s] opera on Dec 2nd (I see it's a <u>Monday</u> this time, not Sunday)[12] & we hope that you can come here before – & – after it – ? [. . .]

[. . .]

I have just done two carols, settings – not arrangements – (one a spring carol with Herrick words) for the new Cambridge Hymnal[13] – which I enjoyed doing. [. . .] The Grammar School in Chelmsford have asked [me] to write a work for the opening of a new school hall next October – I think of resuscitating 'How Samson bore away the Gates of Gaza' (– I wonder if you remember it? as a solo scena[14] –) & making it into a work for chorus & orchestra – which I think would really suit it better.

Grinke has asked me to do a set of violin pieces – (either unaccomp. or with piano)[15] Ricordi want another one or two piano pieces, – I'm going some time to write a harpsichord suite for the Czech harpsichordist Zuzana Ruzikova,[16] the Chelmsford diocese rather want a work for their 50th anniversary![17] & I've got my Prom commission,[18] (– thank goodness I said '65!) – so I seem to have taken on too much at once, really, as I am very slow now, & do like time to scrap endlessly & start again. I've done that all through the clar 5tet & only hope it's right now.

I must stop. We are driving over to lunch with Alan & Isabel Rawsthorne[19] – the first time we shall have met <u>in Essex</u> since they came to live here, years ago now! He has just been in U.S.S.R. Did you hear the new choral work?[20] I liked it – but preferred the solo & orchestral part to the choral.

Do hope we see you before Dec 2nd.
Much love from us both
Your loving
Betty
[. . .]

---

12 Daniel Jones's first opera, *The Knife*, was to be given its first performance by the New Opera Company, at Sadler's Wells Theatre, London, on 2 December 1963.
13 Maconchy's *Down with the Rosemary and Bays: Twelfth Night carol* for two-part chorus, with concluding four-part round (1966), setting Robert Herrick, and *Nowell, Nowell, Nowell* (1966) for 3-part unaccompanied chorus.
14 *How Samson bore away the gates of Gaza*, scena for voice and piano (1937).
15 Violinist Frederick Grinke, for whom Maconchy wrote *Six Pieces* for solo violin (1966).
16 Maconchy's *Notebook* for harpsichord (1965).
17 Maconchy's *Settings of Poems by Gerard Manley Hopkins* for soprano (or tenor) and chamber orchestra (1964); see Letters 177 and 178.
18 Maconchy's *Variazioni concertante* for oboe, clarinet, bassoon, horn, and strings (1964–5); see Letter 183.
19 Composer Alan Rawsthorne and his wife, painter Isabel Rawsthorne (also known as Isabel Lambert).
20 Rawsthorne's *Carmen vitale*, for soprano, mixed chorus, and orchestra (1963).

Williams wrote to Maconchy after Anna's baby, Christopher, was born on 28 October.

168) 12 November 1963

9, Old Village Road, Barry, Glamorgan
Barry 4776
November 12th 1963

Dearest Betty,

I hope Anna's baby arrived without too much delay & that all went well & the baby is lovely. I expect you are with her now. Do give her my love. You will enjoy looking after her & the baby – I know.

It is marvellous how you've always managed to be an absolutely normal, happy woman and a unique composer. And now you have at last been inundated with commissions & requests – which is wonderful news (but I always said it would happen one day).

[. . .] I hope to goodness I can come up for the Festival Hall concert but am dismayed it's on March 7th – though it may be all right for me after all.[21]

My Trumpet Concertino is being in played in North Wales (Hallé tour sponsored by Welsh Committee of Arts Council, conductor Mackerras) on March 8th 9th & 10th. I imagine the rehearsal will be in Manchester before the 7th – and if I go to any of the concerts it will be on the 10th. (The L. S. O. and Monteux[22] are in Barry (!) on the 5th.) Those are the only dates I have fixed for the New Year – isn't it maddening! But I may be able to manage your concert.

I've heard very favourably – at last – from the Trumpeter. [. . .] He says the work is very difficult in unusual ways but is delighted to find lyrical writing for the Trumpet. But I'm afraid he won't get much credit for mastering the difficulties because it won't sound like a virtuoso piece.

One thing I am enjoying & that is scoring it. I haven't enjoyed scoring anything so much for years & can't tear myself away from it. It's marvellous to feel this way once more. The actual composition took me an eternity & there were times when I could have tossed the whole thing to the winds (when I got stuck and felt mentally barren & just couldn't push on) – but now it's finished it seems to hang together & flow quite spontaneously, which is hard to understand.

I'm determined to finish the score and the vocal score of En Famille (after which I shall really bombard the Welsh N. O. C.) before Christmas.

The one snag about these two jobs is that neither has brought in a penny (though, of course, I got paid for the full score of E. F. two years ago) & at my present rate of working they have taken months. (The Trumpeter has promised to

---

21 The Royal Festival Hall concert on 7 March included the London première of Maconchy's *Serenata concertante* for violin and orchestra. See Letter 170.
22 Conductor Pierre Monteux.

look after the parts which is some help.) I suppose I was banking on performing fees to see them through but they've dropped considerably. The situation isn't at all serious (I've always been the careful type) nevertheless I'm being a bit careful at the moment [. . .]

[. . .]

I'm glad you've seen Alan R. again. How extremely well he writes for solo voice (tho' not nearly so well for chorus) I thought 'Death come rock me to sleep' in the new work the finest thing he's written. Full of wonderful sounds and feeling.

[. . .] It's now 11.30 p.m. & time to go to bed (I'm trying to turn over a new leaf & go before midnight.)

[. . .] The best lesson anyone can get in composition is to study early sketches of masterpieces – the before & after is always a revelation. I ruled bar lines for the Trumpet score to the broadcast of Beethoven's 'Leonora' & since I know 'Fidelio' nearly by heart I knew exactly what he'd altered & in every case the alteration was a stroke of genius.

[. . .] I suppose you won't want to come to Dan's rehearsal[23] – no, of course not, – much nicer to spend Sunday at home. In any case it would be wicked for me to come to you now & interrupt when you have so much work to do & you'll want every moment for it. (It would take me several years to get through what you have in hand & I'd have to live like a hermit to cope with it)

All best, love Grace

It's now midnight! (i.e. after reading this through & pausing to think now & again [)]

Any news of Dorrie? I'm ashamed to say I haven't written to her since last Christmas. And not a word from her. G.

[. . .]

169) 5 December 1963

9, Old Vicarage Road, Barry
December 5th 1963

Dearest Betty,

I'm delighted to know that all is well with Anna and Christopher. You must all be very thrilled. I wonder if they'll be coming to you for Christmas. If so you'll have a lovely time.

I was sorry to miss you at 'The Knife' – but in any case it would have been impossible for me to go on Monday because I had a full day's listening to records (for two children's broadcasts) on Tuesday (the only available day for the L. P. grams studio)

---

23 Although Maconchy planned to attend the Monday performance of Daniel Jones's opera, *The Knife* (see Letter 167), Williams had decided to go to the general rehearsal the day before, as the train fare was cheaper on Sunday.

I dashed up on Sunday & got to most of the afternoon rehearsal & of course all the evening dress rehearsal. It seemed to me to be coming off remarkably well [. . .]
[. . .]

I've been reading all the Guild reports & am amazed at the thoroughness & hours & hours of hard work which Executive Members must have put in on behalf of all composers & I only hope all who sit back & reap the benefits feel as grateful as I do.

One thing struck me – since it applies to me, personally & must to most free-lance composers: commission fees are always inadequate when considered as a living wage covering the period of composition. In the past what one lost on commission fees one made up (usually) on repeated performances – but since B. B. C. has cut down so drastically on repeats, it's bound to affect one's acceptance of commissions.

At the moment I can't make up my mind about a commission offered by the 1965 National Eisteddfod – for a 30 mins. work for the Youth Concert – large S. S. A. choir of Secondary & Grammar school girls – with accompaniment for full schools' orchestra.[24] The fee offered was £100 – from their point of view quite a lot – but for several months' work – –.

The secretary said he would try to get it increased to £150 but I don't know whether he'll succeed. Obviously one doesn't look to the B. B. C. for broadcasts of such a work – & the outlook from publishers is bleak. O U. P. say they'd consider a work lasting 20 mins. but couldn't possibly commit themselves until they'd seen the score.

Not much hope there. Last year they turned down [–] because there wouldn't be enough demand for it [–] a Festival Song (about 4 ½ mins – a setting of a Shelley translation of a Homeric Hymn)[25] which I'd written for Croydon Schools Festival for a fee of 6 gns. It cost half the fee to travel up to hear it. Then I've sent it to another publisher – can't remember which but I believe it was Ricordi, anyway it was a firm starting up an educational section from which I'd received a circular letter – & it bounced back almost immediately – no reason given.

In that case I wondered whether their readers were all avant-garde who considered me far too reactionary (but the song wasn't easy)
[. . .]
[. . .] I must stop – had not meant to write anything more than a note – & time is going on & I must get on with scripts (I had a lovely time on Tuesday listening to records of music for toys, dolls, & puppets – for Christmas broadcasts.)

---

24 Williams eventually wrote Benedicite for soprano, mixed chorus, and orchestra (1964).
25 Williams's *Hymn to the Earth* for unison voices and piano (1962).

Don't bother to reply to this because I know only too well what you are up against though I hope you are enjoying it all – & it's marvellous that you've been asked to write so much

With love
Grace

Williams wrote in response to the first broadcast of Maconchy's Serenata concertante *for violin and orchestra, aired on the BBC Home Service on 7 February 1964, performed by Manoug Parikian (violin) with the Birmingham Symphony Orchestra, conducted by Hugo Rignold. A month later, on 7 March, the same performers were to present the London première at the Royal Festival Hall. Williams instead needed to attend the rehearsal for the first performance of her Trumpet Concerto, to be given in Rhyl, North Wales, the following day by Bram Gay (trumpet) and the Hallé Orchestra, conducted by Charles Mackerras.*

170) 9 February 1964

9, Old Village Road, Barry
February 9th 1964

Dearest Betty,

The Serenata really is a most beautiful work full of sensitive and deep thought & sounding like pure gold – so there! More than that I can't say – words are completely inadequate. After what we've had to endure for the last years – except for Britten – & occasionally from Tippett, it was heaven.

I feel it's going to capture London (yes, including Press – it must) at Festival Hall next month.

Isn't it maddening that I'll have to miss it. [. . .]

I'm also furious that I have no Tape recorder – otherwise I could have taped the broadcast (when I go to Marian's (at Bolton) for the rehearsals I must get my brother-in-law to give me advice – he's very knowledgeable about these things. I'm an absolute nitwit)

[. . .]

[. . .] It's a wonderful morning – windows wide open and sun streaming in. I'm having a short respite after seeing to score & string parts & harp of the concerto – which the Trumpeter has photostated on his own machine [. . .]

I've just started some more settings of early Welsh poems – this time at the request of Osian (who asked for them about a year ago)[26] (& he did offer a commission fee) for him to sing to his own accompaniment.

Still no news from Welsh Nat. Opera Co. – but John Moody the producer is very hopeful.

---

26 Williams's *Two Ninth Century Welsh Poems* for baritone and harp (1965), commissioned by harpist Osian Ellis.

Don't bother to reply to this – I really mean it – You must give all your time now to writing more lovely works – love to you both – & to Anna & Christopher if they are still with you – Grace

[. . .]

171) 26 February 1964

> Shottesbrook, Boreham, Chelmsford
> Boreham 286
> February 26th 64

Dearest Grace

Only a line – & most belated – to say THANK YOU & THANK YOU AGAIN for ringing up, – & then writing too about my Serenata. It really transformed my life to know that you really liked it – (music and scoring!) & has made all the difference to me.

I feel so horribly diffident about everything I write these days – (even when I think I do like it & hope it's worth while – when I hear it, – as with the Serenata) Both Manoug & Hugo Rignold were pleased with the broadcast – & both thought it better than they expected. I told Hugo R. what you said about the playing of the orchestra, as it will hearten him & them. I hope they will give it a good perf. at R.F.H. – but it is rather hit-&-miss, I think, – & I felt missed at 1st perf. – but they ought to be more at home in it now.

They rehearse that afternoon in London – [. . .] How I wish you could be there too – & equally how I'd love to hear the new trumpet work. The very best of luck for it. Will anyone make a tape, I wonder? I'd love to borrow it sometime, if so – our nearest neighbours have a tape-recorder & I could play it there (I think I'll have to get one soon!) I have a tape & a record of the Serenata – which you could borrow, or better still hear here! When there is a chance.

My new clar. 5tet is being done in Minehead! (they commissioned it) on March 12th by Gervase de P. & the Dartington 4tet who I've never met.[27] G. de P rang up to say they'd just 'been through it' on Monday (& it was apparently all right) but won't be rehearsing again till the day before the 1st perf! – at Dartington. So I'm going to drive down with him late on 10th ('if you don't mind fast driving' . . .) & hope very much to spend the night with Helen Glatz[28] – to whom I've written – which would be nice: I'll hear the rehearsal on morning of 11th (I've never heard a single note of it yet) & have to give a talk about it that evening in Minehead (to a mostly v. ancient audience who don't like anything later than R. Strauss, & resist strenuously) using a tape, which they hope they can make that morning. I have cold feet, & can you wonder.

[. . .] I'm also doing two Gerard M. Hopkins settings for Sop. & small orch. (to be done in the Cathedral in Chelms. next October.)[29] I hope I shan't have

---

27 Maconchy's Quintet for clarinet and strings was to receive its first performance by Gervase de Peyer (clarinet) and the Dartington String Quartet; see Letter 173.
28 Composer Helen Glatz, who had been a student of Vaughan Williams in the 1930s, lived in Dartington.
29 Maconchy's *Settings of Poems by Gerard Manley Hopkins* for soprano (or tenor) and chamber orchestra (1964), premiered at Chelmsford Cathedral; see Letters 177 and 178.

Section IV.3. Letters 163–173 (July 1963–April 1964)   221

Figure PIV.3.1 Grace Williams, Trumpet Concerto (1963), autograph manuscript, p. 1. (Letter 172). Permission to reproduce kindly granted by Llyfrgell Genedlaethol Cymru/National Library of Wales.

cribbed from you? – I began reading Hopkins again & found I wanted to do them <u>much</u> more than anything else – I'm doing <u>The Starlight Night</u> & <u>Peace</u> – what a wonderful poem it is, isn't it? in fact both of them.

I'm beginning to think of my work for Proms '65 – probably for ob – clar – fag & horn with strings (like the Mozart <u>Sinfonia Concertante</u> or is it called that?[)] which ought to be nice to do – though it will obviously turn out to be <u>chamber music</u> rather than a winner for the Proms![30] (I'm getting more contrapuntal again – do you find it comes in recurrent waves?)

[. . .] All love B.

Christopher is a heavenly baby – & I'm a most doting grandmother! They were all 3 with us after Xmas for 2½ weeks – & A. & Christopher again for a week this month – which was lovely & they come again after Easter. [. . .]

Williams composed this long letter in response to the first performance of Maconchy's setting of words by John Donne, A Hymn to God the Father *(1959), given in a BBC Third Programme broadcast on Sunday, 12 April 1964, by Peter Pears (tenor) and Viola Tunnard (piano), with a detailed account of the rehearsals and first performances of her Trumpet Concerto.*

172) 14 April 1964

9, Old Village Road, Barry, Glamorgan
Barry 4776
April 14th 1964

Dearest Betty,

I heard 'Hymn to God the Father' on Sunday & thought it a very fine setting – (& wondered whether it was linked in any way with the choral setting you did many years ago.[31] I think not – it sounded like a completely new setting) I've been wondering about your performances of the Serenata & the Clarinet 5tet – saw no notices of the Serenata in our provincial editions but can't think they could be anything but excellent. They <u>couldn't</u> go wrong about that lovely work. I'm glad to see the 5tet is to be broadcast in June & hope all was well.

I had a trying time just before my Trpt. Concerto rehearsal; had to arrange and attend an aunt's funeral in N. Wales, then on with Marian to her home in Bolton to alter lots & lots of dynamics in <u>all</u> the parts because they said orch. overpowered trpt. in several places at the February run-through; I also rehearsed with Trumpeter[32] who at first was just playing notes without any meaning at all – so I sang & sang it the way I wanted it to sound & thank goodness he was quick in the uptake. All that week I was feeling rather ill & not eating much – but managed

---

30 The *Variazioni concertante* for oboe, clarinet, bassoon, horn, and strings (1964–5); see Letter 183.
31 The second of Maconchy's Two Motets for double chorus (1931) was also a setting of John Donne's *A Hymn to God the Father*.
32 Bram Gay.

to get to Bradford for the rehearsal on the 7th. I'd been puzzled by what they said about the dynamics & wondered whether it was just because at that first try – (a) the hall was ultra-resonant (b) the soloist had played <u>facing</u> the orch. (in order to get to know the score)

Well, at Bradford, the hall was normal, & he faced the auditorium where I sat &, of course, <u>soared</u> above the orch – & I had to plead to have some of the original dynamics restored. The Hallé were making a nice sound – even tho' it wasn't too expressive – by the end of the rehearsal I could see it <u>would</u> come off.

After all that I just couldn't face planning to go back to N. Wales for the concerts (had had no time to book in anywhere) – so had a day's rest at Marian's – & came home. Since when I've been a bit mentally deranged [(]tho' not certifiably so![)] about the Concerto . . . Reports from Bram (the soloist) were fine. 'You'd have been thrilled if you'd been at Bangor' – & it seems he got a fine reception everywhere. But by that time I'd got very dejected about the work itself – not nearly enough virtuoso writing in it; I should have insisted on more help from him about possible fireworks – – it was all so dead simple – & perhaps corny . . . And I could imagine, somewhere up among the stars a brilliant, scintillating concerto, far beyond my reach.

Then after days of such thoughts I began to cheer up & feel some affection for my score after all – & at last it led to action – I pounced on the weakest spots, injected some vitality into them, & inserted an extra bar in the last page (an extra flourish for trpt – <u>&</u> orch.) So I'll have to face those parts once more & have several days of cleaning them up & altering

Today I heard from William Matthias (a most gifted musician & very promising composer) who'd been at the Bangor concert & at last he gave me the truth. The performance was not satisfactory. Orchestra competent technically – but hadn't got to understand it well enough – or to grasp relationship bet: trpt. & orch. [. . .]

After all the bother, it's only a tiny work – but perhaps worth saving from the scrap heap. Incidentally, I learnt it is far more <u>strenuous</u> for the Trumpet to play liricamente than brillante – it's this relaxed way which involves more risks. I suggested writing a cadenza (actually I did sketch one out) for the end of the finale but Bram said he was just about all in as it was, & cdn't face or risk a cadenza as well.

The Hallé who were anti at first changed their minds by the end of the tour & I've even been asked to write a Trombone concerto! – which I wd never dream of doing – thro' sheer ignorance of the instruments potentialities

[. . .]

Orchestral players are a race apart – cruel as hell if they feel like it – but perhaps the world's not all that kind to them after all – in the middle of everything I realised how young most of them were. You & I & our contemporaries are still at it – but where are the Trombones of yesteryear?

Generations of players must have passed into the limbo of forgotten players since our student days. And the fate of singers is even worse.

Have you finished your Hopkins songs? If so I'd love to see them when you've a copy to spare – <u>also</u> of course, a spare score of the Serenata. How marvellously you seem to be coping with all your commissions – you seem to be working at a tremendous speed. How I envy you – I still crawl along – <u>but</u> thank the lord have at last finished my En Famille vocal score. No news from Welsh N. O. C. – but they've been involved in productions & have a week in Cardiff soon.

The Philharmonia come here in May (with Susskind).[33] This week the National Theatre are in Cardiff – I saw Olivier in Othello last night (& go to Uncle Vanya on Thursday.)[34] [. . .]

[. . .] I <u>must</u> stop – have rambled on far too much – but must add that I took Eryl (who was here with Marian just before Easter) to see the Salzburg Rosenkavalier film[35] (also at Cardiff) – & it made me feel that as soon as they get the sound perfect – which no doubt they will – it will be a marvellous way to hear opera. All the times I've seen Rosenkavalier in Opera houses – but <u>never</u> been close enough to see all the subtleties of the acting – The huge cinema screen was marvellous – & the singing superb – & not distorted by the sound quality (which affected the orchestra far more – like early gramophone recordings)

Love to you all (including Christopher) Grace

[. . .]

Maconchy responded with news of her Quintet for clarinet and strings (1962–3), which received its first performance at the Grammar School in Minehead on 12 March 1964, performed by Gervase de Peyer (clarinet) and the Dartington String Quartet.

173) 20 April 1964

> Shottesbrook, Boreham, Chelmsford
> 20th April 1964

Dearest Grace

It was lovely to get your long letter – & particularly to hear about your Trumpet Concerto: what one does go through as a composer! The odd thing is that we have been doing <u>exactly</u> the same thing – I have also revised my Clarinet 5tet since the 1st perf – (or rather the first five performances on five consecutive days – <u>&</u> B.B.C. recording taken from the 1st perf. at Minehead.) I felt fairly happy with it while rehearsing at Dartington on the Wed. & Minehead on the Thursday for the perf. that evening [. . .] then at the actual performance I suddenly felt flat & that it wasn't as good as I thought – needed more exciting writing for the clarinet, – end not good enough etc. (Everyone else seemed pleased.) Gervase does play

---

33 Conductor Walter Susskind.
34 The National Theatre season included Laurence Olivier in Shakespeare's *Othello* and Chekhov's *Uncle Vanya*.
35 Paul Czinner's 1960 film of Strauss's *Der Rosenkavalier* in a production from the 1960 Salzburg Festival.

superbly & is such a good & intelligent & natural musician. I told him I was sorry I hadn't made it 'a bit more difficult' for him – or something. And after their week of performances he wrote (very nicely – he says he likes the 5tet a lot, & wants to get it into the repertoire) suggesting one or two places where it could have a bit more for the clarinet. This set me off at once on a biggish revision – I felt completely inside the work – : and as a result, I think, of hearing a good deal of his playing. I found myself writing virtuoso clarinet passages which I think do fit in all right – – I've done quite a bit to it – including a new Coda to the Scherzo, a considerable cadenza-passage in the last mvt. & a new ending – and am pretty sure it is a better work.

It's a pity the broadcast is of the original version – which I think is too austere & the string parts a bit bare & thin in one or two places. I hope you'll tell me what you think after the June 23 broadcast? (I've just been invited to E. Berlin – fare paid – [by] the Berlin Radio for a perf. of my Concerto for Oboe, bassoon & strings on June 24th – so shall miss the broadcast myself.) [. . .]

[. . .]

I've been having lovely holidays with Nic at home – [. . .] I think her music is really coming on well. Her exams are in June (& then college entrance in November) & she leaves school at the end of this term – & is doing a production of Figaro in a small hall near here, with a v. enthusiastic group of friends, on August 8th![36] [. . .]

Now Monday morning 27th April

& the third instalment of this letter – I'm sorry it has been so delayed! & I'm now (as for 1st instalment) in a very rattling train . . . N. & I on our way to Ursula's for Figaro rehearsals to-day & tomorrow, & Ben's Midsummer N. Dream[37] tonight. I wish you were to be with us.

[. . .]

I must stop, though I could go on for ages. A heavenly warm spring or summer day – it seems a pity to be coming to London! Though London is lovely in the spring & early summer & N. is in the highest spirits. (She is 17 tomorrow, which is hard to believe) Anna, Francis & Christopher all flourish

I hope you will have time to get down to the sea sometimes now the summer seems to be starting?

Best love always B

---

36 Mozart's opera *The Marriage of Figaro* was presented by the Shottesbrook Youth Players, produced by Nicola LeFanu (who also played 'Cherubina'), designed by Ursula Vaughan Williams, conducted by Jeremy Dale Roberts, with Maconchy as accompanist.
37 Britten's opera *A Midsummer Night's Dream* (1964) was revived at the Royal Opera House, Covent Garden, London.

IV.4 Letters 174–179
(July 1964–January 1965)

During this seven-month period, Maconchy continued working on her Proms commission, *Variazioni concertante* for oboe, clarinet, bassoon, horn, and strings (1964–5). She heard premières of two recent works: *Samson and the Gates of Gaza* for chorus and orchestra (1963–4), given at Edward VI Grammar School, Chelmsford, and her settings for soprano and chamber orchestra of Gerard Manley Hopkins's 'The Starlight Night' and 'Peace' (1964).

Williams was very impressed with her study of Maconchy's *Serenata concertante* for violin and orchestra (1962) while working on her Benedicite for soprano, mixed chorus, and orchestra (1964) and hearing the first broadcast of her *All Seasons Shall Be Sweet* for soprano, SSA chorus, and orchestra (performed with piano) (1959). Neither woman had yet purchased a tape recorder.

In response to a missing letter from Williams, Maconchy wrote describing her visit to East Berlin for a performance of her Concerto for oboe, bassoon, and string orchestra (1955–6) on 24 June 1964.

174) 5 July 1964

Shottesbrook, Boreham, Chelmsford
Boreham 286
5th July 1964

Dearest Grace

A lovely letter to thank you for – which I found when I got back from E. Berlin. I had a really very interesting time there – but was <u>very</u> glad to get home & have been feeling ever since how lucky I am to have such a nice place to live in! E. Berlin looks awful – shattered & only partly rebuilt. Everything scarred & great huge bombed sites still empty – hardly any cars & few people compared to most places. But people <u>look</u> well & seem cheerful – & certainly seem to have enough to eat etc – & clothes better than in Moscow, I thought. The concert went off well – a good perf. of my double concerto, although I wasn't there for a rehearsal [. . .]. I got a good reception – & everyone was <u>very</u> friendly, which was nice

I had one night in Prague on the way, & it was lovely to have a glimpse of it.

I am glad you heard the clarinet 5tet[1] – it was awfully good of you to take such trouble to be able to hear it. It means such a lot to me to have your opinion – I'd awfully like you to hear the revised version as well (hope it will get done sometime – Gervase[2] is keen to do it) & then talk to you about it. The new version is better (though not substantially different, except the end) but it is a small work I feel – & I wonder if it is really interesting enough musically? I hope so! I took ages writing it & had a lot of trouble. In the end I felt the shape was perhaps the best thing about it; it seemed to grow out of the first few bars in spite of having scrapped volumes on the way. [. . .]

[. . .]

[. . .] How exciting writing a Benedicite (marvellous words) for such a huge choir – especially as you have a really good semi-chorus – & a youth orchestra, who are probably very good?

The Chelmsford Grammar School orch have just started on my 'Samson'[3] & I'm to hear a rehearsal soon. The choir are getting going on it, too, I'm told – but unfortunately a great many of them leave at the end of this term! – (the perf. is to be in October)

I'm working at my piece for next summer's Proms ob. clar. horn & fag. with strings[4] – I think I shall call it 'Dibattimenti'.

Very much love always Betty

It was three months before Williams next wrote, belatedly responding to the arrival of the pencil score of Maconchy's Serenata concertante *for violin and orchestra (1962), and a tape of the première.*

175) 1 October 1964

9, Old Village Road, Barry
October 1st 1964

Dearest Betty

I'm so sorry to have been such an age in writing to you about the Serenata.

Soon after it arrived I suddenly got rather ill with an awful attack of depression – very difficult to explain because I'd been absolutely normal & happy, though busy, all through the lovely summer – but there had been several tragedies – road & bathing – connected with people nearby (a small boy of seven, just disappeared in the sea one heavenly afternoon when there wasn't a ripple, just in the spot where we bathe – & no one noticed until it was too late) – then to crown

---

1 BBC Third Programme broadcast of Maconchy's Clarinet Quintet on 23 June 1964.
2 Clarinettist Gervase de Peyer.
3 Maconchy's setting of *Samson and the Gates of Gaza* for chorus and orchestra (1963–4) was to receive its first performance by the school choir and orchestra of Edward VI Grammar School, Chelmsford, in October 1964.
4 The *Variazioni concertante* for oboe, clarinet, bassoon, horn, and strings (1964–5); see Letter 183.

it I was told that one of my best friends, who had an operation last February & whom I thought was getting on nicely had incurable cancer, hopeless from the start. She was away at the time – so I suppose I was free to face up to all the grim details, & sort of began identifying myself with her – & before I knew where I was this ghastly depression took hold of me – which absolutely baffled my other friends because I couldn't tell them what caused it – nothing seemed to have any meaning at all – music unbearable – so in the end I went to my doctor who was very understanding & gave me tablets & a tonic & after about a week it lifted – almost as suddenly as it had come – & I was myself again. [. . .]

[. . .]

Since I got 'cured' I've been racing to finish the pencil score of Benedicite; which I did last night – & now only have nearly 200 pages to copy onto transparencies. (I've done a chorus copy and a vocal score with piano so that they could begin learning it – the orchestra won't need so long). I'm going to Newtown, Montgomeryshire, where it is to be sung for a few days next week to discuss with – & play & sing it to – the music teachers. So I must start practising: The thing that has taken me out of myself more than anything has been the Serenata score which I've played through practically every day (except for the awful week!). It was <u>very</u> difficult at first – but now I really am coping – & enjoying it more & more. It is a <u>lovely</u> score – <u>teeming</u> with melodic & contrapuntal invention & all beautiful in sound. I'm so taken with the score & getting to know it that I haven't <u>yet</u> wanted to hear the tape (which is just as well because the neighbour's tape recorder – not a very good one anyway, is out of action – they say it will play all right but something or other isn't working – so I wouldn't dare risk your tape in it. [. . .]

[. . .]

I hope you are having our wonderful Autumn – we are still stockingless & in summer dresses – & my windows are as wide open as possible. Long may it continue.

With love to you all
Grace
[. . .]

176) 13 October 1964

Barry
October 13th 1964

Dearest Betty,

Marian and her husband were here for the week-end (he was preaching in Newport) & just before they left home I remembered that they had an excellent tape-recorder (original cost £120 – which they got 2nd hand for £30) so I rang them up & asked them to bring it – which they did – & then I had a lovely time on Sunday listening to the Serenata (& a few tapes of mine which I'd never heard.) I was more carried away than ever – the slow movement I rank with the slow mvts. of the Bartok Violin Concerto & Shostakovich Symph. No 5.

It must be recognised as a major work of our time. The person who I think would be interested – & would go all out to give it long rehearsals is Charles Groves. He is a great worker & is getting excellent results from the L'v'pool Phil. [. . .]

If you are willing, I'd love to write to him about the Serenata & I'm pretty certain he'd look at the score & listen to the tape. [. . .]

I had a lovely time last week in Montgomeryshire – lucky with weather – mountain bracken a bright copper & the trees & River Wye very beautiful.

My day with the Music Teachers was fine. I played & sang the Benedicite – answered questions – discussed methods of teaching the more difficult bits – & finally, when they had departed, did a tape-recording, & managed to combine the voice parts & the bare essentials of the accompaniment & – got through without playing any wrong notes! The conductor is going to give a tape to each teacher – so that the tempi will be clinched – & they'll have a good overall idea of how I want it to sound.

One of the teachers is very 'with' the avant-garde composers & went to the Peter Maxwell Davies (whom she calls Max) summer school this year.[5] I imagined she'd put me right beyond the pale & at the start she did her best to cross-question me into insignificance – but I managed to hold my own & soon found she was accepting me.

The rest were dears.

I got home to find a pile of letters – one from Yalding House to [s]ay Peter Gellhorn[6] was going to broadcast my choral suite 'All seasons shall be sweet' (did I give you a score? I have plenty to spare) with B.B.C. Women's Chorus in Music at Night on October 28th.[7] It is published by Welsh Univ. Press in Vocal Score (with note about orch. parts being on hire) & Peter G. was given a copy by Guild for Welsh Music when he adjudicated at Swansea Eisteddfod. It looks as though he hasn't read the note about the orchestra & is going to do it with piano. Naturally I'm glad to have it done at all – but of course would prefer it with chamber orchestra, the way it was composed & it seems unusual for the B.B.C. to do things with piano transcription.

I've written to him about it – no reply yet.

The Penarth Ladies are doing the Shakespeare Lyrics on Welsh Home Service on the 23rd[8] – & did I tell you the Trumpet Concerto is being done on Welsh T. V. in December? – & Barbirolli has set Bram Gay free to play it.[9]

---

5 In the summers of 1964 and 1965 composer Peter Maxwell Davies taught at the Wardour Castle Summer School, founded by Davies, Harrison Birtwistle, and Alexander Goehr.
6 Conductor Peter Gellhorn was a member of the BBC Music Department, housed at Yalding House in Great Portland Street, London.
7 This airing on the BBC Basic Home Service of Williams's *All Seasons Shall Be Sweet* for soprano, women's SSA chorus, and orchestra (1959) was the first broadcast since the first performance in 1960.
8 Williams's Three Lyrics for SSA chorus and piano (1959) was performed on the BBC Welsh Home Service on 23 October 1964 by the Penarth Ladies' Choir.
9 Williams's Trumpet Concerto was broadcast on BBC Wales TV on 4 January 1965, with soloist Bram Gay.

(The London Panel has returned the score but can't give a decision yet – whatever that means – I suppose it will turn it down for Basic broadcasts.)[10]

Am still copying full score of Benedicite when it's finished that'll be the day! [...]

With love to you all

Grace

P. S. Until this morning I've quite liked Sir Alec[11] – felt he was sincere & doing his best – though of course I didn't like his politics. But his message to Wales (pushed under my door) so rattled me (you'd think we never paid any taxes or had Labour M. P.s to fight for us) that I got out all my red pencils & improvised a Labour poster (we have a brilliant young candidate) & stuck it with sellotape on my front window. I don't love Harold Wilson but my goodness we need his brain. The Liberals I salute & wish them well.

[...]

177) 14 October 1964

Shottesbrook
14th October 64

Dearest Grace – I have two letters to thank you for – I've been carrying round an addressed envelope & writing paper for some days – without having yet answered your first, & now by today's 2nd post comes your lovely letter of yesterday ... It was horrible for you being knocked over by that awful fit of depression – I do feel sorry about it – even though it is past now, thank goodness. Real deep depression is so ghastly, & it seems impossible to realise that it will pass – like a cloud lifting – : I think it is worse if it comes apparently without cause – but you had real cause for yours. Well – I'm thankful you are well again – no-one on earth is more courageous than you – but even that can't cure depression, at least not at once – –

It is marvellous of you to have read and played my Serenata so thoroughly & given so much time & thought to it and I hope it is deserving of it. You can imagine how enormously delighted I am at what you say about it – it is <u>wonderfully</u> heartening & cheering. Thank you more than I can say.

[...]

[...] I would be really <u>tremendously grateful</u> if you wrote to Charles Groves about it – & sent him score & tape if he wants them. I've never met him – but respect him very much as a conductor. It is most awfully good of you to think of doing it – with all you have to do.

I would love to have it done at Liverpool – just the thing I'd like best. I've been rather disappointed that no perf. has materialised for it this season – –

---

10 Williams is concerned here about whether the BBC Music Panel in London will permit the Trumpet Concerto to be performed on the Basic Home Service from London.
11 Sir Alec Douglas-Home, of the Conservative party, was then Prime Minister, and his campaign programme had been announced on 8 October 1964 for the election on 15 October.

Section IV.4. Letters 174–179 (July 1964–January 1965)   231

I'm so glad you had such a worthwhile and successful visit to Montgomeryshire: [. . .] Nicola & I are full of admiration, interest & curiosity as to how you made the complete tape of accompt. & voice parts – presumably using two tape-recorders – playing back & adding a voice part each time? You are a marvel!

If there should be a tape to spare for a time we'd <u>love</u> to borrow it – we <u>really are</u> going to buy a tape-recorder – but so far haven't got round to it: at the moment there is no time for anything except keeping the nose to the grindstone. [. . .]

I'm in the middle of my local first performances! Last week was the work I wrote for the Grammar School Choir & Orch (commissioned for the opening of their new – & very good – hall.)[12] [. . .] The young conductor (down from Cambridge last year) was fine – & the boys very nice, & enjoying it. (N. heard one say – 'it's fabulous to sing – you can get your teeth into it'!) Chappel[l]'s are going to publish it.

Next week my two Hopkins settings are being done in the Cathedral, with Mary Wells (wife of Philip Ledger who is conducting) who I think will do them well – (I've only been through them once with her so far,) & the Jacques Orch.[13]

[. . .]

– – Alas! It's now 20th & this letter still on the way . . . The last few days have been rather rushed – [. . .] with musical chores to be done, including boiling down the 2-piano version of my <u>Samson</u> for one piano, for the vocal score, which Chappell's are making a great effort to get out quickly – – & so on. To-day I went to Chappell's to discuss details about it. They've just brought out my 'educational' str. quartet[14] – they are sending you a copy. [. . .]

. . . Such lots more I'd love to go on about – but I think I'd better get this much off – – Anna, Francis & Ch. come for their half-term weekend next week – which will be lovely

Nic sends best love & so does Billy – & lots from me always – take care of yourself – can you get any let-up after copying your full-score on transparencies? A horrid job –

Your loving Betty

[. . .]

Maconchy responded to a missing letter from Williams, in which the latter had reported on sending the score of Maconchy's Serenata concertante *to the conductor Charles Groves and commented on the broadcast on 28 October 1964 of her own choral suite,* All Seasons Shall Be Sweet *for soprano, women's SSA chorus, and orchestra or piano (1959), performed by the BBC Women's Chorus, conducted by Peter Gellhorn.*

---

12 *Samson and the Gates of Gaza* for chorus and orchestra (1963–4), see Letter 174.
13 Maconchy's settings of 'The Starlight Night' and 'Peace' for soprano and chamber orchestra (1964) were first performed at Chelmsford Cathedral on 24 October 1964.
14 Maconchy's Sonatina for string quartet (1963).

178) 4 November 1964

Shottesbrook
Wednesday, November 4th 64

Dearest Grace

First – thank you from my heart for having done all that on behalf of my violin concertante. It's noble of you – & how opportune that C.G. was planning his programme for next season now! – – one hopes he will like it [. . .].

I enjoyed tremendously hearing 'All Seasons' – they are lovely & I gained a lot from having got to know them a bit. But – because of having already formed my own ideas of them, I suppose – I didn't think Gellhorn's tempo & mood was always right – & oh! I longed for the orchestra, as you did. [. . .] This is only a scratch in the train – on my way to hear King Arthur (at Albert Hall!) & Britten Sinfonia da Requiem.[15] [. . .] I have been making some small changes in my [. . .] two Hopkins songs – (or rather in one of them – The Starlight Night –) which went off well in the Cathedral & on the whole I was pleased with them, v. timetaking making changes in scores & parts – as you know! & meantime my Prom work[16] doesn't advance. – – [. . .] Love always Betty

179) 7 January 1965

Shottesbrook, Boreham, Chelmsford
Boreham 286
7th January '65

Dearest Grace

It was lovely to get the very pretty & welcome hanky you sent me – thank you so much for it. & for your card. I was thrilled to hear you were orchestrating your National Anthem for TV[17] – hard indeed – as you say – but it will, I hope, earn very worthwhile returns? I hope you've had a good Christmas & had a spell-off? Which I'm sure you need. We were all together & had a lovely Xmas – Christopher is very attractive – & seems alert & intelligent, we think. Anna & Francis seem to have settled very happily in Rugby – and there is to be another baby early in August!

Nicola has got a place at Oxford – at St. Hilda's which we are very pleased about. [. . .]

You may not have heard that Ina has had a big operation – for a gastric ulcer – but she is very successfully over the operation, & eating again (she had almost

---

15 Purcell's *King Arthur* and Britten's *Sinfonia da Requiem* were performed and broadcast from the Royal Albert Hall, London, on 4 November 1964.
16 *Variazioni concertante* for oboe, clarinet, bassoon, horn, and strings (1964–5); see Letter 183.
17 Williams's orchestration of 'Hen Wlad Fy Nhadau' was broadcast on BBC Wales TV on 4 February 1965.

given up eating altogether! & had had nothing but water for 3 weeks before she went into hospital.)

I wonder when there will ever be a chance of seeing you? do you know that our friendship must be nearly 40 years old! Which year was it you came to R.C.M? is it 39 or 40? We should have a celebration! I think I've got my Prom piece[18] 'in the bag' now – & am scoring it. I'd dearly love to show it to you one day. All love B.

---

18 *Variazioni concertante* for oboe, clarinet, bassoon, horn, and strings (1964–5); see Letter 183.

IV.5 Letters 180–187
(March 1965–December 1965)

During this nine-month period, Maconchy was preoccupied with her work for the 1965 Proms, *Variazioni concertante* for oboe, clarinet, bassoon, horn, and strings (1964–5), and the birth of her second grandchild, Anna's daughter Sarah. She also worked on *Nocturnal* for SATB chorus (1965), and her harpsichord pieces, Sonatina (1965) and *Notebook* (1965). Williams heard performances of various works, including *Penillion* (1955) and the Trumpet Concerto (1963). She was working on *Carillons* for oboe and orchestra (1965, rev. 1973), and heard that her opera, *The Parlour* (1960–61), was scheduled for performance by Welsh National Opera.

Both women continued to see and correspond with their old friends, composers Ina Boyle and Dorrie Gow. As always, they listened to a great deal of new music on BBC radio, and Williams, in particular, was candid about her opinion of composers such as Richard Rodney Bennett, Phyllis Tate, and Thea Musgrave.

Williams wrote to ask about the first broadcast of the revised version of Maconchy's Clarinet Quintet, which was to be aired on the BBC Third Programme on 26 March 1965, in a recorded performance by Gervase de Peyer (clarinet) and the Dartington String Quartet.

180) 17 March 1965

9, Old Village Road, Barry
March 17th 1965

Dearest Betty

I've been looking out for your Clarinet 5tet in the Radio Times. Alun H.[1] told me that Gervase de P., who was in Cardiff some weeks ago, was going to pre-record it for radio as soon as he returned to London. (He told Alun it was a fine work & ought to be widely recognised as such)

I do hope I haven't missed it – there is such a maze of music in the R. T. now that one can so easily miss something important. Why they have to have all the

---
1 Alun Hoddinott.

Section IV.5. Letters 180–187 (March 1965–December 1965)

Network music in the morning I can't think – but I suppose there is a strong reason for having it then & not later in the day – Surely there are far more people free to listen with some measure of concentration between 12 & 6 than between 8 & 2. Mind you there are lots of housewifes who love it as it is – a good friend of mine said 'Isn't it nice having all this lovely music in the morning – –' during which she does all her chores. So far there's only the minimum of contemporary music – but as time goes on I've a feeling they'll have to include it, there just won't be enough classics to fill the programme – as it is there's an awful lot of repetition – I seem to have seen the Egmont Overture[2] in goodness knows how many programmes this last week or so – or is it their policy to plug certain works?

The B. B. C. Welsh Orchestra is to be conducted this summer by a very good Cuban conductor: Alberto Bolet & they are planning several Network programmes with a Spanish & a Welsh work in each (He's doing my old Fantasia (which he did when he was here in the autumn) & Penillion – & I wish he were doing the Trpt. Concerto instead but they seem to have forgotten about their promise to do that – & there isn't much hope now before November.[)]

The Hallé are doing it (with Barbirolli) on a Welsh Tour (including Barry) in May.[3] Before I knew for certain that J. B. was doing it, it was all fixed up & Bram Gay gave J. B. his copy of the score & he took it off to Texas – where he still is. Meanwhile, I've rescored two pages, & made several minor alterations & have the revised conductor's score ready for him when he returns – & two newly photostated revised pages to paste into the score he already has if he prefers to use that one. They say he annotates scores very heavily & re-bows everything. Heaven knows how he'll react when he hears about the alterations! I do really dread meeting him – but what a character he is! [. . .]

([. . .] And did you see 'The Lodger'?[4] I've heard 1½ broadcasts of ['The Lodger'] – couldn't manage the final ½ – & really can't enthuse. I've never read Mrs Belloc Lowndes but imagine it's on about the same plane as Phyllis's music. None of the raw vulgarity of a News of the World treatment of a psychopath of course – but far beneath Britten's or Berg's.[5] But I agree it is far worthier of a Sadlers Wells performance than 'The Mines of Sulphur'[6] – but so are goodness knows how many operas (including three by you know who!) [. . .]

---

2 Beethoven's Egmont Overture (1810).
3 Williams's Trumpet Concerto was to be presented in Swansea on 15 May 1965, in Barry on 16 May, and in Aberystwyth on 17 May, performed by trumpeter Bram Gay with the Hallé Orchestra, conducted by John Barbirolli.
4 The first professional stage production of Phyllis Tate's opera *The Lodger* was given at St Pancras Town Hall on 10 and 11 March 1965. The opera is about Jack the Ripper, with a libretto by David Franklin, based on the book by Maria Adelaide Belloc-Lowndes.
5 Referring to the title character of Britten's *Peter Grimes* and either Jack the Ripper in Berg's *Lulu*, or the title character of his opera, *Wozzeck*.
6 Richard Rodney Bennett's opera *The Mines of Sulphur* (1963) had been given its first performance by Sadler's Wells Opera on 24 February 1965.

I expect you've finished scoring your Proms. work[7] – Do let me know the date of performance.

(My Benedicite is being done on August 3rd[8] – pray heaven we don't have another clash!) I <u>must</u> come to the Prom. & perhaps we can celebrate our 40 years friendship then – No! I've just worked it out & it's not due until September 1966. (I was 20 when I came up to R. C. M. – in 1926) [. . .]

[. . .] I wonder if you'll go to the British Women Composers' Concert tomorrow – I had a notice a day or so ago & wrote a note to Ruth Gipps to thank her for including me & for her enterprise in planning the concert & she wrote back to say it wasn't her doing but all due to the enterprising Roy Wales (whom she has not yet met.)[9] I hope they play your Duo well – & sing my Carol decently.[10] [. . .]

Must stop – it's after midnight
With love to you all
Grace
[. . .]

Williams wrote after hearing the revised version of Maconchy's Clarinet Quintet (1962–3), when it was broadcast on 26 March 1965 by Gervase de Peyer and the Dartington String Quartet.

181) 29 March 1965

9, Old Village Road, Barry
March 29th 1965

Dearest Betty,

I thought it was a lovely performance, in fact one of the most sensitive performances you've ever had – <u>really</u> getting at the heart of your music. Gervase de P.'s wonderful playing must have inspired the 4tet (just as Parikian's playing inspired the C. B. O.).[11] – tho' I've thought for a long time that the Dartington have more intelligence & feeling than most 4tets.

The revision is fine & does a lot to separate the clarinet from the strings, giving just the amount of contrast one wants. Then when it merges with the strings the result (at least when played by Gervase!) is enthralling.

[. . .]

---

7 *Variazioni concertante* for oboe, clarinet, bassoon, horn, and strings (1964–5); see Letter 183.
8 The first performance of Williams's Benedicite was to be on 3 August 1965 at Newtown, during the Royal National Eisteddfod, performed by the Montgomeryshire Secondary Schools' Choir and Orchestra.
9 This concert, entitled 'English Women Composers', was given at London's Commonwealth Institute Theatre by the Pro Arte Singers and Musica Viva Ensemble conducted by Roy Wales and composer Ruth Gipps.
10 Maconchy, *Duo: Theme and Variations* for violin and cello (1951); the carol by Williams has not been identified.
11 Violinist Manoug Parikian's performances of Maconchy's *Serenata concertante* with the City of Birmingham Symphony Orchestra.

All best wishes for your holiday in Italy – hope Nicolai Gedda is there when you are (he gave a recital in Cardiff this season – sang Lieder most beautifully) & Renata Tebaldi who is worth a dozen Callases. Much love Grace

Do forgive this scrappy note – am going to the woods for primroses (I hope!) & pussey willow – it's gloriously hot! – & want to post this on the way – & a friend is calling for me at any moment.

Two months later, Maconchy responded to a missing postcard from Williams, written in anticipation of a BBC Music Programme broadcast on 11 June 1965, of her Penillion, *performed by the BBC Welsh Orchestra, conducted by Alberto Bolet. Maconchy had been over to Ireland where her* Nocturnal *for mixed chorus SATB (1965) had been commissioned for the International Choral Festival, at Cork, and was first performed there on 22 May 1965.*

182) 9 June 1965

Shottesbrook, Boreham, Chelmsford
Wednesday 9th June '65

Dearest Grace.

Lovely to get your p.c. this afternoon – & how forgiving of you to write! when I am still carrying your letters about (first to Italy & then to Ireland!) to answer – & still have not written properly – – oh dear! . . . First how grand to hear Penillion on Friday which I look forward to extremely. I have Christopher here, solo, while Anna & Francis have a few days in Norfolk – the first time they have left him: he is the loveliest & gayest little boy I've ever seen – really extremely nice & the greatest fun, but a complete handful – & I find I get rather exhausted! Old age I fear. . . [. . .]

[. . .]

What a pity Barbirolli got ill before the Hallé tour – but evidently the trumpet concerto went very well. How nice getting such a charming letter from him – a rare thing indeed, I feel sure! He must like it very much, obviously: & so he should

Thursday evening now – another day gone! Spent mostly in the garden with Christopher, as it has been a beautiful day [. . .]

I think I told you I was going over to Cork? For the internat. choral festival. I'd been feeling rather anxious about the adjudicating: – however, in the event, it all went well, & I really rather enjoyed it. [. . .]

[. . .]

We are going to Aldeburgh for a few days on 20th – Peter P. sings my 'Hymn to God the Father' on 22nd.[12]

[. . .]

---

12 Peter Pears (tenor) and Viola Tunnard (piano) gave the first concert performance of Maconchy's *A Hymn to God the Father* (1959) on 22 June 1965 at the Aldeburgh Festival.

Oh dear! This is so dreadfully scrappy & incomplete, & I must go to bed . . . Are rehearsals going well for your Benedicite?[13] My Prom rehearsals[14] look like being a nightmare – I'm having the Scottish orchestra (Glasgow) the 4 soloists from B.B.C. symphony orch (London) & I'll have to be in <u>Rugby</u> for Anna's new baby!

Lots of best love & forgive such a scrappy & self-centred letter your loving Betty

Maconchy's Proms commission, the Variazioni concertante *for oboe, clarinet, bassoon, horn, and strings (1964–5) was first performed during the 1965 Proms, on 10 August at the Royal Albert Hall, London, and broadcast on the BBC Third Programme. The soloists, Terence MacDonagh (oboe), Jack Brymer (clarinet), Geoffrey Gambold (bassoon), and Douglas Moore (horn), played with the BBC Scottish Orchestra, conducted by James Loughran.*

183) 11 August 1965

9, Old Village Road, Barry
August 11th 1965

Dearest Betty,

Thank goodness the Variations came through splendidly on my set last night. <u>Fine</u> music all the way & finely wrought – in many ways a new you (though fundamentally the same) – I think you've found writing for wind a spur to your imagination & <u>all</u> the wind writing was exciting – & the strings of course sounded lovely. My only complaint: I'd have liked it to go on longer – an unusual wish these days – but I felt the music was so serious & involved it could have developed still more – & then the change of Tempo at each new variation would have been more marked – or perhaps the beginning of each variation could have had more spotlight (i.e. the music at end of each variation to prepare the start of the next, throwing it into starker relief.)

[. . .]

I hope you saw Dorrie after your concert – & I hope she writes to tell me all about it. I'll not expect to hear from you just yet because I know you'll be terribly busy coping with Anna. I hope her baby arrived in good time. I had a letter from Ina in which she said you'd had to leave Anna in the hands of her mother-in-law when you flew to Scotland for a rehearsal.

I must fly to post. . .

All best wishes & love & many many thanks for such a fine work
Grace

---

13 See Letter 180.
14 *Variazioni concertante* for oboe, clarinet, bassoon, horn, and strings (1964–5); see Letter 183 and 184.

184) 25 August 1965

at 10 Bath Street, Rugby
25th August '65

Dearest Grace

It was lovely, lovely getting your letter (& pre-prom p.c.) but very sad not seeing you that evening. It would have been heavenly to see you & it was awfully nice seeing Dorrie [. . .]

First – all goes very well here. Anna's baby born on Aug 15th was a daughter – Sarah – a lovely baby, actually pretty – weighing 8¾ lbs – [. . .] Francis is excellent & we share all the jobs. A is feeding Sarah most successfully, but there are disturbed nights, of course, & we've all, except Sarah, had sore throats & coughs, especially F. who looks very tired – so life is real & earnest & no time for anything else. [. . . Nicola] cooked etc most successfully for B. while I've been here, – & is writing music (3 settings of C. Day Lewis.) & a play! She wrote a Serenade for Viola & Cello in 2 days (by request for a concert at St Mary's, Calne) which was very resourceful . . . Nice to be 18 & full of ideas.

Later now. I am delighted and thankful that you liked the Variations. I hardly know myself what to think of them – on the whole they came off just as I meant them to – but do they add up to a really worthwhile work? I have been making some changes – in every spare minute I've had (& there haven't been many) since the performance [. . .][15] It's funny how one thinks of things after a performance that one ought to have thought of before! I think it is the physical impact of the sound of it that is stimulating – (I know it was for my Clar. 5tet.) [. . .]

[. . .]

Goodbye my dear – thank you very much for writing & for listening & for being such a good friend for 40 years.

Much love always –
Betty
[. . .]

On 28 October 1965, Maconchy's Variazioni concertante *for oboe, clarinet, bassoon, horn, and strings (1964–5) was given a second broadcast, from Glasgow, in the BBC Music Programme, performed by Valerie Taylor (oboe), Henry Morrison (clarinet), Barry Morris (bassoon), and Farquharson Cousins (horn), with the BBC Scottish Orchestra, conducted by James Loughran.*

185) [28 October 1965] – postcard

[Williams to Maconchy]
Must write at once after listening to the Variazione They are full of most intense and intricate musical thought – to be listened to again & again & always one

---

15 Detailed explanation of the changes follows.

would get more & more from them. The contrasts were clearer today – & the new build up to VIII fine. V & VII my particular favourites.

[. . .]

I saw some of the Proms. notices & on the surface they were nice but oh dear they hadn't begun to grasp the full meaning of your music. I hope there were others who did. I see you are having several things done this season. Wish I could hear them; but I'm not going to have a moment for months. Just when I'd settled down to write the oboe pieces for B.B.C.[16] I heard right out of the blue that Welsh National Opera were going to do my opera – next May.[17] Endless discussions – they insisted on an English title – & after drawing up long lists of possibles I suddenly saw that the root of all the trouble was The Parlour. [. . .] I am terrified of the months to come – am now converting all the choruses into sol-fa – & to my amazement find it will be very helpful – even though it's driving me crazy. Then I must score the Oboe work (Brass, Percussion, Harp & Strings. All very bell-like & I'm thinking of calling it Carillons for Oboe & Orchestra.)

Then I embark on the band parts of the opera – to be finished by end of March. Arts Council will pay for the copying. When oboe work is finished I'll really snatch a few hours & write a real letter. Best love to you both Grace

All best wishes to Nicola at Oxford.

[. . .]

Some weeks later, Williams responded to missing correspondence from Maconchy, in a lengthy letter that is particularly interesting for raising issues about publishing, commissioning, and retirement, considering the commercial realities of being a composer in her sixties.

186) 7 December 1965

9, Old Village Road, Barry
December 7th 1965

Dearest Betty,

I've been re-reading your last letters – you've written lovely long letters telling me of many exciting things that have been happening to you – how you've found time to write to me or anyone – I don't know, but I am grateful – & feel very ashamed that I haven't written to you – except on fleeting postcards. I think I must be growing more & more snail-like – yet I have got through a lot of work – with no time for anything else.

---

16 Williams's *Carillons* for oboe and orchestra (1965).
17 Welsh National Opera gave the first performance of Williams's opera *The Parlour* at the New Theatre, Cardiff, on 5 May 1966; see Letters 188 and 189.

It is sad I can't hear your new works: the Nocturnal – & the Harpsichord works[18] (how lovely to be lent a harps. I've only played one once & adored it – felt I could go on playing for ever –) & so many new things you've written in recent years – but it's grand that they are all being played & sung – & that the performers [. . .] are so full of enthusiasm. I wish they could all be broadcast – really I get more & more fed up with the Music Programme – nothing much now in the evenings & most people haven't the time to listen during the day. There really is very little British Music in the programmes & there's no excuse for its omission. They are, it's true, doing Composer's Portrait – but at a time when one invariably forgets to listen – but I did manage to remember to listen to Thea M. yesterday – & was rather disappointed – one felt the Triptych[19] had been planned to the nth degree before she began it – & although it has a lot of brilliant orchestration I can't feel it is a spontaneously inspired interpretation of Chaucer at all – not a grain of honest simplicity in it.

I hope you'll get your turn soon.

I'm glad O. U. P. are publishing the Nocturnal (– by the way hasn't Britten just written a Nocturnal?[20] I'm sure I've read that quite recently – & wonder whether the English word will supplant Nocturne.) They've just turned down my Benedicite – after keeping it since August – & I'm a bit downcast because this time there was not the usual bit of consolation – that they liked it but felt it wouldn't sell – just a rather curt rejection – from Christopher Morris (who, I fear, has no use for me.) All he wants from me is another Pearly Adriatic[21] which proved an out & out winner – they sold thousands – & all I got was £5. 5s.

[. . .]

I'm glad I wrote it – but it took six months to do – for a commission fee of £150. So I mustn't accept commissions of that kind again – until I'm a pensioner! (I can retire in February when I'm 60 – but there's that earnings rule that one can't earn more than £5 p.w. – & someone at the N. I.[22] office told me I'd have to retire from composing – i.e. my usual job . . . which can't be true! Anyway I've written them a letter asking for elucidation on several points not explained in their pamphlet – – & have received no reply. I think the questions have well & truly stumped them!) Never mind, all will be well when I'm 65 – pension comes automatically – no stipulation & by then I'll have finished paying into an annuity thing (for self-employed people) & will begin drawing from that.

---

18 Maconchy's *Nocturnal* for mixed chorus SATB (1965), and her harpsichord pieces, Sonatina (1965) and *Notebook* (1965).
19 Thea Musgrave's *Triptych* (Chaucer) for tenor and orchestra (1959).
20 Britten's *Nocturnal after John Dowland*, Op. 70, for guitar, was completed in November 1963.
21 In the early 1950s, Williams arranged three Yugoslav folk songs for SA chorus and piano, titling the third 'The Pearly Adriatic'. They were published by OUP in 1952.
22 National Insurance.

The packing up of Children's Hour[23] has been a sad loss to me – I loved doing those scripts & the pay was excellent. I've just finished the parts of the oboe Carillons & that's all ready for performance, thank goodness [. . .].

[. . .]

Now – when Christmas letters are written – I begin in earnest on the Opera parts. I've done a lot of thinning out in the score – & had awful moments of wishing I could re-score the whole thing! – the Cardiff Theatre has no sunken orch. pit & I realised during their last season that words weren't coming across too well – & it wasn't always the singers' fault. [. . .] Bryan Balkwill will conduct.[24] Everyone says 'Aren't you thrilled!' & all I can say is that a cold shudder runs through me every time I really face up to it. One good thing will be that it will probably turn my hair white – far better than having it streaked with iron grey as it is at present (horrible with my sallow skin.)

I have to finish the parts by the end of March so it will be hard going – but if I'm stuck I'll have to call in help. People are amazed that I'm taking on the copying – but I have to find some sort of job for the coming months & it's better to have one connected with the opera than something entirely different. [. . .]

[. . .]

187) 19 December 1965

Shottesbrook, Boreham, Chelmsford
Boreham 286
19th December '65

Dearest Grace

Very best love and wishes to you for Christmas & always.

I have a lovely long letter from you – & I have enjoyed it so much. . . [. . .] I daren't start to answer properly now – but two things, just – first, what is the date of The Parlour with the Welsh National Opera?

B. & I plan a holiday in Italy in May (a thing we have meant to do for 20 years or so! Just the two of us) & it must not clash with your opera. So be an angel & put the dates on a p.c. I am so thrilled about the opera – & the excellent cast you are having. It's grand.

The other thing is about the Benedicite (the O.U.P. are awful: – they've just turned down a 3-part unaccomp. of mine, written by request for the Vienna choir-boys[25] – who incidentally haven't sung it yet!! – & everybody says how awful the O.U.P. are now) But I don't agree that it isn't worth trying another London publisher. [. . .] Much love Betty.

---

23 The BBC *Children's Hour* was discontinued in 1964.
24 Bryan Balkwill, conductor of Welsh National Opera, 1963–7.
25 Maconchy's *Propheta mendax* for unaccompanied boys' or women's voices (TTA or SSA) (1965). Faber Music published the work in 1967.

APPENDICES
Grace Williams: Works

Indexing a relevant letter, preamble to a letter, or the introduction to a section

Orchestral

    Hen Walia overture (1930) 9, 56, 58
    Suite (*c.* 1931–2) 8, 14
    Movement for trumpet and chamber orchestra (1932) 14, 16, 18, 19
    Concert Overture (1933–4) (I.3), 31, 32
    Four Illustrations for the Legend of Rhiannon (1939, rev. 1940) (I.5), 39, 50, 51, 69, 70, 71
    Elegy for string orchestra (1936, rev. 1940) 51, 55
    Fantasia on Welsh Nursery Tunes for orchestra (1940) (II.1), 54, 55, 57, 58, 64, (II.2), 72, 74, 79, 97, 103, 116, 180, 248, 314, 317, 325, 338
    Sinfonia concertante (1940–41, rev. 1942–3) for piano and orchestra (II.1), 53, 54, 55, 58, 59, 60, 62, 65, 66, 68, 82, 84, 125
    Symphonic Impressions (Symphony No. 1, based on Owen Glendower) (1943, rev. 1952) (II.1), 63, (II.2), 67, 68, 69, 70, 71, 72, 83, 84, 89, (III.1), 94, 96, 97, 110, 111, 118, 127
    Sea Sketches for string orchestra (1944) (II.2), 76, 77, 79, 80, 86, 92, 93, 97, 105, 110, 114, 151, 268, 270, 272, 276, 284, 300, 304, 314, 316, 317, 321, 339
    Violin Concerto (1950) (III.1), 94, 95, 96, 97, 98, 101, 108, 109, 225, 229, 231, 232, 233, 234
    Mountain Sequence for orchestra from the film score for *Blue Scar* (1948) 99
    Polish Polka for orchestra (1948) 99
    Suite for string orchestra (1949) from incidental music for *The Dark Island* 95, 105
    Variations on a Swedish Tune: The Shoemaker for piano and orchestra (1950) 102
    Seven Scenes for Young Listeners (1954) 119
    Penillion (1955) (III.3), 121, 122, 125, 126, 135, 136, 145, 148, 151, (IV.5), 180, 182, 242, 245, 248, 254, 257, 300, 304, 330, 334, 338, 339

xxiv *Appendices – Grace Williams: Works*

Symphony No. 2 (1956, rev. 1976) (III.4), 124, 127, 130, 257, 259, 270, 271, 272, 273, 300, 301, 317, 321, (VI.6), 327, 328, 329, 330, 340, 343, 345, 346, 350, 351
Trumpet Concerto (1962–3) (IV.2), 156, 164, 165, 166, 167, 168, 170, 171, 172, 173, 176, (IV.5), 180, 182, 225, 234, 254, 257, 311, 314, 339, 350
Processional (1962 rev. 1968) (IV.2), 153, 155, 254, 255
Carillons for oboe and orchestra (1965, rev. 1973) (IV.5), 185, 186, (V.2), 202, 210, 211, 212, (V.3), 221, 222, 223, 254, 307, 311, 314, 325, 339
Severn Bridge Variations composite work (1966) (V.1), 192, 193, 196, (V.2), 201, 202, 345, 346
Ballads (1967–8) (V.3), 227, 228, 230, 231, 234, 235, (V.4), 239, 241, 242, 243, 245, 246, 248, 249, 251, 252, 253, 254, 270, 285
Castell Caernarfon (Investiture Processional) (1968–9) 245, 246, 247, 248, 249, (V.5), 255, 257, 258, 259, 262, 263, 266, 274, 276, 279, 295, 302, 303, 314, 315, 350

Chamber

Variations for String Quartet ('Veni Emmanuel') (1920s) 21, 22
Sextet for oboe, trumpet, violin, viola, cello, and piano (1931) 15, 20
Sonatina for flute and piano (1931) 26, 28
Suite for chamber orchestra/nine instruments (1932) 16, 17, 18, 36, 37
Three Nocturnes for two pianos (1953) 121, 125
Diabelleries variations on 'Oh! Where's my little basket gone?' for chamber ensemble (composite work) (c. 1955) 121

Vocal

Two Psalms for soprano and chamber orchestra (1927, rev. ?1934 or 5) 10, 14, (I.4), 35, 270
'Oh! snatch'd away in beauty's bloom' (Byron) for tenor and orchestra (1933) (I.3), 31, 33
'Oh! weep for those that wept' (Byron) for tenor and orchestra (1934) (I.3), 31, 33
Song of Mary for soprano and orchestra (1939, rev. 1940) 61, 84, 107
'Fairground' (Sam Harrison) for tenor and piano (1949) 95
'Flight' (Laurence Whistler) tenor and piano (1949, rev. 1953) 95, 120, 199
'The Lament of the Border Widow' (Anon) for mezzo-soprano and piano (1952) 254
'To Death' (Caroline Southey) tenor and piano (1953) 120
Six Poems by Gerard Manley Hopkins for contralto and string sextet (1958) (III.4), 131, 134, 135, 139, 140, 335, 338, 343, 344
Songs of Sleep (Francis Beaumont & John Fletcher, Thomas Campion, Alfred Tennyson) for soprano, alto flute, and harp (1959) (III.5), 138, 139, 163, 166
Four Medieval Welsh Poems for contralto, harp, and harpsichord (1962) 156, 338, 343, 344

'Lights Out' (Edward Thomas), for tenor and piano (1965) 199
Two Ninth Century Welsh Poems for baritone and harp (1965) 170, 175
'When my love swears' (Shakespeare) for tenor and piano (1967) 227
The Billows of the Sea (Walter Scott; Alfred Tennyson; Anon; John Gay) for contralto and piano (1969) (V.5), 255, 257, 258, 260, 261, 262, 264, 266
Fairest of Stars (John Milton), aria for soprano and orchestra (1973) (VI.4), 308, 311, 313, 314, 317, 320, 326
My Last Duchess (Robert Browning) for baritone and piano (1974) (VI.5), 321, 323, 324, 329, 330, 332

Choral

Gogonedawg arglwydd ('Praise the Lord Eternal') (Black Book of Carmarthen) for chorus and orchestra (1939) 48, 74, 79, 81, 84
'Dacw 'nghariad i iawr yn y berllan' ('See my love in the orchard yonder') for SSA chorus 57
Yr Eos ('The Nightingale') ('Ieuan Ddu') for SSA chorus and piano (1958) 138
All Seasons Shall Be Sweet for soprano, women's SSA chorus, and orchestra/ piano (1959) (III.5), 141, (IV.4), 176, 178, 199
Three Shakespearian Lyrics for SSA chorus and piano (1959) 143, 176, 199, 343
The Flower of Bethlehem/Carol Nadolig (Grace Williams/Saunders Lewis) SATB (1955) 295
Hymn to the Earth (Percy Bysshe Shelley) for unison voices and piano (1962) 153, 169
Benedicite for soprano, mixed chorus, and orchestra (1964) 169, (IV.4), 174, 176, 180, 182, 187
Carmina Avium (various) for SATB chorus, viola d'amore and harp (1966–7) (V.1), 192, 194, 195, 196, 198, (V.2), 199, 203, 211, 213, 214, 215, 216, 295
Missa cambrensis for four soloists, chorus, boys' choir and orchestra (1968–71) 198, 219, 241, 248, 249, 255, 256, 257, 260, 261, 262, 263, 266, 267, (VI.1), 269, 270, 271, 272, 273, 274, 275, 276, 278, 279, 281, 282, 283, 284, 285, 287, 288, 289, 290, 291, 293, 294, 298, 299, 300, 302, 303, 307
The Dancers (Anon; Hilaire Belloc; Thomas Chatterton; May Sarton; Kathleen Raine) for soprano, SSA chorus, string orchestra and harp (1951) 199
Can Gwraig y Pysgotwr (John Blackwell) for women's SSA chorus and piano duet (1969) 270
Ye Highlands and Ye Lowlands (Anon; Robert Burns; Walter Scott) for men's chorus and piano (1972) 289, 295, 300, 302
Ave Maris Stella, SATB chorus (1973) (VI.4), 307, 308, 314, 315, 316, 317, 318, 319, 327, 330, 332, 333, 350, 351
Two interlinked choruses: 'Harp Song of the Dane Women' (Kipling); 'To Sea! To Sea!' (T. L. Beddoes) for SATB, two horns and harp (1975) 330, 332, 333, 335, 336, 337, 338, 339, 341

Stage works

> *Dic Penderyn* (Henry Treece), unfinished opera (1949) 92
> *The Parlour* (Williams, after de Maupassant), opera (1959–61) (III.5), 137, 141, (IV.1), 147, 149, 151, (IV.2), 152, 153, 161, 162, 167, 168, 170, 172, (IV.5), 185, 186, 187, (V.1), 188, 189, 191, 192, 193, 194, 196, 212, 213, 225, 226, 227, 228, 229, 232, 234, 246, 247, 263, 264, 265, 266, 268, 278, 280, 317, 320, 321, 333, 335
> Projected TV opera (never written) (1966–7) 191, 192, 193, 194, 195, 196, 198, (V.2), 199, 203, 204, 210, 212, 213, 219, 220, 227, 232, 234, 235, 238, 266

Arrangements

> *Variations: Breuddwyd Dafydd Rhys* (c. 1934) (I.5)
> Three folk song arrangements (1950) 102, 104
> *Three Traditional Ballads*, arranged for tenor, flute, oboe, and string quartet (1950) 102
> *Twelve Welsh Airs* (1950) 102
> *Three Yugoslav Folksongs*, arranged for unison voices/SA chorus and piano (1952) 186
> *Hen Wlad fy Nhadau,* arranged for Bar, TTBB chorus, and orchestra (melody by James James) (1964) 179

Incidental scores
for radio

> *The Dark Island* (dramatic poem for radio, Henry Treece) (1948) 90
> *Rataplan* (radio fantasy, Henry Treece) (1949) 92, 93
> *The Merry Minstrel* (children's radio, after the Grimm's Brothers), for narrator and orchestra (1949) 95, 104, 116, 117, 225, 237, 242

for films

> *Blue Scar* (1948) 90, 93
> *David*, dir. Paul Dickson (1951) 106
> *A Story of Achievement*, dir. Paul Dickson (1952) 108
> *Fawley Achievement*, dir. Geoffrey Gurrin (1952) 109, 111, 112
> *A Letter for Wales*, dir. Tony Thompson (1960), 147

for drama

> Esther (play by Saunders Lewis), for voice, oboe, clarinet, trumpet, timpani/percussion, harp, and cello (1970) 266, 269, 270, 273

Elizabeth Maconchy: Works

Indexing a relevant letter, preamble to a letter, or the introduction to a section

Orchestral

Fantasy for Children for chamber orchestra (1927–8) 5
Concerto (Concertino) for piano and chamber orchestra (1928, rev. 1929–30) 4, 5, 6, 7, 8, 14, 33, (I.4), 37, 39, 41, (I.5), 149, 150, 269, 270, 271, 275
Theme and Variations (1928) 5
The Land (1929) 8, 19, 33, 34, (I.4), 37, 39, 44, 52, 104
Symphony (1929–30) 11, 13, 15
Suite for chamber orchestra (1930) 11, 12, 13
Comedy Overture (1932–3) 14, 16, 18, 19, 32, 33, 38
Viola Concerto (1937) (I.5), 44
Dialogue for piano and orchestra (1939–41) 48 (II.1), 51, 60, 64, 88, 123, 125
Theme and Variations for string orchestra (1942–3) (II.1), 63, (II.2), 65, 67, 68, 84, 105, 123, 125, 231
Suite from *Puck Fair* (1943) 74, 76, 77, 79, 80, 81, 84, 96, 103, 104, 267
Concertino for clarinet and string orchestra (1945) 83, 84, 86, 90
Symphony (1945–8) 83, 84, 86, 87, 88, 89, 90, (III.1), 94, 95, 97, 100, 101, 103, 108, 111, 118
Concertino for piano and string orchestra (1949) 94, 96, 105, 106, 107, 114
Two Dances from *Puck Fair* (1950) 97, 101
Nocturne (1950–51) (III.2), 105, 110, 111, 112, 144, 145
Concertino for bassoon and string orchestra (1952) 108, (III.3), 114, 118, 165, 259, 262, 264, 328
Proud Thames overture (1952) (III.3), 115, 116, 117, 333
Symphony for double string orchestra (1952–3) 107, 108, (III.3), 118, 119, 123, 127, 130, 317, 321
Concerto for oboe, bassoon, and string orchestra (1955–6) 123, 141, 142, 173
Serenata concertante for violin and orchestra (1962) 147, 150, (IV.2), 152, 154, 155, 158, 161, 165, 167, 170, 171, 172, (IV.4), 175, 176, 178, 181, 209, 229, 232, 233, 270, 299, 302, 338

Variazioni concertante for oboe, clarinet, bassoon, horn, and strings (1964–5) 167, 171, (IV.4), 174, 178, 179, (IV.5), 180, 182, 183, 184, 185, 209, 211, 214, 216, 218, 228, 229, 232, 233, 234, 235, 239, 241, 242, 254, 258

Music for Woodwind and Brass (1965–6) 211, 214, 216, 218, 229, 230, 231, 232, 233

Essex Overture (1966) (V.2), 247, 248, 249, 273

Three Cloudscapes (1968) 212, (V.3), 235, 238, (V.4), 239, 240, 241, 242, 245, 246, 247, 248, 250, 251, 268

Genesis (1972–3) (VI.3), 301, 303, 304, 305, (VI.4), 308, 322

Epyllion for cello and 15 strings (1973–5) 310, 314, 315, 316, 321, 324, (VI.6), 328, 332, 336, 351

Sinfonietta (1976) 332, 334, 337, 339, 342

Chamber

Violin Sonata (1927) 2, 15

Phantasy Quintet for strings (1929) 5, 10

Quintet for oboe and strings (1932) 20, 21, 22, 23, (I.3), 24, 218

String Quartet no. 1 (1933) 24, 26, 30, 32, 33, 34, 121, 122, 123, 316, 330, 333, 350

Six Short Pieces for violin and piano (1934) 35

Prelude, Interlude and Fugue for two violins (1934) (I.4), 36, 40

String Quartet no. 2 (1937) (I.5), 42, 43, 58, 62, 63, 122, 123

Viola Sonata (1937–8) 67

String Quartet no. 3 (1938) (I.5), 45, 52, 113, 122

Country Town for piano (1939) 48, 49

String Quartet no. 4 (1939–43) (I.5), 48, (II.1), 51, 56, 57, 62, 63, 67, 71, 84, 85, 86, 89, 91, 95, 97, 100, 120, 122, 267

Divertimento (initially Serenade) for cello and piano (1941–3) (II.1), 56, 57, 66, 67, 124

Violin Sonata (1943–4) 73, 74, 75, 77, 82, 84, 195, 196, 197, 228

String Quartet no. 5 (1948–9) 89, (II.5), 91, 92, 93, 94, 95, 97, 98, 99, 100, 122, 123, 125, (IV.2), 152, 154, 156, 158, 162, 206, 209, 213, 214, 269, 294, 295, 316, 330, 333, 350, 352

String Quartet no. 6 (1950) (III.1), 95, 104, (III.2), 108, 109, 122

Duo: Theme and Variations for violin and cello (1951) 108, 113, 125, 153, 154, 164, 165, 180, 279, 280

Diabelleries variations on 'Oh! Where's my little basket gone?' for chamber ensemble (composite work) (*c.* 1955) 121

String Quartet no. 7 (1955) 122, 131, 132, 133, 134, 151, 269, 315, 330, 333

String Trio (1956) 128, 129, 132, 151

Variations on a theme from Vaughan Williams's 'Job' for unaccompanied cello (1957) 139

Reflections for oboe, clarinet, viola, and harp (1960–61) (IV.1), 147, 150, 151, 162, 163, 165, 298, 300, 301

Appendices – Elizabeth Maconchy: Works xxix

Quintet for clarinet and strings (1962–3) (IV.2), 155, 156, 161, 166, 167, 171, 172, 173, 174, 180, 181, 184, 189, 211, 213, 214, 239, 240
Sonatina for string quartet (1963) 165, 177
Sonatina for harpsichord (1965) (IV.5), 186, 206, 213, 214, 243, 244, 271
Notebook for harpsichord (1965) 167, (IV.5), 186
Six Pieces for solo violin (1966) 167, 206
String Quartet no. 8 (1966–7) 154, (V.1), 197, 198, (V.2), 205, 208, 209, 210, 211, 216, 217, 218, 219, 220, 237, 238, 269, 294, 316, 330, 333
Preludio, fugato e finale for piano duet (1967) 220, 242, 243, 250, 251
String Quartet no. 9 (1968–9) 253, (V.5), 255, 256, 258, 266, 267, 268, 269, 270, 277, 279, 280, 290, 291, 294, 316, 330, 333, 337, 342, 350
Conversations for clarinet and viola (1969) 259, 271, 298, 300, 301
Three Preludes for violin and pianoforte (1969–70) 259
Music for double-bass and piano (1970) 283, 286
String Quartet no. 10 (1971–2) 290, 291, 292, 293, 294, 295, 296, 300, 301, 302, 303, 304, 316, 328, 329, 330, 333, 337, 342, 352
Three Easy Pieces for violin and viola (1972) 212
Oboe Quartet (1972) 288, (VI.3), 296, 301, 302, 303, 304, 320, 329
Three Bagatelles for oboe and harpsichord (1972) (VI.3), 296, 301, 305, (VI.4), 312
Touchstone for oboe and chamber organ (1975) 310, 326, 327, 328, 332, 348, 349
Morning, Noon and Night for solo harp (1976) 344, 349
String Quartet no. 11 (1976–7) (VI.7), 344, 349, 350, 351, 352

Vocal

'The Woodspurge' (Dante Gabriel Rossetti) for soprano and piano (1930) 16
How Samson bore away the gates of Gaza (Nicholas Vachel Lindsay), scena for soprano and piano (1938) 44, 86, 167
'The Disillusion' (Sheila Wingfield) for voice and piano (1941) 63
Sonnet Sequence (Kenneth Gee) for soprano and chamber orchestra (1946–7) 91, 93
A Winter's Tale (Kenneth Gee) for soprano and string quartet (1949) 91, 94, 137, 138, 139
'Sho-heen sho' Irish lullaby arranged for voice and piano (1955) 299
Four Shakespeare Songs for voice and piano (1956, 1965) 132, 189, 207, 208, 209
A Hymn to God the Father (John Donne) for soprano or tenor and piano (1959) 172, 182, 288, 291
Settings of Poems by Gerard Manley Hopkins for soprano (or tenor) and chamber orchestra (1964) 167, 171, 172, (IV.4), 174, 178
A Hymn to Christ (Donne) for tenor and piano (1965) 288, 291
The Sun Rising (Donne) for tenor and piano (1965) 288, 291

Ariadne (Cecil Day Lewis) for soprano and orchestra (1970–71) (VI.1), 275, 277, 282, 286, 288, 289, 290, 291, 292, 293, 294, 296, 303, 304, 308, 311, 314, 333, 339

Faustus (Christopher Marlowe) scena for tenor and piano (1971) 292, 294

Three Songs for voice and harp (1973) 315, 316, 328, 348, 349

Choral

Two Motets (John Donne) for double chorus (1931) 10, 14, 26, 29, 30, 31, 32, 34, 39, 172

Deborah (unknown) for three soloists, double chorus, and orchestra (1933–4), oratorio 29, 30, 31, 33, 34

The Leaden Echo and the Golden Echo (Gerard Manley Hopkins) for chorus and strings/chamber orchestra (1930–31, rev. 1933–34) 30, 32, 33, 275

Dies irae for contralto solo, chorus, and orchestra (1940–41) (II.1), 53, 54, 56, 57, 58

The Voice of the City (Jacqueline Morris) for female chorus and piano (1943) (II.2), 69, 71, 72, 74, 75, 76, 81

Six Settings of Poems by W.B. Yeats for soprano, chorus, and ensemble (1951) 110

Christmas Morning, children's cantata (1962) 152

Samson and the Gates of Gaza for chorus and orchestra/brass band (1963–4/1973) (IV.4), 174, 177, 242, 310, 314, 315, 316, 317

Nocturnal (Barnes, Thomas, Shelley) for SATB chorus (1965) (IV.5), 182, 186, 189, 216, (V.3), 221, 222, 223, 292, 300, 301, 332

Propheta mendax (eleventh-century Latin poems) for unaccompanied boys' or women's voices in three parts (TTA or SSA) (1965) 187, 195, 196, 197, 220, 227, 228, 341

Down with the Rosemary and Bays: Twelfth Night carol (Robert Herrick) for two-part chorus, with concluding four-part round (1966) 167, 195

Nowell, Nowell, Nowell 'Nowell, sing we all now and some' for 3-part unaccompanied chorus (1966) 167, 206

'I Sing of a Maiden', carol for soprano (or treble) solo and unaccompanied three-part chorus (SAT or TrAT) (1966) 195, 196

'This Day', carol for soprano (or treble) solo and unaccompanied two-part chorus (SA or TrA) (1966) 195, 196

And Death Shall Have No Dominion (Dylan Thomas) for SATB chorus and brass (1968–69) (V.5), 256, 260, 261, 265, 267, 268, 270, 310, 311, 334

Prayer before Birth (Louis MacNeice) for women's chorus (SSAA) (1971) 292, 302, 318, 319, 341, 342

Fly-by-Nights for women's or children's voices with harp or piano (1973) 305, 316, 321

The Isles of Greece (Byron) for chorus and orchestra (1973) 315, 316

Two Epitaphs for SSA chorus (1974) 310, 314, 315, 341, 342

Sirens' Song (William Browne) for soprano solo and chorus (1974) 324, 325, 332, 337, 342

Appendices – Elizabeth Maconchy: Works   xxxi

Two Settings of Poems by Gerard Manley Hopkins for choir and brass (1975) 334, 335, 342, 343, 345, 346, 351

Héloïse and Abelard (Maconchy, after Abelard) for soprano, tenor and baritone soloists, chorus, and orchestra (1976–8) 324, (VI.7), 339, 342, 343, 344, 346, 348, 350, 351, 352

Stage works

Great Agrippa (or the Inky Boys), ballet (1933) 36, 37, 38, 91.4), (I.5), 72

Little Red Shoes, ballet (1935) 14, 29, 37, 39, (I.3)

Puck Fair, ballet (1940) (II.1), 51, 63, 89

The Sofa (Ursula Vaughan Williams, after Crebillon fils), one-act opera (1956–7) (III.4), 127, 129, 131, 132, 133, 136, (III.5), 137, 144, 145, 151, 152, 161, (V.1), 191, 192, 193, 194, 195, 197, (V.2), 202, 204, 209, 210, 211, 212, 213, 226, 229, 243, 246, 247, 268, 344, 348, 351

The Three Strangers (Maconchy, after Thomas Hardy), one-act opera (1957–9) (III.4), (III.5), 137, 140, 151, 152, 161, 194, 195, 200, 201, 202, 203, 209, 218, 219, 220, 224, 228, 235, 247, 248, 249, 261, 262, 263, 264, 270, 271, 274, 275, 286, 287, 344, 348, 349

The Departure (Anne Ridler), one-act opera (1960–61) (III.5), 142, 151, (IV.2), 152, 157, 158, 159, 160, 161, 162, 189, 194, 209, 229, 268, 344, 348, 351

Incidental music for *Witnesses* (Anne Ridler), play (1966) 218

The Birds (after Aristophanes), opera (1967–8) (V.2), 218, 219, 220, 224, 225, 228, 235, 238, 240, 247, 248, 249, 261, 316, 326, 327, 340

The Jesse Tree (Anne Ridler), masque (1969–70) (V.5), 259, 260, 267, (VI.1), 270, 271, 272, 273, 274, 275, 276, 277, 278, 280, 281, 282, 283

The King of the Golden River (Anne Ridler, after Ruskin), children's opera (1975) (VI.5), 324, 326, (VI.6), 327, 328, 331, 332, 334, 335, 336, 340, 341, 342

A Select Bibliography

Writings by Elizabeth Maconchy (arranged chronologically)

'Vaughan Williams as a Teacher'. *Composer* 2 (1959): 18–20.
'A Short Symposium on Women Composers'. *Composer* 6 (1961): 19–21.
'The Image of Greatness: Ralph Vaughan Williams'. *Composer* 15 (1965): 10–21.
'Who Is Your Favourite Composer?' *Composer* 24 (1967): 2–210.
'The Birds'. *Music in Education* 33 (1969): 24–25.
'A Composer Speaks – I'. *Composer* 42 (1971–72): 25–29.
'Serenata Concertante – an Analytical Note', in *Twenty British Composers*, ed. Peter Dickinson. London: Feeney Trust, 1975, 50–53.
'In Conversation with John Skiba'. *Composer* 63 (1978): 7–10.

Writings by Grace Williams (arranged chronologically)

'A Letter from Vienna'. *RCM Magazine* 26, no. 2 (1930): 64–67.
'Vaughan Williams: A Tribute'. *RCM Magazine* 55, no. 1 (1959): 36–37.
'How Welsh Is Welsh Music?' *Welsh Music* 4, no. 4 (1973): 9–12.
'Views and Revisions'. *Welsh Music* 5, no. 4 (1976–77): 9–14.
'Grace Williams: A Self Portrait'. *Welsh Music* 8, no. 5 (1987): 7–16.

Select writings about Maconchy, Williams, and their circle

Beausang, Ita, and Séamas De Barra. *Ina Boyle (1889–1967): A Composer's Life*. Cork: Cork University Press, 2018.
Beer, Anna. 'Maconchy', in *Sounds and Sweet Airs: The Forgotten Women of Classical Music*. London: Oneworld, 2016, 287–324.
Boyd, Malcolm. 'Benjamin Britten and Grace Williams: Chronicle of a Friendship'. *Welsh Music* 6, no. 6 (Winter 1980–81): 7–37.
Boyd, Malcolm. *Grace Williams*. Cardiff: University of Wales Press, 1980, 2nd ed. 1996.
Brüstle, Christa, and Danielle Sofer, eds. *Elizabeth Maconchy: Music as Impassioned Argument*. Studien zur Wertungsforschung. Vienna, London and New York: Universal Edition, 2018.
Cotterill, Graeme. 'Music in the Blood & Fire in the Soul? National Identity in the Life and Music of Grace Williams'. PhD dissertation, University of Wales, Bangor, 2012.
Cotterill, Graeme. 'Shall Nation Speak unto Nation? Grace Williams and the BBC in Wales, 1931–1950'. *Women & Music: A Journal of Gender and Culture* 17 (2013): 59–77.

Appendices – Select writings about Maconchy, Williams, and their circle xxxiii

Davies, Eiluned. '"A Pianist's Note on Grace Williams's *Sinfonia Concertante*'. *Welsh Music* 5, no. 9 (Summer 1978): 22–29.

Davies, Eiluned. 'Grace Williams and the Piano'. *Welsh Music* 6, no. 4 (Spring 1980): 18–25.

Doctor, Jenny. 'The Maconchy Seventh String Quartet and the BBC'. *Musical Objects* 1 (1995): 5–8.

Doctor, Jenny. 'Intersecting Circles: The Early Careers of Elizabeth Maconchy, Elisabeth Lutyens and Grace Williams'. *Women & Music: A Journal of Gender and Culture* 2 (1998): 90–109.

Doctor, Jenny. '"Working for Her Own Salvation": Vaughan Williams as Teacher of Elizabeth Maconchy, Grace Williams and Ina Boyle', in *Vaughan Williams in Perspective*, ed. Lewis Foreman. Albion Press for the Vaughan Williams Society, 1998, 181–201.

Doctor, Jenny. 'Afterword: Channeling the Swaying Sound of the Sea', in *The Sea in the British Musical Imagination*, ed. Eric Saylor and Christopher M. Scheer. Woodbridge: Boydell and Brewer, 2015, 267–77.

Fuller, Sophie. 'Putting the BBC and T. Beecham to Shame: The Macnaghten – Lemare Concerts, 1931–7'. *Journal of the Royal Musical Association* 138, no. 2 (2013): 377–414.

Howes, Frank. 'The Younger English Composers III. Elizabeth Maconchy'. *The Monthly Musical Record* (1938): 165–8.

Leighton Thomas, A. F. 'Grace Williams'. *The Musical Times* 157 (1956): 240–3.

Macnaghten, Anne. 'Elizabeth Maconchy'. *The Musical Times* 156 (1955): 298–302.

Mathias, Rhiannon. *Lutyens, Maconchy, Williams and Twentieth-Century Music: A Blest Trio of Sirens*. Farnham: Ashgate, 2012.

Roma, Catherine. *The Choral Music of Twentieth-Century Women Composers: Elisabeth Lutyens, Elizabeth Maconchy, and Thea Musgrave*. Lanham, MD: Scarecrow Press, 2006.

Siegel, Erica. '"What a Delicious, What a Malicious Imputation!": Gender and Politics in the Reception of Elizabeth Maconchy's *The Sofa*'. MA in Music thesis, University of California, Riverside, 2012.

Siegel, Erica. 'Elizabeth Maconchy: The Early Years, 1923–1939'. PhD dissertation, University of California, Riverside, 2016.

Various. 'Grace Williams – a Symposium'. *Welsh Music* 5, no. 6 (Summer 1977): 15–30, and 5, no. 7 (Winter 1977): 41–60.

Warkov, E. R. 'Traditional Features in Grace Williams's *Penillion*'. *Welsh Music* 7, no. 1 (Summer 1982): 15–24.

Whittall, Arnold. 'Grace Williams 1906–1977'. *Soundings: A Musical Journal* 7 (1978): 19–37.

Index

Editors' notes on the index

This is an index of names, musical works, performing ensembles, organisations, places, and venues found in the letters, section and letter introductions, and footnotes.

For names, the birth and death dates, when known, are shown here in the index, rather than in footnotes. Nicknames and common abbreviations used by Maconchy and Williams are shown as cross-references.

References for Maconchy and Williams themselves are not provided, but compositions by them that are mentioned or discussed in the letters, introductions, or footnotes are indexed (by letter number) in the separate work lists of each composer (Grace Williams: Works, pp. xxiii–xxvi; Elizabeth Maconchy: Works, pp. xxvii–xxxi).

City and country names use terminology from the time of the letters, rather than that of today (e.g. USSR rather than Russia).

In order to keep this index manageable and helpful for the reader, we have not included every name, title, place, venue, etc. found in the letters, introductions and footnotes. Nor have we listed every mention of a term, just those that are most meaningful.

JD and SF

Abbey Opera (London) 431
Aberfan (Wales) 255
Aberystwyth (Wales) 235, 317, 327, 335, 390, 445
Academy of St-Martin-in-the-Fields (London) 414, 422, 441, 447, 454
Addison, John (1920–1998) 183
Adey, Christopher (1943–) 458
'Adrian' *see* Boult, Adrian
Aeolian Hall (London) 16, 79
Aeolian String Quartet 155, 158, 160, 167, 169, 278, 279, 280, 304, 423, 444
Alberni String Quartet 424, 444, 446
Alberta String Quartet *see* University of Alberta String Quartet

Aldeburgh (Suffolk, England) 194, 211, 237, 320, 373, 382
  Aldeburgh Festival 194, 211, 237, 266, 281, 291, 292, 294, 373, 378, 424, 430, 449, 467, 378
Aldwych Theatre (London) 208, 381
Alfred Lengnick & Co. (music publisher) 115, 121, 129, 133, 142, 143, 157, 158
Allegri String Quartet 154, 155, 170, 198, 200–01, 203, 205, 345, 352, 354, 367–8, 382, 383, 389, 444, 466, 475, 476
Allen, Hugh (1869–1946) 3, 6, 26
Alley, John 444

xxxvi Index

America *see* Latin America, United States of America (USA)
Amici String Quartet 173, 174
Ammanford (Wales) 362, 368
Amsterdam (The Netherlands) 20, 106
  see also ISCM Festivals
Andersen, Hans Christian (1805–1875) 19
Andrewes, John 406, 424, 432
'Anna' *see* Dunlop, Anna (née LeFanu)
'Anne' *see* Macnaghten, Anne
Ansermet, Ernst (1883–1969) 442
Aprahamian, Felix (1914–2005) 207, 246
Aristophanes (*c*446–*c*386 BC) 287, xxxi
  The Birds (set by Maconchy) 250, 287–8, 289
Armstrong Gibbs, Cecil (1889–1960) 25, 26, 27, 142
'Arnold' *see* Ashby, Arnold
Arnold, Malcolm (1921–2006)
  Severn Bridge Variations (composite work) 263, 468, 470
  Symphony No. 2 159
Aronowitz, Cecil (1916–1978) 170, 195
Arrau, Claudio (1903–1991) 458
Arts Council of Great Britain 149, 153, 346, 346, 445, 461, 471
  Arts Council Opera Scheme 113–14, 115, 120
  Welsh Arts Council (Committee) 137, 157, 178, 179, 185, 208, 216, 240, 329, 344, 347, 354, 355, 391, 398, 400, 407, 411, 413, 415, 417, 418, 419, 420, 423, 426, 436, 437, 475
Arundell, Dennis (1898–1988) 272
Ashby, Arnold (1917–1994) 130, 139, 140, 144, 161, 177
Association of Welsh Male Choirs 398
Astaire, Fred (1899–1987) 450
  Top Hat 450
Atherton, David (1944–) 347, 355, 361
Auden, Wystan Hugh (1907–1973) 409
Austen, Jane (1775–1817) 440, 470
Australia 467–8, 469, 471, 472
Aveling, Claude (1869–1943) 15
Aveling, Valda (1920–2007) 273, 392, 399, 406, 417
Aymé, Marcel (1902–1967) 249, 270

'B' *see* LeFanu, William Richard
Bach, Johann Sebastian (1685–1750) 22, 112, 150, 415, 442, 448
  Chromatic Fantasy and Fugue, BWV 903 197
  Italian Concerto, BWV 971 197
  Mass in B minor, BWV 232 436
  Cantata, BWV 12: Sinfonia 442–3
  Violin Concerto in E major, BWV 1042 24
Bagenal, Nick (1891–1973) 94–5
Baker, Janet (1933–) 377, 380, 382, 383, 386, 475
Balkwill, Bryan (1922–2007) 242, 245, 249, 293
'Ballet Club Concerts' *see* Macnaghten-Lemare Concerts (London)
Ballymorris (Enniskerry, Ireland) 148, 150
Balzac, Honoré de (1799–1850)
  El verdugo 249, 270, 280, 281
Bangor (Wales) 12, 212, 223, 390, 398
  Bangor University 28, 179, 201, 398
Banks, Don (1923–1980) 258
Barbirolli, Evelyn *see* Evelyn Rothwell
Barbirolli, John (1899–1970) 131, 229, 235, 237, 359
Barenboim, Daniel (1942–) 284, 360
Barker, Noelle (1928–2013) 248, 477
Barlow, Sybil (1902–1985)
  Dance of the Dryads 5
Barnard, Anthony (1891–1963) 16, 37
Barnes, William (1801–1886)
  'Come' (set by Maconchy in *Nocturnal*) 283, xxx
Barrow, John (1931–) 379, 383
Barry (Glamorgan, Wales) viii, 51, 69, 88, 105, 166, 188 (Fig. PIV.1), 216, 235, 260, 262, 265, 280, 322, 325, 364, 384, 396, 402, 431, 459, 474
  Barry Male Voice Choir 381, 390, 398, 402
  Glamorgan Summer School 396, 398
Bartók, Béla (1881–1945) xii, 67, 103, 107, 129, 170, 190, 268, 323, 354
  Concerto for Orchestra 103–4
  Sonata for solo violin 148
  string quartets xii, 190, 297
  Violin Concerto No. 2 126, 129, 228
Bates, Cuthbert (1899–1980) 35
Bath (Somerset, England) 4
  Bath Festival 316, 320, 394, 395, 397, 400
Bauld, Alison (1944–)
  Egg for tenor, flute, cello, vibraphone, and drum ix, 430 (Ex. PVI.5.1)
Bax, Arnold (1883–1953) 85
  Winter Legends, symphonic concerto for piano and orchestra 16
BBC *see* British Broadcasting Corporation
Beatles, The 290, 450

Beaumont, Francis (1584–1616) and
    Fletcher, John (1579–1625)
  'Come, sleep' (set by Williams in *Songs
    of Sleep*) 175, xxiv
Beddoes, Thomas Lovell (1803–1849)
    439, 452
  'To Sea! To Sea!' (set by Williams as
    Two Interlinked Choruses) 439,
    444, 452, xxv
Bedford (Bedfordshire, England) 66, 72,
    92, 95, 97, 249, 257, 318, 329, 356,
    386
Beecham, Lady *see* (1) Humby, Betty
    (2) Hudson, Shirley
Beecham, Thomas (1879–1961) 95, 183–4
Beethoven, Ludwig van (1770–1827) 129,
    257–8
  Adelaïde for voice and piano, Op.46 38
  Fidelio, Op. 72 / *Leonore* 50, 217, 445
  Mass in C, Op. 86 338
  Overture to "*Egmont*", Op. 84 235
  string quartets 129, 371
  Symphony no. 3, Op. 55 'Eroica' 258
Bell, Sebastian (1941–2007) 210
Belloc Lowndes, Marie Adelaide (1868–
    1947) 235
Belsen (Bergen-Belsen concentration
    camp, Germany) 280
'Ben' and 'Benjamin' *see* Britten,
    Benjamin
Bennett, Richard Rodney (1936–2012)
    234, 281–2, 294, 301, 322, 388,
    400, 440
  A Penny for a Song 297, 299, 300
  Epithalamian 280, 282
  Symphony No. 2 282, 299
  The Mines of Sulphur 235, 256, 265,
    299
Berg, Alban (1885–1935) 343
  Lulu 203, 235, 340
  Lyric Suite 477
  Violin Concerto 148, 159, 256, 308
  Wozzeck 47, 235, 301, 302, 380
Berio, Luciano (1925–2003) 190, 254
  Differences 199
  Circles 199
Berkeley, Lennox (1903–1989) 363
  Oboe Quartet, Op. 70 430
Berkman, Louis (1934–1993) 433, 434,
    435, 443, 444
Berlin (Germany)/East Berlin 225, 226
  Berlin Radio 225
Berlioz, Hector (1803–1869) 377, 433
  Symphonie fantastique, Op. 14 304

Bernard, Anthony (1891–1963) 16, 37,
    106, 139
Bernstein, Leonard (1918–1990) 307
Beyond the Fringe 208
Biafra (Africa) 307, 327
'Billy' *see* LeFanu, William Richard
Birmingham (England) 194, 214
  Birmingham Brass 330, 338
  City of Birmingham Symphony
    Orchestra ('C.B.S.O.') 191, 198,
    200, 202, 208, 212, 214, 219, 236,
    245
  University of Birmingham 357
Birtwistle, Harrison (1934–) 229, 424–5
Bishop's Stortford (Essex, England) 288
  Bishop's Stortford College 279, 287,
    315, 316, 317, 363
Bizet, Georges (1838–1875)
  Carmen 302
Blech, Harry (1910–1999) 65, 347
  Blech Quartet 65, 83, 86, 123, 124
Bliss, Arthur (1891–1975) 27, 33, 35, 45,
    70, 76
  Music for Strings, Op. 123 162
Blom, Eric (1888–1959) 153
Bohana, Roy 252, 271, 273–4, 275, 276,
    277, 398, 475
Boissier, Corentin xiii
Bolet, Alberto (1905–1999) 235, 237
Bolton (England) 219, 222
Boosey & Hawkes 44, 338, 352, 368, 424,
    438
  Boosey & Hawkes Concerts 79
Boreham (Essex, England) xix, 147
Boulanger, Nadia (1887–1979) 301, 449
Boulez, Pierre (1925–2016) 164, 307–8,
    360, 392, 401
  Le martineau sans maître 307–8
Boult, Adrian (1889–1983) 6, 16, 17, 27,
    40, 41, 50, 66, 67, 70, 77, 78, 95,
    97, 109, 110, 121, 123, 129, 131,
    148, 263, 359, 394
Bournemouth (England)
  Bournemouth Symphony Orchestra 30,
    38, 39, 195, 414
Boustead, Alan 204
Bowen, Kenneth (1932–) 379–80
Boyd, Malcolm (1932–2001) xi, xiii, xix,
    66, 384
Boyle, Ina (1889–1967) xv, 44, 77, 89,
    100, 101, 131, 144, 150, 151, 162,
    174, 232, 234, 238, 261, 269, 271,
    273, 275, 283, 286–7, 289
  Gaelic Hymns 162

xxxviii *Index*

The spacious firmament on high
 (Addison) 162
Think then my soul (Donne) for tenor
 and string quartet 101
Bradford (West Riding of Yorkshire,
 England) 223
Bradshaw, Susan (1931–2005) 281–2,
 294, 322
Brahms, Johannes (1833–1897) 27, 395,
 427
 A German Requiem, Op. 45 395
 Piano Concerto No. 2, Op. 83 395
 Symphony No. 4, Op. 98 395
 Violin Concerto, Op. 77 16, 395
Braithwaite, Nicholas (1939–) 408
Bright, Clive 424, 455, 459
Brighton (England) 14, 15, 30, 38, 128, 141
Brindle, Reginald Smith (1917–2003) 164,
 179, 398
Bristol (England) 255, 262, 263, 459
 University of Bristol 121
British Broadcasting Corporation (BBC)
 xiv, xvii, xviii, xix, xxii, 5, 11, 17,
 18, 19, 22, 24, 25, 28, 30, 37, 39,
 40, 41, 43, 46, 49, 50, 53, 54, 62,
 64, 66, 67, 71, 72, 73, 74, 78, 80,
 83, 86, 91, 93, 96, 100, 104, 106,
 121, 122, 124, 125, 126, 128, 132,
 135, 141, 142, 143, 147, 151, 153,
 160, 161, 164, 166, 170, 191, 194,
 218, 224, 229, 234, 235, 240, 245,
 249, 250, 261, 263, 266–7, 268,
 274, 275, 283, 284, 289, 291, 298,
 300, 302, 309, 315, 317, 319, 329,
 333, 335, 336, 338, 340, 341, 343,
 347, 355, 368, 370, 371, 376, 379,
 382, 385, 389, 392, 398, 399, 402,
 403, 407, 410, 419, 423, 425, 427,
 431, 432, 437, 439, 442, 444, 450,
 453, 454, 457, 458, 460, 468, 469
 BBC Central Music Advisory
  Committee 197, 205
 BBC commission xiv, 51, 55, 166, 178,
  179, 194, 218, 226, 238, 249, 263,
  315, 317, 318–9, 392, 411, 418,
  444, 452–3
 BBC Maida Vale Studios 109, 126
 BBC Music Library 275
 BBC Reading Panel/Music Panel 66,
  83, 91, 93, 128, 143, 147, 151, 230,
  270, 272, 274, 279, 410
 BBC Written Archives Centre (WAC) xi,
  39, 41, 53, 54, 56, 61, 62, 66, 71,
  73, 83, 91, 93, 96, 99, 106, 122, 126

BBC ensembles
 Augmented Orchestra 120
 BBC Chorus 99, 277, 283, 285, 398,
  410, 412
 BBC Midland Light Orchestra 357
 BBC Northern Orchestra/Symphony
  Orchestra 66, 84–5, 86, 87, 139,
  147, 148, 211, 335, 342, 446
 BBC Northern Singers 342
 BBC Orchestra 16, 50, 53, 62, 68, 70,
  90, 99
 BBC Salon Orchestra 74, 79
 BBC Salon Orchestra Quartet 71
 BBC Scottish Orchestra/Symphony
  Orchestra (Glasgow) 88, 142, 238,
  239, 295, 336, 340
 BBC Singers 91, 420, 427, 444, 446,
  447, 452, 455, 458, 460
 BBC Symphony Orchestra/Concert xvii,
  16, 22, 40, 44, 61, 62, 72, 77, 78,
  95, 109, 110, 121, 123, 149, 151,
  183, 238, 269, 284, 298, 308, 342,
  355, 401, 417
 BBC Training Orchestra 263
 BBC Welsh Orchestra xvii, 51, 55–6,
  70, 98, 119, 125, 128, 131, 138,
  142, 152, 195, 235, 237, 284, 298,
  299, 309, 313, 315, 319, 326, 333,
  335, 336, 351, 358, 379, 395, 425,
  427, 451, 458, 468, 474
 BBC Western Studio Orchestra 43, 44
 BBC Wireless Chorus 48
 BBC Women's Chorus 229, 231, 250, 261
BBC networks & departments
 BBC 1 (TV) 256, 305, 338, 359
 BBC 2 (TV) 380, 409
 BBC Belfast/Station 40, 41
 BBC Cardiff *see* BBC Wales *in*
  British Broadcasting Corporation
  networks & departments
 BBC European Service 70, 83, 88
 BBC Features Programmes 106, 122
 BBC Forces/General Forces Programme
  68, 95
 BBC Glasgow *see* BBC Scotland *in*
  British Broadcasting Corporation
  networks
 BBC Home Service/Basic Home
  Service 61, 62, 70, 77, 85, 88,
  90, 99, 114, 121, 125, 132, 139,
  141, 143, 147, 148, 149, 152,
  160, 166, 195, 199, 210, 219,
  229, 230
 BBC Latin American Service 67, 83

Index xxxix

BBC Light Programme 127, 136, 142, 147, 148
BBC Midland 125, 353
BBC Music Department 67, 70, 96, 125, 126, 128, 164, 229
BBC Music Programme 237, 239, 241, 248, 249, 250, 254, 261, 273, 277, 284, 291, 293, 295, 298, 304, 307, 312, 313, 319, 326
BBC National Programme xvii, 12, 16, 18, 39, 40, 48, 51, 53, 54
BBC Overseas Department 67, 70, 71, 73
BBC Overseas Programmes 67, 70
BBC Radio 1 335
BBC Radio 2 335
BBC Radio 3 333, 334, 335, 336, 340, 341, 343, 347, 353, 354, 355, 358, 359, 360, 364, 367, 368, 374, 376, 389, 395, 397, 398, 401, 403, 407, 409, 410, 413, 416, 417, 420, 425, 427, 429, 430, 431, 432, 433, 434, 435, 437, 439, 442, 443, 444, 446, 448, 451, 453, 454, 455, 458, 460, 462, 466, 467, 471, 475, 478, 479
BBC Radio 4 262, 304, 353, 458
BBC Regional Programmes (London, West) xvii, 16–7, 19, 40, 41, 43, 353
BBC Scotland (Glasgow) 239
BBC Schools Broadcasts/Programmes xvii, 104, 106, 107, 108, 131, 136, 146, 148, 210
BBC Third Programme xxii, 104, 105, 106, 113, 121, 122, 123, 124, 125, 132, 140, 142, 143, 144, 147, 153, 154, 158, 160, 161, 173, 177, 178, 192, 198, 208, 211, 222, 227, 234, 238, 248, 280, 283, 291, 300, 308, 313, 322, 329, 333, 341, 355
BBC Wales (Cardiff, Llandaff) xiv, xvii, 55–6, 61, 70, 119, 125, 126, 128, 133, 137, 146, 149, 165, 178, 179, 263, 269, 273, 277, 289, 292, 293, 295, 296, 298, 300, 302, 309, 315, 317, 347, 356, 395, 401, 403, 411, 412, 418, 427, 432, 444, 447, 452, 453, 458, 460, 468
BBC Wales TV 229, 232, 289, 294, 298, 305, 327, 334–5, 345, 355, 360, 402
BBC Welsh Home Service 119, 122, 210, 229, 333, 341, 345, 383, 431

BBC publications
 Listener, The 127, 131, 156, 169, 170, 204, 327, 340, 341, 405, 417, 450
 Radio Times 273, 297, 304, 321, 337, 364, 383, 390, 407, 408, 426, 427, 428, 429, 431, 444, 461, 464, 468, 470
BBC series & programmes
 A Composer Speaks 376
 BBC Concerts of Contemporary Music 24, 48, 49, 53, 54
 BBC Light Music Festival 163
 BBC Promenade Concerts (London) 5, 11, 20, 57, 61, 62, 65, 72, 77, 78, 81, 83, 90–91, 92, 93, 95, 102, 123, 150, 151, 163–4, 165, 171, 180, 181, 182, 222, 226, 227, 234, 236, 238, 240, 275, 284, 286, 290, 336, 337, 386, 399, 400, 401, 407, 411, 415, 416, 417, 468
 Children's Hour/Welsh Children's Hour 119, 131, 152, 182, 242
 Composer's Portrait 241, 245, 248, 249, 250, 251, 253, 256, 257, 258, 261, 262, 434, 439, 446, 453, 454, 455, 457, 458, 460, 467, 478
 Composers on Criticism 403, 407
 Forsyte Saga, The (1969, BBC1 TV) 333–4
 Music in Our Time 273, 353, 354, 389, 395, 410, 435
 Music Magazine 261, 264, 266–9
 Musica Viva 293, 307
 Omnibus (TV) 338, 359
 The Problem of New Music 248
 St David's Festival 333, 444, 447, 452, 458
 The String Quartet of Today (1975, series) 440
 Thursday Concert/Thursday Invitation Concerts/Tuesday Invitation Concerts 158, 160, 191, 194, 195, 199, 211, 212, 329
 Weekend in Cardiff (1969, Radio 3) 340, 343
 Woman's Hour 121, 458
 Women as Composers (1973, Radio 3) 407, 412, 413, 414–5, 418
 [BBC programmes on British composers] 105, 241, 364
 [other BBC programmes on women/women composers] 88, 184

xl *Index*

[broadcast series of Maconchy string quartets] 147, 154, 155, 156, 160, 403, 413, 423, 424, 439, 444
BBC station headquarters & venues
   BBC Cardiff Station 44, 125, 126, 182, 418
   BBC Manchester studios 338, 341
   Broadcasting House, Concert Hall (London) 27
   Broadcasting House (Llandaff) 263, 269
   Bush House (Aldwych, London) 83
   Maida Vale Studios (London) 109, 126
   Roundhouse (London) 392, 395
   Studio 10 (Waterloo Bridge, London) 17
British Council, The 198, 201, 280
British Music Information Centre, The 289
Britten, Benjamin ('Ben') (1913–1976) xii, 14, 21, 22, 24, 26, 27, 29, 34, 35, 39, 47, 68, 94, 129, 141, 170, 193, 194, 199, 219, 235, 241, 248, 292, 294, 329, 331, 373, 377, 378, 380, 396, 408, 449, 450, 462, 475, 479
   A Midsummer's Night Dream, Op. 64 191, 225
   Albert Herring, Op. 39 145, 204
   Alla Quartetto Serioso: 'Go play, boy, play' 34, 36
   Billy Budd, Op. 50 141, 193, 265, 292
   Canticle V, 'The Death of Saint Narcissus', Op. 89 442
   Cello Suite No. 2, Op. 80 365
   children's operas 462
   Church Parables: *Curlew River*, Op.71, *The Burning Fiery Furnace*, Op.77, *The Prodigal Son*, Op.81 373
   The Golden Vanity, Op. 78 292, 294, 462
   The Holy Sonnets of John Donne, Op. 35 378
   Les Illuminations, Op. 18 68
   Nocturnal after John Dowland, Op. 70 241
   Owen Wingrave, Op. 85 380
   Peter Grimes, Op. 33 235, 373
   Phaedra, Op. 93 475
   Phantasy in F minor for string quintet (1932) 24
   Phantasy for oboe and string trio, Op. 2 25, 26, 39
   Sinfonia da Requiem, Op. 20 232
   Sinfonietta, Op.1 24
   Sonata in C for cello and piano, Op. 65 194
   Spring Symphony, Op. 44 278
   Suite on English Folk Tunes, 'A Time there was', Op. 90 449, 475
   Symphony for cello and orchestra, Op. 68 313
   Two Part-Songs (1932): 'I Lov'd a Lass', 'Lift Boy' 34, 36
   Violin Concerto, Op. 15 68, 408
   War Requiem, Op. 66 194, 197, 205, 404
Broadcasting House (London, Llandaff) *see* British Broadcasting Corporation station headquarters
Bronowski, Jacob (1908–1974) 416, 420–21
Brook, Peter (1925–) 208, 381
Brooke, Gwydion (1912–2005) 147, 151, 158, 336, 340, 342
Brosa Quartet 51, 52, 71
Brown, (Edward) Godfrey (1874–1955) 40, 41
Browne, Sandra (1947–) 428, 431
Browne, William (1590–1645) 436, xxx
Browning, Robert (1812–1889)
   My Last Duchess (set by Williams) 423, 433, 435, xxv
Brussels (Belgium) *see* ISCM Festivals
Brymer, Jack (1915–2003) 238, 397
Bryn-Jones, Delme (1934–2001) 315, 428
Büchner, Georg (1813–1837) 301
Buck, Percy (1871–1947) 290
Budapest (Hungary) 131, 306, 316
   Budapest Symphony Orchestra 306, 321
Budden, Julian (1924–2007) 454
Buesst, Aylmer (1883–1970) 16, 18
Busch, Adolph (1891–1952) 16, 24
   Busch Quartet 16
Bush, Alan (1900–1995) 191
   Diabelleries (composite work) 154–5
Bush House (Aldwych, London) *see* British Broadcasting Corporation station headquarters
Bushey Park (Enniskerry, Ireland) 286–7
Busoni, Ferruccio (1866–1924)
   Rondo Arlecchinesco for orchestra with tenor, Op. 46 107
Byron, Lord (1788–1824) 37, 422, 424
   The Isles of Greece (set by Maconchy) 422, 424, xxx
   'Oh! snatch'd away in beauty's bloom' (set by Williams) 37, xiv
   'Oh! Weep for those that wept' (set by Williams) 37, xxiv
   'So we'll go no more a-roving' (set by Maconchy) 422, 471, 472, 473

Caernarfon (Gwynedd, Wales) 334
  Caernarfon Castle 315, 318–19
Caerphilly (Glamorgan, Wales)
  Caerphilly Festival 265
Cage, John (1912–1992) 409
California (USA) 203, 397
Callas, Maria (1923–1977) 237, 249
Cambridge (England)
  The Cambridge Hymnal (1967) 215, 254, 266
  Cambridge Music Club 396
  King's College, Chapel 266
  King's College, Choir 253–4, 266
  University of Cambridge 231
Camden, Anthony (1938–2006) 410, 413, 418
Camden, Archie (1888–1979) 178, 180, 410
Camden Festival (London) 249, 259, 263, 269, 272, 291, 314
Camden School for Girls (London) 34, 62, 78, 91, 100, 104, 318, 448–9
Campbell, Thomas (1777–1844)
  'The knot there's no untying' (set by Maconchy) 471, 472, 473
Cameron, Basil (1884–1975) 77, 78, 171, 182
Campion, Thomas (1567–1620)
  'The cypress curtain of the night' (set by Williams in *Songs of Sleep*) 175, 211, 213, xxiv
Canada 8, 189, 190, 196, 210
Cantamus Girls' Choir (Mansfield, Nottinghamshire) 414, 422, 429, 462–3, 464
Cantelo, April (1928–) 173, 174, 176
Canterbury (Kent)
  Canterbury Cathedral choir 253
Cape Town (South Africa) 367, 368, 369
Cardew, Cornelius (1936–1981) 290, 399, 400
  The Great Learning 399
Cardiff (Wales) 4, 28, 44, 51, 77, 78, 102, 120, 122, 128, 137, 138, 141, 144, 146, 152, 168, 182, 200, 224, 234, 237, 258, 271, 276, 310, 327, 335, 340, 341, 342, 343, 369, 432, 435, 473
  Cardiff Castle 271
  Cardiff College of Music and Drama 119, 137
  Cardiff Festival of Twentieth-Century Music 252, 271, 273, 298, 313, 377

Cardiff Polyphonic (SATB chorus) 252, 271, 273, 277
  University of Cardiff xxi, 3, 396
  University Ensemble 458, 466
  see also BBC Cardiff Station, BBC Wales, Empire Theatre, National Eisteddfod, New Theatre (Cardiff)
Carewe, John (1933–) 270, 276, 284, 293, 295, 309, 310, 313, 326, 333, 358, 360, 379, 425, 432
Carlsbad (Czechoslovakia) 44, 45
Carnegie Fund 110
Carr, James (1911–1981) 137
Carroll, Lewis (1832–1898)
  The Hunting of the Snark 70
Carter, Elliott (1908–2012) 450
Casa Ricordi (music publisher) 198, 215, 218
'C.B.E.' *see* Commander of the British Empire
'C.G.' *see* Groves, Charles; Royal Opera House (Covent Garden, London)
Chaplin, Charlie (1889–1977) 405
Chappell Music 231, 424, 455, 459, 460
Charles, Prince of Wales 335
  Investiture of the Prince of Wales (1 July 1969) 314, 315, 316, 317, 318–9, 328, 329, 333, 334–5, 336, xxiv
Chart Corner (Seal Chart, near Sevenoaks, Kent) 14, 25, 30, 46, 97, 127
Chekhov, Anton (1860–1904)
  Uncle Vanya 224
Chelmsford (Essex, England) 136, 314
  Chelmsford & Essex Hospital 202, 204
  Chelmsford Cathedral 215, 220, 231
  Edward VI Grammar School (Chelmsford) 215, 226, 227, 231
Cheltenham (England) 352, 356–7, 404
  Cheltenham Festival 121–2, 157, 158, 163, 166, 170, 211, 283, 295, 303, 306, 309, 310, 317, 321, 322, 323, 330, 376, 382, 383, 385, 403, 422, 441, 447, 453, 454, 467
Chester Music (publisher) 89, 352, 460, 461, 464, 467
Chicago (Illinois, USA) 193, 307, 327
Chisholm, Eric (1904–1965)
  Double Trio 24
Chopin, Frédéric (1810–1849) 203, 258
Christie, John Traill (1899–1980), Lucie LeFanu's husband 63, 111
City of Birmingham Symphony Orchestra *see* Birmingham
City Music Society (London) 467

Clark, Edward (1888–1962) 112, 138
Cobbett, Walter Willson (1847–1937) 8
  Cobbett Phantasy Prize 8
  Walter Willson Cobbett Medal for Services to Chamber Music 331, 332
Cockshott, Gerald (1915–1979) 128, 132, 182, 285
Cohen, Harriet (1895–1967) 16, 33, 46, 49, 50, 51
Coleridge, Samuel Taylor (1782–1834)
  'Frost at Midnight' (set by Williams) 179
Coliseum Theatre (London) 371, 409, 430
Colles, Henry Cope (1879–1943) 445
Commander of the British Empire ('C.B.E.') 332, 477
Composers' Guild of Great Britain, The xiv, 119, 120, 157, 173, 174, 177, 182–3, 184, 189, 191, 193–4, 197, 198, 218, 251, 255, 283, 286, 288–9, 330, 336, 390, 420, 421, 437, 443, 453, 477
Connemara (Ireland) 5, 11, 32
Cook, Pamela (1937–2013) 462, 464
Cooke, Arnold (1906–2005)
  Nocturnes 164
Cooke, Helen 446
Cooper Concerts *see* Gerald Cooper Concerts (London)
Cooper, Kathleen (–1957) 138, 138
Cooper, Martin (1910–1996) 128, 161
Copenhagen (Denmark) *see* ISCM Festivals
Copland, Aaron (1900–1990) 450
Copperwheat, Winifred (1905–1976) 105
Cork (Ireland) 109, 237, 392
  Cork Ballet Group 77, 109
  Cork Opera House 77, 98, 109
  Cork International Choral Festival 237, 385
  Cork Symphony Orchestra 109
Covent Garden *see* Royal Opera House (Covent Garden, London)
Coventry (England) 194, 357
  Cathedral Church of St Michael (Coventry Cathedral) 194, 404
  Coventry Festival 194
  University of Warwick (Coventry) 357
Cowdray Hall (London) 54, 100, 101
Cox, Jeremy 454
Craig, Douglas (1916–2009) 250, 264, 279, 281, 343, 353

Craxton, Janet (1929–1981) 211, 376, 378, 392, 399, 401, 403, 409, 414, 434, 438, 441, 442, 446, 471
Crébillon, Claude Prosper Jolyot de (Crébillon fils) (1707–1777) 165, xxxi
Creffield, Roseanne 371, 372
Crichton, Ronald (1913–2005) 384
Cripps, David 309, 326
Criswell, Michael (1962–) 454
Cross, Joan (1900–1993) 115,
Crosse, Gordon (1937–) 282, 357, 363, 430, 462
  Changes: A Nocturnal Cycle, Op. 17 282
  The Grace of Todd, Op. 20 357
  Purgatory, Op. 18 357
  The Story of Vasco, Op. 29 430–31
  Violin Concerto No, 2, Op. 26 355, 357
  Wheel of the World 462
Crossley-Holland, Peter (1916–2001) 125, 132
Croydon (Surrey, England)
  Croydon Philharmonic/Philharmonic Choir/Philharmonic Society 436, 461, 464
  Croydon Schools Festival (Croydon, England) 200, 218
Cruft, Adrian (1921–1987) 255
Crumb, George (1929–) 399, 400–01, 443
  Black Angels (Images I) 440
  Echoes of Time and the River (Echoes II) 399, 400
  Eleven Echoes of Autumn (Echoes I) 443
Cuckston, Alan (1940–) 312
Culham College of Education (Oxfordshire) 372
Culshaw, John (1924–1980) 251, 340
Cundell, Edric (1893–1961) 25, 26, 27, 147
  Serbia 27
  The Tragedy of Deirdre 27
Curzon, Clifford (1907–1982) 62, 63, 77, 78, 79
Czechoslovakia 11, 43, 45, 196, 307, 326–7
  see also Carlsbad, Prague

Da Vinci, Leonardo *see* Leonardo da Vinci
Daily Telegraph Chamber Music Competition (London) 20, 21, 25–8, 37
Dalby, Martin (1942–) 262, 366, 386
Dale, Benjamin (1885–1943) 83
Dallapiccola, Luigi (1904–1975) 55, 328, 340–41, 342, 343, 344, 407

Divertimento in quatro esercizi 54, 340
Ulisse 340, 341
Darlington, Keith 183
Darnton, Christian (1905–1981)
String Trio 24
Dartington (Devon, England) 220, 224
Dartington String Quartet 220, 224, 234, 236, 248
Davies, Andrew 409
Davies, Eiluned (1913–1999) 153, 168, xxxii
Davies, Evan Thomas (1878–1969) 12
Davies, Meredith (1922–2005) 195
Davies, Peter Maxwell (1934–2016) 229, 307, 313, 337, 395, 415–6
  Ave maris stella, Op. 63 410
  Blind Man's Bluff, Op. 51a 395
  Fantasia upon One Note [realization after Purcell] 415
  Revelation and Fall, Op. 31 415–6
Davis, Colin (1927–2013) 313
Dawkes, Hubert (1916–2012) 466
Day-Lewis, Cecil (1904–1972) 239
  'Ariadne on Naxos' (set by Maconchy) 371, 377, 382, 384, xxix
De Nevers, Bernard 129, 130, 133, 151, 158
Debussy, Claude (1862–1918) 5, 7, 28
  Nocturnes (*Nuages, Fêtes, Sirènes*) 7–8, 22, 396
  Pelléas et Mélisande 28, 311, 341
Decca Records 251, 347, 355, 392, 408
  see also Oiseau Lyre, L'
Del Mar, Norman (1919–1994) 256, 417
Delius, Frederick (1862–1934) 6, 28
Dickinson, Peter (1934–) 357
Dickson, Paul (1920–2011) 137
  A Story of Achievement 139, xxvi
  David 137, xxvi
  The Undefeated 137
Dieren, Bernard van (1887–1936)
  Symphony No. 1 (Chinese Symphony) 48, 49
Dobiáš, Václav (1909–1978) 196
Dobrée, Georgina (1930–2008) 307, 308–9
Dods, Marcus (1918–1984) 364, 365
Donne, John (1572–1631) 16, 19, 32, 34, 101, 222, 378, 383, xxix, xxx
Dorchester (Oxfordshire, England) 336, 366, 370–71, 373
  Dorchester Abbey 328, 336, 369, 370, 371, 372
  Dorchester Abbey Festival 336, 346, 352, 354, 357, 358, 366, 371, 372
Dorking 36, 67, 338
  see also Leith Hill Place

'Dorrie' *see* Gow, Dorothy
Douglas-Home, Alec (1903–1995) 230
Downes, Edward (1924–2009) 327, 329
Downton Castle (Ludlow, Shropshire, England) 66
Drake, Bryan (1925–2001) 371, 372
Druckman, Jacob (1928–1996) 435
Dublin (Ireland) 4, 61–2, 63, 64, 77, 101, 106, 281
  see also Ireland, Irish Ballet Club, Santry Court, Trinity College Dublin
Dukas, Paul (1865–1935)
  The Sorcerer's Apprentice 132
Duke's Hall (Royal Academy of Music, London) 346
Dunlop, Anna (née LeFanu) (1939–),
  Maconchy's daughter viii, x, xx, birth 61–2, 63, 64, 65, 66, 68, 72, 76, 81, 82, 85, 88, 90, 93, 94, 97, 98, 101, starting school 102, 103, 108, 109, 111, 118 (Fig. PIII.1), 120, 121, 134, 136, 142, 146, 152, 169, meets husband Francis 173, 184, 189, 195, 198, 199, marriage 202, 204, 208, 210, 212, 214, birth of Christopher 216, 217, 220, 222, 225, 231, 232, 234, 237, 238, birth of Sarah 239, 256, 259, 323, 369, 371, 385, 405, move to Germany 422, 423, 435, back to England 447, 468, 480
Dunlop, Christopher (1963–), Anna's son 210, 212, 214, 216, 217, 220, 222, 224, 225, 232, 237, 259, 323, 369, 405, 423
Dunlop, Francis (1937–2017), Anna's husband 173, 184, 189, 195, 198, marriage 202, 208, 225, 231, 232, 237, 239, 259, 309, 369, 405, 422, 447
Dunlop, Sarah (1965–), Anna's daughter 234, 239, 259, 323, 369, 405, 423
Durham (England) 478
Dushkin, Samuel (1891–1976) 27
Dyson, Ruth (1917–1997) 357

'E.C.O.' *see* English Chamber Orchestra
Eastern Arts Association 477
Edinburgh (Scotland) 41, 43, 46, 49
  Edinburgh Festival 155
  see also Reid Symphony Orchestra (Edinburgh)
Edward VI Grammar School (Chelmsford) *see* Chelmsford

Edwin Evans Memorial Prize *see* Evans, Edwin
Eisteddfod *see* National Eisteddfod
Eisteddfod Choir *see* National Eisteddfod (Barry 1968)
Elder, Mark (1947–) 378
'Eleanor' *see* Ramsbotham, Eleanor Bevan
Elgar, Edward (1857–1934) 27, 28, 394
  Caractacus, Op. 35 437
  The Dream of Gerontius, Op. 38 394
Ellis, Osian (1928–) 195, 211, 219, 377, 406, 424, 432, 442, 466, 467, 471, 473, 474
EMI (record label) 311, 406, 407, 418, 437, 475
Empire Theatre (Cardiff) 77
English Chamber Orchestra ('E.C.O.') 347, 355, 361, 363, 371, 373, 377, 382, 384, 385, 391, 400, 404, 408, 411, 433, 434
English String Quartet 208, 248, 273, 307, 309, 413
Epstein, Jacob (1880–1959)
  Christ in Majesty (in Llandaff Cathedral, Cardiff) 310, 311, 319
'Eryl' *see* Freestone, Eryl (née Evans)
Essex (England) 80, 97, 105, 147, 165, 215
  Essex Youth Orchestra 316, 317, 320, 359, 447, 451, 456, 461, 464
  University of Essex 342, 344
  see also Essex Overture (orchestral work) *in* Elizabeth Maconchy: Works
  see also Bishop's Stortford, Boreham, Chelmsford, Shottesbrook, Stanstead Airport, Wickham Lodge
Evans, David *see* Moule-Evans, David
Evans, Edwin (1874–1945) 112
  Edwin Evans Memorial Prize 111, 112, 113
Evans, Geraint (1922–1992) 249, 335, 395, 428, 431
Evans, Rev. Glyn (1913–2001), *Marian's husband* viii, 188 (Fig. PIV.1), 219, 228, 381, 386, 387–8, 460, 469
Evans, Joy 272, 315
Evans, Marian (née Williams) (1919–2010), *Williams's sister* viii, 17, 66, *birth of Eryl* 91, 96, 119, 124, 150, 188 (Fig. PIV.1), 192, 196, 219, 222, 223, 224, 228, 248, 249, 251, 289, 329, 381, 386, 387–8, 397, 435, 460, 462, 465, 468, 469, 470, 471, 473, 478, 479
Exmoor (England) 63, 384

'F. H.' *see* Royal Festival Hall (London)
Faber Music (publisher) 242, 253, 272, 280, 281, 305, 352
Faerber, Jörg (1929–) 432
Feeney Trust 191, 268
Feldman, Morton (1926–1987) 245, 248, 280, 409–10, 443
  For Frank O'Hara 443
  The King of Denmark 248, 409–10
  Madame Press Died Last Week at Ninety 410
  The Viola in My Life 410
Ferguson, Howard (1908–1999)
  Diabelleries (composite work) 154–5
Ferneyhough, Brian (1943–)
  Prometheus for wind sextet 275, 295
Festival Hall *see* Royal Festival Hall
Festival of Britain 113, 120, 136, 137
  Society of Women Musicians concert 136
  Welsh Committee 136, 137
Finchley Children's Music Group 424, 432
Finnissy, Michael (1946–) 475
Finzi, Gerald (1901–1956)
  Diabelleries (composite work) 154–5
Fischer-Dieskau, Dietrich (1925–) 449
Flagstad, Kirsten (1895–1962) 151
Fleischmann, Aloys (1910–1992) 109
Fletcher, John *see* Beaumont, Francis
Florence (Italy) 407, 435
  see also ISCM Festivals
Foli Scholarship *see* Royal College of Music (London)
Fonteyn, Margot (1919–1991) 341
Forbes, Sebastian (1941–) 328, 345, 398
Forbes, Watson (1909–1997) 169
Foss, Hubert (1899–1953) 14, 15
Foster Dulles, John (1888–1959) 145
Fowler, Jennifer (1939–) 366, 386, 388
France 52, 318
'Francis' *see* Dunlop, Francis
Frank, Alan (1910–1994) 159, 163, 252
Frank, Anne (1929–1945)
  The Diary of a Young Girl (The Diary of Anne Frank) 179, 183
Frankel, Benjamin (1906–1973) 112
Fraser, Norman (1904–1986) 83
Fredman, Myer (1932–2014) 338, 342
Free Wales Army 307, 319, 329
Freestone, David (1944–2016), *Eryl's husband* 276, 317–8, 320, 323,

325, 381, 383, 384, 396, 433,
  449, 463, 465, 472
Freestone, Eleanor ('Elinor'), *Eryl's
  daughter* 440, 449, 463, 465, 476
Freestone, Eryl (née Evans) (1944–),
  Marian's daughter viii, x, xx, *birth*
  91, 96, 119, 126, 150, 188 (Fig.
  PIV.1), 224, 247, *with David* 276,
  277, 289, 297, *marriage* 317–8,
  320, 323, 325, 377, 381, 383, 384,
  396, 420, 421, 431, 433, 438, *birth
  of Eleanor* 440, 449, 462, 463, 465,
  472, 480
Fricker, Peter Racine (1920–1990) 159
  Symphony No. 2, Op. 14 121–2
Fry, Christopher (1907–2005)
  The Lady's Not for Burning 129
  *Ring Around the Moon: A Charade with
  Music* 129–30
Fuchsova, Liza (1913–1977) 192, 193

Gabrieli String Quartet 424, 444, 447–8
Gaddarn, James (1924–2012) 436, 461
Gambold, Geoffrey 238
Gaskell, Helen (1906–2002) 25, 31
'Gatty': 'Black Eyed Susan' *see* Gay, John
Gay, Bram (1930–) 203, 212, 213, 216–7,
  219, 222–3, 229, 235, 289, 333,
  419, 426–7
Gay, John (1685–1732)
  'Sweet William's Farewell to Black-
  eyed Susan' 333
Gedda, Nicolai (1925–) 237
Gee, Kenneth (1908–1986) 113, xxix
Gellhorn, Peter (1912–2004) 229, 231,
  232, 261, 275, 276, 277, 283, 284
Georgian String Quartet 441
Gerald Cooper Concerts (London) 100, 115
Gerhard, Roberto (1896–1970) 329,
  330–31, 354
  Epithalamion 330
  Symphony No. 4 329, 330
German Chamber Music Society (Prague) 8
German, Edward (1862–1936)
  Welsh Rhapsody 334
Germany 167, 199, 318, 412, 422, 434, 441
  at war with, 1939–45 61, 92, *surrender*
  100
[German music culture] 58, 199, 395
Gertler, Andre (1907–1998) 148
Gipps, Lance (1947–) 346
Gipps, Ruth (1921–1999) 236, 346, 404
  Horn Concerto, Op. 58 346
Glasgow (Scotland) 143, 238, 239

see also BBC Scotland (Glasgow), BBC
  Scottish Orchestra (Glasgow) *in*
  British Broadcast Corporation
Glatz, Helen (1908–1996) 220
Glendower, Owen (Owain Glyndŵr) 61,
  74, 77, 80, 82, 84, 86, 88, 124, 142,
  xxiii
Glyndebourne (near Lewes, East Sussex,
  England) 213, 366
Glyndebourne Festival Opera 213, 286,
  366
Glyndŵr, Owain *see* Glendower, Owen
Glock, William (1908–2000) 160, 191,
  194, 371, 372
Goddard, Scott (1895–1965) 156
Godfrey, Dan (1868–1939) 38, 39, 40, 42
Goehr, Alexander (1932–) 229, 279, 282,
  320, 323, 388
  The Deluge 203
Goehr, Walter (1903–1960) 153, 166
Good, Margaret (1906–2000) 68, 80, 81,
  147–8
Goodchild, Mary 31
Goodwin, Noel (1927–2013) 437
Goodwin & Tabb (publisher) 96
Goldsbrough, Arnold (1892–1964)
  Goldsbrough Orchestra 147
Goossens, Marie (1894–1991) 146
Goossens, Sidonie (1899–2004) 146
Gordon, John Barritt ('Jack') (1898–1978)
  19
Gordon-Fleet, Glenys 458
Gotch, Oliver Horsley (1889–1973) 20, 21
Gould, Peter 403
Gow, Colin Clarence (1887–1970),
  Dorothy Gow's brother 145, 375
Gow, Dorothy (1893–1982) xv, 20, 21,
  32, 34, 51, 52, 54, 56, 57, 58, 62,
  66, 92, 74, 88, 93, 101, 114, 115,
  128, 130, 137, 145, 174, 217, 234,
  238, 239, 318, 330, 332, 346, 356,
  375, 392–3, 415, 441, 475–7, 478,
  479–80
  Diabelleries (composite work) 154–5
  Fantasy string quartet 20, 21
  Oboe Quintet 51, 52
  Piece for violin and horn 318, 330, 331,
  332, 392–3
  String Quartet in one movement 114
Graeme, Peter (1921–2012) 195
Grantham (Lincolnshire, England) 62, 66
Greece 189, 280, 412
  see also The Isles of Greece (choral work)
  in Elizabeth Maconchy: Works

xlvi *Index*

Green, Meriel 18
Griffin, Keith 426
Griller String Quartet 25, 29, 31
Grimethorpe Colliery Band 424–5
Grinke, Frederick (1911–1987) 215
Groves, Charles ('C.G.') (1915–1992) 200, 201, 229, 230, 231, 322–3, 325, 332, 356, 398, 418, 420, 422
Gruenberg, Erich (1924–) 351, 352, 428
Guild for Promotion of Welsh Music 329, 333
Guildhall School of Music and Drama (London) 183, 204
Gurrin, Geoffrey
  Fawley Achievement 140, xxvi
Guy, Barry (1947–) 435
Gwynne, David 383

Hadley, Patrick (1899–1973)
  Diabelleries (composite work) 154–5
Haitink, Bernard (1929–) 284
Hallé Orchestra (Manchester) 33, 163, 165, 212, 216, 219, 223, 235, 237, 390, 402, 404, 408
Halsey, Louis (1929–) 436, 455
  Louis *Halsey* Singers 424, 436, 455
Hamburger, Paul (1920–2004) 433, 435
Hamerton, Ann (1900–1997) 164, 178
  The Persian Flute 178
Hamilton, Iain (1922–2000) 159, 164, 190
  Violin Concerto, Op. 15 159
Hampstead (Heath) (London) 93–4, 396
Hampton Court (London) 110
Handley, Vernon (1930–2008) 298, 299, 300, 395, 401, 412, 425, 432
Hardy, Thomas (1840–1928) 157, 253, xxxi
Harkness Fellowship 405, 407, 411, 422, 423, 432, 448
Harper, Heather (1930–) 382, 383, 384, 385, 386, 391–2, 404, 411, 434
Harries, Moelfryn 298, 395, 411, 432
Hartley, Sir Percival Horton-Smith (1867–1957) 16
Hartmann, Karl Amadeus (1905–1963) 109
Harverson, Alan (1922–2006) 414, 438, 446, 471
Harvey, Jonathan (1939–2012) 440
  Ludus amoris (Cantata IV) 338
Haydn, Joseph (1732–1809) 20, 21
  The Seasons 266
  String Quartet, Op.76 No.4 30
Heal's (London) 47

Heath, Edward (1916–2005) 363, 426
Heath, Kenneth 414, 418, 422, 441, 447, 454
Hely-Hutchinson, Victor (1901–1947)
  Sextet 25, 29
'*Henry*' *see* Wood, Henry J.
Henry Wood Promenade Concerts (London) *see* BBC Promenade Concerts *in* British Broadcasting Corporation series & programmes
Henze, Hans Werner (1926–2012)
  The Bassarids 436
  Der junge Lord 341
  Der Prinz Von Homberg 203
Herbage, Julian (1904–1976) 62, 67, 264, 267, 269
Herbert, Muriel (1897–1994) 21
Herrick, Robert (1591–1674) 215, 254, xxx
Heseltine, Philip *see* Warlock, Peter (1894–1930)
Heyworth, Peter (1921–1991) 247
Higgins, F(rederick) R(obert) (1896–1941) 98
Hill, Mary 431
Hill, Ralph (1900–1950) 101
Hill, Rosemary (1927–1989) 302, 303
'Hill's' *see* W. E. Hill & Sons
Hindemith, Paul 402
  There and Back 269, 272
Hinrichsen, Max (1901–1965) 72, 80, 81, 83, 90, 92
H.M.V. (His Master's Voice record label) 126
Hitler, Adolf (1889–1945) 85
Hoddinott, Alun (1929–2008) 149–50, 159, 234, 252, 253, 255–6, 273–4, 275, 276, 277, 293, 313, 334, 335, 340, 347, 377, 379, 396, 402
  The Beach of Falesá, Op. 83 428, 431
  Eryri [Snowdonia] for solo baritone, SATB chorus, and orchestra 334, 335
  Leuenctid y Dydd ('Youth of the Day') 395
  Severn Bridge Variations (composite work) 263, 468, 470
  Symphony No. 1, Op. 7 159
  Symphony No. 5, Op. 81 409
  see also Cardiff Festival of Twentieth Century Music
Holliger, Heinz (1939–) 407, 409
  Cardiophonic for oboe and three tapes 409

Hollingsworth, John (1916–1963) 140, 141, 144
Holst, Imogen (1907–1984) 3–4, 415
Holst, Gustav (1874–1934) 3, 22, 28, 182, 332, 364, 447
The Wandering Scholar, Op. 50 269
Holywell Music Room (Oxford) 33
Hope-Wallace, Philip (1911–1979) 207
Hopkins, Antony (1921–2014) 100, 101, 420
Hopkins, Gerard Manley (1844–1889) 36, 166, 222, 363, 451
    'The Leaden Echo and the Golden Echo' (set by Maconchy, 1930–31) 36–7
    'The Leaden Echo and the Golden Echo' (set by Maconchy, 1978) 363, 371
    'Starlight Night', 'Peace', May Magnificat' (set by Maconchy as *Settings of Poems by Gerard Manley Hopkins*) 220, 222, 226, 410
    'Pied Beauty', 'Heaven Haven' (set by Maconchy as *Two Settings of Poems by Gerard Manley Hopkns*) 451
    'Pied Beauty', 'Peace', 'Spring and Fall', 'No worst, there is none', 'Hurrahing in Harvest', 'The Windhover' (set by Williams as *Six Poems by Gerard Manley Hopkins*) 157, 166, 168, 169, 177, 453, 458
Horovitz, Joseph (1926–) 272
Howarth, Elgar (1935–) 424
Howe, Nesta 249
Howells, Herbert (1892–1983) 6, 331
Howes, Frank (1891–1974) 101, 130, 153, xxxiii
Howgill, Richard 151
Howlett, Neil (1934–) 272, 315
HRH The Prince of Wales *see* Charles, Prince of Wales
Hudson, Shirley (Lady Beecham) 184
Hughes, Arwel (1909–1988) 77, 138, 142, 149, 161, 166, 276, 277, 279, 317, 325, 339
    Gweddi ('A Prayer') 138
Hughes, Ted (Edward James) (1930–1998)
    From the Life and Songs of the Crow 429
    'Song' 429
    The Story of Vasco 430
Humby, Betty (Lady Beecham) (1908–1958) 184
Humperdinck, Engelbert (1854–1921)
    Hänsel und Gretel 65

Hungarian Radio Orchestra *see* Budapest Symphony Orchestra
Hungarian String Quartet/New Hungarian String Quartet 54, 144, 297
Hurwitz, Emanuel (1919–2006) 112, 423–4
    Hurwitz String Quartet 112, 113, 120, 123, 124, 126
Hywel, John (1941–) 398

Ibbs & Tillett (artist management) 383
Ibsen, Henrik (1828–1906)
    Peer Gynt 370
'I.C.A.' *see* Institute of Contemporary Art
'Ina' *see* Boyle, Ina
Institute of Contemporary Arts ('I.C.A.') (London) 139, 140, 153, 420, 423
International Composers' Conference (Stratford, Ontario, 1960) 189
International Society for Contemporary Music (ISCM) 14, 23, 39, 45, 157
    ISCM Festivals 14, (Vienna 1932) 20, (Amsterdam 1933) 20, 22, 23, (Florence 1934) 36, 37, 39, (Prague 1935) 43, 44, 45, 49, 50, (Paris 1937) 51, 52, (1944) 89, (London 1946) 103, (Copenhagen 1947) 106, (Amsterdam 1948) 106, (Brussels 1950) 120, 122, (London 1962) 203
Investiture of the Prince of Wales (1 July 1969) *see* Charles, Prince of Wales
Ireland xxi, 3, 4, 7, 8, 11, 12, 32, 76, 101, 109, 134, 147, 148, 237, 261, 271, 281, 286–7, 338, 393, 402, 405, 477
    see also Ballymorris, Bushey Park, Connemara, Cork, Dublin
Ireland, John (1879–1962) 20, 83
    Piano Concerto 20, 426
'Iris' *see* Lemare, Iris
Irish Ballet Club (Dublin) 63, 64
Isaacs, Leonard (1909–1997) 132
ISCM *see* International Society for Contemporary Music
Italy 179, 199, 237, 242, 318, 436, 464
    see also Florence, Siena, Sicily, Venice
Ives, Charles (1874–1954) 448, 450

Jacob, Gordon (1895–1984) 6, 22, 48, 68, 83
    Diabelleries (composite work) 154–5
    String Quartet No. 2 21, 22
Jacob, Sydney (?–1958) 22

xlviii *Index*

Jacobs, Arthur (1922–1996) 247
Jacques, Reginald (1894–1969) 93, 110
　Jacques String Orchestra 93, 110, 231, 297, 302
James, Eirian (1952–) 458
Janáček, Leoš (1854–1928)
　From the House of the Dead 267
　Jenúfa 30, 246, 473
Jenkins, Rae (1903–1985) 79, 152, 269, 351, 352, 451
Jeremiáš, Otakar (1892–1962) 8, 9
Jirák, Karel Boleslav (1891–1972) 7, 8–9, 193
Johnson, Robert Sherlaw (1932–2000) 328, 345
Johnstone, Maurice (1900–1976) 164
Jones, Daniel (1912–1993) 149, 159, 179, 255, 323, 333, 379, 409
　Cloud Messenger 138
　Investiture Processional Music 333, 334, 335
　Severn Bridge Variations (composite work) 255, 263, 468, 470
　Symphony No. 2 162
　Symphony No. 4 'In memoriam Dylan Thomas' 161, 162
　Symphony No. 8 409
　The Knife 215, 217–8
Jones, David Lloyd *see* Lloyd-Jones, David
Jones, Delme Bryn (1934–2001) *see* Bryn-Jones, Delme
Jones, Granville (1922–1968) 122, 123, 139
Jones, Gwyneth (1936–) 335
Jones, Gwynn Parry (1891–1963) 30, 38, 40
Jones, Philip oboist (1933–1987) 261, 269, 270–71, 277, 279, 284, 295, 309, 326, 410
Jones, Philip trumpeter (1928–2000) 327
　Philip Jones Ensemble 275, 327
Jones, Richard Roderick (1947–) 328, 341, 450
Jowitt, Roy (1938–2012) 309, 326
Joyce, Robert (1927–2018) 379

Kabalevsky, Dmitry (1904–1987) 144–5, 192
'K.A.W.' *see* Wright, Kenneth
Keefe, Bernard (1925–) 441
Keller, Hans (1919–1985) 194, 385, 401, 425, 440, 441
'Ken' *see* Wright, Kenneth
Kennedy, Robert F. (1925–1968) 319

Kennedy Scott, Charles (1876–1965) 162
Kent (England) xxi, 14, 66, 127
　University of Kent 398
　see also Canterbury, Chart Corner
Kern, Patricia (1927–) 453
Khachaturian, Aram (1903–1978) 192
King, Thea (1925–2007) 211, 248
King's Choir *see* Cambridge
King's College *see* Cambridge
King's Lynn Festival 351, 363, 366, 371, 376, 377, 380, 382, 383, 384, 385, 416
Kipling, Rudyard (1865–1936) 439, 450, 452, 454
　'Harp Song of the Dane Women' (set by Williams as *Two Interlinked Choruses*) 333, 444, 447, 450, 452, 454, xxv
Kitchin, Margaret (1914–1998) 122, 136
Kitson, Charles Herbert (1874–1944) 198
Kneller Hall (Royal Military School of Music) 333
Koussevitsky prize 121
Krenek, Ernst (1900–1991) 190
Kubelik, Rafael (1914–1996) 129, 131, 284
Kurtz, Eugene (1923–2006) 435

'L. C. C.' *see* London County Council
Lambert, Constant (1905–1951) 46, 48, 53, 79
Lambert, Isabel *see* Rawsthorne, Isabel
Landowska, Wanda (1879–1959) 312
Langridge, Philip (1939–2010) 371, 372, 378, 434
Latin America 67, 190
　see also Latin American Service *in* British Broadcasting Corporation networks
Lawrence, D. H. (1885–1930) 203
Lawrence Turner Quartet 51
Ledger, Philip (1937–2012) 231
Lee, Clifford 373, 376
Lee, Vernon (1856–1935)
　'Dionea' 185
LeFanu, Anna *see* Dunlop, Anna (née LeFanu), *Maconchy's daughter*
LeFanu, Lucie (1901–1996), *William's sister* 31, 63, 111
LeFanu, Nicola (1947–), *Maconchy's daughter* viii, x, xii, xiii, xv, xviii, xix, xx, xxi–xxii, *birth* 105, 106, 108, 109, 110, 115, 118 (Fig. PIII.1), 141, 146, 150, 152, 154, 158, *growing musical interests* 189,

198, 199, 200, 208, 225, 231, *at St Hilda's, Oxford* 232, 239, 240, 245, 249, 251, 252, 253, 258, 278, *lessons with Alexander Goehr* 279, 282, 287, 293, 295, 304, 309, 312, 316, *course at Siena with Petrassi* 320, *at RCM* 323, 328, 331, 336, 338, *study with Thea Musgrave* 341, 346, 350 (Fig. PVI.1), 351, 356, 357, *shortlisted for Radcliffe Music Award* 366, 369, 376, 386, 388, 389, 391, 397, *study in USA* 399, 401, 405, 406, *awarded Harkness Fellowship* 407, 411, 412, 413, 414, 415, 417, 418, 422, 423, 424, 432, 434–5, 436, 438, 441, *teaching at St Paul's Girls' School, London* 447, 448, 460, *to Australia* 467–8, *with David Lumsdaine* 469, 471, 472, *return to London* 478, 480
   But Stars Remaining for solo soprano 434–5
   Il cantico dei cantici II 389
   Chiaroscuro 354, 357
   Clarinet Quintet 366, 386, 388
   Dawnpath 468
   The Hidden Landscape 405, 407, 417, 420, 479
   Preludio I 320
   Rondeaux for tenor and horn 434
   The Same Day Dawns 451
   Soliloquy 248, 249, 252, 253, 270, 279, 410
   Trio 275, 309
   Variations for oboe quartet 374, 376, 378, 389, 410, 434–5
LeFanu, Victor Charles, *William's uncle* (1865–1939) 148
LeFanu, William Richard ('Billy') (1904–1995), *Maconchy's husband* viii, xix, xx, *engagement* 7, *librarian of Royal College of Surgeons* 8, *marriage* 11, 12, 15, 16, 23, 26, 27, 28, 29, 30, 34, 45, 51, 56, 62, 64, *evacuation to Downton Castle, Shropshire* 66, 70, 74, 76, 77, 78, 80–81, 93, 94–5, *to Wickham Lodge, Essex* 97, 98, 101, 102, 108, 109, 110, 113, 114, 115, 118 (Fig. PIII.1), 129, 134, 136, 138, 142, 146, 148, 151, at *Shottesbrook, Boreham, Essex* 154, 166, 174, 189, 202, 203, 208, 210, 239, 242, 245, 249, 262, 275, 279, 281, 286, 287, 295, 303, 304, 309, *retirement* 325, 332, 336, 358, 372, 386, 387, 391, 393, 402, 412, 421, 422, 424, 432, 438, 478, 480
Leighton Thomas, A. F. 161, xxxiii
Leith Hill Place (Dorking, England) 99
   see also Dorking
Lemare, Iris (1902–1997) 14, 18, 19, 23, 32, 33–4, 35, 45, 53, 136, 206, 314, 467, 472, 477
   Lemare Concerts 51
   see also Macnaghten-Lemare Concerts
Lengnick *see* Alfred Lengnick & Co. (music publisher)
Leningrad (USSR) 192
Lennox, David 272, 273
Leonardo da Vinci (1452–1519) 143, 259, 420
Leppard, Raymond (1927–) 363, 382, 383, 384, 385, 391, 392, 400, 404, 411, 433, 434, 446
Levan, Topsy 174
Lewis, Anthony (1915–1983) 194
Lewis, Arnold 411
Lewis, Cecil Day *see* Day-Lewis, Cecil
Lewis, Idris (1889–1952) 61, 66, 68, 69, 72, 90, 125, 128
Lewis, Jeffrey (1942–) 449
Lewis, Saunders (1893–1985) 355, 390, xxv
   Esther 355, 360, xxvi
Lidka, Maria (1914–2013) 100, 101, 254, 368
Ligeti, Gyorgy (1923–2006) 441, 443
   String Quartet No. 2 440, 441, 443
Lind, Deirdre 365
Lindsay, Nicholas Vachel *see* Vachel Lindsay, Nicholas
Lindsay Singers, The 385
Lindsay String Quartet 424, 444, 467
Listener, The see British Broadcasting Corporation publications
Liverpool (England) 275, 323, 327, 332
   Liverpool University Chamber Music competition 275, 293, 295
   Royal Liverpool Philharmonic Orchestra 79, 200, 201, 230, 325, 327, 332, 356, 362, 368, 394, 395
'Liz' see Elisabeth Lutyens
Llandaff (north Cardiff, Wales) 200
   Howell's School, Llandaff 463

Index

Llandaff Cathedral 200, 201, 310, 311, 316, 319, 379–80, 394
Llandaff Cathedral Choral Society 379
Llandaff Festival 197, 200, 201, 260, 265, 310, 316, 317, 319, 327, 329, 340, 344, 346, 376, 379–80, 384, 394–5
Welsh Llandaff Society 401–2
see also Broadcasting House (Llandaff) in British Broadcasting Corporation station headquarters; BBC Wales in British Broadcasting Corporation networks & departments
Llandudno (Wales) 249, 250, 356
Lloyd-Jones, David (1934–) 395
Lockspeiser, Edward (1905–1973) 71
L'Oiseau Lyre see Oiseau Lyre, L'
London (England) xii, xiv, xxi, 3, 5, 7, 8, 14, 17–8, 19, 30, 32, 34, 37, 44, 45, 54, 65, 66, 68, 74, 78, 79, 80, 83, 84, 85, 87–8, 90, 92, 93, 94–5, 96–7, 102–3, 104, 105, 106, 107, 114, 120, 125–6, 128, 133, 137, 141, 150, 160, 183, 205, 219, 220, 225, 249, 269, 282, 286, 288, 305, 318, 320, 338, 341, 342, 347, 351–2, 356, 361, 362, 371, 372, 378, 382–3, 384, 391, 396, 412, 413, 419, 420, 423, 431, 434, 443, 444, 448, 478
Inner-London Education Authority 431
London Chamber Orchestra 16, 106, 139
London Contemporary Music Centre 54, 100, 101, 111, 112, 113, 115, 119–20, 121, 123, 132, 138, 142
London County Council competition prize for Coronation Overture 148, 149, 150
London Mozart Players 347
London Oboe Quartet 376, 378, 403, 414, 430, 434, 442
London Philharmonic Orchestra 51, 77, 79
London Sinfonietta 409
London String Trio 164
London Studio Strings 358, 364
London Symphony Orchestra 12, 18, 41, 161, 162, 171, 192, 216, 327, 329, 335, 359, 407, 418, 419, 420, 421, 431, 475, 476
London Virtuosi 410
see also Abbey Opera, Academy of St-Martin-in-the-Fields, Aeolian Hall, Aldwych Theatre, BBC venues, Camden Festival, Camden School for Girls, City Music Society, Coliseum Theatre, Cowdray Hall, Duke's Hall, Gerald Cooper Concerts, Guildhall School of Music and Drama, Hampstead, Hampton Court, Heal's, Institute of Contemporary Arts, ISCM Festivals, Macnaghten-Lemare Concerts, Mercury Theatre, Morley College, National Gallery Concerts, National Theatre Company, Park Lane Group, Purcell Room, Putney, Queen Elizabeth Hall, Queen's Hall, RBA Galleries, Royal Academy of Music, Royal Albert Hall, Royal College of Music, Royal Festival Hall, Royal Opera House, Sadler's Wells Opera, Sadler's Well Theatre, St George's Church Hanover Square, St Mary Abbots Theatre, St Pancras Town Hall, St Paul's Girls' School, Southlands Training College, Victoria & Albert Museum, W. E. Hill & Sons, Westminster Abbey, Westminster Cathedral, Wigmore Hall
Long, Kathleen (1896–1968) 19
Lord, Roger (1924–2014) 327
Loughran, James (1931–) 238, 239, 336, 340, 342, 390, 402, 404, 408
Louis Halsey Singers see Halsey, Louis
Loveland, Kenneth (1915–1998) 255, 322, 323, 325, 346, 379, 381, 384, 458
Lovett, Leon (1935–) 167
Lowe, John (1906–1966) 125, 132
Lowenbach, Jan 203
Lubbock, John 477
Lubbock, Mark (1898–1986) 184
Lubotsky, Mark (1931–) 408
'Lucie' see LeFanu, Lucie
Luff, Enid (1935–) 449–50
Lumsdaine, David (1931–), Nicola LeFanu's husband 469, 471, 472, 478
Lutosławski, Witold (1913–1994) 441, 443
String Quartet 440, 441
Lutyens, Elisabeth (1906–1983) xiii, xv, 14, 45, 45, 47, 48, 141, 143, 332, 341, 353, 364, 373, 374, 387, 397, 413, 449–50, 477
Diabelleries (composite work) 154–5

The Dying of Tanneguy du Bois 45, 46, 47, 48
Helix, Op. 67 No. 2 322
Infidelio, Op. 29 412
Isis and Osiris, Op. 74 477
'Lament of Isis on the Death of Osiris' from *Isis and Osiris*, Op. 74 364
A Phoenix, Op. 71a 364
Quincunx, Op. 44 332
The Tides of Time, Op. 75 373
The Tyme doth Flete, Op. 70 329
Lyn, Harry van der 252, 264, 273–4, 276

'M.' *see* Thomas, Mansel
'M. U.' *see* Musicians' Union
McCabe, John (1939–2015)
  Rain Songs 312
MacDonagh, (John Alfred) Terence (1908–1986) 51, 238
MacGibbon, Margot (1906–1998) 121, 140
  MacGibbon String Quartet 121, 139, 140, 155, 156
Mackerras, Charles (1925–2010) 216, 219
Macnaghten, Anne (1908–2000) 14, 15, 19, 20, 23, 25, 26, 31, 39, 47, 71, 73, 101, 130, 139, 140, 143, 144, 145, 153, 154, 161, 248, 453, 471, 477
  Macnaghten String Quartet 14, 15, 20, 30, 31–2, 33, 39, 71, 153
  Macnaghten Concerts (London) 153, 154, 177, 278, 279, 345, 445, 453, 471, 477
  Macnaghten-Lemare Concerts (London) 14, 19, 20, 21, 23, 24, 30, 32, 33, 34, 43, 44, 45, 477
Macneice, Louis (1907–1963)
  'Prayer Before Birth' (set by Maconchy) 385, 401, 429, xxx
Maconchy, Elizabeth Violet (1907–1994)
  see xxxv
  see also Elizabeth Maconchy: Works, xxvii–xxxi
  see also Maconchy Archive *in* Oxford: St Hilda's College
Maconchy, Gerald Edward Campbell (1875–1922), *Maconchy's father* 14
Maconchy, (Mary) Maureen (Barbara) (1902–1991), *Maconchy's sister* 8, 31, 32, 36, 47, *birth of Richard* 49, 62, 90, 91, 96, 97, 109, 184
Maconchy, Sheila Campbell (1910–1945), *Maconchy's sister* 8, 31, 32, 49, 50, 56, 61, 66, 79, 100

Maconchy (née Poë), Violet Mary (1878–1940), *Maconchy's mother* 7, 8, 15, 16, 29, 49, 61, 66
Maderna, Bruno (1920–1973) 190
Mahler, Gustav (1860–1911)
  Symphony No. 2 284
  Symphony No. 5 308
Major, Margaret 211, 279
Makarova, Nina (1908–1976) 192
Malcolm, George (1917–1997) 197, 312
Manchester (England) 134, 216, 467, 478
  see also BBC Manchester studios, Hallé Orchestra
Manduell, John (1928–) 277, 279, 295, 382, 422, 441
Mangeot, André (1883–1970) 73
Manning, Jane (1938–) 364, 434
'Mansel' *see* Thomas, Mansel
Mansfield choir *see* Cantamus Girls' Choir
Margaret, Countess of Snowdon (Princess Margaret) (1930–2002) 263
'Marian' *see* Evans, Marian (née Williams)
Marlowe, Christopher (1564–1593)
  Dr Faustus (set by Maconchy) 385, xxix
Marriner, Neville (1924–) 447, 454
Martin String Quartet 155
Masaryk, Tomáš Garrigue (1850–1937) 11
Masters, Robert (1917–2014) 198, 211
Matheson, Muir (1911–1973) 137
Mathias, Rhiannon xiii, xxxiii
Mathias, William (1934–1992) 211, 396, 410
  Concerto for Orchestra, Op. 27 323
  Divertimento, Op. 7 355
  Elegy for a Prince, Op. 59 395–6
  Prelude, Aria and Finale, Op. 25 355
  Wind Quintet, Op. 22 211
Mattie, *Williams's housecleaner* 176
Maupassant, Guy de (1850–1893) 246, 298
  Boule De Suif 249, 250, 251–2, 253, 256, 262, 273, 281
  '*En famille*' (set by Williams as *The Parlour*) 173–4, 197, 209, 246, xxvi
'Maureen' *see* Maconchy, (Mary) Maureen (Barbara), *Maconchy's sister*
Maw, Nicholas (1935–2009) 363
  The Rising of the Moon 366
  Severn Bridge Variations (composite work) 263, 468, 470
Mayer, Dorothy Moulton (1886–1974) 145
Mayer, Robert (1879–1985) 145
Melos Ensemble 195, 273, 296
Memphis Recording Company 71
Mendelssohn, Felix (1809–1847)
  Elijah, Op. 70 449

lii *Index*

Menotti, Gian Carlo (1911–2007)
   The Medium 361
Menuhin, Yehudi (1916–1999) 308
Mercury Theatre (London) 139, 140
Merritt, Kathleen (1901–1985) 114, 122, 132, 136, 147
   Merritt String Orchestra 114–5, 122, 132, 135, 136, 147
Messiaen, Olivier (1908–1992) 307
   Chronochromie 307
Messina, Cedric (1920–1993) 249, 253, 256, 265, 280, 298, 302, 303, 370
Metcalf, John (1946–) 449–50
Miles, Maurice (1908–1985) 158, 161, 162, 178
Milhaud, Darius (1892–1974) 113, 114, 431
Minehead (Somerset, England) 220, 224
   Minehead Grammar School 224
Minton, Yvonne (1938–) 383
Mitchell, Donald (1925–2017) 281
Montgomery, Bob 455
Montgomeryshire *see* Newtown (Montgomeryshire, Wales)
Monteux, Pierre (1875–1964) 216
Monteverdi, Claudio (1567–1643) 352
   L'incoronazione di Poppea 213
   Il ritorno d'Ulisse 400
   Vespers (1610) 400, 412
Montreal (Canada) 203
Moody, John (1906–1993) 219, 245
Moore, Douglas 238
Morgan, Joseph 77
Morley College (London) 266, 269, 271, 275, 406, 477
Morris, Christopher (1922–2014) 241
Morris, Jacqueline 85
   'The Voice of the City' (set by Maconchy) 80, 85, xxx
Morris, Wyn (1929–2010) 327, 332
Morrison, Colin 145
Morrison, Helen ('Nelly', 'Nellie') 145, 475–6, 477
Moule-Evans, David (1905–1988) 3–4
Moscow (USSR) 226
Mozart, Wolfgang Amadeus (1756–1791) 11, 54–5, 112, 150, 245, 408, 427
   Die Entführung 11
   Don Giovanni 11, 112, 286, 448
   Idomeneo 251
   Le nozze di Figaro/The Marriage of Figaro 11, 50, 225, 297
   Requiem, K. 626 284
   Sinfonia concertante, K. 364 222

'Mummy' *see* Maconchy (née Poë), Violet Mary
Munich (Germany) 109, 278
   see also Musica Viva (Munich)
Murray, Len (1922–2004) 435
Murrill, Herbert (1909–1952) 126, 127, 128
Musgrave, Thea (1928–) xv, 234, 283, 296, 301, 329, 331, 340, 341, 343, 413, 415, 460
   The Abbott of Dimmock 341
   Chamber Concerto No. 3 296
   Clarinet Concerto 341
   Concerto for Orchestra 329, 341, 408
   Night Music 340, 343
   Sinfonia 211
   The Decision 296, 300, 301, 303, 315
   Triptych for tenor and orchestra 241
Musica Viva (Munich) 109
Musicians' Benevolent Fund 476, 478
Musicians' Organisation of Peace 145
Musicians' Union ('M.U.') 266, 278, 335, 336, 352, 357
Musorgsky [Moussorgsky], Modest (1839–1881) 28
   Boris Godunov 28
   Khovanshchina 30

'N' *see* LeFanu, Nicola
NFMS *see* National Federation of Music Societies
'N, Mrs' *see* Mrs Newnham
National Council of Women of the USA 158, 163
   International Contest for Women Composers 158
National Eisteddfod (Bangor 1931) 12, (1932) 18, (Cardiff 1960) 179, (Swansea 1964) 229
   (Royal) National Eisteddfod (Newtown 1965) 218, 236, 246, 354
   (Royal) National Eisteddfod (Barry 1968) 257, 260, 265, *Eisteddfod Choir* 274, 280, 284, 285, 292, 302, 303, 311, 317, 319, 322, 323, 325
   (Royal) National Eisteddfod (Ammanford 1970) 362, 369
National Federation of Music Societies ('NFMS') 422
National Gallery Concerts (London) 65, 71
National Theatre Company (London) 224
National Youth Orchestra of Wales/Welsh Youth Orchestra 152, 155, 317, 459
Neaman, Yfrah (1923–2003) 289, 297, 298, 299, 300

Neel, Boyd (1905–1981) 93, 122
'Nelly', 'Nellie' *see* Helen Morrisson
Nendick, Josephine (1940–) 395
Neuhaus, Max (1939–2009) 248
New London Quartet 155
New Opera Group/Company 166, 168, 178, 181, 183, 184, 204, 205, 206, 215, 296, 300, 412
New Philharmonia Orchestra 336, 342
New Theatre (Cardiff) 240, 242, 245, 248, 249, 428
New York (New York, USA) 476
Newnham, Mrs, *Williams's housecleaner* 176, 312, 313, 321, 362, 419
Newtown (Montgomeryshire, Wales) 228, 229, 231, 236
  see also National Eisteddfod (Newtown 1965)
Neyder, Anton 281, 291
'Nic' and 'Niccy' *see* LeFanu, Nicola
Northern Sinfonia 347
Norwich (England) 309, 372, 385
Notariello, Antonietta and Felicity 336
Novello (music publisher) 426

Octavia Travelling Scholarship *see* Royal College of Music
Ogdon, John (1937–1989) 252, 273, 276, 313
  see also Cardiff Festival of Twentieth Century Music
Ogilvie, Frederick (1893–1949) 64
Oiseau Lyre, L' (record label) 391, 392, 404, 434
Olivier, Laurence (1907–1989) 224
Opera for All *see* Welsh National Opera
Orchestra Nova 342
Oxford (England) 20, 309, 336, 346, 352, 366, 370, 386, 389, 390, 396, 438, 439, 454
  New College 189
  Oxford Ladies' Musical Society 139, 140
  Oxford University Music Club 33
  Oxford University Press ('O.U.P.') (music & hire library) 14, 136, 157, 158, 159, 163, 164, 214, 241, 242, 275, 352, 406, 427, 428, 431, 439, 450, 463
  Schola Cantorum 286
  Somerville College 365
  St Hilda's College 166, 232
    Maconchy Archive xix, xx, 30, 351, 385, 403, 406, 413

University Church of St Mary the Virgin 436, 454
University of Oxford 166, 232, 240, 278, 282, 316, 320, 357
see also Holywell Music Room (Oxford)

Padmore, Elaine (1947–) 413, 415, 418, 453
Palestrina, Giovanni Pierluigi da (1525–1594) 410
Palmer, Ernest (1858–1948) 5
Parikian, Manoug (1920–1987) 212, 214, 219, 220, 236, 355
Paris (France) 7, 51, 52
  Paris Cinema 83
  see also ISCM Festivals
Park Lane Group (London) 373, 376
Parry, Thomas (1904–1984) 317
Pashley, Ann (1937–2016) 366, 367, 371, 372
Patron's Fund *see* Royal College of Music
Paul, Gwendo (1906–c.1997) 6
Pears, Peter (1910–1986) 94, 131, 206, 222, 237, 294, 377, 424, 442, 467, 471, 472, 473
Penarth Ladies' Choir 229
Penderecki, Krzysztof (1933–)
  St Luke Passion 286, 287, 290
Performing Right Society ('P.R.S.') 158, 283, 292, 294–5, 297, 298, 300, 319, 335, 404
Perkin, Helen (1909–1996) 20–21, 426
Petrassi, Goffredo (1904–2003) 320
Peyer, Gervase de (1926–2017) 195, 220, 224, 227, 234, 236, 273, 275, 303
Pini, Antony (1902–1989) 74, 79
Piper, John (1903–1992) 311
Plaistow, Stephen 385
Pleeth, William (1916–1999) 68, 71, 81
Poe, George Leslie (1846–1934), *Maconchy's grandfather* 4, 5
Poland 367, 368, 369
Poldi, *Maconchy's household help* 64
Ponsonby, Robert (1926–) 437
Poole, John 420, 425, 427, 444, 452, 453, 454, 455, 458
Porter, Andrew (1928–2015) 320, 372
Poston, Elizabeth (1905–1987) 70, 73, 254, 413, 415
Pougnet, Jean (1907–1968) 74, 79
Poulenc, Francis (1899–1963)
  Aubade, Op. 51 8
  Dialogue of the Carmelites, Op. 159 33
Pousseur, Henri (1929–2009) 254

Prague (Czechoslovakia) xx, 3, 7, 8, 11, 12, 17, 19, 21, 28, 29, 30, 41, 44, 45, 49, 50, 192, 193, 196, 203, 226, 326–7, 352, 363
  Prague Philharmonic Orchestra 8
  Prague Radio 9
  Prague Radio Symphony Orchestra 390
  see also German Chamber Music Society (Prague), ISCM Festivals
Previn, André (1929–2019) 359
Price, Janet (1938–) 250, 261, 262, 379, 383, 411, 415, 418, 420, 427, 431
Price, Margaret (1941–2011) 280, 335, 428, 431
Prince of Wales *see* Charles, Prince of Wales
Princess Margaret *see* Margaret, Countess of Snowdon
Pritchard, John (1921–1989) 142
Promenade Concerts, Proms (London) *see* BBC Promenade Concerts *in* British Broadcasting Corporation series & programmes
Prospect Theatre Company 341
'P.R.S.' *see* Performing Right Society
Puccini, Giacomo (1858–1924)
  Gianni Schicchi 209
  Il tabarro 302
Purcell, Henry (1658/9–1695) 415
  Fantasias 30, 352, 415
  King Arthur 232
Purcell Room (South Bank Centre, London) 278, 346, 373, 376, 399, 433, 434, 443, 444, 456
Putney (London) 14, 476

Queen Elizabeth Hall ('Q.E.H.') (South Bank Centre, London) 296, 385, 391–2, 406, 411, 432, 436, 438, 446
Queen's Hall (London) 11, 16, 40, 79

'R.T.' *see* Radio Times *in* British Broadcasting Corporation publications
Radcliffe Music Award/Prize 325, 328–9, 331, 334, 336, 344, 345, 347, 366, 376, 382, 386, 388
Radio Times see British Broadcasting Corporation publications
Rainier, Priaulx (1903–1986) 413
Ramsbotham, Eleanor Bevan (1892–1952), *Dorothy Gow's partner* 34, 88, 101, 115, 130, 145
Randell, Anthony 358, 361

Rands, Bernard (1934–) 435
  Ballad I 395
  Mésalliance 392
Raverat, Gwen(dolen) (née Darwin) (1885–1957) 19
Rawsthorne, Alan (1905–1971) 169, 215, 258, 276
  Carmen vitale 215
  Diabelleries (composite work) 154–5
Rawsthorne, Isabel (Isabel Lambert) (1912–1992) 215
Raybould, Clarence (1886–1972) 62, 64, 72, 80, 139, 142, 143, 459
RBA Galleries (Royal Society of British Artists) (London) 113
Read, Ernest (1879–1965) 149
  Ernest Read Children's Concerts 149, 150
Redman, Reginald (1892–1972) 43, 44
Reid Symphony Orchestra (Edinburgh) 41, 43, 46, 51
Rhyl (Flintshire, Wales) 219, 390
Ricordi *see* Casa Ricordi (music publisher)
Riddick, Kathleen (1907–1973) 106, 136, 161
  Riddick String Orchestra 106, 136, 161
Riddle, Frederick (1912–1995) 65, 74, 79
Ridler, Anne (1912–2001) 173, 181, 207, 278, 328, 336, 346, 351, 369, 371, 423, 436, 439, 454, 461, 465, xxxi
Rignold, Hugo (1905–1976) 214, 219, 220,
Ritchie, Margaret (1903–1969) 146
Roberts, Jeremy Dale (1934–) 225
Roberts, (William Henry) Mervyn (1906–1990) 127
Robinson, Christopher (1936–) 338
Robinson, Stanford (1904–1984) 19
Robles, Marisa (1937–) 252, 273, 274, 276
Rolston, Thomas (1932–2010) 388
Rooper, Jasper (1898–1981) 94
Ross, Katharine 454
Rossetti, Dante Gabriel (1828–1882) 21, xxix
Rossini, Gioacchino (1792–1868) 282
  Cenerentola 205
  Le comte Ory 297
Rostropovich, Mstislav (1927–2007) 194
Rothwell, Evelyn (later Barbirolli) (1911–2008) 158, 178, 180, 392, 399, 406, 417
Roundhouse (London) *see* British Broadcasting Corporation venues
Rowe, Percy 54
Roxburgh, Edwin (1937–) 445
Royal Academy of Music (London) 5, 413
  see also Duke's Hall

Royal Albert Hall (London) 68, 77, 79, 83, 151, 213, 232, 238, 255, 256, 290, 417, 422, 424, 468
Royal College of Music (RCM) (London) xxi, 3, 5, 6, 8, 18, 19, 21, 22, 34, 48, 49, 155, 198, 236, 268, 290, 318, 323, 331, 355, 356, 360, 361, 363, 479, 480
  Foli Scholarship 4
  Patron's Fund 5, 6, 15, 18, 20, 27, 44
  Octavia Travelling Scholarship 7, 8
Royal College of Surgeons (RCS) 8, 98
  Library of the RCS 8, 66
Royal Festival Hall ('F.H.', 'R.F.H.') (South Bank Centre, London) 148, 149, 150, 151, 166, 183, 216, 219, 220, 329, 336, 342, 409
Royal Liverpool Philharmonic Orchestra *see* Liverpool
Royal National Eisteddfod *see* National Eisteddfod
Royal Opera House (Covent Garden, London) ('C.G.') 133, 201, 225, 249, 256, 313, 341, 381, 419
Royal Philharmonic Orchestra ('R.P.O.') 142, 153, 158, 161, 335, 398, 409, 420, 421, 423, 424, 428, 432, 441
Royal Philharmonic Society 68, 166
Rseszow (Poland) 96
Rubbra, Edmund (1901–1986) 341
Rugby (England) 232, 238
Ruskin, John (1819–1900)
  The King of the Golden River (set by Maconchy) 423, 436, 439, xxxi
Rutland, Harold (1900–1977) 124, 125
Růžičková, Zuzana (1927–2017) 215

Sackville-West, Vita (1892–1962) 11
Sadler's Wells Opera (London) 172, 177, 185, 235, 245, 249, 256, 294, 296, 409, 430
Sadler's Wells Theatre (London) 177, 181, 183, 184, 203, 204, 205, 206, 215, 245, 249, 267, 293, 294, 296, 297, 300, 341, 412
St Asaph Festival (Flintshire, Wales) 410, 412, 420
St David's Festival *see* British Broadcasting Corporation series & programmes
St George's Church, Hanover Square (London) 424, 432
St George's Chapel, Windsor Castle (Windsor, England) 396
St Hilda's College *see* Oxford
St Mary Abbots Theatre (Kensington, London) 431
St Mary's Calne (Wiltshire, England) 111, 239
St Pancras Festival *see* Camden Festival
St Pancras Town Hall (London) 235, 249, 272
St Paul's Girls' School (London) 447, 448, 449
Salisbury (Wiltshire, England) 413, 468
  Salisbury Cathedral 451, 464, 466, 468
Salon Orchestra and Salon Orchestra Quartet *see* British Broadcasting Corporation ensembles
Salzburg (Austria) 50, 255
Salzburg Festival 224
Sanders, John (1933–2003) 352
Santry Court (near Dublin) 4
Santry Parish Church 11
Sargent, Malcolm (1895–1967) 5, 129, 149, 151, 152, 153, 274
Schoenberg, Arnold (1874–1951) 48, 380, 460
  Erwartung 390
  Pierrot Lunaire 79
Schola Cantorum *see* Oxford
Schubert, Franz (1797–1828) 444
Schulhoff, Erwin (1894–1942) 8, 9, 19, 193
Schumann, Robert (1810–1856) 427
  Dichterliebe 294
Schwarz, Rudolf (1905–1994) 183, 347
Scotland 153, 238, 295
  see also BBC Scotland *in* British Broadcasting Corporation networks
  see also Edinburgh, Glasgow
Scott, Walter (1771–1832)
  'Rosabelle' (set by Williams in *The Billows of the Sea*) 333, xxv
Sculthorpe, Peter (1929–2014) 328, 345
Seal, Richard (1935–) 414
Searle, Humphrey (1915–1982) 112, 159, 323, 329
Sedivka, Jan (1917–2009) 161
Seiber, Mátyás (1905–1960)
  Ulysses 138
Severn suspension bridge 263
Shakespeare, William (1564–1616) 77, 124, 168, 180, 181, 190, 229, 259, 268, 292, 333, 433, 472
  Falstaff 77, 405
  Henry IV 77, 124
  Henry V 405
  King Lear 208

Macbeth 405
A Midsummer Night's Dream 381
Othello 224
Richard II 341
'Sigh, no more ladies,' 'Orpheus with his lute,' 'Blow, blow thou winter wind' (set by Williams in *Three Lyrics from the Plays of Shakespeare*) 261, 463, xxv
'Take, O take those lips away', 'The Wind and the Rain', 'Come away, death', King Stephen (set by Maconchy in *Four Shakespeare Songs*) 248, 267, 268, xxix
'When my love swears', sonnet no. 138 (set by Williams) 292, xxv
Shawe-Taylor, Desmond (1907–1995) 446
'Sheila' *see* Maconchy, Sheila Campbell, *Maconchy's sister*
Shelley, Percy Bysshe (1892–1922) 200, 218
Hymn to the Earth (set by Williams) 200, xxv
'To the Night' (set by Maconchy in *Nocturnal*) 283, 284, 286, xxx
'A widow-bird sate mourning for her love' (set by Maconchy in *Three Songs*) 422, 471, 472
Sherlaw Johnson, Robert (1932–2000) 328, 345
Shingles, Stephen 397
Shore, Bernard (1896–1985) 53, 54,
Shostakovich, Dmitri (1906–1975) 193, 199,
Symphony No. 5, Op. 47 228
Shottesbrook (Boreham, Essex) xix, xx, 147
Shottesbrook Youth Players 225
Sibelius, Jean (1865–1957)
Symphony No. 2, Op. 43 87
Sicily (Italy) 328
Siena (Italy) 320, 323
Sinclair, Monica (1925–2002) 272, 291
Skalkottas, Nikos (1904–1949) 245
Slatford, Rodney (1944–) 373, 376
Sliwinski, Zen 66, 67, 69, 71, 87, 88, 89, 90, 96, 97, 98, 99, 351, 367, 368, 369, 370
Smetana, Bedřich (1824–1884)
Prodaná nevěsta/The Bartered Bride 78
Smith, Bill (1894–1968) 293
Smith, Michael 458
Smyth, Ethel (1858–1944) 184
Snell, Howard (1936–) 418, 419, 421, 426

Snowdon, Lord *see* Armstrong-Jones Anthony
Soames, René (1903–1985) 146
Society for the Promotion of New Music (SPNM) xiv, 144, 174, 346, 391, 406, 413, 421, 423, 436, 439, 440, 441, 443, 445, 455, 468, 477, 478
Society of Women Musicians ('S.W.M.') 29, 30, 31, 136
Solti, Georg (1912–1997) 479
Somerset (England) 5, 384
Souster, Tim (1943–1994) 322
South America *see* Latin America
Southampton (England) 140, 247, 352
University of Southampton 357
Southern Arts Festival 371
Southern Cathedrals Festival 413, 451, 464, 468
Southey, Caroline (1786–1854)
'To Death' (set by Williams) 153, xxiv
Southlands Training College (London) 14, 34, 449
Soviet Friendship Society 144
Spencer, Sylvia (1909–1978) 29, 30, 31
Stalingrad (USSR) 80, 85, 87
see also The Voice of the City (choral work) *in* Elizabeth Maconchy: Works
Stamford (Lincolnshire, England) 69, 87, 88
Stanstead Airport (Essex, England) 288
Stevens, Bernard (1916–1983) 113, 114, 131
Ricercar 162
Stevenson, Ronald (1928–2015) 399, 400
The Continents/Piano Concerto No. 2 399
Stockhausen, Karlheinz (1928–2007) 407, 409
Ylem 409
Strauss, Johann (1825–1899) 273
Strauss, Richard (1864–1949) 220, 433
Der Rosenkavalier 224
Salome 11
Stravinsky, Igor (1882–1971) 27, 28, 170, 308, 331, 416
Duo concertant 27, 28
In memoriam Dylan Thomas 331
Le sacre de printemps 22, 47
Petrushka 22, 127, 416
Pulcinella Suite 27
Susskind, Walter (1913–1980) 224, 420, 421, 428
Swansea (Wales) 229, 235, 263, 327, 392, 427

Swansea Festival 157, 163, 165, 328, 329, 333, 334, 342
  see also National Eisteddfod
Swayne, Giles (1946–) 447
Switzerland 14, 61, 66, 79, 100, 128, 198
'S.W.M.' *see* Society of Women Musicians
Sykes, John (1909–1962) 34
  Litanie 34, 36

Tate, Phyllis (1911–1985) xv, 234, 235, 252, 413, 415
  A Secular Requiem (The Phoenix and the Turtle) 333–4
  The Lady of Shalott 313
  The Lodger 235
  The Phoenix and the Turtle 333–4
Tavener, John (1944–2013) 462
Taylor, Muriel (?–1971) 198, 211
Tchaikovsky, Pyotr (1840–1893)
  The Sleeping Beauty 341
  Symphonies Nos. 1, 4, 5 and 6 395
Tear, Robert (1939–2011) 250, 261, 262, 267
Tebaldi, Renata (1922–2004) 237
Tennyson, Alfred (1809–1892)
  'Sweet and Low' (set by Williams in *Songs of Sleep*) 175, xxiv
  'Sweet and Low' (set by Williams in *Billows of the Sea*) xxv
  'The Lady of Shalott' 179, 313
Theodorakis, Mikis (1925–) 292
Thomas, Dylan (1914–1953) 161, 330
  'And death shall have no dominion' (set by Maconchy) 328, 330, 331, 343, 345, xxx
  'Do not go gently into that good night' 331
Thomas, Edward (1878–1917)
  'Will you come?' (set by Maconchy in *Nocturnal*) 283, 284, xxx
  'Lights Out' (set by Williams) xxiv
Thomas, Hugh 449
Thomas, Mansel (1909–1986) 70, 85, 98, 122, 125, 128, 130, 131, 133, 134, 137, 141, 149, 164
Thomas, Mary (1932–1997) 415–16
Thomas, Megan 43, 44
Thompson, Tony
  A Letter for Wales 191, xxvi
Thomson, James (1700–1748) 179
Three Choirs Festival 330, 337, 338, 394
Thurston, Frederick ('Jack') (1901–1953) 102, 106, 110
Tippett, Michael (1905–1998) 170, 201, 219, 284, 307, 313, 388, 389–90, 397

King Priam 201
The Knot Garden 389
Severn Bridge Variations (composite work) 263, 468, 470
Symphony No. 2 170
The Midsummer Marriage 313, 473
Tofield, George 309, 326
Toscanini, Arturo (1867–1957) 87
Tovey, Donald Francis (1875–1940) 41, 43, 46, 49
Trau, Sela (1898–1991) 83, 161
Treacher, Graham 295, 296, 297, 359, 447
Treece, Henry (1911–1966) 113, 114, 125
  The Dark Island 109, 135
  Rataplan 113
Trimble, Joan (1915–2000) and Valerie (1917–1980) 154
Trinity College, Dublin 283, 286, 289
Troutbeck, W. H. 156, 446
Trowell, Brian (1931–2015) 340, 341, 347
Tucker, Norman (1910–1978) 172, 177
Tudor Singers, The 35, 39
Tunnard, Viola (1916–1974) 222, 237
Turetzky, Bertram (1933–) 435
Tusler, Leslie 402

'Uncle Ralph' *see* Vaughan Williams, Ralph
Union of Soviet Socialist Republics (USSR) 112–13, 191, 192, 215, 416
  see also Leningrad, Moscow, Stalingrad
United States of America (USA) 71, 87, 113, 145, 150, 158, 163, 190, 210, 211, 212, 213, 248, 323, 327, 396, 381, 406, 414, 424, 432, 435, 441, 445, 448, 450, 469, 476
University of Alberta String Quartet 382, 388, 403, 447
University of Birmingham *see* Birmingham
University of Cambridge *see* Cambridge
University of Oxford *see* Oxford
University of Wales Press 69, 175
University of Warwick (Coventry) *see* Coventry
Uppingham (Rutland, England) 62
'Ursula' *see* Vaughan Williams, Ursula
USSR *see* Union of Soviet Socialist Republics

Vachel Lindsay, Nicholas (1879–1931)
  'How Samson Bore Away the Gates of Gaza' (set by Maconchy for soprano and piano, 1938) 54, xxix

Valéry, Paul (1871–1945) 259
Varèse, Edgar (1883–1965) 190, 307
  Arcana 307
Vaughan Williams, Adeline (1870–1951), *Vaughan Williams's first wife* 338, 394
Vaughan Williams, Ralph ('Uncle Ralph') (1872–1958) viii, ix, *teacher of Maconchy and Wiliams at RCM* 3, 6, 7, 15, 19, 23, 24, 26, 27, 28, 36, 44, 45, 46, 47, 48 (Ex. Pl.4.1), *wartime in Dorking* 67, 68, 71, 82, 89, 98, 99, 101, *75th birthday* 106, 107, 110, 112, 124, 128, 129, 130, 133, 140, 141, 143, 154, 155, 156, 157, 166, *death* 171–2, 176, 177, 185, 220, 268, 286, 332, 338, 339, 359, 394, 397, 398, 433, 453, 466, xxviii, xxxii, xxxiii
  Diabelleries (composite work) 154–5
  Fantasia on a Theme by Thomas Tallis 316
  Job 48, 89
  A Pastoral Symphony/Symphony No. 3 48, 397
  Riders to the Sea 177
  A Sea Symphony/Symphony No. 1 394
  Serenade to Music 339
  The Shepherds of the Delectable Mountains 89
  Sinfonia Antarctica 397
  Symphony No. 5 89, 299
  Symphony No. 6 110, 394
  Symphony No. 9 171
  Two-Piano Concerto 394
  Omnibus: Ralph Vaughan Williams — A Portrait of an English Composer 338, 339, 359
  Ralph Vaughan Williams Trust 357, 392, 453
Vaughan Williams, Ursula (1911–2007), *Vaughan Williams's second wife* 165, 171–2, 225, 246, 264, 270, 304, 343, 394
  The Sofa (libretto) 165, 270, xxxi
Vega, Aurelio de la (1925–) 190
Vellère, Lucie (1896–1966) 163
Venice (Italy) 245, 246, 407
Vercors (Jean Bruller) (1902–1991)
  Le silence de la mer 249, 292
Verdi, Giuseppe (1813–1901)
  Requiem 310
Veress, Sándor (1907–1992) 52
  String Quartet No. 2 51, 52
Victoria & Albert Museum (London) 297

Vienna (Austria) xxi, 3, 7, 8, 11, 13, 20, 28, 42, 47, 51, 57, 58, 145, 282, 363, 445, xxxii
  Vienna Boys Choir 242, 253, 255, 256, 281, 291, 294, 463
  see also ISCM Festivals
Vinci, Leonardo da *see* Leonardo da Vinci
Virtuosi of London *see* London Virtuosi
Visconti, Luchino (1906–1976)
  Death in Venice 381
Vishnevskaya, Galina (1926–2012) 404

W. E. Hill & Sons (London) 356
Wadham, Dorothy (1895–1990) 24, 39
Wagner, Richard (1813–1883) 6, 107, 151, 259, 409, 470
  Die Meistersinger von Nürnberg 246, 371, 479
  Der Ring des Nibelungen 133, 380, 426–7
  Göttterdämmerung 151, 251
  Siegfried Idyll 316
  Tristan und Isolde 38, 133, 151, 340, 381
Wales xii, xix, xxi, 3, 55, 63, 85, 105, 137, 138, 191, 216, 219, 222, 223, 230, 255, 256, 263, 289, 302, 309, 335, 347, 356, 359, 390, 401–2, 412, 416, 434, 445, 451, 457, 458
  Archbishop of Wales (Glyn Simon) 329
  see also Free Wales Army, National Eisteddfod, National Youth Orchestra of Wales, Charles Prince of Wales, University of Wales Press
  see also Aberfan, Aberystwyth, Ammanford, Bangor, Barry, Caernarfon, Caerphilly, Cardiff, Llandaff, Llandudno, Newton, Rhyl, St Asaph Festival, Swansea, Wrexham
Wales, Roy 236
Wallfisch, Peter (1924–1993) 254
Walmesley, Claire 433
Walsh, Stephen (1942–) 395
Walters, Gareth (1928–2012) 355
  Divertimento 355
Walton, William (1902–1983) 149
  Belshazzar's Feast 44
  Façade 79
  Orb and Sceptre 149
  String Quartet in A minor 198, 201
  Violin Concerto 68
Warburton, Ernest (1937–2001) 279, 315, 467
Ward, Henry 278, 366, 371, 372, 373
Ward, Joseph (1932–) 272, 291, 315

Warlock, Peter (Philip Heseltine) (1894–1930) 73
Warrack, Guy (1900–1986) 88, 318
Washington D.C. (USA) 203
Watanabe, Akeo (1919–1990) 427
Watts, Helen (1927–2009) 168, 169, 170, 327, 333, 334, 337, 342, 344, 379, 383, 453, 466, 467
Weil, Terence (1921–1995) 170
Welbeck String Orchestra 178
Weldon, George (1908–1963) 163, 165, 166
Wellesz, Egon (1885–1974) 7, 12, 20, 23, 169, 282, 301, 309
Wells, Mary (1935–) 231
Wells-next-the-Sea (North Norfolk) 369, 385
Welsh Arts Council *see* Arts Council of Great Britain
Welsh National Opera/Welsh National Opera Company 179, 234, 240, 242, 245, 246, 249, 250, 262, 264, 279, 289, 291, 293, 294, 298, 316, 329, 343, 345, 353, 428, 473
  Opera for All 253, 281, 329, 379
Welsh Youth Orchestra *see* National Youth Orchestra of Wales
Westminster Abbey (London) 205
Westminster Cathedral (London) 400
Westrup, J(ack) A. (1904–1975) 46
Wetherell, Eric (1925–) 301, 379
Whewell, Michael (1923–1977) 143
Whistler, Laurence (1912–2000)
  'Flight' (set by Williams) 153, xxiv
White, Eric Walter (1905–1985) 346
Whiting, John (1917–1963) 297, 299
Whittington, David 454
Wickham Lodge (Wickham Bishops, Essex, England) 98, 105, 147, 150
Wicks, Allan (1923–2010) 253, 255
Wigmore Hall (London) 100, 101, 139, 345, 352, 403
Willcocks, David (1919–2015) 253, 266
Williams, Emlyn (1905–1987)
  The Corn is Green 305
Williams, Gareth, *Williams's nephew* 472
Williams, Gerrard (1888–1947) 26
Williams, Glyn (1908–1976), *Williams's brother* viii, 188 (Fig. PIV.1), 457, 459, 460, 472
Williams, Grace (1906–1977) *see* xxxv
  see also Grace Williams: Works, xxiii–xxvi
Williams, Marjorie, *Williams's sister-in-law* viii, 188 (Fig. PIV.1)
Williams, Rose Emily (née Richards) (1873–1962), *Williams's mother* viii, 53, 84, 96, 104, 131, 150, 167, 176, 177, 181, 182, 183, 188 (Fig. PIV.1), 189, 192, 196, 197, 198, 201
Williams, Shirley (1930–) 426
Williams, William Matthews (1876–1957), *Williams's father* viii, 128, 131, 150, 157, 188 (Fig. PIV.1)
Williamson, Malcolm (1931–2003) 301, 337
  From a Child's Garden (Robert Louis Stevenson) 313
  The Violins of St Jacques 300
Williamson, Stanley (1921–2010) 338, 359
Wilson, Catherine (1936–) 204, 205, 206, 207
Wilson, Harold (1916–1995) 230, 363, 423, 426, 435
Wilson, Marie (1903–after 1983) 298
Wilson, Steuart (1889–1966) 46, 83, 125, 126, 127
Wingfield, Sheila (1906–1992) 77, xxix
Winter, Keith (1940–) 396, 398
Wissema String Quartet 346
'W.M.A.' *see* Workers' Music Association
Wood, Henry J. (1869–1944) 5, 11, 24, 27, 62, 63, 72, 73, 74, 78, 81, 83, 247, 339, 373
Wood, Hugh (1932–) 440, 441
Wood, Robin (1924–2004) 161
Woodgate, Leslie (1900–1961) 48, 99
Woodhead, Joan 66
Woodhouse, Charles (1879–1939) 44
Worcester (England) 213, 337, 338, 342, 343, 353
  Worcester Cathedral Choir 330, 338
Workers' Music Association ('W.M.A.') 85, 90, 91
Worshipful Company of Musicians 331
Wortham, Hugo Evelyn (1884–1959) 26, 27
Wrexham (Wales) 327, 356, 390
Wright, Kenneth ('Ken', 'K.A.W.') (1899–1975) 54, 55, 61, 66, 67, 73, 76, 123, 125, 126, 127, 128
Wynne, David (1900–1983) 379
Wyss, Sophie (1897–1983) 54, 67, 68, 77, 105, 106, 129, 142

Xenakis, Iannis (1922–2001) 321, 329

Young, Douglas (1947–) 442
  Landscapes and Absences 442

'Zen' *see* Sliwinski, Zen
Zorian, Olive (1916–1965) 105
  Zorian String Quartet 105

Printed in the United States
By Bookmasters